THE WORD
MADE SELF

❖

THE WORD MADE SELF

Russian Writings on Language, 1860–1930

THOMAS SEIFRID

Cornell University Press
Ithaca and London

Parts of this book appeared in "Khaidegger i russkie o iazyke i bytii,"
Novoe literaturnoe obozrenie 51:3 (2002): 64–75.
© *Novoe literaturnoe obozrenie,* Moscow, 2002. Used here by permission.

First published 2005 by Cornell University Press
Printed in the United States of America

Library of Congress Cataloging-in-Publication Data
Seifrid, Thomas.
   The word made self : Russian writings on language, 1860-1930 / Thomas Seifrid.
      p. cm.
   "Parts of this book appeared in Novoe literaturnoe obozrenie 51:3 (2002)."
   Includes bibliographical references and index.
   ISBN 0-8014-4316-4 (cloth : alk. paper)
   1. Language and languages--Philosophy.   2. Philosophy, Russian--History.
I. Title.
   P107.S45 2005
   400--dc22

                                                          2004023506

Cloth printing   10 9 8 7 6 5 4 3 2 1

for Martin

Contents

Acknowledgments

IT IS IMPOSSIBLE TO CONDUCT RESEARCH as involved as that which went into this book without incurring debts, which I here gratefully acknowledge.

A National Endowment for the Humanities Summer Stipend made it possible for me to travel to Russia in 1995 and consult important materials to which access would otherwise have been difficult if not impossible. A Simpson Humanities Grant, awarded through the College of Letters, Arts and Sciences at the University of Southern California, enabled me to buy a new computer that made working with my increasingly large and numerous files a far pleasanter task. Ongoing research support from the same College of Letters, Arts and Sciences made possible another trip to Russia in 2000 and has facilitated the purchase of books and other needed materials all along.

I am indebted to many individuals as well. Caryl Emerson provided insightful, critical, and sympathetic commentary on the manuscript of a sort an author can usually only dream about. John G. Ackerman at Cornell University Press kept interest in this project alive despite the many other pressing claims on his time (and Cornell University Press in general should be commended for its staunch support of publishing in the area of Russian studies). Galin Tihanov and Robert Bird generously shared their ideas, their enthusiasm for Russian philosophy, and their impressive bibliographical knowledge. Nicoletta Misler brought me a copy of Florenskii's study of names, *Imena,* at a crucial juncture, while Elizabeth Durst provided me with one of Shpet's *Filosofskie etiudy.* To my colleagues in the Department of Slavic Languages and Literatures at USC I am indebted for years of rewarding interaction.

I would also like to thank (if I may) the several climbing partners I have had over the years, who have held their share of falls and led routes when I didn't feel up to it, and whose camaraderie has helped to keep me sane: Alex Watts-Tobin, Tony Bird, John Dambros, Johan and Elvira Burger, and especially Miklós and Krisztina Peterfy.

Most of all I thank my wife, Lena, and son, Martin, who make everything worthwhile.

T.S.

THE WORD
MADE SELF

Introduction

Russia's Preoccupation with Language in the Modern Era

THAT RUSSIANS HAVE TENDED TO PROFESS a near-religious, if not indeed fetishistic, veneration for the power of language—for the Word—is well known, as are the particularly intense declarations of that veneration which appeared in the first part of the twentieth century. Gogol may have written *Dead Souls* in order to redeem Russia, and Dostoevsky may have spoken of "beauty" (which for him included verbal beauty) as having the power to save the world, but Andrei Bely enthused over nothing less than the literal magic of words and urged that the force of primitive incantations be recreated in Symbolist poetry. Seeking to emancipate the word from its burden of quotidian reference, the Futurists similarly proclaimed the "self-sufficient word" and set out to write a poetry of "the word as such"—while their Formalist allies worked to enshrine this principle in criticism. Only a few years later, in his 1922 essay "On the Nature of the Word," the poet Osip Mandelstam wrote in a gnomic vein that the Russian word should be viewed as "active flesh, resolving itself in event . . . sentient and breathing flesh," while in Mikhail Bakhtin's hands the relations between words acquire something of the intensity, at once bureaucratic and personal, of life in a communal apartment: for him words can harbor intentions, anticipate responses to themselves, cast "sidelong glances," even contain "loopholes."[1]

Beyond this circle of celebrated examples one finds if anything an even deeper preoccupation with the nature of language in Russian intellectual culture of this period (roughly, 1860–1930). The discussion arises within such varied movements as linguistics, philosophy, the Russian religious renaissance, the Symbolist and Futurist movements in literature, Formalist

1. Osip Mandel'stam, "O prirode slova," in *Sobranie sochinenii v trekh tomakh,* vol. 2, *Proza* (New York: Inter-Language Literary Associates, 1971), 245–46; Mikhail Bakhtin, "Slovo v romane," in *Voprosy literatury i estetiki. Issledovaniia raznykh let* (Moscow: Khudozhestvennaia literatura, 1975), 98, 106; Bakhtin, *Problemy poetiki Dostoevskogo* (Moscow: Sovetskaia Rossiia, 1979), 271.

literary theory, and the abiding middlebrow culture of Russia's "thick journals." The range of genres in which the problems are treated is similarly broad, from Aleksandr Potebnia's studies of Russian grammar proper to his forays into the philosophy of language, from phenomenological philosophy (the works of Gustav Shpet and Aleksei Losev) to theologically oriented philology (Sergei Bulgakov's *Filosofiia imeni* [The philosophy of the name] and many of the writings of Pavel Florenskii), from popularizing cultural theory such as Vladimir Ern's *Bor'ba za Logos* (The battle for logos) to the poetic manifestos of Symbolists, Acmeists, and Futurists.

What is less obvious is that this fairly diffuse group of writings, whose effusions over the significance of language at first glance might seem to constitute an unthinking cultural reflex, forms an unexpectedly coherent body of writings oriented toward a set of concerns transcending the disciplinary focus of the particular works that contain them and in this way embodying a response to other, more deeply embedded, issues in Russian culture. This study will argue that Russian writings on the nature of language in the late nineteenth and early twentieth centuries manifest just such a coherence: that read in conjunction, across their disciplinary boundaries, they can be seen to emanate out of a project larger than that explicitly identified in any one of them. It is as if they all partake of certain overarching tasks, or, to use terms more familiar to cultural analysis in the West, form a "discourse paradigm" despite their lack of overt, public unity.[2]

What binds together the sudden profusion of Russian writings about language in the later nineteenth and early twentieth centuries, I believe, is the effort to provide a model of the self or of selfhood that is grounded in language and that finds in language the prototype for what the self should

---

2. V. I. Postovalova glosses "*sverkhzadachi,*" "overarching tasks"—actually a Stanislavskian term—as "those issues in the cultural or spiritual life of society toward which an author orients himself, be it consciously or unconsciously"; see her "Poslemslovie," in A. F. Losev, *Filosofiia imeni* (Moscow: Izd. Moskovskogo universiteta, 1990), 243. The situation of Russian writings on language at the turn of the century closely resembles that described by Katherine Arens for nineteenth-century psychology (which, drawing on Kuhn and especially Foucault, she labels a "discourse paradigm"); see her *Structures of Knowing: Psychologies of the Nineteenth Century,* Boston Studies in the Philosophy of Science, 113 (Dordrecht: Kluwer Academic, 1989), 4. Among philosophers and psychologists in the nineteenth century, Arens suggests, "Their own articulations of the problems they addressed are often strikingly similar in terminology and formulation despite the discord in their stated purposes." This is so despite the fact that, because it was practiced by professionals in many fields, the commonality of terms among nineteenth century "psychologies" was obscured (ibid., 32, 44). Another way of characterizing the cohesive forces within this tradition would be to use Wittgenstein's notion of "family resemblances" among objects within a group, which involve no single trait shared by all but arise on the basis of contiguous relations, as in the series abc–cde–efg; see his *Philosophical Investigations,* 3rd ed., trans. G. E. M. Anscombe (Englewood Cliffs, N.J.: Prentice-Hall, 1958), 31.

be.[3] In the obvious sense that language is produced and used by humans, and therefore is in some way an emanation of selves, virtually any statement on the nature of language relies at least implicitly on such a model. But what I have in mind throughout this study is the non-self-evident, and therefore nontrivial, ways in which Russian writers of this period attempt to bind a concept of language to one of selfhood, indeed sometimes to represent language as constituting a kind of self in its own right—something they did, incidentally, well in advance of Heidegger's better-known declaration of language as the "home of being." In fact I would argue that it is precisely *because of* this language-oriented search for selfhood that "language" has traditionally been so hallowed in the Russian context. This impulse is a broadly European as well as a Russian one, but it has exerted particular attraction within the Russian tradition. It is especially apparent in the tendency of certain Russian writers to attribute to "the word" such values as self-consciousness, self-reflection, perception, intentionality, and so forth; yet it is much more than just allegorized psychology, insisting throughout on the linguistic nature of the self it seeks to define (it is always a *speaking* self that is involved; the nature of language is always felt to be essential to the nature of the self). The impulse was perhaps shaped in part by the relative lack of other concepts of selfhood, whose development for a variety of reasons was otherwise attenuated in the Russian context.[4] Like most intellectual movements in the relatively cosmopolitan Russia of its day, it draws on western European (especially German) thought of the nineteenth and early twentieth centuries but also relies significantly on Orthodox doctrines of Trinitarianism and Christology and, with them, a centuries-old Russian tradition of speculation on the nature of language.

3. By "selfhood" I mean the seat of subjectivity as well as the set of problems involved in establishing personal identity, such as whether a self has unity, and if so, whether that unity resides in the mind or in the body; the nature of self-knowledge and its role in anchoring identity; the nature of memories and their role in anchoring identity; mind's relation to the world, and so forth. For a useful overview of these issues see Terence Penelhum, "Personal Identity," in *Encyclopedia of Philosophy*, vol. 6, ed. Paul Edwards (New York: Macmillan and Free Press, 1967), 95–107.

4. It may be overstating the case somewhat to claim that Russia "lacked" a definition of the self—there was most certainly a theological definition, and by the mid-nineteenth century Russian literature was abundantly rich in fictional versions of selves. But the very late emergence of anything resembling professional philosophy in Russia postponed concerted speculative writing on the topic until the latter part of the century. In any event, from the decade of the Great Reforms until ideological conformity was imposed under the Soviets one can note a flurry of such efforts in one disciplinary mode or another to define the self. For an informative sampling see Andrzej Walicki, "Positivism and Psychology," in *A History of Russian Thought from the Enlightenment to Marxism,* trans. Hilda Andrews-Rusiecka (Stanford: Stanford University Press, 1979), 357–62. For an interesting exploration of how a Russian intellectual movement attempted, unsuccessfully, to avoid the notion of the self, see Daniel Rancour-Laferriere, "Why the Formalists Had No Theory of the Literary Person," *Wiener Slawistischer Almanach,* Sonderband 31, *Psychopoetik* (1992): 327–37.

These writings on language in the late nineteenth and early twentieth centuries constitute a chapter in Russia's intellectual history that has been largely overlooked. But the underlying agendas of the Russian effort to define selfhood within language, as well as its presuppositions and its strong predilection for taking thought about language in certain directions rather than others, have exerted considerable influence on the ways in which Russians have dealt with and theorized about verbal phenomena in the twentieth century. To the extent that the movements affected by this tradition, such as Russian Symbolism, Formalism, and Futurism, the structural linguistics of Roman Jakobson, the writings of Mikhail Bakhtin, and later Soviet structuralism and semiotics, have influenced thought outside of Russia, its repercussions have been wide indeed. Moreover, as I argue at several points, some of the Russian philosophical concerns that initially appear of only local (not to say provincial) significance turn out also to shed light on some of the underlying roots and agendas of Western thought about language in the modern era, as the particularly congenial examples of Hegel, Heidegger, Gadamer, and, on occasion, Wittgenstein, make clear.

In Chapter 1 of this study I consider some of the ways in which language has been thought of, in both the West and in Russia, as more than a mere instrument of communication, especially in the German Romantic line of thought about the centrality of language to human self-definition that begins with Herder and then becomes increasingly emphatic over the course of the nineteenth century. I next examine the ways in which the pivotal figure for modern Russian philosophy of language, a linguist named Aleksandr Potebnia (1835–91), imported German Romantic ideas while subtly fusing them with Russian notions about the self whose origins lie in patristic teachings on Christology and Trinitarianism. This discussion is followed, in Chapter 2, by a survey of Russia's rich verbal culture of the early twentieth century (theory of literature, poetic manifestos, utopian treatises proposing a new language, and so forth), which shows how many of Potebnia's concerns were sustained within it. Chapters 3 and 4 are then devoted to closer examinations of the most extensive contributions to the philosophy of language in twentieth-century Russia, with an eye to their particular efforts to identify language and the self. Chapter 3 looks at the protean writings of Pavel Florenskii, as well as the treatise on the nature of names (*Filosofiia imeni*) written by his erstwhile student—and fellow Orthodox priest— Sergei Bulgakov. Both Florenskii and Bulgakov make self-conscious efforts to link their theories of language to Orthodox thought, but both, as I show, are complex figures whose thought at nearly every step responds to a variety of Modernist influences, Western as well as Russian. The potent, if now largely forgotten, intrusion of phenomenology into Russian thought in the early twentieth century, and its contribution to Russian philosophy of language, is the subject of Chapter 4. Here I look closely at how Gustav Shpet and Aleksei Losev in varying ways adapted Husserl's phenomenology to their projects for identifying ontologically secure forms of selfhood. In the Conclusion I repeat the exercise of Chapter 2, but this time look to the writings of thinkers who are peripheral to, and whose most significant works post-date, the era under consideration (Vygotsky, Voloshinov, Bakhtin, Jakobson) in order to show how enduring was the enterprise Potebnia set in motion when he attempted to define the self in linguistic terms, even as it ranged far afield.

Chapter 1

Potebnia and the Revival
of Russian Thought about Language

THE MODERN PHASE OF RUSSIAN WRITING about language arguably begins in the 1860s, with Aleksandr Afanas'evich Potebnia (1835–91), a Ukrainian linguist and professor at Khar'kov (now Khar'kiv) University who wrote widely on the psychological, esthetic, and cultural implications of human speech. Some of his psychological notions were later mocked by the Formalists (who nonetheless drew on them at the same time), but his writings exerted considerable influence on the ways Russians thought about literature and language in the late nineteenth and early twentieth centuries. What made Potebnia so pivotal a figure was that he introduced into the Russian context the Romantic theory of language that had been developed in Germany by Wilhelm von Humboldt, but did it in such a way as to suggests its affinities (and perhaps also its underlying genetic link) with certain expectations of language that had informed Russian thought since the Middle Ages.

Potebnia's writings on language will be examined later in this chapter, but it is impossible to understand his contribution to the Russian tradition without first considering some of the broader contexts informing this line of inquiry as a whole. What follows in no way pretends to be an exhaustive account of the philosophy of language in Europe (which would be massive). It is, rather, an attempt to survey key moments and significant tendencies in the persistent European—including eastern European—effort to link language and self. Once again, the position I take in this discussion is that, apart from the empirically obvious fact that language emerges from human mouths (though when one considers age-old debates over the divine versus human origins of speech it becomes clear that not even this provenance can be taken philosophically for granted), none of the assertions made or implied about the relation of language to our selfhood is intrinsically obvious, outside of the particular philosophical context in which it appears. This does not mean that there is really no such relationship, nor that we cannot come close to defining it; but, like any intellectual endeavor, writings on the nature of language are informed by all sorts of secondary predilections, latent concerns, and often unacknowledged habits of analogization, whose articulation (if we manage it) can tell us something about the underlying structures shaping this area of human thought.

Early Greek speculation on the nature of language—and given the importance of Greek thought to the Orthodox tradition ancient Greek ideas should be considered no more "Western" than they are "Eastern"—was metaphysical in character rather than grammatically descriptive or "linguistic" in the sense in which we would now use that term. One particularly important issue for the Greeks concerned the origins of language, whether it arose out of *physis* (nature) and therefore should be regarded as established by some order external to human endeavor (but perhaps organizing and controlling it), or as the result of pure convention or human invention (*nomos* or *thesis*), its meanings therefore perhaps provisional and nonessential. A closely related issue was that of whether, once one has language, linguistic phenomena are best thought of as forming an internally coherent whole (*analogia*), in which case the world and the self might form such wholes as well, or whether the elements of language are irregular in form and distribution (*anomalia*), constituents of a fluctuant and unsettled universe.[1] Both these concerns can be sensed in one of the most celebrated examples of Greek thought on language, Plato's *Cratylus,* which explores the nature of referentiality. In this dialogue Socrates approvingly cites Cratylus to assert that there is a natural propriety of appellation for things that exist, so that names serve to point out the quality of the things they denote and one can, via a name, "[lay] hold of an entity, so as to imitate existence." This is so, he reasons, because names are produced by the "artificer of names," who ensures that they are true. Socrates thus sees language as enjoying a direct link with essence, as a result of which explorations of language can lead to knowledge of true being. Hermogenes, however, counterargues that there is no "propriety of appellation other than through convention and common consent," so that examinations of words will lead us to nothing other than knowledge of how this has been done. Socrates meanwhile spins out a series of etymological commentaries in support of his position—a line of inquiry which was later to interest several Russian thinkers—which, however, may in fact be intended parodically, so that Plato's ultimate views are difficult to pin down.[2]

When it arose in this richly speculative context, the idea of grammar, in the sense of morphological description of a language, was in fact an

---

1. R. H. Robins, *A Short History of Linguistics,* 4th ed. (London: Longman, 1997), 23.

2. Plato, *Cratylus. Parmenides. Greater Hippias. Lesser Hippias,* Loeb Classical Library vol. 167 (Cambridge: Harvard University Press, 1992), 372, 365, 293, 284. Regarding the possibly intentional absurdity of some of Socrates' etymologies, see H. N. Fowler, "Introduction to the *Cratylus,*" ibid., 4.

innovation, and rather than viewing it as a methodologically inevitable idea that evolved over time into the self-evidently justified discipline of linguistics, we would not be misguided in viewing it as just one more part of philosophical speculation on the nature of language. Plato already felt it necessary to parse *logos* (sentence, but also order-informed thought) into *onoma* (name or subject) and *rhema* (predicate), and Aristotle enriched this scheme in the grammatical sketch of Greek offered in the *Poetics,* where he discusses syntax in connection with solecism. But the first comprehensive effort at a grammar of Greek was that of Dionysius Thrax, written somewhere around 100 B.C., which was followed by the more extensive *Téchne grammatike* (of disputed Alexandrian authorship), whose more extensive categories were soon taken over by Varro (116–27 B.C.) and applied to Latin. Varro's efforts (which, incidentally, gave us the erroneous label of "accusative" for a case the Greeks had termed something like "causative") were then superseded in the fourth century A.D. by Donatus's, and around A.D. 500 by Priscian's Latin grammar.[3] The result of these assorted taxonomizing endeavors was the sense of language as a complex, abstract, but also essentially ordered and rule-governed system of significations that remains with us to this day.

As I have suggested above, such grammars are in fact not speculatively mute but can be thought of as elaborations on the idea of language as self-sufficient form. Heidegger was well aware of this aspect of Greek linguistic thought, and comments regarding their derivation of terms like *ptōsis* (case) and *enklisis* (declension) that for the Greeks, language is obviously taken as another thing that is, a *being* among others. The way in which the Greeks generally understood beings in their Being must have made itself felt in the conception and definition of language. Only on this basis can we grasp these terms, which, as modus and casus, have long since become hackneyed labels that tell us nothing.[4]

But the impulse to probe the nature of language more deeply did not die with the proliferation of grammars. In fact the next significant outburst of speculation on the nature of language, which took place in the Middle Ages, arose precisely out of a sense that the kind of descriptive taxonomy represented by Priscian was insufficient and that philosophical rather than morphological explanations ought to be sought even for the rules of grammar.[5] The result was a series of treatises written in the thirteenth and

---

3. See Robins, *Short History of Linguistics,* 37–42, especially the chart on 42 outlining the development of grammatical categories from Plato to the present.

4. Martin Heidegger, *Introduction to Metaphysics,* trans. Gregory Fried and Richard Polt (New Haven: Yale University Press, 2000), 62.

5. Robins, *Short History of Linguistics,* 89–90.

fourteenth centuries that sought to integrate the grammatical description of Latin with the categories of scholastic philosophy (which is to say Aristotelian philosophy, filtered through Aquinas and Catholic theology).[6] Prominent among the authors of such grammars were the "Modistae," so called because they wrote treatises *de modus significandi.* They held that things as existents possess various properties or modes of being (*modi essendi*); that the mind abstracts these *modi essendi* from things and considers them as *modi intelligendi*; and that language then permits these mental abstractions to be communicated via the *modi significandi.*[7] Because these categories were felt to reflect accurately reality and the powers of the human mind, in their relation to the variety of spoken languages they represented something like an ideal geometry in relation to empirically occurring shapes. From this concept arose that of a universal grammar underlying all languages and embedded in universals of human thought (interestingly, such notions had not concerned earlier grammarians whose attentions had been confined to Latin and Greek, whereas medieval grammarians, increasingly aware of the multiplicity of European vernaculars, began to search more concertedly for an underlying principle of unity). One corollary of this belief is the conviction that if one could accurately describe grammar as such, one would gain profound insight into the human mind and through that the structure of the world. Related to the notion of universal grammar, but having its own complex derivation from Platonic and neo-Platonic philosophy (including, notably, the *Cratylus*), was the great medieval debate over the referential status of words. On the (neo)Platonic side stood the "realist" belief that predicate terms such as "man" (as in "Socrates was a man") or "rational" ("man is rational") stand for universals existing in their own right, apart from the particulars of which they are predicated; while on the other stood the "nominalist" surmise, skeptical of Platonic universals and testimony to a dawning empiricism, that the world consists only and exclusively of particulars, so that names for anything else are mere linguistic conventions.[8] Ultimately these issues have to do with the consequentiality of language, with the relation between human speech and the order of the created world—as it happens, an abiding concern in the Russian context as well.

In the post-Renaissance sixteenth, seventeenth, and eighteenth centuries, debates over the nature of language were shaped by the tension between empiricism and rationalism that characterized philosophy as a whole in that era. The rationalist view of language, heir to the Modistae and Realism,

---

6. Ibid., 88.
7. Ibid., 91–92.
8. Ibid., 100–101.

promoted the notion of a universal thought structure manifesting itself in all languages but existing independently of any particular one of them. The Port Royal grammarians of the mid-seventeenth century, for example, expounded a general theory of grammar based on the universal laws of human reason and attempted to reveal the unity underlying the separate grammars of different languages. Since, they assumed, the laws of reason were the same for the whole of humanity, then the basic laws of grammar must be the same for all languages. Language for the Port Royal grammarians was the outward manifestation of the laws of reason, and its forms, categories, and combinatory rules were therefore the reflections of mental acts.[9] Subsequent writers in this vein, such as James Harris, author of *Hermes or a Philosophical Enquiry Concerning Language and Universal Grammar* (1751), and James Burnett (Lord Monboddo), author of the six-volume *Of the Origin and Progress of Language*, drew philosophical support from Descartes's belief in innate ideas rather than the age's opposing alternative, Lockean empiricism—and this rationalist line of thought has continued to inspire theories of language down to the modern era, such as Hjelmslev's 1928 *Principes de grammaire générale* and Chomsky's theory of generative grammar, which insists on the innate and universal nature of linguistic structure.[10] A still more striking offshoot of this line were the numerous projects, representing a kind of dream of the utopian debabelization of language, for so-called universal languages or "real characters," which sought not merely to account for the nature of existing languages or to assemble a common language out of parts of them, like Esperanto, but to create a new philosophical language altogether in which universal ideas could be perfectly expressed in symbols created expressly for that purpose (for example, Leibniz's *Specimen calculi universalis,* Bishop John Wilkins's *Essay towards a real character and a philosophical language,* and many others, including, in the heady aftermath of the Bolshevik revolution in Russia, Ia. Lintsbakh's 1919 *Printsipy filosofskogo iazyka* [Principles of philosophical language]).[11]

Meanwhile the Enlightenment's countervailing tendency toward empiricism—which in the realm of language translates into a sense that language cannot convey us to any metaphysical knowledge, in that we can only know of it what we see and hear before us—had fostered work on descriptive phonetics and the grammatical description of individual languages until, in the later eighteenth century, the discovery of Sanskrit by Europeans stimulated

---

9. T. A. Amirova et al., *Ocherki po istorii lingvistiki* (Moscow: Nauka, 1975), 214, 223–24.

10. Robins, *Short History of Linguistics,* 133, 141. Chomsky makes his philosophical affinities explicit in his *Cartesian Linguistics. A Chapter in the History of Rationalist Thought* (1966; reprint, Lanham, Md.: University Press of America, 1983).

11. Robins, *Short History of Linguistics,* 130–32. See also chap. 6 of J. R. Firth, *The Tongues of Men* (London: Watts, 1937).

the vigorous investigation of genetic relations among what were now recognized as the Indo-European languages. In 1786, in a paper presented to the Royal Asiatic Society in Calcutta, Sir William Jones claimed that Sanskrit was more refined than Latin and Greek, and that all three had "sprung from some common source."[12] Another, possibly more influential, impetus appeared in Friedrich Schlegel's *Über die Sprache und Weisheit der Indier* (On the language and wisdom of the Indians) of 1808, which went further than Jones by arguing the derivation of Greek, Latin, Persian, and German from Sanskrit or its source.[13] The 1810s, a particularly energetic period, saw the publication of Franz Bopp's study of Sanskrit in comparison with Greek, Latin, Persian, and German (1816), Rasmus Rask's treatise on the origins of Icelandic (1818), and Jakob Grimm's investigation of the grammar of Germanic languages (1819), while in 1820, in Russia, Vostokov published his study of the Slavic languages (*Rassuzhdenie o slavianskom iazyke* [Dissertation on the Slavic language]). Not long after, August Pott's *Etymologische Forschungen auf dem Gebiet der indogermanischen Sprachen* (Etymological research in the sphere of Indo-Germanic language) [1833–36]) consolidated these foundations of modern comparative and historical studies in linguistics.

The reconstruction of a hypothetical Indo-European language and the comparative-historical studies that accompanied it without a doubt represent the signal achievement of nineteenth-century linguistics.[14] To that extent Indo-European studies also represent one of the most important chapters in human thought about what language is, concentrated in the question of how it has evolved. Parallel to these investigations, however, there persisted efforts to define the ontology of language and formulate a general theory of language in its relation to thought—impulses that even some of the comparative and historical studies had been unable to resist as they sifted through their copious empirical data (Friedrich Schlegel, for example, was led to muse on the intellectual superiority of "organic," by which he meant inflected, languages).[15] These efforts raised few issues that were new, but what changed in the nineteenth century was the degree to which language came to be incorporated within descriptions of the self and its mental life; and it was nineteenth-century western European, particularly

12. Robins, *Short History of Linguistics*, 140, 168.

13. Anna Morpurgo Davies, *Nineteenth-Century Linguistics*, vol. 4 in Giulio Lepschy, ed., *History of Linguistics* (London: Longman, 1998), 68.

14. V. A. Zvegintsev, *Istoriia iazykoznaniia XIX–XX vekov v ocherkakh i izvlecheniiakh*, chast' I (Moscow: Prosveshchenie, 1964), 28–29. See also Holger Pedersen, *Linguistic Science in the Nineteenth Century. Methods and Results*, trans. John Webster Spargo (Cambridge: Harvard University Press, 1931).

15. Amirova et al., *Ocherki po istorii lingvistiki*, 319.

German, thought that provided the immediate stimulus for the writings on language that so vividly characterize Russian cultural life in the *fin-de-siècle* and early twentieth century.

Both rationalist philosophy and the ancient sources on which it drew had posited a close relation between thought and language, but had tended to relegate language to a secondary, instrumental role in the relationship (nowhere better exemplified than in the notion that a philosophically more efficient language could be devised *ad hoc*).[16] Condillac altered this scheme in his 1746 *Essai sur l'origine des connaissances humaines* (*Essay on the Origins of Human Knowledge*) when he suggested the fundamental necessity of language to thought by arguing that only the use of signs, first and foremost linguistic signs, makes it possible for us to deploy any thoughts more complex than the simplest ideas supplied to us by our sensory perceptions. It is signs that allow us to abstract, juxtapose, and conjoin simple ideas, and it is these activities, which result from reflection and experience, rather than the reception of sensory impressions and the ideas they trigger, that represent the active workings of the human mind. These signs serve as "chains to the different combinations of simple ideas" that we make. Memory is particularly reliant on such signs. Thus for Condillac language is not thought as such, but it serves as thought's indispensable catalyst. Moreover, Condillac is motivated by an impulse that was to resurface in such movements as Quine's ordinary language philosophy, namely, to examine the use we habitually make of words in order to discern something of the principles informing our ideas (Condillac credits Locke with this impulse, and in fact presents his entire essay as an embellishment on Locke's 1690 essay on human understanding). His ultimate aim is akin to that of the would-be creators of universal language, albeit less extreme: to eliminate ambiguous speech and the use of concepts sanctioned only by custom, in the hope of removing philosophical error from language.[17]

The genuinely pathbreaking innovation in describing the relationship between language and the self, however, was made by Johann Gottfried Herder, in his 1772 *Abhandlung über den Ursprung der Sprache* (*Essay on the*

16. Gadamer calls this the "instrumentalist devaluation of language that we find in modern times"; see Hans-Georg Gadamer, *Truth and Method,* trans. Joel Weinsheimer and Donald G. Marshall (New York: Continuum, 1998), 403–4. See also Buzuk's similar remark that, for all the differences in their views of whether an essential link exists between language and thought, Aristotle and the Stoics, on the one hand, and the Alexandrine grammarians, on the other, shared the assumption that language is no more than an external tool (*orudie*) for the expression of thought. For Buzuk, it was not until Humboldt that this assumption was challenged; see P. A. Buzuk, *Ocherki po psikhologii iazyka* (Odessa: Knigoizdatel'stvo A. A. Ivasenko, 1918), 111.

17. Étienne Bonnot de Condillac, *An Essay on the Origin of Human Knowledge. Being a Supplement to Mr. Locke's Essay on the Human Understanding,* trans. Thomas Nugent (1746, 1971; Delmar, N.Y.: Scholars' Facsimiles and Reprints, 1998), 110, 120, 53.

Origin of Language), one of the great trio of eighteenth-century treatises on language and mind (the other two being Condillac's essay and Rousseau's *Essai sur l'origine des langues* [*Essay on the Origin of Languages*] of the 1750s).[18] Instead of the previously assumed relationship of hierarchy, in which thought/reason and its categories preceded linguistic expression and the categories of grammar, Herder posited a common origin and parallel development. In his account language and thought are inseparable; language is the tool, the content, and the form of human thinking—a definition that makes language an organic part of the self, at least to the extent that thinking is considered central to selfhood.[19] Herder rejected the popular explanations that language originated in exclamations arising out of sensations (outcries of emotion), as both Rousseau and Condillac had asserted (animals utter such noises, too, Herder remarks, but such noises are not language), or that language was a divine gift (no God needs to invent language).[20] Instead he claims that humans, as reflective beings, invented language in order to make sense of the world around them.[21] For Herder language was an instrument, but it was one without which the end it served could not exist. "Thus language appears as a natural organ of reason, a sense of the human soul, as the power of vision . . . built for itself the eye" [*sic*]; "I cannot think the first human thought, I cannot align the first reflective argument without dialoguing in my soul or without striving to dialogue."[22] So central is language to Herder's concept of human identity that we are, in his account, "creatures of language."[23] One significant corollary of this idea was that, since language and thought are interdependent, the thought patterns and literatures of different peoples could be understood only through their own language—hence the preoccupation with national speech, literature, and identity that Herder bequeathed to the Romantic age. This notion was important also to Humboldt, and resurfaced in more recent times

---

18. John H. Moran in his afterword to the English translation of Rousseau's essay says that parts of the essay were begun in 1749, the rest finished in the mid-1750s but withheld from publication. Rousseau viewed language as, if not essential to the self, nonetheless a handy adjunct to the self's most important element, the passions. In his account language is the means invented by humans for the expression of pre-rational feelings (in the sense that for Rousseau one feels before one can think). Its natural mode was oral, poetical, and metaphorical rather than written, prosaic, and literal (writing altered language by substituting exactitude for expressiveness). In Johan Gottfried Herder and Jean-Jacques Rousseau, *On the Origin of Language,* trans., with afterwords, by John H. Moran and Alexander Gode (Chicago: University of Chicago Press, 1966), 80–81.

19. Johann Gottfried Herder, "Essay on the Origin of Language," in *On the Origin of Language* (1966; reprint, Chicago: University of Chicago Press, 1986), 155.

20. Ibid., 127.

21. Ibid., 119.

22. Ibid., 127, 128.

23. Ibid., 143.

in the once-influential linguistic relativity thesis associated with Whorf, Sapir, and Boas.[24]

By far the most influential extension of Herder's assertion that language is essentially involved in selfhood was Wilhelm von Humboldt's monumental *Über die Verschiedenheit des menschlichen Sprachbaues und ihren Einfluss auf die geistige Entwicklung des Menschengeschlechts* (1836; *On Language: The Diversity of Human Language-Structure and Its Influence on the Mental Development of Mankind*), a lengthy essay he wrote as the introduction to a three-volume study of the Kawi language spoken on the island of Java (*Über die Kavi-Sprache auf der Insel Java* [1836–1840]). For Humboldt, though language and thought can artificially be considered apart from one another, language is "the formative organ of thought," the means through which "entirely internal" intellectual activity is externalized and made perceptible to the senses.[25] In contrast to the conception of language as separable instrument embraced by the rationalists, Humboldt's metaphor of "organ" makes language integral to the self and its metaphorical body. "Thought and language are . . . one and inseparable from each other. But the former is also intrinsically bound to the necessity of entering into a union with the verbal sound; thought cannot otherwise achieve clarity, nor the idea become a concept."[26] In the historical life of humankind there are even certain "paths of the spirit" (that is, philosophical developments) that are unthinkable until there arise languages in which to think them, these languages themselves thus representing milestones in humankind's development (this is the "mental development of mankind" referred to in his title; Humboldt was very interested in this idea of the fitness of certain languages to certain types of thought, and believed that inflected languages, in particular Sanskrit, were philosophically superior to others, such as Chinese, which he felt left all grammatical form to the work of the mind).[27] At the same time, with characteristic Romantic emphasis on spontaneous outflow, Humboldt claimed that language arises not out of the premeditated aim of creating an aid to communication but as an "involuntary emanation of the spirit" generated by an "inner need of man"; it is "a thing lying in his own nature,

24. Robins notes that this idea is anticipated in the medieval doctrine of nominalism; *Short History of Linguistics,* 102. For insight into some of Herder's contradictions and shortcomings, as well as into the intellectual context of his essay, see Paul B. Salmon, "Also Ran. Some Rivals of Herder in the Berlin Academy's 1770 Essay Competition on the Origin of Language," *Historiographia Linguistica* XVI (1989):1/2, 25–48.

25. Wilhelm von Humboldt, *On Language: The Diversity of Human Language-Structure and Its Influence on the Mental Development of Mankind,* trans. Peter Heath (Cambridge: Cambridge University Press, 1988), 46.

26. Ibid., 54–55.

27. Ibid., 44; see also 100, 145, 230.

indispensable for the development of his mental powers and the attainment of a worldview."[28]

Humboldt's account also shows with particular clarity how certain ideas about the self could shape a theory of language; that is to say, the extent to which certain properties attributed to language—such as self-containment, boundedness, unity, coherence, inwardness versus outwardness—may be traced to underlying notions about selfhood. Indeed in many ways Humboldt describes language as if it *were* a self. As he states in his famous adversative definition, language is not *ergon* or "dead product" such as grammarians might analyze but the *energeia* or activity through which humans form concepts and express them to one another, which is to say that language is not a thing but one of the processes comprising the life of the self (in the German terms Humboldt also uses, language is not *Erzeugtes* but the generative process of *Erzeugnung*).[29] Although some forms of language acquire an "incomplete, mummy-like preservation" in writing, language in the proper sense is never a fixed object but an "ever-repeated mental labour of making articulated sound capable of expressing thought."[30] Indeed, so closely is language to be identified with subjectivity that no matter how much we might "fix and embody, dismember and dissect" it through analysis, there will always remain in it some unknowable residue "wherein the unity and breath of a living thing resides."[31] Humboldt even suggests that thought concretized in the form of actual words and utterances is already "dead product," so that "the soul must continually try to make itself independent of the domain of language, for the word, after all, is a *constraint* upon its ever more capacious inner sensitivity"; the soul should regard the word as a mere "resting place" for its inner activity[32]—as if genuine language were some state existing just prior to articulation as such. There is no more stasis in language, Humboldt asserts, than there is in the "ceaseless effulgence of human thinking itself."[33]

Humboldt's pronouncements on the social nature of language, a point on which Condillac had also dwelt, develop in a similar vein. Language for Humboldt always originates in dialogue, whose importance to him (as opposed to the meaning it held for Russians like Shpet, Florenskii, and to some extent Bakhtin) seems to lie less in a principle of communality than of indeterminacy and process. A word for Humboldt does not convey a

28. Ibid., 24, 27.
29. Ibid., 48–49.
30. Ibid., 49.
31. Ibid., 51.
32. Ibid., 92.
33. Ibid., 143.

fixed concept, "it merely provokes the user to form such a concept under his own power. . . . Men do not understand one another by actually exchanging signs for things, nor by mutually occasioning one another to produce exactly and completely the same concept; they do it by touching in one another the same link in the chain of their sensory ideas and internal conceptualizations, by striking the same note on their mental instrument."[34] The result is the engendering of "matching but not identical" concepts in each mind.[35] As he puts it in a celebrated statement, "all understanding is always at the same time a not-understanding, all concurrence in thought and feeling at the same time a divergence."[36] For Humboldt "language" is always prior—ontologically and even temporally—to anything we could identify as its empirical product.

Humboldt also treats language as something directly involved in the ontology of selfhood by describing the articulatory process as a bodying forth of something arising internally, in the spirit, into the outward, material realm. Just as thought yearns to move from darkness into light, from confinement into the infinite, he argues, "so sound streams outward from the heart's depths, and finds a medium wonderfully suited to it in the air . . . whose seeming incorporeality is also a sensuous counterpart to the mind."[37] Sound enters into language-making because as mental striving "breaks out through the lips" its acoustical product is returned to the speaker's ear. The result is something like a self harmoniously poised between inner and outer worlds. "Thus the presentation becomes transformed into real objectivity, without being deprived of subjectivity on that account. Only language can do this."[38] Language here is almost entirely subsumed within an account of selfhood. Humboldt essentially has little to say about language that is not also or really a statement about the self.

Most of all, perhaps, one senses Humboldt's pronouncements on language are influenced by an underlying model of selfhood when he describes the role language plays in the psychological processes that lead us toward self-consciousness and self-awareness. For Humboldt, who was still influenced by Enlightenment epistemology (that is, the assumption that there are two levels of human awareness, one a flow of "presentations" from the external world to the mind, the other a consciousness of or reflection on them), human consciousness operates within an indeterminate and formless

34. Ibid., 151–52.
35. Ibid., 152.
36. Ibid., 63.
37. Ibid., 55.
38. Ibid., 56.

flux of thoughts and perceptions.[39] In using—or rather in generating—language, however, we reflect on this flow, organize it, and deploy a sign (word) that lends unity to it. "The indeterminate working of the power of thought gathers itself together in a word. . . . Now it is an individual thing [*ein individuelles Wesen*], or determinate character and determinate form."[40] What is interesting here is Humboldt's tendency to transfer the principle of identity-conferring unity from consciousness as such to its linguistic vehicle, so that it is now the *word* that possesses unity and awareness: once language is placed at the center of the self, the qualities of selfhood centripetally migrate to it. Nowhere is this mapping of selfhood onto language clearer than in Humboldt's assertion that language is an "internally connected organism," possessing not only subordinate parts but also "laws of procedure . . . directions and endeavours" that may be compared with the physiological laws determining the workings of the human body.[41] One even senses something of this mapping in his adaptation of Herder's celebrated idea that the language and culture of a particular nation form an epistemological screen intervening between its members and the world they inhabit (something Humboldt labels a "*Zwischenwelt*").[42] Humboldt uses this idea in part to account for the "linguistic diversity" heralded in the title of the preface to his study of Kawi, but his discussion emphasizes not the grammatical, morphological, or phonological traits that would have interested comparative linguists but, again, modes of knowing that connote the self-like qualities of completeness, self-reference, and identity. National languages are possessed of a guiding principle, a leitmotif, a unity conferred on them by an underlying national "feeling" or "impulse," and the very metaphor he uses for this phenomenon points toward origins in thought about the self: "*Charakter der Nation*," "*Charakter der Sprache*."[43]

Humboldt's metaphoric reference to language as an "organism," in fact, points up an influential current in nineteenth-century thought that is also indicative of some of the conceptual paths Russian thinking on language

39. See Martin L. Manchester, *The Philosophical Foundations of Humboldt's Linguistic Doctrines*, Amsterdam Studies in the Theory and History of Linguistics Science, Studies in the History of the Language Sciences, vol. 32 (Amsterdam: John Benjamins, 1985), 37, 46.

40. Quoted in Manchester, *Philosophical Foundations*, 37.

41. Humboldt, *On Language*, 21, 90.

42. Ibid., 157. For related ideas in nineteenth-century psychology, see Arens, *Structures of Knowing*. Arens identifies a body of ideas she terms "conceptual psychology" and associates with a range of figures from Herbart to Wundt, Dilthey, and Mach, as the dominant paradigm in nineteenth-century psychology, describing it as emphasizing the epistemological role played by mental constructs, as well as their historicity, fluidity, cultural specificity, and conventionality (see in particular 105, 219–21, 338–39).

43. Manchester, *Philosophical Foundations*, 116; see also Humboldt, *On Language*, 50. Incidentally these phrases already appear in Condillac, *Essay on the Origin of Human Knowledge*, 283.

was to take ("indicative" because while the patterns are similar, some of the sources are different): that of organicism.[44] In his Vienna lectures of 1808 August Schlegel drew a seminal distinction between "mechanisms," which are formed out of parts externally appropriated and artificially assembled, and "organisms," which carry their own motivation and impulse for development within them. For Schlegel organic form is therefore innate, whereas mechanical form is an accidental addition.[45] Before long organic metaphors had spread throughout German philosophy and had become one of the dominant ways of interpreting human experience. In the case of language, into thought about which Cassirer credits Schlegel with introducing the notion of "organic form," the organic metaphor gave rise to prolific attribution of the qualities of living beings to verbal phenomena.[46] In particular German thought in this period tended to see the organism, with its combination of unity and cyclical development, as the prototype for all dynamic wholes—which meant that to the extent that language was conceived as such a whole, it began also to be thought of as resembling a living being, and very often a kind of self. With this came the expectation of certain traits, such as a propensity to undergo constant change and cyclical development (in 1833–36 Pott, for example, described languages as having life cycles), self-containment, and motivation by an internal rather than external force. In this line of thought the principle of organization in an organism was held to be innate, the organism representing a unity guaranteed by the mutual dependence and interrelatedness of its parts.[47] The tendency was thus to see language as developing according to its own internal laws, as constituting an autonomous entity demanding its own discipline of study (similar assumptions, minus the explicit acknowledgment of organicist thinking, underlie the Russian Formalists' view of the literary work of art).[48] The conceptual paradigm of organicism could exert profound influence even when it was meant metaphorically, as Davies claims is the case in

44. Chomsky points out that Humboldt was influenced by Romantic discussions of mechanical versus organic form; *Cartesian Linguistics,* 22–3.

45. Davies, *Nineteenth-Century Linguistics,* 86.

46. Cassirer's remark is in his *Philosophy of Symbolic Forms,* quoted in Davies, *Nineteenth-Century Linguistics,* 86. Davies, however, notes the extent to which the idea was already in the air—in Herder, in Schelling. Of course, as we have seen, the kind of structural metaphors one finds in organicism go back quite far: the Port Royal grammar, for example, describes signs as having an "outside," consisting of sounds or letters, and an "inside," consisting of meanings or the ways in which people use sounds to express thoughts; Amirova et al., *Ocherki po istorii lingvistiki,* 214. Amirova et al. explicitly draw a parallel between this aspect of the Port Royal conception of language and Chomskian deep versus surface structure (ibid., 231). One also recalls the *Beseda* together with its Orthodox patristic precedents and parallels in Augustine.

47. Davies, *Nineteenth-Century Linguistics,* 86–87.

48. On the lack of a notion of personhood in Formalism see Rancour-Laferriere, "Why the Formalists Had No Theory of the Literary Person," 327–37.

Humboldt; but in the second half of the century, in the works of such figures as August Schleicher and Max Müller, the metaphor comes to be taken
literally and is brought to "extreme consequences": "language now becomes
a real organism with a life of its own independent from that of the speaker."[49]

Some sense of the seductive powers wielded by this organicist paradigm
can be gathered from a 1945 essay by Cassirer, in which he argues that Humboldt's version of organicism served as an important precedent for an "organic" view of language that became influential in the twentieth century in
the form of nothing less than structural linguistics, a body of thought one
ordinarily thinks of as remote from metaphysical speculation. By "organic"
Cassirer means a conception of language as a coherent whole whose parts
are mutually dependent, rather than as an aggregate of detached, isolated
facts.[50] He opposes this view to the empirical-inductive studies predominant in the nineteenth century, whose "spell," he claims, was broken by the
1900 publication of the first volume of Husserl's *Logische Untersuchungen*
(*Logical Investigations*; though, see above, Schlegel really broke the spell a
century earlier).[51] Cassirer suggests that organicism is the same view as the
"holism" underlying paleontology, which enables scientists in that field to
reconstruct an entire organism if they possess even one of its parts, guided
by the belief that there are no accidental components in organisms. He
traces it back ultimately to Goethe's use of the term "*Gestalt*," and its associated "morphological idealism," in his ruminations on the changes plant
types undergo in the natural world (specifically, forms arising out of form-
lessness) and notes that when psychologists much later began to break away
from the Humean tradition and to regard psychic life as something more
than a mere aggregate of sense-data or "simple ideas," they could find no
better term for the integrated whole they were attempting to define than
"*Gestalt*."[52] Cassirer insists that in the case of linguistics the "organic" quality is formal and methodological rather than ontological (Schleicher, he
notes, erred in taking the comparison of language with an organism literally and ontologically); but one can nonetheless also see the notion of
morphologically ideal *Gestalt* or organicism that Cassirer describes—which
appears in Goethe, then Humboldt, then resurfaces in Husserl and goes on
from there to underlie structural linguistics—as none other than a metaphor for the self, which furthermore underlies *both* Romantic organicism
and structuralist "holism."

Another nineteenth-century philosopher whom it would be impossible
to overlook in this context is Hegel. Although Hegel only occasionally

49. Davies, *Nineteenth-Century Linguistics*, 88, 104.
50. Ernst A. Cassirer, "Structuralism in Modern Linguistics," *Word* 1 (April 1945): 110.
51. Ibid., 102.
52. Ibid., 105, 120.

touches on issues having to do with language, he figures importantly in the history of the ideas I am tracing here as the author of what was arguably the most significant account of selfhood in the nineteenth century, his *Phenomenology of the Spirit.* He was also enormously influential on Russian thought from the 1840s onward, and even after the waning of his intellectual hegemony toward the nineteenth-century's end continued to hold sway in the twentieth through such thinkers as Bakhtin and Lukács.[53]

Hegel defines the self as a form of emergent and self-reifying consciousness, and the enormous attraction his writings exerted had in part to do with the way his discussion in works like *The Phenomenology of the Spirit* deftly straddles several frames of reference at once: his remarks on the nature of consciousness present themselves as a definition of the metaphysical concept of spirit as such, detached from any individual embodiment; but they also add up to his seminal doctrine of how sense or idea unfolds within world history, while at the same time offering themselves as a possible account of the mental or psychological life of the individual.

Particularly consonant with the views of language that became important in Russia during the late nineteenth and early twentieth centuries are Hegel's remarks on the divisions experienced within the self in the course of its development, his account of how spirit (or the self, or self-consciousness) undergoes a partial extrusion of itself and then reassimilates this reified part of itself into its life-process. This moment of emptying or self-extrusion is also that in which consciousness becomes aware of itself, and in which self-consciousness arises. The fundamental act that leads to this state of affairs is one that "divides spirit into spiritual substance on the one side, and consciousness of the substance on the other."[54] This act also gives rise to a contradiction in which the self, which is spirit, must now confront a part of itself that has entered the world of things; but this thinglike part of the self is now paradoxically recuperated as an organic, even essential, component of the self. "This self that is turned into a thing, is in fact the return of reality into itself; it is a being-by-itself that is there for its own sake, the existential form of spirit. . . . Being-by-itself on its own account is, strictly speaking, the loss of self, and alienation of self is really self-preservation."[55] Or, as Hegel puts it more clearly in his preface to the *Phenomenology*: "The spirit . . . becomes an object, for the spirit is this movement of becoming

53. See Edward J. Brown, *Stankevich and His Moscow Circle, 1830–1840* (Stanford: Stanford University Press, 1966); and Galin Tihanov, *The Master and the Slave. Lukács, Bakhtin, and the Ideas of Their Time* (Oxford: Oxford University Press, 2000).

54. Georg Wilhelm Friedrich Hegel, *The Phenomenology of the Spirit,* in *The Philosophy of Hegel,* ed. Carl J. Friedrich (New York: Modern Library, 1953), 414.

55. Ibid., 456.

something other for itself, i.e., an object for its self, and then to sublimate this otherhood."[56]

This doctrine of the self's objectification is relevant in the context of this study because the Russians often regard language, as Hegel himself does, as precisely this kind of reification of the spirit that exits into otherness only in order to be reabsorbed within the organic entity of the self—indeed, as the preeminent example of such reifications. It is, Hegel tells us in the *Phenomenology*, "the existence of a pure self as self; in speech the particular self-existent self-consciousness comes as such into existence, so that its particular individuality is something for others. . . . Language contains the ego in its purity; it alone expresses the 'I' as self. Its existence in this case is, as existence, a form of objectivity which has in it the true nature of existence."[57] In other words, for Hegel language is the reified *form* in which the self has its existence, an idea we will encounter again in the writings of such Russians as Gustav Shpet, Pavel Florenskii, Aleksei Losev, and even, as I will argue, Roman Jakobson. In this line of thought language is "a way of existing which is directly self-conscious existence."[58] What brings Hegel even closer to the Russian tradition of thought about language is the likely source for this idea about the self seeking its form in language. As Walter Kaufmann points out in his commentary to this text, what Hegel has here presented in metaphysical terms is in fact a sublimated version of the Christian account of the Trinity:

> "The spirit is this movement" alludes to the Holy Spirit: God the Father become God the Son—he becomes something other for himself, an object for himself—but then this otherhood is canceled and yet preserved in the Holy Spirit. Spirit is that which is not static, nor unstained self-identity; on the contrary, it is of its very essence that it is dynamic, is development, is sublimated otherhood.[59]

For good measure one could add, and there is no contradiction here, that Hegel's account of spirit is also a sublimated version of the cosmology elaborated by the Neoplatonists, who regarded the world and all it contains as the products of successive manifestations or exitings of essence from "the One"—a doctrine that, as we will see, often paralleled that of Christianity in Russian thought.[60]

56. Georg Wilhelm Friedrich Hegel, Preface to the *Phenomenology of the Spirit*, in *Hegel: Texts and Commentary*, trans. and ed. Walter Kaufmann (South Bend, Ind.: University of Notre Dame Press, 1977), 56.

57. Hegel, *Phenomenology of the Spirit*, 446.

58. Ibid., 481.

59. In Hegel, Preface to the *Phenomenology of the Spirit*, 57.

60. On the affinities between Hegel's "emanationist" view of things and the Neoplatonists, especially Plotinus, see Charles Taylor, *Hegel* (Cambridge: Cambridge University Press, 1975), 102.

Although it shares with its western European counterpart an origin in Greek thought, and although in the post-Petrine era (from the eighteenth century onward) it largely followed Western initiatives, Russian thought on the nature of language has a different—and rich—history of its own that must be taken into account when considering Russian writings on language of the *fin-de-siècle* and early twentieth century.

Russian, or more broadly Orthodox Slavic, speculation on the nature of language goes back at least to the ninth century, when the use of Old Church Slavic spread among the eastern and southern Slavs together with controversy surrounding its appropriateness, versus that of Greek, Hebrew, or Latin, as a vessel for the liturgy and scriptures.[61] At this early stage, recorded Slavic awareness of language consisted mostly of a "Cyrillo-Methodian" doctrine which held that there were scriptural warrants for using any language for Christian worship,[62] though this doctrine was sometimes applied in intricate ways (for example, when mounting an apology for Old Church Slavic against the rival claims of the supranational Greek language, the defenders of its use tended to treat it as a weapon for the defense of ethnic self-identity; but among the Slavs themselves Old Church Slavic came to be treated as a rigidly codified, supranational language in its own right, suppressive of local dialects).[63]

If it is true that grammatical and metaphysical categories have long enjoyed a relationship of mutual infection (see, for example, the argument that Aristotelian metaphysical categories are essentially expressions of grammatical functions of the Greek language),[64] then even early attempts at grammatical descriptions of the Slavic language(s), such as the *Os'm' chestii*

61. Robert Mathiesen notes that the use of OCS was linked with the Slavs' drive toward political independence from the eastern part of the Roman empire and for the autocephaly of their churches; see his "The Church Slavonic Language Question: An Overview (IX–XX Centuries)," in Riccardo Picchio and Harvey Goldblatt, eds., *Aspects of the Slavic Language Question*, vol. 1, *Church Slavonic—South Slavic—West Slavic* (New Haven: Yale Concilium on International and Area Studies, 1984), 45–65. Some of the most important medieval Slavic writings on language are collected in V. Jagić *Codex Slovenicus Rerum Grammaticarum*, Slavische Proplyäen, Band 25 (1896, reprint; Munich: Wilhelm Fink Verlag, 1968). For a survey of Russian conceptions of grammar in medieval writings on language from the (rather narrow) viewpoint of structural linguistics, see Dean S. Worth, *The Origins of Russian Grammar. Notes on the State of Russian Philology Before the Advent of Printed Grammars* (Columbus, Ohio: Slavica, 1983).

62. Mathiesen, "Church Slavonic Language Question," 52.

63. Harvey Goldblatt, "The Church Slavonic Language Question in the Fourteenth and Fifteenth Centuries: Constantin Kostenečki's *Skazánje izъjavljénno ō pismenex*," in Picchio and Goldblatt, eds., *Aspects of the Slavic Language Question*, vol. 1, *Church Slavonic—South Slavic—West Slavic*, 68.

64. Emile Benveniste argues that Aristotle's choice of categories is determined by the Greek language, i.e., by the Indo-European grammatical pattern; see his *Problèmes de linguistique générale*, vol. 1 (Paris: Gallimard, 1966), 63–74. See also Naftali Prat, "Orthodox Philosophy of Language in Russia," *Studies in Soviet Thought* 20 (1979): 9.

slova (The eight parts of speech, known in Serbian and Russian manuscripts
of the fourteenth to seventeenth centuries),[65] which describes Slavic morphology in terms of the categories of noun, verb, participle, article, pronoun, preposition, adverb, and conjunction, may not be innocent of
metaphysics; nor, as we have seen, is the very notion of "grammar," which
is to say, of "language as form," which Kolesov argues was brought to Rus'
by this document.[66] But genuine philosophical reflection on language
seems to have begun in earnest among the Slavs in the fourteenth and fifteenth centuries, when the Cyrillo-Methodian metalinguistic doctrine was
radically amended by a "Euthymian" one. Named after Euthymius of
Trnovo, who served from 1375 to 1393 as the last patriarch of medieval Bul-
garia, this doctrine was closely linked with the so-called Hesychast movement in Orthodox theology (on which more below), and is largely without
parallel in the West.[67] In the particular case of Russia, it arrived as a part of
the "second South Slavic influence" occasioned by the migration to Russian
lands of Balkan scholars fleeing the Turkish advance into their homelands.[68]
In keeping with a Hesychast belief in the distinction between the unknowable Divine Essence (*ousia*) and its accessible manifestations in the form of
"energies" (*energeiai*), the Euthymian metalinguistic doctrine held that written letters are not intermediary symbols but direct manifestations of the Divine Presence, so that every "orthograph" is a visible representation of the
Divine Word.[69] This idea was further developed by Euthymius's pupil Con-
stantine Kostenečki, for whom language was an "instrument of divine revelation through the means of graphic signs whose origins and spiritual
function must be discovered even before one can regulate their empirical
use."[70] It was this doctrine that generated the apprehension among late medieval Slavic scribes, familiar to Russianists from its especially vivid application by the Old Believers during the religious Schism of the seventeenth
century, that an accidental slip of the pen or tongue might yield a heretical
statement. Out of it also grew a fairly elaborate set of orthographic rules

---

65. Silvia Toscano, "Orthodox Slavdom," in Giulio Lepschy, ed., *History of Linguistics*, vol. 3,
Renaissance and Early Modern Linguistics (London: Longman, 1998), 125–27.

66. Vladimir V. Kolesov, "Traces of the Medieval Russian Language Question in the Russian
Azbukovniki," in Picchio and Goldblatt, eds., *Aspects of the Slavic Language Question*, vol. 2, *East
Slavic* (New Haven: Yale Concilium on International and Area Studies, 1984), 91.

67. See Goldblatt, "Church Slavonic Language Question," 69; Mathiesen, "Church Slavonic
Language Question," 56, 62. Toscano considers the advent of Hesychasm to mark the "birth of
philology" among the Slavs; "Orthodox Slavdom," 127.

68. Toscano, "Orthodox Slavdom," 131.

69. Goldblatt, "Church Slavonic Language Question," 74. Or, in Mathiesen's semiological definition, "the connection between a *significans* and a *significatum* is not arbitrary and conventional
but necessary and inherent in the *significans*"; "Church Slavonic Language Question," 58.

70. Goldblatt, quoted in Toscano, "Orthodox Slavdom," 129.

(known as *antistoecha* [in Russian, *antistikha*]) intended to safeguard against such error by ensuring that distinctions be made among homophonous grammatical or lexical forms.[71] Language (or at least Old Church Slavic) in this view ceased to be a mere vehicle of communication but in a wholly earnest way came to be viewed as itself constituting "a sort of icon representing Orthodox theology."[72] One interesting corollary was that graphic signs came to be viewed not as indexes of language but as language itself,[73] another that writing was privileged over speech, since written texts in Old Church Slavic were held to be not records of but models for spoken speech.[74]

In Russia the development of this Euthymian doctrine was partly interrupted by a remarkable group of Muscovite and Novgorod heretics in the later fifteenth and sixteenth centuries, who anticipated the secularizing trend that was to replace it.[75] Embracing an ideology close to that of the European Renaissance which emphasized the importance of knowledge for its own sake—"*izhe kotoryi glupyi, u boga ne mozhet' byti*" ("for whoever is stupid cannot approach God")[76]—these writers occupied themselves with a variety of scholarly rather than strictly theological problems, including that of grammatical description. The most intriguing of their works is the so-called *Laodikiiskoe poslanie* (Laodicean epistle) of the late fifteenth century, written by the Moscow heretic deacon Fedor Kuritsyn in a cipher known only to a few initiates, which aimed to present encyclopedic information on the Russian language, in alphabetic order (Kuritsyn was also

71. Mathiesen, "Orthodox Language Question," 63, 59. Kostenečki argued that if one wrote "*edinorodnii si*" ("the only-begotten ones") instead of the correct "*edinorodnyi sy sn^*" ("the only-begotten Son"), one would commit the Nestorian heresy of dividing Christ into two persons; see Goldblatt, "Church Slavonic Language Question," 74.

72. Mathiesen, "Orthodox Language Question," 60.

73. Goldblatt, "Church Slavonic Language Question," 75, quoting Riccardo Picchio, "Church Slavonic," in Alexander M. Schenker and Edward Stankiewicz, eds., *The Slavic Literary Languages: Formation and Development* (New Haven: Yale Concilium on International and Area Studies, 1980), 1–33.

74. Mathiesen, "Church Slavonic Language Question," 59; Toscano, "Orthodox Slavdom," 127–28.

75. On the heretical sects see N. A. Kazakova, *Antifeodal'nye ereticheskie dvizheniia na Rusi XIV-nachala XVI veka* (Leningrad, 1955); cited in Roman Jakobson, "One of the Speculative Anticipations. An Old Russian Treatise on the Divine and Human Word," *Selected Writings*, vol. 2 (The Hague: Mouton, 1971), 369. Mathiesen points out that the Schism that shook the Russian Church in the early seventeenth century was essentially a conflict between the Euthymian and Meletian views of OCS ("The Church Slavonic Language Question," 63). For a "case study" of how these two views (here presented as textual versus grammatical) influenced interpretations of the OCS verb forms for "to be," see V. Zhivov and B. Uspenskii, "Grammatica sub specie Theologiae. Preteritnye formy glagola 'byti' v russkom iazykovom soznanii XVI-XVIII vekov," *Russian Linguistics*, vol. 10, no. 3 (1986): 259–79.

76. Quoted in Kolesov, "Traces of the Medieval Russian Language Question," 100.

author of the *Napisanie o gramote* [Treatise on grammar], which argued the human rather than divine origins of speech).[77] Yet even in these secularizing works metalinguistic description did not escape metaphysical or even theological entanglements. For example, Russian scribes writing as late as the seventeenth century—but drawing on an Orthodox compilation of translations from the tenth—often resorted to a ternary system for classifying linguistic phenomena because they "tried to comprehend the general and particular grammatical categories through the prism of their Christian view of the world, which projected them onto the ternary grid: *svjatoe* ('holy'),—*srednee* ('middle')—*padšee* ('fallen')."[78] Thus the paradigmatic series angel-man-devil (that is, high-middle-low) was seen to replicate itself in the distribution of such linguistic phenomena as singular-dual-plural number and masculine-neuter-feminine gender.[79] The heretics rejected this ternary principle in favor of such oppositions as vowel-nonvowel, masculine-nonmasculine, which seem presciently to anticipate the marked/unmarked binary oppositions of structural linguistics. They did so, however, not because this struck them as a more accurate way to describe language, but because the essence of their heresy lay in a rejection of the doctrine of the Holy Trinity, which is to say, they were rejecting the particular hypothesis of Divine Being that underlay the ternary system.[80]

It was precisely on these grounds that the heretics were attacked when their movement was forcibly suppressed and Russian metalinguistic doctrine reverted aggressively to Euthymian precepts. The reaction in fact produced one of the philosophically boldest of the early Russian works on language, the anonymous *Beseda o uchenii gramote,* which is found in Muscovite manuscripts of the sixteenth and seventeenth centuries.[81] Aimed specifically at countering the anti-trinitarianism and "humanism" of Kuritsyn's *Napisanie,* the *Beseda* asserts what was to become one of the most influential analogies between language and self in the Russian context. After an opening explication of the nature of the Trinity—the Divine Self—the work argues that its structure is replicated within the human self as well, in the form of psyche (analogous with the Father), word (Son), and reason

77. Ibid., 8–9; Toscano, "Orthodox Slavdom," 132.

78. Kolesov, "Traces of the Medieval Russian Language Question," 95.

79. Ibid., 94. Binary systems of classification were also available to late medieval Russian scribes, however. Kolesov attributes the ternary system to a work he identifies as the *Bogoslovie.* The same tenth-century collection of translations from the Greek that contained it, however, also contained a work called the *Dialektika* (written by John of Damascus and translated by John Exarch the Bulgarian) that deployed a binary system; see Kolesov, "Traces of the Medieval Russian Language Question," 94.

80. Kolesov, "Traces of the Medieval Russian Language Question," 95.

81. Jakobson, "One of the Speculative Anticipations," 369; see also Jagić, *Codex Slovenicus Rerum Grammaticarum,* 385–98.

(Holy Spirit). The most significant among these human components turns out, moreover, to be the word. Just as for the Orthodox fathers Christ is "twice-born," because he is eternally generated by the Father but also incarnated on earth among men, so does the word exist through some "incomprehensible birth," abiding "unknown near the soul," only to be "born again through a second, fleshy birth," during which it "emerges from the lips and reveals itself by the voice to the hearing."[82] Thus the word is conceived to be not only intimately linked with the self but inherently self-like in its properties, indeed as replicating the essential actions of the Divine Self within the individual. Actually this type of analogy was also known in the West, even if explicit awareness of it did not survive as long there as it did in Russia. Wolfson, who annotates Jakobson's presentation of the *Beseda,* points out the parallels between the double birth of the word as described in the Russian work and a Stoic doctrine distinguishing between "internal" and "uttered Logos," and notes that both Marius Victorinus and Augustine imputed a similar triune structure to the self (consisting of existence, life, and intelligence for the former; memory, understanding, and will for the latter).[83] Such an analogy between language and the self seems in particular to underlie Humboldt's remarks on speech sounds as material externalizations of something originating in the mind. It is also conceivable, if one wishes to speculate, that this analogy may also have been one of the ultimate sources of the organicist paradigm so influential in the nineteenth and early twentieth centuries—perhaps exerting its influence via the intermediary of Hegelian thought.

This type of medieval speculation on the nature of language eventually gave way to a "Meletian" doctrine (after Meletii Smotrytskii, author of a Slavic grammar of 1619), which tended to confine itself to what we would now recognize as purely linguistic concerns and which treated Old Church Slavic as a secularly "classical" language along the lines of Latin.[84] But the impulse to see language as connected with other important things beside itself remained subtly influential in Russia even after the sixteenth century—and was indeed to some extent consciously revived in the Russian writings

---

82. Ibid., 373.

83. Ibid., 372–73; also Harry Austryn Wolfson, *The Philosophy of the Church Fathers,* vol. 1, Faith, Trinity, Incarnation (Cambridge: Harvard University Press, 1964), 299–300, 361. Toscano, meanwhile, attributes this conception of language to the Orthodox Church fathers Gregory of Nyssa, Anastasius Sinaites, Gennadius Scholarius, and others, and points out that it also figures in such texts as the *Os'm' chestii slova,* Kostenečki's *Skazanie,* Iosif Volockij's *Prosvetitel',* and Zinovij Otenskij's *Istiny pokazanie;* "Orthodox Slavdom," 144, n. 21.

84. Kolesov, "Traces of the Medieval Language Question," 110, Mathiesen, "Church Slavonic Language Question," 61.

on language of the late nineteenth and early twentieth centuries with which this study is concerned.

Thus, although the most significant achievements in Russian linguistics of the seventeenth and eighteenth centuries were the grammars by Smotrytskii and Lomonosov, together with the treatises on the emerging literary language by Trediakovskii, Lomonosov, and Karamzin, a number of works from this period explore more evidently philosophical concerns (something which may in part be attributed to the fact that in Russian gymnasia universal grammar was taught in a series with logic, psychology, philosophy, and ethics).[85] For example, Radishchev's 1792 "O cheloveke, o ego smertnosti i bessmertii" (On man, his mortality, and his immortality) meditates in the spirit of Rousseau, Condillac, and Herder (whom he cites) on the miraculous gift speech represents. Radishchev invokes the nature of language as evidence for the metaphysical qualities of the self: language provides strong proof for the immortality of the soul, he states, because only an ignorant person could claim that speech is corporeal. Sound is corporeal, because it is nothing but the movement of air striking our ear drums; but the word is not to be identified with its corporeal signifier; it is something spiritual and living. "The word goes into the soul," Radishchev states, "while the sound disappears within the ear."[86] Again, what is characteristic here is the mediation of linguistic issues through recourse to notions about the self. In a similar vein was a work published in 1810 by I. Ornatovskii— like Potebnia after him, a professor at Khar'kov University—titled "Noveishee nachertanie pravil rossiiskoi grammatiki, na nachalakh vseobshchei osnovannykh" (A modern outline of the rules of Russian grammar, based on general principles), as well as an 1811 study by I. F. Timkovskii, yet another member of the Khar'kov faculty, titled "Opytnyi sposob k filosofskomu poznaniiu rossiiskogo iazyka" (Experimental means to a philosophical knowledge of the Russian language).

Even the nineteenth century in Russia, otherwise dominated by comparative-historical studies (such as A. Kh. Vostokov's 1820 "Rassuzhdenie o slavianskom iazyke, sluzhashchee vvedeniem k grammatike sego iazyka, sostavliaemoi po drevneishim onogo pis'mennym pamiatnikam" [Dissertation on the Slavic language, serving as an introduction to its grammar, compiled on the basis of its ancient written monuments], which appeared just after major works by Bopp, Rask, and Grimm) and heavily indebted to German models, betrays similar traces of the speculative urge. In part due to the influence of the Slavophile movement, Russian historical studies

85. F. M. Berezin, ed., *Khrestomatiia po istorii russkogo iazykoznaniia*, 2nd ed. (Moscow: Vysshaia shkola, 1977), 12.

86. Ibid., 27.

tended to emphasize the Romantic rather than Enlightenment-empirical strain in what they borrowed from Germany. As a result they tended to be less concerned, once they had established the morphological and syntactic relations among the Slavic languages, with reconstructing the Indo-European language than they were with characterizing the unique qualities of Russian language and culture along lines laid down by Herder and Humboldt. In effect the effort was to look for reflections of the national identity in the nation's language. Thus F. I. Buslaev sought to discover in the Russian language traces of the early attitudes, culture, and mores of the nation (in works such as "O prepodavanii otechestvennogo iazyka" [On teaching the language of the fatherland], 1844; "O vliianii khristianstva na slavianskii iazyk" [On Christianity's influence on the Slavic language], 1844; "Opyt istoricheskoi grammatiki russkogo iazyka" [Attempt at a historical grammar of the Russian language], 1858), while I. I. Sreznevskii sought to identify the development of Russian proper out of the family of Slavic languages with the period in which Russia "assumed its separate position among the nations of Europe."[87] Nowhere is this tendency more evident than in the writings of K. S. Aksakov, son of the writer S. T. Aksakov, who very likely influenced Potebnia. Aksakov argued that Russian grammar had its own "foundation and reason" and should not be analyzed according to the alien categories of languages like Latin.[88] For Aksakov the Russian language is the dwelling place of the "spirit of the nation" and is a living form whose parts are bound together by a common purpose ("O grammatike voobshche" [On grammar in general]); the word is "spirit embodied in the flesh of sound" ("*dukh, voplotivshiisia v zvukovuiu plot'*") whose true "inner life," moreover, consists in the meaning of its etymological root (this in particular may have influenced Potebnia).[89] To be sure, these are not much more than Romantic-organicist clichés, but they suggest that the inclination to view language as in some way manifesting characteristics of selfhood (albeit national in scope) were at least in the air at mid-century.

Moreover, Humboldt's influence on Russian intellectual life was fairly well established even before Potebnia so energetically adapted his ideas on the nature of language. K. P. Zelenetskii, whose *Sistema i soderzhanie filosofskogo iazykoucheniia s prilozheniem k iazyku russkomu* (System and content of philosophical linguistics in application to the Russian language [1841]) appeared only a few years after the posthumous publication of Humboldt's major works in 1836–39, follows Humboldt in drawing a distinction

---

87. I. I. Sreznevskii, *Mysli ob istorii russkogo iazyka. Chitano na akte Imp. S.-Peterburgskogo universiteta 8 fev. 1849 g.* (Moscow: Gos. uchebno-pedagogicheskoe izdatel'stvo, 1959), 35.

88. Berezin, *Khrestomatiia,* 94

89. Ibid., 146, 150.

between the outer and inner sides of language and argues that "external factors" such as soil and climate influence the way of thinking of a people,
which in turn is reflected in its language. He also follows Herder in rejecting the (Rousseauian) thesis of language's origins in exclamations, an argument in which Herder had laid the ground for asserting the link between
language and thought; calls "thought which presupposes the word" humankind's "first existential act"; and says that human self-consciousness
could only have expressed itself in the form of a sentence (the first one
specifically being "*Ia esm'*," "I am").[90] Despite being influenced by Becker's
Organismus der Sprache and its "biological" view of language, I. I. Davydov's
Opyt obshchesravnitel'noi grammatiki russkogo iazyka (Attempt at a comparative grammar of Russian [1852]) paraphrases Humboldt's idea that language is a record of development of the human spirit, as well as his thoughts
on the interplay between individual and social factors in the formation of
language.[91] M. A. Tulov's works on linguistic categories and Russian phonology are also steeped in Humboldt's and Steinthal's conception of language
as the product of national spirit (his ideas concerning etymology are very
close to those Potebnia was to develop, though this may just as likely be a
response to as it is an anticipation of the latter).

By the second half of the nineteenth century Russia thus had both an in-
digenous and a Western-influenced tradition of philosophical speculation
on language, neither of which was a novelty. Nonetheless, if one were to
search for the point at which the modern Russian interest in the nature of
language begins to coalesce, one would have to locate it in the writings of
the Ukrainian linguist Aleksandr Afanas'evich Potebnia (1835–91). Though
Potebnia can be derivative and even self-contradictory—at least when held
to the stricter standards of twentieth-century philosophy (see, for example,
Bibikhin's mostly anachronistic belittling of him)—his writings bring together a variety of impulses in the philosophy of language that were to prove
enormously fertile in the Russian context. Potebnia was nurtured in the
comparative and historical emphases that predominated Russian linguistics
in the middle of the nineteenth century (he was supposedly inspired to
study language by Sreznevskii's 1849 lecture, "Mysli ob istorii russkogo
iazyka" [Thoughts on the history of the Russian language]), and he shared
some of its representatives' interests in the distinctive features of the Russian language; but his writings inaugurate a pronounced turn toward a more

90. Ibid., 78.
91. Ibid., 57.

philosophical theorization of what language is, and this turn was to exercise a surprisingly far-reaching influence on Russian thought about language and indeed Russian verbal culture in the late nineteenth and early twentieth centuries (in the broader sense of the Russian term *slovesnost'*, rather than linguistics proper). He accomplished this turn by introducing Humboldt's ideas into the Russian context, filtered in part through the "psychological tendency" in linguistics associated with post-Humboldtians like Steinthal, Lazarus, and Wundt.

Potebnia did more than just paraphrase Humboldt and his successors, however, and, as will be seen, the ways in which he departs from his German sources are as interesting as those in which he remains faithful. But even had he done nothing more than transpose Humboldtian thought into the Russian context, his writings would have been inaugural for the tradition I am addressing here because they provided a set of terms and concepts in which to discuss language and the self simultaneously. They introduced into the Russian context an emphasis on such ideas as the role speech plays in consciousness, on the experience of speech, the role of language in cognitive life, and so forth—that is, they established a native precedent for speaking simultaneously about language and about the self in ways that were immediately congenial to the late nineteenth century. It was primarily Potebnia who made available to modern Russian thought a doctrine, not just of language or "the word" as something important to philosophy, but of language as central to a concept of the self, indeed, as the very key to establishing selfhood.[92] In so doing he updated native Slavic traditions of thought about language by fusing them with more recent German influences—in so doing exposing some of the common roots of both.

Potebnia's starting point is the ontology of language outlined in Humboldt's monumental *On the Diversity of Human Language-Structure and Its Influence on the Mental Development of Mankind* (1836), and as the title of his own most important work on the philosophy of language indicates (*Mysl' i iazyk* [Thought and language], 1862), his ideas can be viewed largely as an elaboration on Humboldt's assertion that language and thought are

---

92. Potebnia's eclectic joining of linguistics, poetics, and psychology had meaningful precedents in European thought. Chomsky notes that in the case of what he calls "Cartesian linguistics"—that which asserts the presence in the mind of innate ideas and a universal grammar, which tradition he describes as running from Descartes through Humboldt—"we are dealing with a period that antedates the divergence of linguistics, philosophy, and psychology. The insistence of each of these disciplines on 'emancipating itself' from any contamination by the others is a peculiarly modern phenomenon" (*Cartesian Linguistics* 76, n. 4). It is interesting that Chomsky claims that what Humboldt meant by "inner form" is in fact generative grammar (Ibid., 87, n. 39). For a rebuttal of this view, see Eugenio Coseriu, "Semantik, Innere Sprachform und Tiefenstruktur," *Folia Linguistica. Acta Societatis Linguistica Europaeae* 1970 (4): 53–63.

essentially linked.[93] Thus early in the work he declares Humboldt's key insight to have been that language is the "organ which forms thought" and asserts that only through words can concepts form (in the latter case echoing Herder as much as Humboldt).[94] In keeping with this perspective much of the emphasis in Potebnia's reiteration of Humboldt falls on the contingent, dynamic, fluctuant, or tentative nature of linguistic phenomena, which serves in his account to underscore their origins in the self, at least in the self as conceived in the post-Romantic nineteenth century. He thus predictably invokes Humboldt's adversative definition of language as *energeia,* or activity, rather than *ergon,* or thing, if anything intensifying Humboldt's sense of process in his Russian gloss: the Russian word "*deiatel'nost'*" that Potebnia uses to translate Humboldt's *energeia* ("*ne delo, a deiatel'nost'*") differs from both the Greek term and the German gloss Humboldt sometimes provides it (*eine Erzeugnung*) by suppressing connotations of the object upon which the activity is performed. If the Greek and German terms can be translated roughly as "the doing [of something to something]," Potebnia's term is more like "the doing-ness" of language.[95] Potebnia also points

93. Potebnia and other Russians who experienced Humboldt's influence in the 1860s did so in response to a double stimulus. P. Biliarskii's translation of Humboldt's *magnum opus* in 1859 rendered it something of a contemporary to Potebnia's generation, while Humboldt's ideas experienced something of a revival among German linguists in the 1860s, in particular in the so-called "psychological movement" associated with Heymann Steinthal, M. Lazarus, and Wilhelm Wundt. This group sought to develop a theory of language within what was arguably becoming the dominant doctrine of selfhood of that age, psychology. Its members sustained an interest in the kind of *Völkerpsychologie* important to both Herder and Humboldt, but tended to diminish the element of subjectivity in language by demoting it to something closer to the instrumental status it had in Port Royal grammar: for them speech was first and foremost a form of mental activity, and linguistics nothing but a branch of psychology concerned with the role language plays in concept formation. Potebnia, incidentally, studied directly with Steinthal, the leader of this neo-Humboldtian "psychological" school, in Berlin in 1862; see M. K. Gidini, "Slovo i real'nost'. K voprosu o rekonstruktsii filosofii iazyka Gustava Shpeta," in *G. G. Shpet/Comprehensio. Vtorye Shpetovskie chteniia* (Tomsk: Vodolei, 1997): 87, n. 14. On the "psychological tendency" see Amirova et al., *Ocherki po istorii lingvistiki,* 362–87; Zvegintsev, *Istoriia iazykoznaniia XIX–XX vekov,* 23–34; V. N. Iartseva et al., eds., *Lingvisticheskii entsiklopedicheskii slovar',* (Moscow: Sovetskaia entsiklopedia, 1990), s.v. "Psikhologicheskoe napravlenie." See also Clemens Knobloch, *Geschichte der psychologischen Sprachauffassung in Deutschland von 1850 bis 1920,* Reihe Germanistische Linguistik, 86 (Tübingen: Max Niemeyer Verlag, 1988), 67–119, 268–73, and Davies, *Nineteenth-Century Linguistics,* 202–4.

94. A. A. Potebnia, *Mysl' i iazyk,* in his *Estetika i poetika* (Moscow: Iskusstvo, 1976), 57. Over the course of his career Potebnia tended overwhelmingly to assume an organic link, if not full identity, between language and thought. Nonetheless, inconsistencies appear. In the later *Iz lektsii po teorii slovesnosti,* for example, he claims that thought exists prior to and apart from language; see A. A. Potebnia, *Estetika i poetika* (Moscow: Iskusstvo, 1976), 538. On the inconsistencies see V. Bibikhin, "V poiskakh suti slova. Vnutrenniaia forma u A. A. Potebni," *Novoe literaturnoe obozrenie* 14 (1995): 23–34; and Amirova et al., *Ocherki po istorii lingvistiki,* 388, 391.

95. Potebnia, *Mysl' i iazyk,* in his *Estetika i poetika,* 56. For further interesting discussion of related Greek terms, in particular of *logos* as intellect versus *ergon* as the intractable world, see Adam Millman Parry, *Logos and Ergon in Thucydides* (New York: Arno Press, 1981), 13, 15–21, 83–86.

out that for Humboldt language operates not with a set of discrete entities (fixed meanings, referents, traits) but through antinomies, such as freedom versus necessity of expression, individual versus national character of meaning, divine versus human origins, and so on, which suggest the dynamic nature of linguistic meaning.[96] He further follows Humboldt in seeing the essential workings of language as taking place in the fluid cognitive moments that precede or attend the use of words without quite being identified with them.[97] In linguistic communication, he asserts, no *transmission* of ready-made thought from speaker to listener takes place. Instead speech serves cognition by awakening an analogous thought-process in the mind of the listener: "To name with a word is to create a new thought in the sense of a transformation, in the sense of a regrouping of the former store of thoughts under the pressure of a new impression. . . . To speak does not mean to convey one's thought to another but only to stimulate in the other his own thoughts."[98] So "unfinalized" is this process, to use a Bakhtinian term, that for Potebnia (as for Humboldt) when language is at work "all understanding is misunderstanding," and every new use of a word constitutes a new word.[99]

For both Potebnia and Humboldt—as, indeed, also later on for Bakhtin—this model of speech as cognitive interchange strongly implies the social basis of language ("*obshchestvo predshestvuet nachalu iazyka*"), something Humboldt refers to as *Wechselrede*.[100] In being made available to others, one's own thought joins thought processes shared by the whole of humanity, the thought of an individual requiring supplementation by another if it is to avoid error and attain completion.[101] Thus "only on the lips of another can the word become comprehensible to the speaker," and the process is even described as involving a complex interplay of subjectivity and objectivity echoing the remarks in Humboldt noted above:[102] objectivity increases as the speaker hears his own word on another's lips, while subjectivity is also enhanced because the subjective element embedded in the word has now been expanded to include another self.[103] As Potebnia

96. Ibid., 58.

97. F. M. Berezin remarks that Potebnia rejects the reduction of words to mere indices of ideas and offers instead a model for the "non-simple transmission of thought in words"; see his *Russkoe iazykoznanie kontsa XIX–nachala XX v.* (Moscow: Nauka, 1976), 17.

98. Potebnia, *Iz zapisok po teorii slovesnosti*, in his *Estetika i poetika*, 540–41.

99. Potebnia, *Mysl' i iazyk*, in his *Estetika i poetika*, 57–66, 140.

100. Ibid., 111–12. On Humboldt, see John Fizer, *Alexander A. Potebnja's Psycholinguistic Theory of Literature. A Metacritical Inquiry*, Harvard Ukrainian Research Institute Monograph Series (Cambridge: Harvard University Press, 1986), 21.

101. Potebnia, *Mysl' i iazyk*, in his *Estetika i poetika*, 58.

102. Berezin, *Russkoe iazykoznanie*, 30.

103. Potebnia, *Mysl' i iazyk*, in his *Estetika i poetika*, 58.

remarks in a later work, in this manner the word serves as a link between otherwise enclosed and isolated selves.[104]

All the same, Potebnia's theory tends to relegate this communicative and social function to second place, behind the much more important event of self-cognition that unfolds within language. What takes place in speech, he asserts, is that we come to be aware of the nature of our own thought processes. Direct knowledge of the self is impossible, he claims; but the primary action exerted on the speaker by the use of a word is to divide the speaker's mental world immediately into "I" and "not-I" and thus lay the foundation for self-consciousness.[105] The word then becomes something of a mirror allowing the speaker to apperceive his own thoughts: "The word . . . is first and foremost a means for understanding the speaker, for apperceiving the contents of his thought."[106] Even the passive listener to an utterance experiences an awakening of self-examination correspondent to that of the speaker. The word performs this function, Potebnia suggests, because in themselves, outside of language, our internal states are inchoate and can be made clear to us only if they find expression in language. Our conscious life takes place within a stream of fugitive perceptions, and only when our impulse toward self-awareness causes a deposit to be left in the form of articulate sound can perceptions become objectified and cognized as thought, held before our inner gaze ("*Zvuk stanovitsa namekom, znakom proshedshei mysli. V etom smysle slovo ob"ektiviruet mysl', stavit ee pered nami*").[107] Only in language do we know our thoughts; language completes our self-expression and self-definition.

The import of such statements in Potebnia's account is clearly less to make some claim about the structure of language than it is to declare linguistic phenomena to be the emanations of living subjectivity: for Potebnia as much as for Humboldt the events of language are also the events of being. Indeed, in this regard Potebnia makes some interesting departures from Humboldt that if anything strengthen an emphasis on subjectivity. As Fizer suggests, Humboldt was a Hegelian who saw the process of speech as one by which abstract, transcendent "spirit" permeates human consciousness through the medium of language; in his reworking of Humboldt,

---

104. Potebnia, *Iz zapisok po teorii slovesnosti*, in his *Estetika i poetika*, 307.

105. Ibid., 305–6; Potebnia, *Mysl' i iazyk*, in his *Estetika i poetika*, 170.

106. Potebnia, *Mysl' i iazyk*, in his *Estetika i poetika*, 139.

107. Quoted in O. Presniakov, *Poetika poznaniia i tvorchestva. Teoriia slovesnosti A. A. Potebni* (Moscow: Khudozhestvennaia literatura, 1980), 63. Florenskii makes the following comment on this idea: "The word is placed before us in the manner of an object, is *thrown before* us as something *outside of* us" ("[*Slovo*] stavitsia nami predmetno, metaetsia pred, *pred nami kak nechto vne nas*"; see "Stroenie slova," in his *U vodorazdelov mysli*, prilozhenie k zhurnalu *Voprosy filosofii*, vol. 2 (Moscow: Pravda, 1990), 351.

however, Potebnia redefined this Hegelian metaphysical "spirit" psychologically, as individual mental activity. As a result, the epistemic subject, which
was later to be banished as far as possible from structural linguistics, moves
to the center of Potebnia's thoughts on language.[108]

The most striking moment in Potebnia's account of language and subjectivity, however, is his development of Humboldt's concept of "inner form."
One of Humboldt's aims had been to account for the relation between
sound and meaning in language, and to this end he had posited "inner
form" as the mechanism whereby extra-linguistic content—things out there
in the world—gets correlated with the nexus of sounds that constitutes language. In Humboldt's writings this term appears only a few times and seems
not to have meant much beyond the syntactic and semantic organization
any given language possesses (Humboldt speaks loosely of an outer form
consisting of phonetic structure and two strata of inner form consisting of
grammatical and conceptual structures),[109] though as a part of his idea of
language as a "*Zwischenwelt*" mediating between human consciousness and
the world it could be regarded as a more consequential anticipation of the
linguistic relativity thesis of Whorf and Sapir. But Potebnia makes the concept of inner form central to his theory of language and transforms it in
ways that reveal both the peculiarities of his own ideas and the influence of
older currents of Russian thought about language that he was, consciously
or not, in the process of reviving.

The most obvious departure from Humboldt in Potebnia's account is
that, whereas Humboldt's "inner form" designates a function of language as
a whole (his term is *innere Sprachforme*), Potebnia speaks of the inner form
of the *word,* for which he posits a tripartite structure: "In the word we distinguish: its *outer form,* that is, its articulate sound, its *content,* which is objectified by means of sound, and its *inner form,* or nearest etymological
meaning, that means by which the content is expressed."[110] At first glance
this sort of particularizing interest in structure seems odd in an account of
language otherwise so taken with Humboldtian event-ness. Something of a
precedent for this shift might have been provided by Humboldt himself,
who suggested a basic analogy between the individual word and language as
a whole,[111] but a good deal more is attributable to the psychologizing detour Humboldt's concept took through the theory of Steinthal, Potebnia's
immediate German mentor.

---

108. Fizer, *Potebnja's Psycholinguistic Theory,* 16, 49.
109. Manchester, *Philosophical Foundations,* 90.
110. Potebnia, *Mysl' i iazyk,* in his *Estetika i poetika,* 175.
111. Fizer, *Potebnja's Psycholinguistic Theory,* 30.

Steinthal borrowed his psychological concepts from Johann Friedrich Herbart, who, writing in the 1810s, had described the workings of the mind within the framework of Enlightenment epistemology and Newtonian physics.[112] In Herbart's model of the psyche, ideas are like atoms moving within the arena of the mind, and cognition is the process by which the sum of ideas already present ("perceptions" or "presentations") comes mechanically into contact with, adjusts to, and absorbs new perceptions. For Steinthal the question then was what role *language* plays in these psychic events. His answer was to define the word as "representation, or the presentation of a presentation" ("*Vorstellung, oder Anschauung der Anschauung*").[113]

What stands out in this Herbartian model of the psyche is its spatial literalism, its conception of the mind as a finite space across which the discrete entities of ideas carom in mechanical fashion. The trope is taken up by Steinthal, whose conception of the mind, as Knobloch remarks, replicates that metaphysics of the soul (*Seelenmetaphysik*) beloved of the nineteenth century, according to which the soul is an inner space (*innerraum*) furnished with assorted forms or structures (*Gebilde*).[114] The spatial literalism of Herbart's model is evident in Potebnia as well. What gives the word its power to produce understanding, he asks? The answer lies in its ability to serve in the individual as the intermediary between a new perception, or whatever occupies the foreground of consciousness at a given moment, and the prior reserves of thought located outside of immediate consciousness. "In creating a word . . . the impression one has received undergoes new changes, it is as it were perceived yet again, that it, it is *apperceived*" ("apperception" in Herbart and Potebnia refers to the participation of known masses of perceptions in the formation of new thoughts).[115]

But Potebnia does not restrict himself, as Steinthal for the most part does, merely to describing the role language plays among the events taking

---

112. See Richard Lowry, *The Evolution of Psychological Theory: A Critical History of Concepts and Presuppositions,* 2nd ed. (New York: Aldine, 1982), 66–68; and Manchester, *Philosophical Foundations,* 46.

113. Quoted in Knobloch, *Geschichte der psychologischen Sprachauffassung,* 269. For all the clumsy physicality we might now see in Herbart's description of the psyche, his contribution to psychology was to overcome the longstanding assumption of immobile and indivisible mental capacities (on this see Buzuk, *Ocherki po psikhologii iazyka,* 116).

114. Knobloch, *Geschichte der psychologischen Sprachauffassung,* 271.

115. Potebnia, *Mysl' i iazyk,* in his *Estetika i poetika,* 142–43, 122. Moreover this very process works in a manner reminiscent of syntax. There exists a certain element representing the previously accumulated reserves of life experience, which plays the role of predicate; on the basis of this old representation or perception there arises a certain other perceived element which plays the role of subject (Berezin, *Russkoe iazykoznanie,* 26).

place within the Herbartian room of the psyche. What he does in his definition of "inner form"—and it is difficult to say whether this represents a
bold conceptual step, a moment of provincial clumsiness, or somehow
both—is to transfer the qualities of finitude and boundedness directly to
the word, that is, to identify the word with the bounded space of the psyche that constitutes the self in Herbart's scheme. Instead of designating a
function of language, as Humboldt does when speaking of "inner form,"
Potebnia posits the existence of a discrete entity, something reified, literal,
possessed of structural totality (an outer form, inner form, and content).
Chudakov thus speaks of the way in which for Potebnia the word transforms perception into a "bounded mental particularity."[116]

Moreover, Potebnia transfers to this entity the very processes of cognition and self-consciousness that in Steinthal and Herbart constitute the
vital workings of the mind (and by separating "content" from "inner form"
in his tripartite model of the word, he neatly sets aside issues of referentiality, leaving himself free to offer a definition of "inner form" that is primarily psychological, cognitive, and epistemological in nature). In particular
Potebnia emphasizes the experience of self-knowledge made available
through the word's "inner form," which consists in the epistemological
awareness language provides of the relation between what we know and
what we know *about* what we know (Berezin calls this a "second knowledge," "*vtoroe znanie*"):[117] "The *inner form* of the word is the relation of the
contents of thought to consciousness; it shows us how a person perceives his
own thought"; "it is not the image of an object, but the image of an image,
that is, a *representation*."[118] It is as though, behind all the mechanistic talk
of "masses" of existing perceptions experiencing "pressure" from new ones,
and so forth, Potebnia were instinctively reviving the more subjective sense
of "apperception" found in Leibniz (the mind's reflexive apprehension of its
own inner states) and Kant (consciousness unifying the subject's experience
and therefore serving as the basis for the very possibility of experience and
thought).[119] For Potebnia and Humboldt, however, as opposed to Herbart,
Leibniz, and Kant, such self-knowledge is impossible without the word,
which thus becomes selfhood's anchor in the world.

In what seems one of Potebnia's more curious decisions, the source of
much criticism of his philosophy of language, he also identifies this "inner

116. A. P. Chudakov, "A. A. Potebnia," in *Akademicheskie shkoly v russkom literaturovedenii,* ed.
P. A. Nikolaeva et al. (Moscow: Nauka, 1975), 313.

117. Berezin, *Russkoe iazykoznanie,* 28.

118. Potebnia, *Mysl' i iazyk,* in his *Estetika i poetika,* 115, 147.

119. On Leibniz and Kant see Simon Blackburn, *The Oxford Dictionary of Philosophy* (Oxford:
Oxford University Press, 1994), 21.

form" of the word with its "nearest etymological meaning."[120] The proba-
ble reasons behind this are several. Steinthal's own version of the "inner
form" of language was a historical rather than a structural account of the
way in which perceptions lead, via language, to self-consciousness: first
there occurs a purely reflexive moment in which a concept is onomatopo-
etically matched with a sound; then the mind selects characteristic attributes of the object, brings them to the fore of consciousness, and affixes them
in the *etymon* or root of the word. Over time the image-like quality of this
meaning is gradually worn away, until one is left with an arbitrary, purely
mechanical link between word and object.[121] Another influential factor
would certainly have been that, as a man of his century who had been profoundly influenced by Sreznevskii's 1849 lecture on the national factors that
shaped the Russian language and Buslaev's similarly Russocentric views,
who was moreover an avid collector of folk tales, songs, and sayings, Potebnia would have inclined toward the kind of Herderian explorations of national identity seemingly afforded by investigations into the origins of
Russian words.[122] In this vein K. S. Aksakov had already, in 1839, declared
the root's meaning to constitute "the inner, genuine life of the word," and
etymological roots in general to represent the "true springs from which
flows the whole life of the word, the whole language of the people" (Potebnia clearly takes over some of this Romantic vocabulary).[123] Nor should
one overlook the ur-precedent underlying all these doctrines, which established etymology as a key heuristic device in the philosophy of language—
Plato's *Cratylus,* in which Socrates and his interlocutors explore the
etymologies of various Greek words in an effort to determine whether the
relation between word and referent is arbitrary or essential.

Whatever the source of Potebnia's preoccupation with etymology, however (and Steinthal seems the most likely factor), the use to which he puts
it in his account of language clearly derives from his emphasis on selfhood.
Part of Potebnia's ideas concerning the role etymology plays in "inner form"
comes, again, from the mechanistic psychology of Herbart as refracted
through Steinthal: certain traits of an object inevitably stand out more
forcefully in our perception than others, argues Potebnia, just as one's gaze

120. Later Potebnia was to downplay the role of etymology in favor of a functional lexical definition of inner form as "that least meaning, without which the word cannot be itself," "the nearest or formal meaning" (Amirova et al., *Ocherki po istorii lingvistiki,* 405; see also M. G.
Iaroshevskii, "Poniatie vnutrennei formy slova u Potebni," *Izvestiia AN SSSR. Otdelenie literatury
i iazyka,* t.V, vyp. 5 [1946]: 395–99).
    121. Knobloch, *Geschichte der psychologischen Sprachauffassung,* 114.
    122. Presniakov, *Poetika poznaniia i tvorchestva,* 30.
    123. Aksakov, "O grammatike voobshche," quoted in Berezin, *Khrestomatiia po istorii russkogo
iazykoznaniia,* 150.

pauses more readily on the bright spots of a surface; over time convention happens to have fixed these as the word's central meaning.[124] But in fact lurking within this historical-psychological theory is an epistemological one. For Potebnia this etymologically conferred inner form is not just the passive winner in some perceptual lottery but the means by which we become aware of the unity of sensory images and thereby gain *knowledge of* that unity, as a fact about the world. "In addition to the factual unity of the image the inner form provides knowledge of that unity"; through inner form the word becomes "the means for cognizing the unity of a sensual image."[125] This is what Potebnia means when he declares inner form to be not the image of an object but the image of an image.[126] As the one stable element in the shifting mass of perceptions the mind encounters, it functions to reassure us of what Kant called the "synthesis of the manifold," and the claims Potebnia makes for it are correspondingly large.[127] By recognizing the invariant element in recurring perceptions of a given person, he argues at one point—and it is precisely this kind of invariant that is taken up by language as inner form—we "lay the foundation" for the category of "substance" ("*substantsiia*"), of the thing-in-itself. A step is thus taken toward the knowledge of truth ("*istina*"), Potebnia remarks, which, if it is not yet that very knowledge, nonetheless points to its existence somewhere on the horizon.[128] The apperception at the heart of inner form, Potebnia states, is identical with the type of thought termed a "judgment" ("*suzhdenie*").[129] The word's inner form thus serves as a record of the mind's encounter with the world and, in effect, as an index to what we are justified in knowing or asserting about the world.

But, to borrow a term from John R. Searle, for Potebnia the ontology of this inner form is not a third-person ontology, it is a first-person ontology, and Potebnia's accounts of its origins and its workings strongly assert its links with subjectivity.[130] In the case of the inner form's history, the link has to do with its supposed origins in poetry. Potebnia insists that the etymological

124. Potebnia, *Mysl' i iazyk*, in his *Estetika i poetika*, 128. This idea appears in Herder, too. In attempting to reconstruct the origins of language he speaks of the "ocean of sensations" in our minds, out of which we single out one wave, arrest it, and fix our attention on it—a process he calls apperception. He then speculates that some early human, upon seeing a sheep, must have reflected on its bleating as its distinguishing mark and remarked to himself, "Yes, you are that which bleats." Johann Gottfried Herder, "Essay on the Origin of Language," in *On the Origin of Language*, 115, 117. Exactly how this gives rise to the German word for sheep is left unclear.

125. Potebnia, *Mysl' i iazyk*, in his *Estetika i poetika*, 147, 153.

126. Ibid., 147.

127. Kant is quoted in Fizer, *Potebnja's Psycholinguistic Theory*, 3.

128. Potebnia, *Mysl' i iazyk*, in his *Estetika i poetika*, 154–55.

129. Ibid., 147.

130. John R. Searle, *The Rediscovery of the Mind* (Cambridge: MIT Press, 1998), 17, 151–73.

meaning at the word's core (the "*oko*" or eye within the Russian word "*okno*," the root "**stl*," "to spread," within "*stol*") was originally born out of an aesthetic act that denoted some object by means of a poetic trope (specifically, a metaphor, "*sravnenie*").[131] In fact the claim Potebnia makes is stronger than that: the word initially *was* a poetic work—"every word . . . necessarily passes through a state in which that word is a work of poetry."[132] Etymology thus opens the door to the phenomenon of symbolism, "*obraznost'*," which for Potebnia underlies linguistic signification in general: it points to the "word's originary poetic nature" ("*iznachal'naia poetichnost' slova*") and through that to the associations and perceptions characteristic of an earlier, mythic stage of language (the notion of a lost "poetic" stage in the evolution of language was in fact a commonplace and appears in both Rousseau and Condillac).[133] Although this stage of knowledge has long been superseded, its essential cognitive operations remain alive, or are in principle recoverable, in modern language.[134]

The psychological theory Potebnia offers to explain this poetic moment in word formation—which he presents as both historical and still validly descriptive of how human consciousness works—is similarly informed by a sense of the fluid life of the self. The reason that words were initially aesthetic acts, Potebnia states, is that the very process of cognition is one of comparison: when some cognitive unknown (X) comes into contact with our reserves of knowledge about the world (A) the mind generates an image (a) that represents the point of contact between them.[135] Inner form is what registers this inherently comparative, metaphorical *tertium comparationis* of cognition. For example, the Russian word "*iazvit'*" means to inflict wounds (*rany, iazvy*); but "*iazva*" (ulcer) denotes "*to, chto bolit*" (that which hurts) and "*bol'*" (pain, hurt) in turn denotes "*to, chto zhzhet*" (that which burns). Thus the inner form of "*iazvit'*" contains an image of burning, and Potebnia posits as the ultimate origin the Sanskrit verb "*indh*," "to burn" ("*zhech'*"), which he explains as arising out of "the feeling accompanying the perception of a flame."[136] Thus out of all the possible ideas and feelings

---

131. On this subject see Fizer, *Potebnja's Psycholinguistic Theory*, 29–50.

132. Potebnia, *Iz lektsii po teorii slovesnosti*, in his *Estetika i poetika*, 530.

133. The reference to the word's originary poetic qualities is in Chudakov, "A. A. Potebnia," 317; on the mythic stage of language see Potebnia, *Mysl' i iazyk*, in his *Estetika i poetika*, 165.

134. As Presniakov points out, although it is only later in Potebnia's career that he moves overtly from linguistics into poetics, he tends from the outset to work from ideas about the nature of the poetic work of art toward insights into the nature of language; see his *A. A. Potebnia i russkoe literaturovedenie kontsa XIX–nachala XX veka* (Saratov: izd. Saratovskogo universiteta, 1978), 83.

135. Potebnia, *Iz lektsii po teorii slovesnosti*, in his *Estetika i poetika*, 367; see also Presniakov, *Poetika poznaniia i tvorchestva*, 58.

136. Potebnia, *Mysl' i iazyk*, in his *Estetika i poetika*, 115.

associated with wounding, what has been singled out as synecdochically definitive is the sensation of burning. What such an account notably preserves is the traits of indeterminacy (since instead of a simple mapping of word onto referent, Potebnia's theory pictures a single trait extracted from a sea of possible perceptions) and contingency (since the original poetic-referential act opted, in an exercise of will, for this one trait when it could have chosen myriad others), as well as, perhaps, a kind of hidden intentionality in the word (which turns out to make something like cognitive decisions), which had been hallmarks of Humboldt's subjectivizing account of language.

Figurative expressions thus turn out to be an essential component of thought as well as the historical source of language.[137] "The only reason that the word is the organ of thought and the necessary condition for all subsequent development of one's understanding of the world and oneself is that it is originally a symbol, an ideal, and therefore possesses all the properties of a work of art."[138] Ontologically language and poetry are the same thing, the poetic work being merely a more elaborate version of a word, possessing the same three-part structure and serving an identical purpose. Both arise out of subjective intentions—*energeia*—which are directed toward producing a synthetic representation of reality.[139] Indeed, it is this synthetic representation rather than *ratio* as such that Potebnia sees as the purpose of the word's inner form, which is to say, of speech and even cognition in general.[140] In *Mysl' i iazyk* he remarks that it is the human capacity for "non-utilitarian delight" ("*neutilitarnoe naslazhdenie*") that explains our possession of speech and separates us from the animals, and this set of beliefs would seem to explain Potebnia's surprisingly hostile attitude, much like that of an art-for-art's-sake aesthete, toward the "civic" school of literature and criticism in the Russian 1860s and 1870s.[141] To be sure, Potebnia grants that this poetic quality in language is subject to attrition or "forgetting" over time, the word entering a "second type of existence" as this happens.[142] He calls language that has lost its imagery in this way "prosaic" and says that it serves the purposes of a scientific cognition based on laws of identity and empirical facts. But he displays a tellingly inconsistent attitude

137. Ibid., 119.
138. Ibid., 196.
139. Ibid., 190.
140. Fizer, *Potebnja's Psycholinguistic Theory,* 9.
141. See ibid., 95–96, 102. Boris M. Gasparov similarly notes that Potebnia's 1862 *Mysl' i iazyk* was conspicuous in its *avoidance* of the era's politically charged debates over the nature of the Russian language and the grammars that describe it; see his "The Language Situation and the Linguistic Polemic in Mid-Nineteenth-Century Russia," in *Aspects of the Slavic Language Question,* vol. 2, East Slavic, 302.
142. Potebnia, *Iz lektsii po teorii slovesnosti,* in his *Estetika i poetika,* 535.

toward this evolutionary event, on the one hand implying that the loss of inner form is inevitable and even necessary, and that neither poetic nor prosaic cognition is to be valued over the other; on the other hand doubling back within a few pages of such arguments to assert the centrality of "poetry" to human experience and moving quickly to suggest, as if total loss were unthinkable, that the erosion of imagery within words can be compensated for by the creation of new words and the use of imagery at the level of the sentence rather than the word.[143]

The influence of Romantic aesthetics is obvious in all this, but the word/poetry analogy may also have suggested itself so readily to Potebnia because in his account the "inner form" of the word, as the bounded domain within which the essential activities of consciousness take place, really functions as a synonym for the self, a kind of mini-theater of human self-awareness and encounter with the world. With language thus transformed into the site of selfhood, the idea of language as mere instrument of communication is left far behind.

That said, Potebnia's theory of language would remain a provincial doctrine, heavily indebted to its German idealist sources, were it not for the resonances one can discern in it of certain other influences that form an important substratum of Russian culture and thought.[144] For there is another plausible factor in the particularizing bent of Potebnia's thought, and it can be seen in the potent ambiguity inhabiting the word "*slovo*" in the Russian tradition: "*slovo*" can mean lexical unit, like the standard use of English "word," German "*Wort*," or French "*mot*"; or it can mean something like "speech" or "discourse," that is, the workings of language in general. It is this ambiguity that allows Potebnia to plunge in the very first sentence of his *Mysl' i iazyk* into a remark on the relation between "*mysl'*" and "*slovo*," and to use "*slovo*" and "*iazyk*" more or less interchangeably throughout the work. If we non-native Russianists are used to this ambiguity, we are more familiar with its broadening implications, that is, we are used to pointing out that in Russian "*slovo*" often really means "speech" or "language" or "discourse."[145] In Potebnia, however, the ambiguity works in

---

143. Ibid., 369–70.

144. Prat, in fact, links the two traditions: "Russian religious philosophy carries on the tradition of Platonism which dominates Orthodox theology" but it was also heavily influenced by German philosophy, "especially [by] the mighty neo-Platonic stream which ran from the great mystics of the Middle Ages to Schelling and Hegel" ("Orthodox Philosophy of Language," 1).

145. See, for example, the entry for "discourse, word [*slovo*]" in the glossary appended by Emerson and Holquist to M. M. Bakhtin, *The Dialogic Imagination. Four Essays,* trans. Caryl Emerson and Michael Holquist, University of Texas Press Slavic Series, No. 1 (Austin: University of Texas Press, 1981), 427. On the multiple meanings "slovo" acquires in Bakhtin's writings, see also Alexandar Mihailovic, *Corporeal Words: Mikhail Bakhtin's Theology of Discourse* (Evanston: Northwestern University Press, 1997), 38.

precisely the opposite direction: to introduce an emphasis on particularity and structural totality, to posit the existence of a discrete, reified entity in which are concentrated the vital workings of language.

Behind this semantic ambiguity stands a whole philosophical and theological tradition devoted to definitions of *logos* and involving language, speech, Reason, (neo)Platonic idea, and even the personhood of Christ. This tradition is distinct from the concepts in linguistics and the philosophy of language outlined earlier in this chapter but runs parallel to them through both western and eastern European thought (witness the analogies, noted above, that are asserted between language and the Trinity in both the Muscovite *Beseda o uchenii gramote* and Augustine). What made Potebnia's doctrine of inner form so productive in the Russian context was the way in which it subtly, quite possibly unconsciously, linked this patristic and Neoplatonic line of thought with that of Romantic organicism as interpreted by Herder and Humboldt. Ultimately these strains of thought have common origins, but by the nineteenth century they were felt to be distinctly different.

An overview of Slavic patristic Neoplatonism will help to explicate something of the "past" of Potebnia's concepts of "inner form" and "the word" as models of selfhood and in so doing illustrate the kinds of ideas, resident in native Russian doctrines of *logos,* that Potebnia set in motion as his ideas gained currency around the turn of the century. In fact, it is precisely this Russian tradition (or more accurately this Russian redaction of Neoplatonism) that explains many of the departures—always particularizing and personifying—from German sources noted above in Potebnia: it is the magnetic field that bends the otherwise straight beam of concepts radiating out of German idealism.

As Gustav Shpet, one of Russia's most significant philosophers of language in the 1910s and 1920s, notes in passing in his 1927 *Vnutrenniaia forma slova* (The inner form of the word), a work clearly mindful of Potebnia if also conspicuously neglectful of him, Humboldt's concept of "inner form" can ultimately be traced back to Plato's concept of *eidos* (form) as the ideal prototype informing but also transcending the objects we find in the world.[146] This is true in the general sense that the kind of thought represented by

146. Gustav Shpet, *Vnutrenniaia forma slova (Etiudy i variatsii na temy Gumbol'dta)* (Moscow: Gos. akademiia khudozhestvennykh nauk, 1927), 54–55. Shpet also credits Humboldt with transferring the concept of "inner form" into language. There is some truth to this claim: Humboldt has more specific things to say on the nature of language in this connection than do such forerunners as Plato, Plotinus, Giordano Bruno; but the linguistic idea is not lacking in the earlier tradition, and Shpet virtually ignores the whole tradition of *logos* addressed by S. N. Trubetskoi in *Uchenie o Logose v ego istorii,* in his *Sochineniia,* Filosofskoe nasledie, t. 120 (1906; Moscow: Mysl', 1994).

Humboldt's and Potebnia's theories would be unthinkable without the close links established in Greek philosophy among the concepts of *eidos* (form), *idea* (idea, ideal), and *logos* (word, utterance; both the content and form of what is spoken), as the result of which the word comes to be seen as the manifestation of universal (divine) Reason, the embodiment of a principle of cosmic unity, "the opposite of everything unaccounted for, unverbalized, lacking sense or form."[147] The desire to assert the unity of thought and language in Humboldt and Potebnia can trace its origins ultimately to this complex, as can Potebnia's assumption that the word must somehow lead to cognition of essential truths (cf. the Cynics' notion, identical to Cratylus's view in the eponymous Platonic dialogue, that the true definition of a thing resides in its name, which "explains what the given thing was or is").[148] More specifically, Potebnia's preoccupation with the word's synecdochical focus on a single trait of an object, implicitly the most central or essential, ultimately derives from the Platonic concept of the *eidos* as the absolute ideal or form that provides things with the rationale for their existence—as Shpet suggests for Humboldt's related concept of "inner form."

Still closer to Potebnia's description of the word is the concept of *logos* as Aristotle developed it in his attempt to emend the dualism of Plato's metaphysics. Transferring the prototypical *eidos* out of the transcendent realm into the thing it defines, he declared it to be an inwardly residing concept determinative of that thing's final appearance and form (the form of a living body, Aristotle said, is its soul).[149] Thus is something like a complete being, at once self-like and word-like, posited as the key entity in both existence and thought (Aristotle furthermore treated its progressive unfolding as a process of *uttering*).[150] The Stoics of the third century B.C. took this process of ontologization and personalization of *logos* even further. In an effort to assert that being and thought are one—and that this unity centers in language or at least in something accessible within language—the Stoics conjectured that the body and soul had arisen from a single basis, the

147. Trubetskoi, *Uchenie o Logose,* 72; see also L. F. Il'ichev et al., eds., *Filosofskii entsiklopedicheskii slovar'* (Moscow: Sovetskaia entsiklopedia, 1983), s.v. "Logos."

148. Trubetskoi, *Uchenie o Logose,* 62.

149. Ibid., 75.

150. Il'ichev, *Filosofskii entsiklopedicheskii slovar',* s.v. "Eidetizm." There are inevitable echoes of this in Potebnia: for example, in his claims that the word leads to knowledge of the category of "substantive" and through that to awareness that truth ("istina") exists; that the inner form of the word induces the concept of the object's unity and generality in the face of its perpetually changing features; and that the auditory "external form" of the word is not crude material but material already subjected to thought (*Mysl' i iazyk,* in his *Estetika i poetika,* 154–55, 178). Something like a Platonic or Aristotelian sense of "prototype" also seems to underlie Potebnia's discussions of etymology—akin to the way in which for Plato in the *Cratylus* "a correct name expresses the essence of the named object, not through its phonetic or visible form which differs from language to language but through the idea or eidos" (Prat, "Orthodox Philosophy of Language," 3).

ethereal *"pneuma,"* or breath, or spirit, which is at once mental and corpo-real, and whose proximity to the act of articulating speech is apparent. For the Stoics this *pneuma* was at once the fiery element of life and *logos,* in the sense of divine reason containing the law of all things, which animates the world and is identical with it in substance.[151] This cosmic *logos* furthermore generates, through a process akin to uttering, subordinate forms, called "spermatic *logoi,*" which lead an independent existence and whose purpose is to define the classes and species that instantiate separate living forms.[152] As a result within each of us there resides a *logos* that is human reason but also an emanation of the divine reason inhabiting the world as a whole (moreover this *logos* forms our "inner word," as opposed to the uttered, pro-nounced words that symbolize it, a distinction later taken up not only in philosophy but in patristics as well).[153]

But Potebnia's thought owes an even greater debt (unsurprising, given his background, but nowhere explicitly acknowledged) to a subsequent phase in the tradition of thought about *logos,* namely the complex of ideas that was Hellenistic, Christian, and ultimately Eastern Orthodox thought. Much of the particularizing and personalizing impulse in his theory, much of its attraction to themes of boundedness, identity, and self-cognition, can be traced to these sources. Nor was Potebnia the last to incur this debt. One characteristic feature of the Russian writings on language with which this study is concerned is that in the exemplary texts—in the works of Floren-skii, Bulgakov, Losev, for example—one repeatedly finds the discussion of language somehow oddly contaminated by anthropomorphizing ideas whose proper home seems to lie elsewhere. That elsewhere very often turns out to be the Eastern Orthodox doctrines of *Logos,* which have retained their influence throughout centuries of Russian culture.

The important step from the ancient Greeks to the Orthodoxy more im-mediately influential in the Russian context can be found in the thought of Philo (ca. 20 B.C.–ca. A.D. 50), a member of the Jewish diaspora in Alexan-dria, whose philosophy blended Platonic idealism with Judaic monotheism. The Platonic element in Philo's thought consists in assertions to the effect that *logos* represents divine energy and reason, the "soul" that pierces all things, differentiating them and generating concrete beings out of eternal prototypes; but this understanding is also linked in his thought with concepts of "law" (*nomos*) and Wisdom derived from the Old Testament

---

151. Trubetskoi, *Uchenie o Logose,* 82.

152. Prat comments that "in neo-Platonism the Platonic-Aristotelian doctrine on the *Nous* as prime mover and its energies is combined with the Stoic notion of 'seminal reasons,' pervading the cosmos and developing the 'internal' logos into 'uttereds.' This meaning of 'logos' is very im-portant for the later Orthodox philosophy of language" ("Orthodox Philosophy of Language," 2).

153. Trubetskoi, *Uchenie o Logose,* 85–89.

(Mosaic monotheism).[154] "Law" for Philo is a principle of universal reason and moral regulation, that rational word which "dictates that which should be and forbids that which should not." As Divine Wisdom it is also the source of all truth and goodness, the breath of God's power, pure excrescence of His glory, reflection of His eternal light, and pure mirror of His actions.[155]

What marks an even more distinct turn in Philo's thought from the Greek tradition is his personification of *logos* as a *being* serving as an intermediary between two worlds. For Philo, God is infinitely remote from the created world and transcends any thought, word, image, concept, or definition of him, so that we can only know what he is not (the apophatic theology of the Orthodox Church owes much to Philo). There exist divine powers, however, that mediate between God and the world, and in which he reveals himself and his acts. As mediaries they are at once of God and of the world, but they are distinct from both God and the world, and, unlike the still rather impersonal "spermatic *logoi*" of the Stoics, are conceived of as beings very much like angels in the Old Testament tradition. Chief among these beings is *Logos,* whom Philo personifies as a "second God," the image of the Father but also a prototype of the world and so a "heavenly man" (at this point it makes sense to capitalize the term to designate a concrete being as distinct from an abstract principle):[156]

> And the Father who created the universe has given to his archangelic and most ancient Word a pre-eminent gift, to stand on the confines of both, and separated from that which had been created from the Creator. . . . And the Word rejoices in this gift, and, exulting in it, announces it and boasts of it, saying, "And I stood in the midst, between the Lord and you"; neither being uncreated as God nor yet created as you, but being in the midst of these extremities, like a hostage, as it were, to both parties.[157]

154. Ibid., 175.
155. Ibid., 123, 127, 146, 290.
156. Ibid., 161, 166, 176; Il'ichev, *Filosofskii entsiklopedicheskii slovar'*, s.v. "Filon Aleksandriiskii."
157. Philo, "Who Is the Heir of Divine Things," in *The Works of Philo. Complete and Unabridged,* trans. C. D. Yonge (n.p: Hendrickson Publishers, 1993), 293. Philo's conception of the Divine Word apparently derives from a broader set of rabbinical teachings about intermediaries (i.e., separate beings) between God and man, among which are the Spirit of God, the Voice of God, the Glory of God, the archangel Metatron, and in particular, Memra, the (personified) Word of God (Trubetskoi *Uchenie o Logose,* 293). S. V. Troitskii, in his attack on the twentieth-century resurgence of the *imiaslavie* doctrine, cites as a damning precedent for the doctrine this same Hebraic notion of "Memra," the Word of God that exists as a separate being from God and mediates between God and the created world. For Troitskii this is a form of idolatry. See S. V. Troitskii, *Ob imenakh bozhiikh i imiabozhnikakh* (St. Petersburg: Sinodal'naia tipografiia, 1914), 92–94.

In Philo's doctrine this *Logos* has three stages of existence: first as a thought of God, then as an incorporeal being created by God prior to the creation of the world (and used by God to create the world, so that *Logos* serves as the agent of creation), and finally as immanent in the world after its creation.[158] The moment of incarnation in the last stage is important to Philo in his discussions of human ontology, which characteristically emphasize the indwelling of spirit in matter and cite as precedent the same phenomenon in language. Upon entering the created world, *Logos* clothes itself in flesh, and, since the *Logos* dwells partially in each of us, the relation of our souls to our bodies is an extension of that between *Logos* and the world.[159] Speech, Philo remarks in an interesting passage, is the garment God has given us to cover our nakedness.[160]

The notion of a personified and incarnated *Logos,* of course, reaches its apogee in Christian theology, which identifies the person of Christ with eternal *Logos* and considers Christ's earthly existence as the unique reification of that Divine Word.[161] In fact the identification of Christ as *Logos* occurs in only one of the gospels, that of John. Judaism had its concepts of Wisdom, identified with the Law of Moses, which preexisted the created world, and of a similarly preexistent Messiah. These had already played a role in the writings of the apostle Paul, who saw the revelation of the Law of Moses and the birth of Jesus as successive stages in the earthly revelation of the preexistent Wisdom, who was for him by implication the Holy

---

158. Wolfson, *Philosophy of the Church Fathers,* 364.

159. Trubetskoi, *Uchenie o Logose,* 177; Wolfson, *Philosophy of the Church Fathers,* 366, 368.

160. Philo, "On Dreams, that They are God-Sent," in *Works of Philo,* 374.

161. As P. P. Gaidenko points out, Russian philosophers in the early twentieth century often differed radically in their views on the relation between ancient Greek and Christian concepts of *logos.* Trubetskoi and Vladimir Solov'ev saw profound affinity between the two, whereas Lev Shestov, citing Nietzsche in his defense, saw irreconcilable differences (between Greek logic and "madness," philosophy and faith, Athens and Jerusalem; see Gaidenko, "'Konkretnyi idealizm' S. N. Trubetskogo," in Trubetskoi, *Sochineniia,* 14–15). For Trubetskoi himself, the advent of Philonic and Christian anthropomorphic concepts of *Logos* heralded the appearance of the very concept of the individual self, which Greek thought had not worked out on its own (since for Plato, Socrates, and Aristotle the soul concretized in individual beings is still in essence something universal; 22). In any event, in the atmosphere of the early-twentieth-century Russian religious renaissance Trubetskoi's defense of his *magnum opus* on the history of *Logos* was considered a major cultural event (see notes to Trubetskoi by Gaidenko and D. E. Afinogenova, 718). For a discussion of some of the correspondences between Christian (especially Catholic) theology and notions of language, see Kenneth Burke, *The Rhetoric of Religion. Studies in Logology* (Boston: Beacon Press, 1961). Among much else, Burke suggests that many of the statements made in theology about God can be applied, *mutatis mutandis,* to words, and points out parallels between concepts of the Trinity and the incarnation (especially in Arian doctrine) and those of the word and uttering (1, 13).

Spirit.[162] The remarkable step the fourth gospel takes is to substitute *Logos* for this Wisdom/Holy Spirit/Messiah, and thereby, as has been argued, to identify the Messiah with the *Logos* of Philo's philosophy.[163] At the same time it is important to remember the distinctly *verbal* identity this claim attributes to Christ: for through the Christ of whom John writes the word of the prophets (that is, the promise of redemptive incarnation) becomes the Word of Christianity, embodied and personified *Logos*—a perlocutionary event *par excellence.*[164] Thus, for example, in Theophilus, an early Christian theologian, the begetting of the Son by the Father was explicitly the "uttering" of the *Logos,* while in the fourth century Zeno of Verona described the Son as "[coming] forth from the mouth of God" just prior to the creation of the world.[165] Conversely, to say, as Clement of Alexandria does (borrowing from Philo), that the *Logos* is "the image of God," "divine," the "archetypal light of light," and so forth is to impute these qualities to language as well, just as the Greek definition of *logos* as a principle of cosmic reason tended to make order and logic the essence of language.

As one moves into the more specific terrain of Orthodox Christology and Trinitarianism, the intersections of key issues among theology, ideas concerning language, and ideas concerning selfhood multiply still more.[166] In the relatively profane context of Potebnia's and other modern-day Russian theories of language, the precise theological meanings of these doctrines are less important than the terms they make available to speculation about the nature of selves in relation to language—they provide a model of (divine) selfhood that is also in an essential way a word.

Thus one could view later, secular attempts at working through the paradoxes of selfhood as taking up essentially the same kinds of problems as those addressed in the more properly theological veins of Christology and Trinitarianism. Issues having to do with the precise boundaries of the self in relation to consciousness and with the self's continuity over time are especially relevant here. In the case of the Trinity the dilemma facing early theologians was to adhere to monotheism, thereby countering charges of

162. Wolfson, *Philosophy of the Church Fathers,* 159, 177.

163. Ibid., 176–78, 364. On the more general debts of the Gospel of John to preceding traditions, see C. H. Dodd, *Historical Tradition in the Fourth Gospel* (Cambridge: Cambridge University Press, 1963).

164. Trubetskoi, *Uchenie o Logose,* 250.

165. Wolfson, *Philosophy of the Church Fathers,* 194, 197.

166. See Mihailovic's excellent study of similar theological themes in Bakhtin's writings, especially on the role incarnational models played for him, on the concept of logos, and on the repercussions in modern Russian thought of the Chalcedonian definition of Christ's divine/human natures as "non-fused and inseparable" (*nesliianno i nerazdel'no*); *Corporeal Words,* 1–7, 17–24, 126.

polytheism leveled by Judaism and (later) Islam, while at the same time accounting for three somehow distinct personae encompassed in the godhead. The solution arrived at, after a very involved history, was to posit a single *ousia* or essence that was undivided but nonetheless possessed of three distinct hypostases, each of which was held to be singular and subsisting in its own being, and which functioned within the godhead as manifestations of personhood (here defined roughly as a distinguishing quality—"it is the 'person' of the hypostasis called Father to be unbegotten, that of the hypostasis called 'Son' to be begotten," and so on).[167] In the case of Christology, the debates over which were if anything even more complex than those over the Trinity, the aim was to preserve the transcendence of deity while embracing the myth of incarnation. Following disputes among those asserting the exclusive deity of Christ, those asserting a complete rift between his deity and human form, and so forth, the Orthodox branch of Christianity finally settled on the Chalcedonian formula that identified him as possessing two *natures* within one *person* or *hypostasis*—thus opting for a paradox that acknowledged dualism but subsumed its threat within a principle of unity.

One might hesitate to make too much in this context of Potebnia's tripartite word (or "triune," as Fizer goes so far as to call it), were it not for the fact that, unlike Humboldt, who speaks of language in general, Potebnia combines sound, meaning, and self-knowledge within a unitary word, which thus resembles something more like the Trinity.[168] In his native tradition one can also bracket Potebnia between the seventeenth-century *Beseda o uchenii gramote,* which invokes precisely the analogies of the Trinity and human personhood (soul, reason, and body) to explain the nature of words; and Potebnia's twentieth-century successor Florenskii, who in *his* account of inner form claims that trinitariness (*troichnost'*) is characteristic of both language and of being, and who relates the opposition of external to internal form in the word to that between body and soul.[169] And, as suggested above, it seems plausible to conjecture that concepts of the sign or word in the *Western* tradition, with their core of meaning/intention negotiating its relations with material otherness, might in similar ways also be covert models of the self.

Further evidence for an affinity with the doctrines of Christology can perhaps be found in the curious but persistent overtones of a kenotic

---

167. On these issues see Jaroslav Pelikan, *The Spirit of Eastern Christendom (600–1700),* vol. 2 in *The Christian Tradition* (Chicago: University of Chicago Press, 1974), 77–79, 81–82.

168. Fizer, *Potebnja's Psycholinguistic Theory,* 30.

169. Florenskii, "Stroenie slova," in *U vodorazdelov mysli,* 347.

plot—Christ's descent into worldly incarnation, followed by his resurrection and transfiguration—that find their way into their accounts of the
speech act in Humboldt, Potebnia, and others. These accounts all occur
within discussions of the relations between subjectivity and objectivity,
and all posit an exit from, followed by a return to, the subject. Comment-
ing on how subjective activity fashions an *object* in thought, Humboldt
states that as the workings of the senses combine with those of the mind,
"the presentation is ejected, becomes an object *vis-à-vis* the subjective
power, and, perceived anew as such, returns back to the latter." This cannot happen without language, for "in [language] the mental striving breaks
out through the lips in language, the product of that striving returns back
to the speaker's ear. Thus the presentation becomes transformed into real
objectivity, without being deprived of subjectivity on that account."[170]
Potebnia reproduces this very passage in *Mysl' i iazyk,* as does Shpet in
Vnutrenniaia forma slova, who (paradoxically, given his general antipathy
to religious thought) provides a particularly vivid Russian gloss: "*imenno v
[iazyke] dukhovnoe stremlenie proryvaet sebe put' cherez guby i vozvrashchaet
svoi produkt k sobstvennomu ukhu*" ("it is precisely in language that spiritual strivings rend a path for themselves out through the lips and then return their product to one's own ear").[171] One can compare the interplay
of subjectivity and objectivity in such remarks with Pseudo-Dionysius,
who refers to the paradoxical attributes of dividedness in God—that is,
His departures from primordial Unity out into the world—as "blessed ex-
trusions of the Godhead into the out-there" ("*blagolepnye vykhody bogo-
nachaliia vo-vne*").[172] The modern passages share none of Dionysius's
mysticism; but they are nonetheless permeated by an awareness of the logic
of Christology.

Nor, in discussing the parallels between the philosophy of language in
Russia and its possible theological substratum, can one overlook icons (as
we will see, Losev makes this connection explicit). In Orthodoxy, an icon is
held to be not just the depiction of a scene but the physical embodiment of
a divine prototype that in worship serves as an intermediary between the
transcendent and worldly realms—much as for Potebnia the word is not a
mere *signans* of some *signatum* but the site on which consciousness works
out the relationship between itself and the world. The theological discussions that surround icons in history, moreover, come very close to ideas

---

170. Humboldt, *On Language,* 56.

171. Potebnia, *Mysl' i iazyk,* in his *Estetika i poetika,* 58; Shpet, *Vnutrenniaia forma slova,* 16.

172. Dionisii Areopagit, *O bozhestvennykh imenakh. O misticheskom bogoslovii* (St. Petersburg:
Glagol, 1994), 73.

about language: the essential paradox of the icon has to do with "circum-scribing" the infinite in finite form, the precedent for which is the doctrine of *Logos* or the incarnated Word, and Pelikan notes that in the eighth- and ninth-century polemics over the appropriateness of icons, iconoclasts de-clared the worship of icons an "acute hellenization" of Christian theol-ogy.[173] Thus, in addition to the ideas he was consciously adapting from Humboldt, Steinthal, and others, icons may well have provided Potebnia with an intuitive precedent for such notions as the reification of prototypes, the existence of a concrete form that might serve as intermediary between disparate realms, and for the circumscription of unboundedness within a bounded form.

My point in reproducing these sometimes esoteric ideas is not to argue that Potebnia relied on them consciously as he wrote *Mysl' i iazyk,* still less to suggest that he should be regarded as a crypto-theologian or even mys-tic (claims that do apply, at least in part, to some of his successors in the tradition). Rather it is to suggest that some of the impulses operating in Potebnia's thought are cognate with, and perhaps even descended from, the issues outlined above. For the secular Potebnia the "word" is in no way a cosmic person; but it is very much the seat of selfhood and it is dis-tinctly called on to serve consciousness as an intermediary between the vast unknown and the known (recall his claim that "inner form" is the *ter-tium comparationis* mediating between stored experience and what is newly encountered). Similarly, when Potebnia states that through the word human beings "create a new world out of the chaos of [their] im-pressions," he certainly means this with a measure of irony; but the irony itself reflects an awareness of precisely what myth of verbal incarnation is being invoked (note that John 1:1–5 also links the Word of God with the creation).[174]

In fact in the long run the great contribution that Neoplatonism made to Russian thought on language was not that it sustained an aura of religios-ity but that it suggested that thought about the nature of the self ought to be absorbed *within* thought about language. But, if they are valid, the kinds of parallels indicated above suggest why Potebnia's theory proved so fertile for subsequent Russian writing about language. It brought to light these very intersections between modern systems of thought originating in the West and the Neoplatonism that was really the only long-standing native intellectual tradition dealing, however indirectly, with selfhood in any kind

---

173. Pelikan, *Spirit of Eastern Christendom,* 107.
174. Potebnia, *Iz zapisok po teorii slovesnosti,* in his *Estetika i poetika,* 302.

of speculative detail. Potebnia's ideas were fertile in this sense, most obviously for the philosophers of the Russian religious renaissance, who set out to revive the very traditions only latently represented in Potebnia (for example, Florenskii, Bulgakov, to some extent the Symbolists and Acmeists); but they proved fertile, too, for their nonreligious counterparts, such as Shpet, Jakobson, the Formalists, and Bakhtin, who mined the tradition for secular insights into language and the self.[175]

175. On the Symbolists and religious thought, see Irina Paperno, "O prirode poeticheskogo slova. Bogoslovskie istochniki spora Mandel'shtama s simvolizmom," *Literaturnoe obozrenie*, no. 1 (1991): 29–36. Jakobson represents an interesting detour in this intellectual history. As Holenstein has shown, Husserl's phenomenology profoundly influenced Jakobson's theory of language. But Husserl was in turn one of the modern thinkers significantly influenced by Humboldt's philosophy of language (Cassirer is another; see Iartseva, *Lingvisticheskii entsiklopedicheskii slovar'*, s.v. "Gumbol'dtianstvo").

Chapter 2

Russia's Culture of Logos *in the Early Twentieth Century*

POTEBNIA'S PRIMARY CONTRIBUTION to Russian thought was to provide it with a doctrine of language as something possessing the form and behavior of a self, and as occupied with a constant process of coming to know both its own interiority and the relation of that interiority to the surrounding world. His model had appeal as a psychologizing explanation of language, which is to say that it treated language within the then-dominant way of understanding mental processes (still pre-Freudian, influenced by Herbart and Wundt), and within those processes accorded it an essential role. The Romantic (German idealist) emphasis on fluidity, indeterminacy, and process in Potebnia's ideas reassured one that mental and verbal life were open, mutable, and evolving, rather than rigid, hierarchical, and mechanistic, as conceived of in Enlightenment models of the self.[1] In fact, Potebnia's theorizing is so given over to outlining this general view of language that it has little use as a guide to the specifics of any particular language—one would be at a loss to know what to *do* with his model in the way of linguistic analysis. Instead his model serves primarily to tell us what our selves are like (they are image-producing, articulating seekers after epistemological knowledge), and how self-like is the primary manifestation of our mental life, which is language.

What makes Potebnia so interesting from the standpoint of Russian culture in a broader sense is the way in which, as we have seen, key elements in his scheme suddenly enabled a kind of heightened traffic between metaphysical notions deriving from Neoplatonic thought in its Russian Orthodox rescension, on the one hand, and the latest developments in Western, especially German, philosophy and psychology, on the other. Serious philosophy of language in Russia, a good deal of which draws on themes first

---

1. Consider in this vein Vetukhov's remark that later, when Potebnia became interested in the shift from nominal to verbal forms in the evolution of the Russian sentence, he revealed how "Human thought, which had once represented all things and processes as substance, gradually abandoned that category and learned to cast the impressions it received in the form of attribute and energy"; A. Vetukhov, "A. A. Potebnia (†29 noiabria 1891 g.)," (Warsaw: Tipografiia Varshavskogo okruga, 1898), 43–44.

addressed by Potebnia, really gets under way only in the 1910s and 1920s. But Potebnia's ideas already exerted a more impressionistic influence in the late nineteenth and early twentieth centuries. Repercussions of his ideas appear in that era in the form of conscious efforts by disciples to extend his ideas, but also reverberate throughout the many speculations on the nature of language that were produced by a wide variety of cultural figures in the Russian *fin-de-siècle*. Together these intellectual strands form the Russian culture of *logos* within which the writings of Shpet, Losev, Florenskii, and others in the first decades of the twentieth century arose.

The most direct offshoot of Potebnia's ideas in the *fin-de-siècle* was the writings of a group of students and other adherents from Khar'kov whose collective output is sometimes referred to in Russian scholarship as "Potebnia-ism" (*potebnianstvo*) but is perhaps more accurately identified as the "psychological tendency" in Russian literary criticism. Represented by such figures as D. V. Ovsianniko-Kulikovskii, A. Gornfel'd, V. Khartsiev, T. Rainer, and B. Lezin, the group concentrated its efforts on the journal *Voprosy teorii i psikhologii tvorchestva* (Questions in the theory and psychology of art), which was devoted to exploring the psychic processes taking place within the creating or aesthetically perceiving subject.[2] This apparent turn away from questions of language proper toward aesthetics and literature was not entirely unmotivated, given Potebnia's designation of an "image-like quality" (*obraznost'*) as the chief trait of the word's inner form, as well as his writings on the links between language and art (one should also recall the generally aestheticizing bent of Potebnia's thought, which was a reaction against the sociological emphases of mid-nineteenth century Russian culture). The movement was in any event everywhere subtended by a tendency toward what Presniakov calls the "absolutization of language," a trait that was in fact to become, not without Potebnia's influence, characteristic of the dawning era as a whole.[3]

The writings of these Potebnians tended to pursue an eclectic rather than focused agenda, and were often as much interested in adapting Potebnia to current intellectual vogues (such as neo-Kantianism and Mach's empirio-criticism) as they were in developing the ideas themselves. But this very dispersive quality was perhaps a sign that it was as much the *issues* Potebnia had opened up as it was his intellectual legacy proper that mattered, and

2. P. A. Nikolaeva et al., eds., *Akademicheskie shkoly v russkom literaturovedenii* (Moscow: Nauka, 1975), 304; Presniakov, *A. A. Potebnia i russkoe literaturovedenie*, 142.

3. Presniakov, *A. A. Potebnia i russkoe literaturovedenie*, 143.

"potebnia-ism" was influential in the development of Russian philology despite the fact that its significance was subsequently eclipsed by such flashier movements as Formalism and the avant-garde.[4]

A good example of how some of Potebnia's more dutiful followers sought to extend his ideas can be found in A. P. Pogodin's *Iazyk, kak tvorchestvo* (Language as creation [1913]). Pogodin presents his study as an elaboration on the precepts found in his mentor's *Mysl' i iazyk* and begins by reciting the fundamental positions of the Humboldt/Potebnia view of language: it represents the constant creative activity of thought and therefore is the expression of self-knowledge; speaking consists not just in producing articulate sounds but in "thinking in words"; the word consists of an outer form and inner content, the latter originating in visual or auditory imagery.[5] He then applies this doctrine to the field of psychology by examining such issues as the development of speech in infants, the likely mental world of animals, and, most extensively, aphasia and other speech disorders (Pogodin had, incidentally, also published a monograph entitled *Vnutrenniaia rech' i ee rasstroistva* [Inner speech and its disturbance] in the November 1906 issue of *Zhurnal ministerstva narodnogo prosveshcheniia*, some of which might have served as background material for Jakobson's later writings on aphasia). In all this Pogodin does little more than rewrite the relevant experimental observations in Potebnian vocabulary, as in his explanation of aphasia as a rift between "inner speech" and its full outward expression ("amnesiac aphasia is the rupture of the link between the inner and outer word; only the latter is a symbol, whereas the former remains merely a complex of sounds").[6] As Presniakov points out, his work consists largely of lengthy quotations from French and Swiss psychologists; but it shows how eager Potebnia's followers were to map his vision of the linguistically constituted self onto any phenomena it could be considered to explain.[7]

A closely related example is the writings of B. A. Lezin, editor of *Voprosy teorii i psikhologii tvorchestva*, who was more interested in the philosophical and psychological aspects of Potebnia's legacy and whose primary concern was to show that Potebnia had anticipated contemporary developments in these areas. It was Lezin's "Khudozhestvennoe tvorchestvo kak osobyi vid

4. Ibid., 151. For a straightforward (psycho-)linguistic extension of Potebnia's ideas, see Buzuk's overview of issues having to do with language and thought, which incorporates Wundt's "willful" theory of language formation (i.e., the belief that the word is a means for cognition, but it arises out of the intentional use of an articulatory gesture to signify something, which use spreads through the speech community and becomes a word); Buzuk, *Ocherki po psikhologii iazyka*.

5. A. P. Pogodin, *Iazyk, kak tvorchestvo. Voprosy teorii i psikhologii tvorchestva*, t.IV (Khar'kov: n.p., 1913), 3, 5.

6. Ibid., 49.

7. Presniakov, *A. A. Potebnia i russkoe literaturovedenie*, 149.

ekonomii mysli" (Artistic creativity as a special way of economizing thought, in *Voprosy teorii i psikhologii tvorchestva* 1911, vol. 1) which famously, if somewhat unfairly, earned Potebnia the contempt of the Formalists (in general it was under this aegis of the "psychology of artistic creation" that the Formalists rejected Potebnia and identified him with everything passé in thought about language and art by their Futurist allies).[8] Lezin argued that Potebnia's concept of "inner form" had anticipated Mach's ideas about perception, and that Potebnia's description of the processes of abstraction and generalization at work in language affirmed the "law of the economy of forces" propounded by Mach and Aveniarius.[9]

The work of the literary critic D. V. Ovsianiko-Kulikovskii illustrates the extension of "potebnia-ism" into broader philological realms. In his *Theory of Poetry and Prose* of 1909 he developed Potebnia's ideas about the relation between poetry and prose as divergent principles in the nature of language as well as successive phases in its development. Like Potebnia, Ovsianniko-Kulikovskii posited an analogy between the word and the poetic work, and therefore defined literature as a form of "mental activity" leading to cognition of the world, within which the poetic and the prosaic represent two complementary forms.[10] In his account mental images can be categorized as "typical," "symbolic," or "schematic," and form a continuum extending from more poetic to more prosaic, with the prosaic forms exhibiting an erosion of the symbolizing impetus of "inner form" in its more vigorous manifestations (he also developed a theory of the important role played by metonymy, synecdoche, and metaphor in poetic thought, based on the assumption that different types of image originate in different types of cognition). Just as Potebnia's emphasis on the eventness of the speech act had led him to assign the recipient of a verbal message an important role in the formation of its meaning, Ovsianniko-Kulikovskii anticipated "reader-response" criticism by writing of the reader's "co-creativity" in the artistic text.[11] As suggested by the examples of Mandelstam, for whom the interlocutor is essential to the act of poetic creation, and Bakhtin, for whom the dialogic speech act is an inherently ethical event, this became one of the most productive of Potebnia's ideas in the Russian context. A fair amount of Ovsianniko-Kulikovskii's work, however, is concerned with the theoretically less innovative task of postulating psychological "types" within the development of Russian literature, such as the "Pushkinian," with its alleged

8. See, however, Rancour-Laferriere's insightful remarks on Formalism's conspicuous avoidance of the concept of personhood; Rancour-Laferriere, "Why the Formalists Had No Theory of the Literary Person," 327–37.

9. Presniakov, A. A. Potebnia i russkoe literaturovedenie, 143.

10. Nikolaeva et al., *Akademicheskie shkoly,* 359.

11. Presniakov, A. A. Potebnia i russkoe literaturovedenie, 144–47.

emphasis on detached observation, and the "Gogolian," which emphasized "experiment" with reality.[12]

One of the ways in which Potebnia's ideas about language were beginning to move outward from this circle of adherents into the broader context of Russian literary culture can be sensed from an exchange that took place in the pages of Russia's "thick journals" between A. Gornfel'd, one of Potebnia's Khar'kov students, and the literary critic F. Batiushkov, a student of Veselovskii. Gornfel'd opened the debate with a sally entitled "Muki slova" (The word's torments), published in 1899.[13] He intended his title ironically, as a parody of the frequent claims made by contemporary "decadent" poets that significant thought is ultimately inexpressible in language—a reprise of the neoromantic idea, best known in the Russian context from Tiutchev's poem "Silentium," that in poetry one ought ideally to "be silent, hide oneself, and keep [one's feelings] secret." For Gornfel'd the primary defense against this kind of speculative irresponsibility lay in the fundamental link between word and thought as it had been defined by Potebnia. The neoromantics, Gornfel'd suggests, misconstrue the Humboldt/Potebnia claim that "all understanding is misunderstanding" because each listener must recreate the meaning conveyed in a speaker's words. Granted, in Potebnia's scheme the meanings of words are flexible; but the boundaries of misunderstanding are not infinite. The meaning of a word is the "thought" it represents within the language, and departures from this meaning can only go so far.[14] Moreover, because its semantic functions are carried out within the larger network of meanings that is the language as a whole, the word represents a "first science," a first attempt to lend the nature of a system to the world.[15] Gornfel'd cites Lotze's observation that when we ask for and receive the name of a thing, we are reassured that the designated object has already been assigned a place in the scheme of things by "general reason." Possession of a name testifies that an object is known and cognized. The existence of language thus assures us of the orderly nature of reality. "Disarray and disorder are intolerable to the spirit; thought thirsts after a system— and finds it first of all in language."[16] The "torments" poets profess to endure, Gornfel'd concludes, are those of genre or medium rather than language, in which all thoughts are potentially expressible. For Gorn'feld,

12. Nikolaeva et al., *Akademicheskie shkoly,* 369, 371.

13. It is interesting to note that Gor'kii used to recommend "Muki slova" to beginning writers; see Presniakov, *A. A. Potebnia i russkoe literaturovedenie,* 155.

14. A. G. Gornfel'd, "Muki slova," *Russkoe bogatstvo* (1899), 84–86.

15. Ibid., 93. Here Gornfel'd points out Humboldt's claim that languages embody worldviews, which he implies means systematized accounts of reality. In thinking of semantics in this vein he both echoes Potebnia and anticipates Shpet.

16. Ibid., 93–94.

Potebnia's conception of language thus assures us that language is adequate to the self, which is ultimately rational, and no experiments in verse contradict this fact.[17]

Batiushkov responded to this "positivist-conservative" statement (in which one can detect a rehearsal for the skirmishes, typical of our own day, between an E. D. Hirsch or John Ellis with the post-structuralist Derrida, De Man, and company) by taking up the central issue of the relation between language and thought. Gornfel'd, he remarks, thinks that efforts by decadent poets to sever the two are doomed to failure by the essential unity of form and content; but what he fails to take into account is that content might be developed apart from its "material wrapping."[18] Batiushkov then rejects the very premise of Humboldt's and Potebnia's view of language: contrary to what they believed, he asserts, the word is not a "condition of thought" (*uslovie mysli*) but merely thought's conventional form (*uslovnaia forma*).[19] With the minor exception of onomatopoeia, there is no immediate connection between the word's acoustic signifier and its meaning.[20] Content and form are separable in language (and in poetry) because language and thought are not identical and should not be confused with each other. Beyond this nominalism, of course, lay Futurism, with its utopian aspiration to "liberate" form from conventional meaning, and behind the debate in general one can discern more fundamentally divergent beliefs about the relation of language to the self: for Gornfel'd it forms an essential part, its systematic nature assuring us of our own and the world's rational character; for Batiushkov there emerges the possibility that the self might be conceived without reference to language and might therefore be liberated from rationality. But what is significant in the present context is the degree to which the debate took Potebnia's theory of language as its point of departure.

Fervent interest in the nature of the word also spread far beyond this immediate circle of Potebnia's students into early-twentieth-century Russian

---

17. Gornfel'd also criticized attempts by Belyi, Bal'mont, and others at the other end of the spectrum of semantic speculation to attach absolute meanings to individual letters, regardless of their context; see Presniakov, *A. A. Potebnia i russkoe literaturovedenie*, 154. See also Gornfel'd's sardonic response to Bely's *Glossolalia*, "Nauchnaia glossolaliia," in *Boevye otkliki na mirnye temy* (Leningrad: Kolos, 1924), 140–54.

18. F. Batiushkov, "V bor'be so slovom," *Zhurnal ministerstva narodnogo prosveshcheniia* (1900), No. 2, otd. 2, 212.

19. Ibid., 211.

20. Ibid., 214.

culture as a whole, where it affected such grand movements in Russian letters of the era as Symbolism, Acmeism, and Futurism. If the interest was not due to Potebnia alone, his voice nonetheless played a much more prominent role in it than we have tended to recognize—not least his synecdochal refocusing of attention from language as a whole to the more readily anthropomorphized "word"—and in the examination of language the influence of his blending of German idealist with older, Eastern Orthodox impulses was considerable.

Among the cultural figures most exuberant in their pronouncements on the ontological necessity of the word or of language in this era is Andrei Bely. The general qualities of his statements, their heterogeneous and sometimes inconsistent borrowings from philosophy and mysticism, are well known, but what bears consideration here is the extent to which he derives some of his seemingly idiosyncratic positions, in particular the assorted vivifying and anthropomorphizing metaphors he deploys in his descriptions of language, directly from Potebnia—a debt he actually acknowledges with almost hyperbolic gratitude.

Russian Symbolism in general tended to search for word-like phenomena at the heart of reality. In *Po zvezdam* (Among the stars), for example, Viacheslav Ivanov says of Baudelaire that he was a "realistic symbolist" because he knew that "for those who can hear it there sounds in nature the myriad-voiced eternal word," and states that insofar as any object contains a "hidden reality" it is already a symbol.[21] The Symbolist notion, derived in large part from Solov'ev, that the symbol is precisely that site in the cosmos on which the transitory combines with the eternal, also resonates with patristic doctrines of *Logos*.[22] But among the Symbolists it is Bely who offers the most explicit and extensive theorizations on the nature of language.

To begin with, Bely published an ecstatic posthumous review of Potebnia's works in the journal *Logos* and frequently invoked Potebnia's legacy to legitimize statements he regarded as foundational for Symbolism (in his writings on language Bely frequently cites *Mysl' i iazyk*, as well as *Zapiski po russkoi grammatike*, together with an extensive list of Potebnia's German sources, often taken directly from Potebnia: Steinthal, Grimm, Becker,

21. Quoted in James West, *Russian Symbolism. A Study of Vyacheslav Ivanov and the Russian Symbolist Aesthetic* (London: Methuen, 1970), 53–54.

22. See for example the definition offered by Volynsky (A. L. Flekser) in *The Battle for Idealism* (1900) of Symbolism as "the fusion of the phenomenal and the divine worlds in artistic representation"; quoted in West, *Russian Symbolism*, 108. Fizer suggests that what attracted the Symbolists to Potebnia was his definition of the word as something empirically tangible on the level of morphology while anagogic (that is, tending to uplift the mind toward spiritual things) and the level of semantics (*Potebnja's Psycholinguistic Theory of Literature*, 120).

Humboldt, Lotze, Lazarus).[23] The *Logos* article makes bold claims for Potebnia as one of the founders of Symbolism. Early readers of Potebnia missed the element of daring in his writings, Bely says, which had to do with their treatment of such fundamental issues as the origins and meaning of language, myth, and poetic creativity. Potebnia treated such issues with an originality that qualifies him as one of the great European linguists of his age.[24] The "work" Potebnia carried out was "in essence" the same as that of Nietzsche (!): by showing that at its core the word is an image or symbol, he made clear the "irrational roots of the self" operating in verbal creation (the immediate linking of self and word here being symptomatic). The way in which acoustic shell links up with inner form in Potebnia's theory represents "the living, in essence irrational, symbolism of language."[25] This means that every word is in principle a metaphor. Potebnia's contribution to the philosophy of language was thus to show that creativity is historically prior to cognition, and that the work of cognition in language has come full circle and returned to metaphor.[26]

In general Bely's writings on language and the symbol represent a sustained effort to show that language, especially the language of Symbolist poetry, is continuous with essence—an impulse characteristic of many Russian writers in this area. His starting point in Potebnia is the idea that the word functions principally as a means to cognition. As a symbol, the word represents a union that is comprehensible to me of two otherwise incomprehensible essences, he states in "Magiia slov" (The magic of words), echoing, however distantly, the Herbartian psychological ideas in Potebnia about the mind's accommodation of "unknown" mental data within the store of the known.[27] In "Emblematika smysla" (The emblematics of sense) he similarly says that the symbol combines the aims of cognition "with something lying beyond the bounds of cognition," then declares on the basis of this that the time has now come for the "theory of cognition" to give way to a "theory of creativity."[28]

Bely's most significant debt to Potebnia, however, has to do with his adaptation of the concept of "inner form," in which he advances a mystical theory of the symbol that, minus its woollier elements, is essentially a

---

23. See, for example, Andrei Belyi, *Simvolizm* (Moscow, 1910; reprint, Munich: Wilhelm Fink Verlag, 1969), 572–73, though see also Rainov's claim that Gornfel'd had pointed out the affinity between Potebnia's ideas and the aesthetics of Symbolism before Bely's *Logos* article (which he erroneously dates 1912–13); T. Rainov, *Aleksandr Afanas'evich Potebnia* (Petrograd: Kolos, 1924),16.
24. Belyi, "Mysl' i iazyk. Filosofiia iazyka A. A. Potebni," *Logos* (1910), 241.
25. Ibid., 250.
26. Ibid., 257.
27. In Belyi, *Simvolizm,* 430.
28. Ibid., 67, 79.

metaphysics of verbal structure. In some of the footnotes to "Magiia slov" he makes an excursus into the Potebnia/Humboldt idea of language as a form of energy rather than as a thing (see for example the very Humboldt-ian remark that "living speech is an eternally flowing and creating form of activity"; he then cites Potebnia's concept of "inner form" in order to assert that this energy of language is connected with the poetic image).[29] The "symbolism of language" is precisely what is expressed through the word's inner form, he asserts.[30] The essence of this doctrine is that the formal unity of sign and referent in the word can be taken as metaphysical evidence of the potential unity of the world as a whole (for example, of its phenomenal and noumenal realms).[31] This claim represents a subtle twist on medieval realism, which held that names for things and categories of things are justi-fied because those things and categories truly exist in the world, prior to their naming. Here the certitude is projected in the reverse direction, from the word to the world: if the word obtains as unity, so too must the reality it represents. "The image of the whole of reality, which is given in an ab-stract term, is a metaphysical concept," he remarks; "this reality, given in an image of value, is the manifest appearance [*lik*] of the world's unity."[32] "For that reason the very concept of unity is given in emblematic terms; what from the perspective of cognition we call the emblem of emblems, as the absolute limit for constructing any concepts, is the Symbol."[33] Bely's state-ments in this vein often betray a keen desire to tap into the ontological essence lodged within the word. "Unity makes itself known to us in the form of a symbol," he claims, "and for that very reason, when we treat of it in terms of cognition or creation, we speak of it in the language of symbols. It is in this sense that we should understand the proposition, 'Unity is a Symbol' "—in other words, language and symbols are natural objects for metaphysical study because they enjoy a privileged link with essence.[34] "By eliminating any form of psychologism from the word [a maneuver cognate, incidentally, with Husserlian phenomenology as well as Formalism] we in-vest it with *sui generis* existence; the word becomes Logos; logical reality it-self is a *sui generis* ontology."[35] Indeed, in "Magiia slov" Bely suggests that the word is the *only* reality of which we have a sure grasp, an island of on-tological certitude in an ocean of hypothesis and ambiguity. "The worlds of

29. Ibid., 435.

30. Ibid., 574–76. In its appropriative gesture Bely's statement is not unlike Chomsky's later claim that Humboldtian inner form is nothing other than Chomskian deep structure.

31. See, e.g., Belyi, "Emblematika smysla," in *Simvolizm,* 107.

32. Ibid., 91.

33. Ibid., 92.

34. Ibid., 98.

35. Ibid., 120.

abstract concepts, like the worlds of essences, no matter what we may call them (matter, spirit, nature), are not real; they do not even exist without the word; the word is the only real ship on which we sail from one unknown to another."[36] Therefore only when I *speak* am I truly conscious of myself.[37]

As some of the passages I have quoted indicate, Bely often translates his metaphysical account of the symbol into terms deriving from the religious doctrine of *Logos* (in fact he refers to his theory of the symbol as a "powerful stream of Eastern mysticism" flowing into the hermetic world of nineteenth-century European art).[38] He deploys this terminology in the figurative or ironic manner one finds in Solov'ev, in the sense that what he intends is more a philosophical expansion of Christian concepts than a devout adoption of them; but apart from the doctrine of a personal God he takes over a good deal of Eastern Christian metaphysics. Art is capable of conveying us to the living *image* of cosmic unity, Bely claims, using a term ordinarily used in Russian orthodoxy to refer to the image or visage of Christ or saints in icons ("*lik,*" etymologically related to the Russian *litso,* "face"), and this image is merely the anthropomorphic form of *Logos.*[39] The unity of disparate natures—divine spirit and mundane flesh—central to the Christological doctrines of the Church and, in Orthodoxy, of sacred icons, here becomes a metaphor for the way in which art (especially Symbolist poetry) serves to body forth the otherwise elusive or unrevealed unity of the cosmos. "Symbolic unity," Bely says, sounding Jakobsonian for a moment, "is the unity of the cognitive series within the creative series. . . . In religious terms artistic creation conveys us toward divine manifestation; the *Logos* of the world assumes human appearance [*Lik*]. . . . The task [of theurgy] is to reveal unity in the human image [in *Lik*], to transform the word (principle) into flesh (into the content of our reality); speaking figuratively [an intentional pun: "*na obraznom iazyke*" also means "in terms of images"] this means to transform the Word into Flesh."[40] To make the source of his references even clearer, Bely then cites the foundational text of Christian Logology, the opening of the Gospel of John: "In the beginning was the Word."

Bely invokes this line of "Eastern mysticism" independently of his philological borrowings from Potebnia, but what he has essentially done—as others like Losev, Florenskii, and Bulgakov would do after him—is to make explicit one of Potebnia's most powerful but unacknowledged subtexts. He

36. Belyi, "Magiia slov," in *Simvolizm,* 436.
37. Ibid., 440.
38. Belyi, "Emblematika smysla," in *Simvolizm,* 143; he also cites Trubetskoi's survey *Uchenie o Logose*—e.g., *Simvolizm,* 126.
39. Ibid., 79.
40. Ibid., 94.

also extends this rhetorical gesture into a series of broader anthropomorphizing descriptions of language—typically emphasizing such themes as the
incarnation or the death and rebirth of language—which, while free of distinctly religious terms, nonetheless clearly draw on the doctrine of Christ's
incarnation that stands at the center of the Christian concept of *Logos.* Thus
in "Magiia slov" he declares the creative word (that used in art) to be "an
incarnated word (a word-as-flesh)" and to be authentic only in that sense.[41]
Fusing both Potebnian and religious subtexts he calls the "living word
(word-as-flesh)" a "flourishing organism," whereas the word-as-term (*slovo-
termin*) is a "dead crystal formed as a result of the completed process of
decay of the living word." The "common prosaic word, that which has lost
its quality of acoustic and painterly imagery and not yet become an ideal
term, is a putrid, decaying corpse," and we are now surrounded by such decaying words, which poison us until the longed-for rebirth of the word that
Symbolism will usher in.[42] That this metaphor exerted significant influence
within Russian culture of this period is evident from such echoes as
Shklovskii's invocation of it in the title of his essay "Voskreshenie slova"
(The resurrection of the word), to be brought about by Futurist verse, and
Gumilev's oft-quoted poem of 1921, "Slovo" (The word), which laments the
fact that humanity has forgotten the divine nature of the word and has set
as its boundaries "the meager bounds of the natural world" ("*skudye predely
estestva*"): "And like bees in an abandoned hive / Dead words have a foul
smell" ("*I, kak pchely v ul'e opustelom / Durno pakhnut mertvye slova*").[43]

Another evident concern of Bely's is with what might be called the ontological efficacy of language, or, as Austin would have called it, its perlocutionary force: its ability not only to represent reality but also to change it.
Particularly important in this regard is the act of naming, which Bely, echoing doctrines like medieval realism that assert an essential link between
name and referent, describes as capable of constituting reality—though it is
also characteristic of Bely to vacillate ambiguously between this kind of
mystical ontologism and a neo-Kantian subjectivism which holds that language creates only within one's private worldview; hence it is often unclear
in his statements whether the objects he refers to are real existents or elements in a purely mental world. "Language is the most powerful instrument of creation," he declares in "Magiia slov"; "when I name an object
with a word I confirm its existence. Every cognition already flows out of an
act of naming. Cognition is impossible without the word."[44] He even

41. "Magiia slov," in *Simvolizm,* 434.
42. Ibid., 436.
43. Nikolai Gumilev, *Stikhotvoreniia i poemy* (Leningrad: Sovetskii pisatel', 1988), 312.
44. Belyi, "Magiia slov," 429.

makes the audacious claim that "the word . . . creates causal relations that only later come to be recognized" and that "If there were no words neither would the world exist."[45] The neo-Kantian influence becomes evident when Bely suggests that the "creation" in question is of a mental image rather than of something external to the self, as when he says that "the word creates a new, third world—the world of sound symbols, by means of which the mysteries of the world lying outside of me are illuminated" or "In sound a new world is created *within the bounds of which I feel myself to be* the creator of reality; then I begin to name objects, i.e. *secondarily* to recreate them for myself"; or even "all cognition is an illusion which follows from the word."[46]

But the ontological yearning nonetheless reasserts itself whenever Bely speaks of the incantatory powers of language and writes enthusiastically about ancient folk beliefs (practices, as he would have it) involving charms and the magical use of language. Here he again draws explicitly on Potebnia, in this case on examples Potebnia had given of "folk creativity in language." As Presniakov points out, however, Potebnia's interest had been purely historical—he was concerned to show that the creation of images was especially relevant to the early development of language and culture— whereas Bely wants to suggest that the incantatory powers of language can be revived.[47] These are the powers the word possesses when it is still a "living word" and these are the powers he believes language will regain when it is reborn in Symbolist verse. Bely's fascination with (folk) incantation was in fact widespread among the Symbolists (who may have been drawn to this idea of the magic, incantatory powers of the word because of the way it imputes to language a kind of selfhood evincing itself in will, movement, action). In 1908, two years before Bely's collection of essays appeared, Blok had published "Poeziia zagovorov i zaklinanii" (The poetry of spells and incantations) in which he muses on the fervent "belief in the word" characteristic of the "ancient soul." What supported the practice of incantations, Blok argues, was the lack of any assumption that man was separate from

---

45. Ibid., 431, 429.

46. Ibid., 430, 431, 438 (emphasis added). It is interesting that Bely suggests that this world-creating practice of naming originates in a sense of fear before a hostile and incomprehensible world, much as Rousseau suggests that "man's first motives for speaking" were passions, such as fear before strangers who seemed enormous and whom primitive man therefore named "giants" ("Essay on the Origin of Language," 22–23): "by the sound of the word I tame these elements; the process of naming spatial and temporal phenomena with words is a process of incantation," "by creating words, by naming unknown phenomena with sounds we conquer and charm these phenomena; all life rests on the living power of speech"; and he goes on to give the very Rousseauian example of "taming" the rumbling of thunder ("grrrrrr") by calling it "*grom*" (Belyi, "Magiia slov," in *Simvolizm*, 431, 435).

47. Presniakov, *A. A. Potebnia i russkoe literaturovedenie*, 157.

nature, out of which flowed a belief in the indivisibility of subject and object, word and deed (Blok in his turn cites Potebnia's study of Ukrainian folk songs, his opinion that the casting of spells may have arisen out of something even more primordial than ancient religious beliefs, and his description of incantations as a situation in which "what is depicted" and "what depicts" are only weakly distinguished).[48] But despite its implicit suggestion that this state of affairs ought to be revived, Blok's discussion remains mostly historical. Five years later than Bely, Bal'mont also took up the theme of incantations in his symptomatically titled *Poeziia kak volsheb-stvo* (Poetry as magic [1915]). If we could but rediscover in ourselves the primordial force of spell-casting, Bal'mont pleads, then "that sound-sculpture called the Word would reveal its innermost voice and speak magically to us"; and he implicitly links this idea with the doctrine of *Logos* when he argues that "if the whole life of the world is an unfathomable miracle arising out of nonbeing through the force of a creative word, then our human word, with which we measure the universe and rule over the elements, is the most magical miracle of all that is valuable in our human life."[49]

Closely related to Bely's fascination with the (purported) magical power of words is his belief in universal sound symbolism—an interest one also finds in Bal'mont and Khlebnikov—to which he devoted his 1917 *Glosso-laliia–Poema o zvuke* (Glossolalia—a poem about sound). The title features the Greek word for the "gift of tongues" granted to the apostles at Pentecost, and Bely, who had a lively interest in religious sects, may have been influenced by D. G. Konovalov's study of religious ecstasy among Russian sectarians, which also inspired some of the Futurists' claims for a new language.[50] Armed with the theosophical writings of Rudolph Steiner, dictionaries of Indo-European roots, and occasionally dipping into Potebnia's *Mysl' i iazyk*, Bely unfolds a series of investigations into the idea that sounds or even letters have absolute meanings, and that the fundamental sounds of all

48. Aleksandr Blok, "Poeziia zagovorov i zaklinanii," in *Sobranie sochinenii v vos'mi tomakh*, t.5 (Moscow-Leningrad: Khudozhestvennaia literatura, 1962), 37, 43, 45–46, 48.

49. Konstantin Bal'mont, *Poeziia kak volshebstvo* (1915; reprint, Letchworth-Herts, England: Prideaux Press, 1973), 54–55, 52.

50. Vladimir Markov suggests that Konovalov serves as the "unnamed source" of some of Kriuchenykh's examples of sectarian speaking in tongues and in general as one of the inspirations for Futurist *zaum*; in his *Russian Futurism. A History* (Berkeley: University of California Press, 1968), 202. If so this is despite the predominantly physiological, rather than linguistic or mystical, interest Konovalov displays toward his subjects (he discusses, e.g., increases in heart rate, the appearance of perspiration during states of religious "ecstasy," and so forth) as well as the tone of clinical neutrality verging on skepticism that he adopts toward the sectarians claims vis-à-vis their ecstatic babble ("a collection of incomprehensible words or distorted foreign words . . . nonsense sounds"). D. G. Konovalov, "Religioznyi ekstaz v russkom misticheskom sektanstve," chast' I, vyp. I, "Fizicheskie iavleniia v kartine sektantskogo ekstaza" (Sergiev Posad: Tipografiia Sv.-Tr. Sergievoi Lavry, 1908), 170.

languages can be shown at root to denote the same ideas or qualities. Thus, to give just one example, he asserts that one can still discern the motif of "streams of light" congealed in the roots *zi-si-zis-sis-zir-sir-ris-riz* despite the obscuring accumulation of other meanings over the centuries. Hence in Russian one finds "*vzir*" and "*vzirat*'" (to gaze), while in Assyrian there is "*Siherach*" (the rising sun); "*siianie*" (radiance) in Russian and "*ciel*'" in French, and on to "*zhizn*'" (life) and "*zizanah*" (to give birth) in Zendish and even "*Osiris*" and "*Ch-ris-os.*"[51] What joins this desire to find an absolute set of meanings in language with a belief in language's incantatory powers is, again, the longing for a direct link with essence: if linguistic signification is not "arbitrary" in a Saussurian sense, and sounds enjoy an essential link with their referents, then by divining the roots of language we can gain direct access to the essence of the world. Moreover, for Bely the speculative etymologies of *Glossolalia* are meant not just as hypotheses about the unity of languages but as prophetic anticipation of the day when the "language of languages" underlying the babel of the world's tongues will reassert itself and language will enter into its full ontological rights: "The ability to read a sound is only the first hint at the *language* of languages; and we know that the second coming of the Word will take place."[52] "May the brotherhood of nations come about: the language of languages will tear asunder languages; and then the second coming of the Word will happen."[53] If the ideal of a universal language recalls the aspirations of seventeenth- and eighteenth-century philosophers with their "real characters," the reference to a "second coming" makes clear that Bely's vision is even more heavily indebted to the Christian doctrine of *Logos*.

Even the theoretical proclamations of the Russian Futurists, Symbolism's rebellious successors, reveal the influence of Potebnia's ideas about language, despite the fact that, as Steiner points out, their cherished notion of *zaum* ("trans-sense" language or poetry) aimed largely at emphasizing what Potebnia would have called the "outer form" of the word and may be construed as having "attacked the very heart of Potebnia's aesthetic system."[54] But for all the superficial denigration of Potebnia by the Futurists and Formalists, a consideration of even something as simple as the key terms in the Futurist vocabulary—the "word as such," the "self-oriented word," the insistence on neologism as the basis of poetry—already begins to suggest a debt, even if a reactive one, to Potebnia. And as an aesthetic theory vesting its hopes for

---

51. Andrei Belyi, *Glossolaliia. Poema o zvuke* (1917/1922; Tomsk: Vodolei, 1994), 35. For Gornfel'd's scathing review of these speculations, see his "Nauchnaia glossolaliia."

52. Belyi, *Glossolaliia*, 89.

53. Ibid., 95.

54. Peter Steiner, *Russian Formalism: A Metapoetics* (Ithaca: Cornell University Press, 1984), 144.

the world's renewal in experimentation carried out within language, Futurism clearly partakes of the "absolutization" of language characteristic of the era in general. Aleksei Kriuchenykh's examples of *zaum,* for example, may celebrate the pure exteriority of linguistic sounds liberated from sense (for example, the famous "*Dyr bul shchyl*") but his artistic declarations strike notes more reminiscent of Potebnia. The claim in "Deklaratsiia slova, kak takovogo" ("declaration of the word as such") that existing natural language has become outworn and that artists have the right to create a new one clearly draws on Potebnia's account of how initial "poetic" impulses in language decline into "prosaic" ones.[55] Elsewhere Kriuchenykh uses "language that has not yet frozen" as a synonym for *zaum,* recalling the general view in Humboldt and Potebnia that language is a form of energy rather than a thing.[56] Kriuchenykh also echoes Potebnia when he suggests that new words should be formed and new combinations of words arranged "according to their *inner laws,* which reveal themselves to the speechmaker."[57]

A still more significant Futurist expatiator on the nature of language is Velimir Khlebnikov. Whether it is true or not, as the admittedly partisan Rainov claims, that Khlebnikov drew on Potebnia's ideas in elaborating his theory of *zaum,* Khlebnikov exemplifies the chiliastic hopes attached to language in Russia of the early twentieth century—the ways in which language came to be viewed as much more than a utilitarian tool for communication.[58] Khlebnikov often enough speaks of language as if it were an organism, a kind of self in its own right; but he is even more emphatic in his insistence that language is a necessary complement to, or even condition of, the self. For Khlebnikov it is in language that the deracinated and wandering self will one day find its true home—will come to inhabit meaning.

The guiding sense in Khlebnikov's various writings on language, which he lends the flavor of something quasi-biblical, kabbalistic, allegorical, or "Egyptian," is one of symbolic systems as seductively opaque surfaces beneath which swarm esoteric absolute meanings—a kind of delirium of precise denotative systems such as language or numbers that might displace our unredeemed world or at least be revealed to underlie and govern it (occasionally he also mentions music, as when he proposes a "Futurist scale" combining music, number, and language in "Nasha osnova" [Our basis], making one think of the similar interest in mathematics of Pavel Florenskii and Aleksei Losev).[59] At times he treats these meanings as mysteries still

55. A. Kriuchenykh, "Deklaratsiia slova, kak takovogo," in Vladimir Markov, ed., *Manifesty i programmy russkikh futuristov,* Slavische Propyläen (Munich: Wilhelm Fink Verlag, 1967), 63.

56. "Delaratsiia zaumnogo iazyka," in ibid., 179.

57. "Novye puti slova," in ibid., 68 (emphasis added).

58. Rainov, *Aleksandr Afanas'evich Potebnia,* 16.

59. Velemir Khlebnikov, "Nasha osnova," in *Tvoreniia* (Moscow: Sovetskii pisatel', 1987), 629.

hidden from us, as when he states in "O sovremennoi poezii" (On contemporary poetry) that "the strange wisdom [of magical speech] can be broken down into the truths contained within separate sounds: *sh, m, v,* and so forth. For the present we do not understand them . . . but there is no doubt that these lines of sounds are the series of world truths that pass before the twilight of our souls."[60] At other times he proposes specific meanings of words and sounds, often based on spurious phonetic or etymological reasoning, as in the passage in "Ka" in which the narrator reasons that the semantic relation of "*bes*" (demon) to "*bremia*" (burden) must be the same as that of "*ves*" (weight) to "*vremia*" (time), then concludes from this that time and weight are revealed as "two different devourings of one and the same force."[61] An imaginary dialogue in "Uchitel′ i uchenik" (Teacher and student) proposes something similar (the idea that the preposition "*bez*" [without] means "called forth by pain" and "*bog*" [god] means a being toward whom one should experience fear), calling it, in a markedly Potebnian vein, "the inner declension of words."[62] Language for Khlebnikov is not an instrument, but a reservoir of meanings—and, as even his descriptive terms make clear (things are "hidden within" sounds), like the selves it might redeem it has *interiority.*

What these beliefs lead Khlebnikov to propose is a millenarian project for uncovering the true esoteric roots of language and on their basis constructing an entirely new, universal tongue.[63] Underlying this aim is the now familiar perception, couched in organic metaphor, of the "death of language," which Potebnia transmitted to Russians from Humboldt and the German romantics (and which we have seen in Bely and others). Meaning can be either "pure" or "quotidian," Khlebnikov states in "Nasha osnova."[64] The everyday meaning of a word masks its pure meaning, just as the sun's light prevents us from seeing the stars. But if we can set aside quotidian language we may be able to perform the "Copernican revolution" of uncovering the "self-sufficient word." Or, the current state of language is described as "bookish petrification" against which "word-creation" will militate.[65] Moreover, like Condillac, Khlebnikov claims that there exist "poorly constructed words" that the project of "word-creation" will destroy in order to

60. Ibid., 634.

61. Ibid., 525.

62. The full title is "Uchitel′ i uchenik. O slovakh, gorodakh, i narodakh. Razgovor I" (Teacher and student. On words, cities, and peoples. Conversation I), in Khlebnikov, *Tvoreniia*, 585.

63. Markov notes the similarity between this aim and philosophical languages of the eighteenth century (*Russian Futurism,* 303); Steiner characterizes Khlebnikov's aspiration as the desire to return to "an original language of pure rationality" (*Russian Formalism,* 205).

64. Khlebnikov, *Tvoreniia,* 624.

65. Ibid., 627.

build new ones in their place. Like Bely, he locates the precedent for such creativity in folk language ("whoever knows the Russian village knows about words formed for an hour and having the lifespan of a moth"), including incantations, which he calls "*zaum* in folk speech"; but his most earnest prescriptions as to how this should be done are quite idiosyncratic.[66] Notwithstanding his statement in "O sovremennoi poezii" that we do not yet know the absolute meanings of sounds, in "Khudozhniki mira" (Artists of the world) he proposes a series of glosses based on the idea that the units of language all denote spatial relations: "*v*" in all languages denotes rotation around a point, "*kh*" means a closed curve, "*sh*" means the fusions of several planes into one, and so forth, in a manner very reminiscent of Bely's *Glossolalia*.[67] The task facing "artists of thought" is to build a new alphabet out of such concepts, and new "buildings of words" out of these units of thought.[68] In this task they should be guided by the fact that the first sound in a word "directs" all the others in it, like the leader of a labor collective,[69] and that words beginning with the same consonant are united around the same concept[70]—a notion reminiscent of Potebnia's remarks about how our perception best retains the letters that come toward the beginning of a series *a,b,c,d,e*. Moreover, the Russian language has a messianic role to play in all this utopian language-building: can Russians not permit themselves the right to create a new language, just as Lobachevskii created a new, non-Euclidian grammar, Khlebnikov muses in "Kurgan Sviatogora" (Sviatogor's burial mound)?[71] Or, in the same essay, it is the Slavic languages as a group that the wind will whorl together like so many beautiful leaves into a single "circle-maelstrom" of the Slavic word.[72] Once these tasks have been accomplished, *zaum* will provide a "future language of the world," overcoming the current division and enmity among men.[73]

Nor was Khlebnikov alone in the heady days following the Bolshevik revolution in his desire to establish a universal language. In fact he was far outdone in this regard by Ia. Lintsbakh, whose *Printsipy filosofskogo iazyka*.

66. "Kurgan Sviatogora," ibid., 580; and "O stikhakh," ibid., 633.

67. Presniakov points out that Potebnia was skeptical of such attempts at defining sound symbolism and believed they were convincing only to the person proposing the particular set of symbolic meanings; *A. A. Potebnia i russkoe literaturovedenie*, 166.

68. Khlebnikov, "Khudozhniki mira," in *Tvoreniia*, 621.

69. Ibid., 622.

70. Khlebnikov, "Nasha osnova," in *Tvoreniia*, 628.

71. Ibid., 580.

72. Ibid. This belief was also shared by Zdanevich; see Markov, *Russian Futurism*, 357. In Khlebnikov's case, however, see also his proposal in the second letter he wrote to a group of Japanese students, in which he proposes the creation of a universal language based on numbers, to be called "Iazyk chisel Venka Aziiskikh Iunoshei" (The language of numbers of the wreath of Asian youths); in *Tvoreniia*, 606.

73. Khlebnikov, "Khudozhniki mira," ibid., 622.

Opyt tochnogo iazykoznaniia (Principles of philosophical language: an experiment in precise linguistics [1919]) sets out, drawing inspiration from Leibniz, to demonstrate that it is indeed possible to construct an ideally efficient and universally comprehensible language based on mathematics. For Lintsbakh contemporary linguists are no more advanced than alchemists who merely "collect antiquities," whereas it is possible to apply mathematics in order to produce the gold of a perfect future language.[74] Lintsbakh's language would replace lexicon and syntax with geometry and algebra; it would denote mental representations in the form of geometric drawings and concepts in the form of formulae.[75] The specimen Lintsbakh proceeds to develop over some 250 pages of discussion purports to eliminate anything extraneous or retarding in the written representation of speech and to subordinate the laws of logic to mathematical operations (since the fundamental operations of logic are positing and denying, which can be replaced symbolically by addition and subtraction). In the end he arrives at a beautifully abstract representational system of such abstruse complexity that it would take a musicologically minded mathematician even to begin to master it. Lintsbakh proposes ways to represent thought diagrammatically in three dimensions, in order to approximate the simultaneity of thought and transcend the linearity of the written line—which impetus does not prevent him from making interesting claims about film and its linearity as the universal language of the subconscious—all this carried out in the name of ideal parsimony and speed, Ockham's razor wielded in the service of the Revolution and its semiotic utopia.[76]

The relation of the Formalists, the Futurists' half-siblings, to Potebnia's thought and what it represented in the philosophy of language were also complex. We tend to remember them as theoreticians of literature who set their careers in motion with a strident rejection of Potebnia's idea that art consists in "thinking in images," but early Formalist writings appeared almost under the aegis of Potebnia, at least as Potebnia had been adapted by the Symbolists and Andrei Bely. The idea that genuinely scientific study of literature must begin with the study of poetic language as a species unto itself can be traced to Potebnia via Bely, and the Formalist opposition of poetic to prosaic language is essentially an absolutized version of the complex

74. Ia. Lintsbakh, *Printsipy filosofskogo iazyka* (Petrograd: n.p., 1916), iii–vi.
75. Ibid., ix.
76. For Lintsbakh's comments on film see, e.g., ibid., 68, 95.

interaction Potebnia had described within language between poetic and prosaic impulses.[77]

A good example of early Formalist indebtedness to Potebnia can be found in Shklovskii's "Voskreshenie slova," originally a speech given at the Stray Dog cabaret in Petrograd.[78] The speech reveals in particular the extent to which Shklovskii's celebrated ideas about poetry's revivifying psychological effects were initially couched in terms drawn from Potebnia. "Every word at its root is a trope" is the Potebnian paraphrase with which Shklovskii begins; then he adds, using Potebnia's guiding metaphor of language as organic being, "words are now dead, and language resembles a cemetery, but the newly born word was alive and image-laden."[79] In general the article is steeped in the organic metaphors—a striking trait in a supposedly form- or matter-oriented avant-garde theoretician—that Potebnia had taken over from Humboldt and German linguistic thought of the nineteenth century. What happens when words become familiar, he continues, invoking Potebnia's structural model, is that we cease to experience their *inner* (figurative) and *outer* (acoustic) sides.[80] He cites Potebnia's "Iz lektsii po teorii slovesnosti" on the "loss" of form the word experiences as it progresses from its poetic to its prosaic stage and suggests that there has taken place an analogous "death of the forms of art."[81] The Futurist verbal experiments that Shklovskii intended his speech to justify are then described as having arisen out of a desire to deal in "living form and the living, not the dead, word."[82] Shklovskii's title is meant metaphorically, even provocatively; but, as in the case of Bely, the allusion it makes to *Logos* (the resurrection of Christ) is a virtually inevitable, rather than happenstance, connection for Russians dealing with these concepts in this era, and a further religious (specifically, iconic) note sounds when Shklovskii claims that the Futurists break down and distort the word in their poetry "out of a desire to give it a face" ("*zhelaia dat' emu litso*").[83] Shklovskii's apology for Futurist experiment in poetry, in other words, derives to a striking degree from a Potebnia-inspired sense of word or language as a (once) "living" being, destined for rebirth.

---

77. On Formalist adaptations of Potebnia see Presniakov, *A. A. Potebnia i russkoe literaturovedenie*, 67–68.

78. Steiner, *Russian Formalism*, 151.

79. Viktor Shklovskii, "Voskreshenie slova," *Texte der Russischen Formalisten*, Band II (Munich: Wilhelm Fink, Verlag, 1972), 2.

80. Ibid.

81. Ibid., 4, 6.

82. Ibid., 12.

83. Ibid.

Shklovskii strikes similar chords in "O poezii i zaumnom iazyke" (On poetry and trans-sense language), a retrospective view from the late 1910s of the original scandal stirred by Futurist *zaum*. In a manner reminiscent of Potebnia's views on the poetic principle within language, Shklovskii argues that *zaum* is not a recent innovation but a principle latent within language at all of its stages and evident even before Futurism in such phenomena as esoteric aesthetic languages, children's speech, folk incantations, and the "speaking in tongues" of Russian sectarians (he cites Konovalov's celebrated study).[84] Even "Potebnia," the article in which he brashly attacked Potebnia's views on language and art, is indebted to its ostensible target. Shklovskii claims that by focusing on the cognitive function of language Potebnia overlooked the true function of art, which is to render things palpable, and that he failed to see imagery as just one in a series of devices through which palpability can be attained. But the very idea that the *telos* of poetry lies in a psychological experience of palpability can be seen as deriving from Potebnia's discussions of the effects utterances produce in the minds of their recipients (and possibly from the significant attention devoted to the psychology of artistic experience by Potebnia's students); and the fact that Shklovskii feels compelled in 1916, some twenty-five years after Potebnia's death, to storm the castle of *potebnianstvo* indicates how influential Potebnia's ideas were. Tension between loyalist *potebniantsy* and the prodigal post-Potebnia Formalists was to resurface in polemics as late as the 1920s, when Formalism's heyday coincided with the publication of the first volume of Potebnia's collected works.[85]

If the Potebnia-oriented remarks in Shklovskii's essays represent not moments of rhetorical incaution but symptomatic features in the development of his (and Formalism's) ideas, then the notorious Formalist "exteriorization" of language and art, and parallel excoriation of Potebnia for his supposedly sentimentalist emphasis on "inner form" and "poeticity," may be somewhat disingenuous. As Rancour-Laferriere has argued, the ironic result of Formalist "efforts to displace the person from literature" by insisting on the autonomy of the literary text and the processes that generate and shape it (thereby neglecting "any literary entity . . . which might conceivably utter the pronoun 'I' "), "was to permit the person to appear elsewhere, as if in compensation."[86] Thus Shklovskii's assorted remarks on narrative structure do not really negate the importance of literary character, and Eikhenbaum

---

84. Viktor Shklovskii, "O poezii i zaumnom iazyke," *Poetika. Sborniki po teorii poeticheskogo iazyka* (Petrograd: 18-ia Gosudarstvennaia tipografiia, 1919), 13–26.

85. Presniakov, *A. A. Potebnia i russkoe literaturovedenie*, 174–77.

86. Rancour-Laferriere, "Why the Formalists Had No Theory of the Literary Person," 327, 334.

could not escape suggesting the importance of Gogol's *skaz* narrator.[87] Still more revealingly, for Rancour-Laferriere, did personhood creep back into Formalist pronouncements in abundant personifying discussions of the literary device as "hero," of a genre's orientation (*ustanovka*) that "searches" for the right form or perishes when it fails to find one—in general a tendency to treat the *text* as a person that Rancour-Laferriere traces down through structuralism and post-structuralism as well and terms a "fallacy of misplaced personification."[88] But the habit of treating a verbal artifact as if it were a self is precisely one of the key reflexes that the Formalists likely absorbed from Potebnia. To take just the example of Shklovskii, his cherished psychological effect of "palpability" is but a short knight's move away from the cognitive function Potebnia believed was central to language. Indeed, if the principal effect of "palpability" is to make us aware of our essential nature, which is mental vitality, then it is very close to Potebnia's emphasis on the self-knowledge we gain through the word. And in Formalist assertions that art or language is dead, or will experience rebirth, or "orients" itself toward something, or "inherits" poetic principles indirectly from its "uncles" rather than "father," Potebnia's personified word—a myth in its own right—is alive and well.[89]

The particular veneration of the "word" that characterizes Russian culture in the late-nineteenth and early-twentieth centuries finds something like its apotheosis in the several eloquent essays the poet Osip Mandelstam devoted to the themes of culture, the nature of the word, language, and poetry. One of the salient features of the essays is their tendency to concretize and personify the "word," which I have suggested owes much of its impetus, if not its ultimate origins, to Potebnia. What these personifying claims work toward in Mandelstam is the construction of an alter-ego or alter-self which is also the embodiment of the whole of (Russian) verbal culture—and surrogate martyr of its various travails. Nor is the kenotic note in

87. Ibid., 331–34.
88. Ibid., 334.
89. In a 1923 essay entitled "The 'Society for the Study of Poetic Language' and Potebnia," I. Plotnikov also argued that the Formalists tried to hide an otherwise obvious debt to Potebnia, whose insistence on the study of form over content had freed the study of literature from its subservient attachment to social-historical concerns and thus paved the way for Formalism ("'Obshchestvo izucheniia poeticheskogo iazyka' i Potebnia," *Pedagogicheskaia mysl'*, No. 1 [1923], 31–32). For Plotnikov, Potebnia's "system" was the first modern literary science, and the shortcomings for which Shklovskii takes Potebnia to task are largely due to Potebnia's simply not having had time to develop a poetics of external versus internal (image-bound) form (Plotnikov, ibid., 40).

Mandelstam's myth of the Word a mere idiosyncrasy, because, as Irina Paperno has shown, he draws quite consciously on esoteric eastern doctrines of *Logos* and names that came to the attention of Russian intellectuals circa 1910.[90]

At the simplest level Mandelstam's veneration (or "absolutization," in Presniakov's term) of the word is evident in his use of it as a synecdoche for poetry or even the whole of verbal culture, and in his corresponding treatment of it as an actor on the stage of history. In "Slovo i kul'tura" (The word and culture) he declares, overturning Marx, that the basis of social structure is formed not by class conflict but by one's attitude toward the word: people are now divided into friends and enemies of the word, he states, and he defines the Soviet state as one that "negates the word."[91] The true historical moment at present is not that of the Bolshevik revolution but of a "heroic era" in the "life" of the word, one in which the word has become as real as "flesh and bread" and in which the word also "shares the fate of flesh and bread—suffering."[92] Russia risks falling at any moment into an abyss of nihilism that would amount to "separation from the word."[93] At the same time the era is witnessing the phenomenon of *glossolalia* (which for Mandelstam is not quite that of Bely or the Futurists, but rather the abundant variety of poetic output: "In a sacred trance poets speak in the language of all times and all cultures"). In this regard the "word" has become a thousand-reed pipe, animated with the breath of all centuries at once.[94]

Like the Futurists, but in conscious opposition to the Symbolists, who were always in the end looking beyond the word toward the transcendent states to which it might convey them, Mandelstam insists on the word's autonomy. But much more consciously than the Futurists, and very much in the spirit of Potebnia's writings, he seeks to define an autonomous word that is a living being, a self, rather than pure external form. Foundational to this enterprise is his notion of "nominalism" (like Bely's, a self-conscious updating of the medieval doctrine) that amounts to an assertion of the word's absolute independence and right to self-definition.[95] Why

---

90. It is interesting to note that in Mandelstam's poems only about four of the approximately twenty-five mentions of "slovo" treat it in this generalizing fashion. The rest clearly speak of particular words, not the Word. See Demetrius J. Koubourlis, *A Concordance to the Poems of Osip Mandelstam* (Ithaca: Cornell University Press, 1974), 501.

91. Osip Mandel'shtam, "Slovo i kul'tura," in *Sobranie sochinenii v trekh tomakh*, 223, 226.

92. Ibid., 225.

93. Ibid., 248.

94. Ibid., 227.

95. Bely offers some interesting remarks in this regard in his *Logos* article on Potebnia. Potebnia, Bely claims, strove to establish the "self-value of the word" ("Mysl' i iazyk. Filosofiia iazyka

should the word be identified with the object it denotes, Mandelstam asks in "Slovo i kul'tura"; is the thing really the master of the word? Rather, the word is Psyche—in Greek mythology, the human soul that migrates from body to body. The "living word" does not denote an object; instead like Psyche it freely chooses its referent as if choosing a residence, "wander[ing] around the thing freely, like the soul around a body it has cast off but not forgotten."[96] In other words the principle of nominalism frees the word to operate like a self. Later, in "O prirode slova" (On the nature of the word), he identifies "nominalism" as a defining trait of the Russian language and glosses the term as "a concept of the reality of the word as such" and of its "inner freedom."[97] It is the opposite of utilitarianism but at the same time provides a safe haven from the entropic forces perennially undermining Russian culture: "every word in Dal'’s dictionary is . . . a winged fortress of nominalism, fitted out with the spirit of Hellenism for tireless battle with the formless element, the nonbeing that everywhere threatens our history."[98]

Mandelstam's abundant personifications of the word and embeddings of it within a larger narrative (Psyche seeking a place to dwell, the word suffering the trials of history) are clear enough evidence of an orientation toward selfhood in his thought on language, but, as the soul-body metaphor suggests, his essays also look more directly back to Potebnia by emphasizing the word's interiority. In "Slovo i kul'tura" he describes poems as "living through their *inner image,* through that impress of form which precedes the written poem. Not a word yet exists, but the poem sounds. That is the *inner*

A. A. Potebni," 249); and the "ideal" for the word in Potebnia's eyes is "autonomy, i.e., the maximal blossoming of inner form" (*ibid.,* 250). Mandelstam's "nominalism" in fact bears at best a loose relation to a strict philosophical sense of the term. As Freidin suggests, Mandelstam was probably attracted to the idea of the arbitrariness of the sign, which had been championed by Moscow linguists who had been reading their Saussure; Gregory Freidin, *A Coat of Many Colors. Osip Mandelstam and His Mythologies of Self-Presentation* (Berkeley: University of California Press, 1987), 172. Freidin locates the immediate source of Mandelstam's interest in nominalism in the neo-Kantianism of the Freiburg school (ibid., 173). In his remarks this idea then becomes a kind of manifesto for the freedom of the poetic word from obligatory otherworldly meanings of the kind that Symbolism had sought to read into poetic speech. But the medieval nominalism of Roscelin, Abelard, and William of Ockham arose as a rejection of the Platonic doctrine that universals enjoy real, objective existence; *Concise Encyclopedia of Philosophy of Language,* ed. Peter V. Lamarque (Oxford: Elsevier Science Ltd./Pergamon, 1997), s.v. "Nominalism." Mandelstam's allegorizing narrative of meaning as personified soul runs directly counter to the empiricist thrust of their views.

96. Mandel'shtam, "Slovo i kul'tura," 226.
97. Mandel'shtam, "O prirode slova," in *Sobranie sochinenii v trekh tomakh,* t. 2, 246.
98. Ibid., 251.

image, which is what the ear of the poet perceives."[99] Again in "O prirode slova" he asserts that there is no difference between "word and image," because "the word is already a sealed image."[100] Considering the word in these terms removes the vexing issue of form versus content, of whether semantics or sound has priority. A verbal representation is a complex system, Mandelstam states, and rather than thinking of it in outdated psychological terms as something objectively given in the mind it should be thought of as "one of man's organs," exactly like the liver or heart—a clear echo of one of the central claims in both Potebnia and his source Humboldt that language is the "organ of thought."[101] Mandelstam sometimes even reads this self-like interiority into phenomena only tangentially related to the word. What makes Bergson's philosophy superior to the theory of evolution, he claims in "O prirode slova," is that it reveals the "inner connectedness" of things rather than the external sequence represented by causality.[102] The Russian language has always been "inwardly united" and marked by its quality of "inner freedom."[103]

Mandelstam may also have drawn from Potebnia another distinctly self-like trait he attributes to the word, his notion that poetry must always consist in dialogue. It was, after all, through Potebnia's paraphrase of Humboldt that an awareness of such notions as the contingency of verbal meaning, its inherence only in dialogue between two interlocutors (all understanding is misunderstanding, my meaning is completed only after it returns to me from the lips of another, and so forth), had entered the Russian context. Mandelstam's "O sobesednike" (On the interlocutor) could be read as an application of these ideas to the writing of poetry. What frightens us most about the insane, he observes, is their indifference toward us—their gaze that fails to see us, their senseless speech. Contrary to assorted myths about poets fleeing the crowd in order to write in isolation, poets need listeners. In fact, what Symbolism ignored was the "juridical" side of the speech act, the fact that if I speak, others are in a certain sense obligated to listen to me.[104] For Mandelstam poets may find their true interlocutor not among their contemporaries but in Boratynskii's "reader in posterity";

---

99. Mandel'shtam, "Slovo i kul'tura," 226–27 (emphasis added). That Potebnia is the likely source of this passage has been noted by many before me. Paperno points it out ("O prirode poeticheskogo slova," 32), citing Freidin, *Coat of Many Colors*, 162, and noting that it was first suggested by A. Bem in his review of Mandelstam's essay in the Prague journal *Volia Rossii* (1923), nos. 6–7, 159–60.

100. Mandel'shtam, "O prirode slova," 254.

101. Ibid., 255. Paperno also points out the link with Potebnia in this passage (but does not mention Mandelstam's use of the concept of "organ"; "O prirode poeticheskogo slova," 33).

102. Mandel'shtam, "O prirode slova," 242.

103. Ibid., 245–46.

104. Mandel'shtam, "O sobesednike," in *Sobranie sochinenii v trekh tomakh*, t. 2, 233–34.

but in his view the guiding principle remains that "there is no lyric without dialogue."[105]

The aspect of Mandelstam's metapoetical essays that reveals the most about his cultural context, however, is his notion of the incarnated word. As Paperno has shown, cross-fertilization between poetry and theology was characteristic of Russian culture in general in the early twentieth century, and significantly informed Mandelstam's articulation of the reasons for his departure from Symbolism. A particularly important moment in the evolution of Mandelstam's views was shaped by the theological disputes set in motion by a group of Russian monks on Mt. Athos, the so-called "*imiaslavie*" debate, which came to public attention in Russia in 1912–13, during the "crisis" of Symbolism.[106] In their enthusiasm for esoteric symbols the Symbolists had seized on the theurgic implications of the monks' claim that words *are* their referents, in the same way that for Orthodoxy icons *are* the divine figures they represent. Mandelstam offered a more nuanced, "protestant" dissent from this kind of verbal mysticism, insisting on the poetic word's equally authentic existence as a simple object-term in natural language.[107] But theological terms nonetheless appear throughout his essays. Thus, to speak, as "Utro Akmeizma" (The morning of acmeism) already does, of "conscious sense, Logos" as the only element of the word yet to be absorbed into the concept of "form," and to declare that "Logos demands only equal rights with other elements of the word," is to combine Potebnia's idea of the word's structure with a personification of the word that clearly derives from Christian doctrine.[108] "Slovo i kul'tura" makes this influence even clearer when it describes the word as having now become "flesh and bread" and prophesies that whoever "lifts up the word and shows it to the era, as the priest does the eucharist, will be a second Joshua."[109] In "O prirode slova" the essence of the Russian language, which Mandelstam claims has enabled Russian culture to preserve its unity through the vicissitudes of history, is defined as a certain "Hellenism" transmitted to it from Byzantium rather than from the West.[110] The "mystery" of this Hellenism consists in the phenomenon of "free incarnation," which has enabled the Russian language to become nothing less than "flesh that makes sounds and

---

105. Ibid., 235, 239.
106. Paperno, "O prirode poeticheskogo slova," 30.
107. Ibid., 33, 35.
108. Mandel'shtam, "Utro akmeizma," in *Sobranie sochinenii v trekh tomakh*, t. 2, 321.
109. Mandel'shtam, "Slovo i kul'tura," 226.
110. Mandelstam also sounds a Herderian note when he declares that the unity of Russian literature inheres in the "language of the *narod.*" By Mandelstam's era the idea is a perfectly conventional piece of Romantic inheritance, but one could probe the Herderian concept itself to see whether it itself does not contain a latent notion of selfhood as that entity which enables language.

speaks"[111]—a self if there ever was one. It is in this context that Mandelstam offers his definition of the "Hellenistic" Russian word as "active flesh, resolving itself in event,"[112] which fuses the Christian myth of incarnation (the word becomes flesh, and this leads to "event") with a Humboldtian sense of language as activity or *energeia* ("active flesh").

Moreover, as Paperno argues, it is very likely that Mandelstam found precedent for his argument in two celebrated works that identified a similar "synthesis" as characteristic of the era that witnessed the birth of Christianity. F. F. Zelinskii's *Religiia ellenizma* (The religion of Hellenism), published in 1922 but known in educated circles from university lectures long before then, argued that it was the mutual interaction and antagonism within the culture of Hellenism between principles of secularism and sacralism that gave birth to the new religion of Christianity.[113] Somewhat earlier, Trubetskoi's magisterial *Uchenie o Logose v ego istorii* (first published in 1900 but reissued in 1906 as the fourth volume of his collected works, which were completed in 1912) had argued that it was only in Christianity that Greek ideas about language had fused with the Hebrew monotheistic belief in a personal God to produce the New Testament concept of Logos.[114] It was through this prism of concepts combining Russian philology (including in significant measure Potebnia) and theology that Mandelstam saw the postrevolutionary period in Russia as a tragically "heroic" era giving birth to a new poetic word: one vulnerable and set upon by the external world (this is one connotation of its interiority) but also poised to carry out a sacrifice that might preserve the Hellenistic light of Russia's culture from the brutal darkness it now faced.

Although not a direct response to Potebnia, Vladimir Ern's collection of philosophical essays *Bor'ba za Logos* (The struggle for Logos [1911]) shows the extent to which the Platonic and Eastern Orthodox doctrines of "logos" that are latent in Potebnia's arguments, and that are treated metaphorically in Mandelstam's writings, were beginning to receive explicit attention in early twentieth-century Russia in the circle of philosophers and theologians forming the so-called "Russian religious renaissance." A minor figure in the history of Russian philosophy, Ern nonetheless reveals some of its most important interests by virtue of having been close to its intellectual center. He

111. "Slovo i kul'tura," 245.
112. Ibid., 246.
113. Paperno, "O prirode poeticheskogo slova," 34.
114. Ibid., 34.

was a personal friend of the leading religious thinkers of the late nineteenth and early twentieth centuries. He attended gymnasium in Tiflis with Florenskii, as a philosophy student at Moscow university attended lectures by S. N. Trubetskoi and L. M. Lopatin, knew Sergei Bulgakov, E. N. Trubetskoi, and Nikolai Berdiaev, and died, if one can count that, in the apartment of Viacheslav Ivanov. He also participated in the 1906 founding of the "Religious-Philosophical Society Dedicated to the Memory of Vladimir Solov'ev" in Moscow, in the subsequent creation by its members of a "Free Theological University," and in 1916 was elected to the Moscow Psychological Society (in which Gustav Shpet also took part).[115]

Ern's guiding philosophical interest from an early age was Platonism, particularly Platonic ontologism as it had developed in Russian and Italian philosophy. More specifically, his ideas crystallized in the course of polemics with writers, especially S. L. Frank, associated with the neo-Kantian-leaning journal *Logos,* published by Musaget from 1910 to 1915. His principal aim was to search for a middle way between the skepticism of neo-Kantianism and the materialist denial of metaphysics that was equally strong in certain Russian circles at the time. He sought to define that path in terms of the holistic ontologism of Eastern doctrines of "logos" and "manifestation," even while continuing to make fashionable references to the opposition between Apollo and Dionysius, quoting Viacheslav Ivanov as he did so. *Bor'ba za Logos* is a product of this search. It is less an original contribution to philosophy—Ern was not alone in his desire to find a philosophical perspective between the extremes of materialism and neo-Kantianism—than a compendium of ideas current within the Russian religious renaissance that shows how central the notions of language and selfhood (represented in the concept of "logos") were becoming to that movement.

The opening essays outline the negative boundaries of Ern's philosophical position. He first laments pragmatism's preoccupation with "only that which can be felt with the hands, smelled, seen" but notes ironically that at least this represents a change from the "scholastic flights" of neo-Kantianism or the still broader tendency it represents of immanentism.[116] He then offers a critique of Berkeley as the founder of immanentism: the flaw of "new philosophy" (that is, everything since antiquity and the Middle Ages), Ern asserts, injecting patristic vocabulary, has been to separate itself from "nature as essence" and thereby revert to a mechanistic worldview that

115. See A. P. Alekseev et al., eds., *Filosofy Rossii XIX–XX stoletii (biografii, idei, trudy)* (Moscow: Kniga i biznes, 1993), 210; A. D. Sukhov, ed., *Sto russkikh filosofov* (Moscow: Mirta, 1995), 308–10.

116. Vladimir Ern, *Bor'ba za Logos. Opyty filosofskie i kriticheskie* (Moscow: Put', 1911), 11. The essays in the volume were based on lectures delivered circa 1907–10 to the Solov'ev religious-philosophical society and to a student society devoted to the memory of S. N. Trubetskoi.

eliminates the living *physis* of antiquity together with its herd of organic cohorts: *eidos*-es, entelechies, spermatic *logoi,* as well as the no less living *natura archetypa* and *natura creata creatans* of patristic and medieval doctrine.[117] Berkeley's division of the world into *res cogitans* and *res extensa* turns it into something inert and reduces our knowledge of the world to nothing more than a subjective picture.[118] In Hume's hands this is elaborated into a full "meonic myth" (that is, negating, illusionistic), according to which the world is nothing but an illusion. This "meonism" that appears in Berkeley and blossoms in Hume finally entrenches itself in Kant's transcendentalism, which Ern regards as the culmination of (Western) rationalism.

In the central parts of the collection Ern turns to a passionate defense of Russian thought before this alien and mortifying doctrine. He takes care not to assert any simplistic identification of Orthodoxy with one and Catholicism with the other, but he locates the salvific quality of Russianness in nothing less than the strain of "logism" he finds predominant in the culture.[119] *Ratio,* the principle dominant in the West, leads to philosophically unjustified abstraction, schematism, and blind subjectivism (he throws in the mechanization of modern life for good measure). Its defining characteristic as a "meonistic" philosophy is "the negation of nature as Essence"—it denies both the ontological priority of the created world and the fact that that world exists as a manifestation of the divine self, principles often felt within this tradition to be exemplified in the "word."[120] The opposing principle, which flows out of the hellenic philosophy of the East and survives as an underground current of veneration within Russian culture, is that of the Word or *Logos* (here Ern cites such key figures in Orthodox philosophy of language as Dionysius the Areopagite, Maximus the Confessor, and Gregory of Nissa).[121] Indeed, Ern describes the low-profile persistence of this current in a manner very close to the claim this study has made about the coherence over more than a century of interest in word and self in Russia: "but there is also such a thing as an inner tradition, subterranean, subconscious, which, being unbroken within appears broken from without." It is for this reason, he remarks, that apparently disparate philosophical developments can reveal

---

117. Ibid., 27.

118. Ibid., 28.

119. This part of the collection is a critical review of the first Russian issue of the international philosophical journal *Logos* (1910), which was strongly oriented toward contemporary German philosophy. For a list of the journal's contents, see its revived Russian successor *Logos* 1 (1991): 186–87.

120. Ern, *Bor'ba za Logos,* 92, 121, 128.

121. Ibid., 76.

an inner unity on closer consideration.[122] The essence of *Logos* as a philosophical principle for Ern lies in its ontologism and transcendence: it is not a mere subjective-human fiction but a metaphysically real part of Divine nature.[123] Moreover, when a philosopher rises to "Logistic" consciousness he erases in himself the rift between thought and essence because he recognizes himself as a part of the divine Essence.[124] Rationalism sees the self as irrational and therefore perceives the world under the category of thing; "logism," on other hand, sees through to the divine image of God residing within the self and therefore perceives the world under the category of personhood.[125] Its entire view of creation is personalistic, because it views the entire cosmos in terms of a manifesting self, the primary exemplum of which is the divine Word.

That the instinct shaping Ern's treatment of such sweeping philosophical issues was to ground them in a concept of language was, as we have seen, characteristic of most of the significant movements in Russian culture in the late nineteenth and early twentieth centuries—the era that followed Potebnia. The kind of effort Ern represents to define an endemic Russian doctrine of *logos* in the context of modernist thought was to receive far more extensive treatment in the works of the philosophically minded theologians Pavel Florenskii and Sergei Bulgakov, whose contributions to the philosophy of language form the subject of the next chapter.

122. Ibid., 107.
123. Ibid., 82.
124. Ibid., 83.
125. Ibid., 357–58.

Chapter 3

Orthodox Essentialism
and Its Dialogue with Modern Thought

THE SUDDEN OUTPOURING OF WRITINGS on the nature of language in *fin-de-siècle* Russia belongs to the broad current of revived philosophical idealism that arose there as a reaction against the materialism and positivism that had predominated in intellectual circles in the mid-1800s. As we have seen, by the turn of the century this current had spread out from the academy into popular, or at least educated, culture, particularly through the Symbolist movement in Russian literature and the language-conscious elements of Futurism and Acmeism. An important rallying point of this idealist reaction was the moral demand that the self or personality—in Russian philosophical parlance, *lichnost'*—be restored to its central position in philosophy. In his study of the history of Russian psychology, David Joravsky remarks that in this period "the Russian educated public was obsessed with the problem of the self," especially with "the sense of incongruity between ourselves as natural objects and ourselves as conscious subjects."[1] This was also the era in which the "problematic of psychology" became important in Russian intellectual life, and it was this era that saw the establishment of institutions such as the Moscow Psychological Society (1889), Moscow University's Psychological Institute (1912), and the influential journal *Voprosy filosofii i psikhologii* (Questions of philosophy and psychology); it is interesting to note that, as the title of that journal suggests, psychology entered Russian intellectual life more as a philosophical issue than as a medical one, and key figures such as A. I. Vvedenskii were emphatic in their insistence that it not depart that domain.[2]

1. David Joravsky, *Russian Psychology. A Critical History* (Oxford: Basil Blackwell, 1989), 191, 166. See also Mihailovic, *Corporeal Words*, 99–111.

2. On the "problematic of psychology," see Gidini, "Slovo i real'nost'," 54; on psychological societies see Joravsky, *Russian Psychology*, 95, 159. There were precedents in the Russian intellectual context for this early twentieth-century mixing of philosophy and psychology, including an interest in ancient Greek thought. Florovskii mentions P. S. Avsenev, a professor at the Kiev Theological Academy who taught a kind of romantico-theosophical philosophy that combined Schellingian mysticism with Russian asceticism, Plato, and Plotinus; Prot. Georgii Florovskii, *Puti*

In Potebnia's era idealists in search of selfhood had defined their views by rejecting the positivism with which Russian thought had experienced such heady infatuation, but which for some now appeared a mechanistic creed that reduced life to mere physicality. In the twentieth century, however, this renascent idealism itself entered a period of crisis in which it found itself anxiously defending its positions not only against materialism but also against the radically opposed doctrine of neo-Kantianism, whose tenets seemed to deny the reality of the created world by treating it as a mere emanation of subjectivity (witness, for example, the collections *Problemy idealizma* [Problems of idealism (1903)] and *Vekhi* [Signposts (1909)], as well as the "crisis" of Symbolism in 1910). What characterizes the idealist reflex in this later period is the effort to find a position between these two extremes, in particular by turning to one or another form of essentialism or ontologism. As an antidote to neo-Kantian subjectivism the idealists of the early twentieth century emphatically asserted the reality of the world outside the epistemological subject; but they also wanted to resist the erosion of personhood through its dissipation in purely external conditions. They yearned for a concrete metaphysics rather than an abstract metaphysics of a Hegelian type, and this led them to posit an essentialist personalism as the basis of everything.[3]

In Russian philosophy this trend is especially characteristic of the so-called "Russian religious renaissance" associated with such figures as Vasilii Rozanov, Lev Lopatin, Sergei and Evgenii Trubetskoi, Nikolai Berdiaev, Semën Frank, Nikolai Losskii, and Vladimir Ern, which self-consciously

---

russkogo bogosloviia (1937; Vilnius: Vil'niusskoe pravoslavnoe eparkhial'noe upravlenie, 1991), 241. Florovskii also notes the significance to Russian thought of the journal *Voprosy filosofii i psikhologii,* which recorded the philosophical searchings of the most important idealists of the era and registered such things as early Russian responses to Nietzsche, and of the closely related Moscow Psychological Society which published, e.g., Solov'ev's "*Ob upadke srednevekovogo mirosozertsaniia*"; Florovskii, *Puti russkogo bogoslavia,* 331, 453, 492. He further remarks that the mixing of such disparate philosophical currents at the turn of the century was characteristic of Russian intellectual life in general, with its "many-tiered" arena in which the ideas of several centuries typically co-exist; (Florovskii, 500). On the role of the Moscow Psychological Society as the "philosophical center of revolt against positivism in the Russian Silver Age," which moreover drew on Kant's defense of the autonomy of the self to develop a personalist doctrine of the self as ontologically rooted in transcendent being, see Randall Allen Poole, "The Moscow Psychological Society and the Neo-Idealist Development of Russian Liberalism" (Ph.D. diss., University of Notre Dame, 1995), 2, 38, 196–97, 201. Evtuhov also points out that the Moscow Philosophical Society, with its journal *Voprosy filosofii i psikhologii,* was the home of neo-idealism in early twentieth-century Russia (though there were parallel developments in the universities); Catherine Evtuhov, *The Cross and the Sickle: Sergei Bulgakov and the Fate of Russian Religious Philosophy, 1890–1920* (Ithaca: Cornell University Press, 1997), 57.

3. S. M. Polovinkin, "P. A. Florenskii: Logos protiv khaosa," in *Filosofiia* 2 (1989): 15.

sought to revive Eastern Orthodox traditions of thought.[4] But the Russian religious renaissance also gave rise to one of the most concentrated episodes of thought concerning language in modern Russia—which should come as no surprise if, as I have argued, much of the search for "selfhood" in modern Russia is bound up with the philosophy of language. While the writings of this movement sometimes appeal to Western readers because their abundant and often exotic spiritual motifs seem familiar from such classics of Russian literature as Gogol and Dostoevsky, from a philosophical perspective they can appear awkwardly conservative, the outpourings of thinkers who sought escape from the pressures of life in the twentieth century by turning to a romantically fabricated spiritual past—or, at their worst, a retreat from the modern world into nationalist sentiment. Whether such a charge is accurate in reference to the movement as a whole is too large a topic to deal with here. But it is manifestly inaccurate when applied to the movement's writings on language. In fact, one could argue that the way certain figures in the Russian religious renaissance engage modern philosophy's "linguistic turn" represents the movement's distinctly modernist face. Most significant in this regard are the writings of Pavel Florenskii (1882–1937) and Sergei Bulgakov (1871–1944), which arise out of an interchange between self-consciously retrospective but also astutely contemporary modes of thought about language, the self, art, culture, and even the human body.

Florenskii's intellectual background and affinities reflect the cultural complexities of the Russian religious renaissance as a whole. Like Bulgakov, whose treatise on language is also discussed in this chapter, he sought his identity in the modern era by entering the priesthood. In 1914 he conspicuously turned down the offer of a position in the secular world of Moscow University, where he had studied in the department of physics and mathematics, to attend the Moscow Theological Academy (*Moskovskaia dukhovnaia akademiia*). When he was later hired to teach there he primarily taught the "history of worldviews" but also developed an interest in the so-called "ontological school in Russian theology" (or as it has also been called, the "school of believing reason," associated with such faculty at the academy as F. A. Golubinskii, V. D. Kudriavtsev-Platonov, A. I. Vvedenskii, and

---

4. See Evtuhov's discussion of this philosophical moment in "The Silver Age as History," introduction to her *Cross and the Sickle,* 1–17. Evtuhov captures the tendency of these thinkers to polarize the philosophical scene when she comments on Sergei Bulgakov's intellectual development later in the same study: "Bulgakov now believed that Soloviev had found a resolution to the 'two nightmares' of contemporary philosophy—'mechanistic materialism' and 'idealistic subjectivism' " (138).

archimandrite Serapion Makshin).[5] Florenskii's philosophical thought deals with paradigms that clearly descend—despite pronounced divergence on some points—from Vladimir Solov'ev's religiously oriented "philosophy of all-unity," and virtually all his philosophical writings have an explicit theological cast to them, from the voluminous *Stolp i utverzhdenie istiny* (1914; *The Pillar and Ground of the Truth*), written on the eve of his entry into the Moscow Theological Academy and steeped in Orthodox mysticism, to his essays on aesthetics, which typically concentrate on religious art such as icons.[6]

Yet both Florenskii's cultural background and his thought, including his writings on language, are more complex than his willfully cultivated image of himself as an Orthodox mystic might suggest.[7] His professional interests ranged well beyond theology—he also made noteworthy contributions to philosophy, aesthetics, mathematics, physics, and what would now be called materials sciences—and his writings are correspondingly protean. Of himself and his worldview circa 1925–26, he wrote (in the third person) an entry in an encyclopedic dictionary: "He has developed a contrapuntally structured worldview out of several propositional themes closely related to each other, but his worldview does not yield to concise systematic exposition."[8] His turn toward theology was preceded by four years of study in mathematics at Moscow University, where the prevailing interests were as much philosophical (of Old Testament–mystical as well as neo-Pythagorean leanings) as technically mathematical, and whose members saw themselves as forming the "Moscow Philosophical-Mathematical School."[9] In this setting Florenskii wrote a thesis on "Discontinuity (*Preryvnost'*) as an Element of a Worldview" (the term "discontinuity" reflecting the department's interest in philosophical extensions of Georg Kantor's set theory) under the direction of N. V. Bugaev, with whose son Boris—the poet Andrei Bely—he attempted to join a monastery in March 1904 (their request to Bishop

5. Polovinkin, "P. A. Florenskii," 17–18; Episkop Anatolii [Kuznetsov], "Mirosozertsanie sviashchennika Pavla Florenskogo i nasha sovremennost'," in Michael Hagemeister and Nina Kauchtschischwili, eds., *P. A. Florenskii i kul'tura ego vremeni/P.A. Florenskij e la cultura della sua epoca* (Marburg: Blaue Hoerner Verlag, 1995), 476.

6. On Florenskii's philosophical influences, see S. S. Khoruzhii, "O filosofii sviashchenika Pavla Florenskogo," in P. A. Florenskii, *Stolp i utverzhdenie istiny (I)*, prilozhenie k zhurnalu *Voprosy filosofii* (Moscow: Pravda, 1990), vi.

7. Regarding the cultivated self-image, see, for example, the photograph in Michael Hagemeister, "P. A. Florenskii: Zhiznennyi put' v fotografiiakh i dokumentakh," in Hagemeister and Kauchtschischwili, *P. A. Florenskii i kul'tura ego vremeni*, 548, in which Florenskii poses in front of an icon of the Redeemer, holding a cross, eyes meditatively closed.

8. Polovinkin, "P. A. Florenskii," 6.

9. See P. A. Nekrasov, *Moskovskaia filosofsko-matematicheskaia shkola i ee osnovateli* (Moscow: n.p., 1904).

Antonii Florensov was declined).[10] He was also a close acquaintance of Viacheslav Ivanov, whose theoretical writings on the nature of symbols influenced his views on language (both Bely and Ivanov continued to visit Florenskii after university, circa 1910, when he was married and serving as a priest in Sergiev Posad), and the Futurist poet and visionary Velimir Khlebnikov nominated him as one of his "chairmen of the earth."[11] His first articles appeared not in religious outlets but in Merezhkovskii's review *Novyi put'* (New path) and in the Symbolist journal *Vesy* (Scales).[12] He also knew Valerii Briusov and Maksimilian Voloshin, and was acquainted with the avant-garde artists Popova, Tatlin, Grishchenko, and Vesnin.[13] Even *Stolp i utverzhdenie,* which Florenskii defined as an exercise in theodicy and submitted as his master's thesis to the Moscow Theological Academy, abounds in references to secular philosophers such as Nietzsche, Renan, Cohen, Bolzano, Georg Kantor, and Russell (to cite only a few of the contemporaries in the work's staggeringly erudite bibliography) and produces the distinct impression, as Berdiaev put it, of having been written not by a monk but by a contemporary of Merezhkovskii, Ivanov, Blok, and Bely.[14] Moreover, as Bonetskaia suggests, the main impulse discernible in the religious-philosophical inquiries of *Stolp i utverzhdenie* is not so much gnostic certitude or implicit faith in salvation or prayer as it is the work's "cognitive pathos," Florenskii's restless probings of the boundaries and possibilities of thought.[15] If in the end Rosenthal's observation remains apt that what Florenskii did in his intellectual career was to find precedents for Symbolist "God-seeking" in the doctrines of the early Church, thus drawing Russian religious quests of the early twentieth century back into the Church, he

10. Vladimir M. Piskunov, "Pavel Florenskii i Andrei Belyi. (K postanovke problemy)," in Hagemeister and Kauchtschischwili, *P. A. Florenskii i kul'tura ego vremeni,* 89.

11. Maria S. Trubacheva and Sergei Z. Trubachev, "Sergiev Posad v zhizni P. A. Florenskogo," in Hagemeister and Kauchtschischwili, *P. A. Florenskii i kul'tura ego vremeni,* 25.

12. Bernice Glatzer Rosenthal, "Pavel Florensky as a 'God-Seeker,' " in Hagemeister and Kauchtschischwili, *P. A. Florenskii i kul'tura ego vremeni,* 67.

13. See A. G. Naslednikov, "Ot sostavitelia," preface to Pavel Florenskii, *Ikonostas. Izbrannye trudy po iskusstvu* (St. Petersburg: Mirfil/Russkaia kniga, 1993), viii. In addition to such Modernist literary acquaintances Florenskii was close in this period to more religiously oriented philosophers such as Rozanov, Sergei Bulgakov, Vladimir Ern, M. N. Novoselov, V. A. Kozhevnikov (Igumen Andronik [A. S. Trubachev], "P. A. Florenskii. Zhiznennyi put'," in Hagemeister and Kauchtschischwili, *P. A. Florenskii i kul'tura ego vremeni,* 3, 6), and the young A. F. Losev (Trubacheva and Trubachev, "Sergiev Posad," 25).

14. Quoted in Milivoe Iovanovich, "'Stolp i utverzhdenie istiny' P. Florenskogo: Siuzhet, zhanr, istoki," in Hagemeister and Kauchtschischwili, *P. A. Florenskii i kul'tura ego vremeni,* 444; see also Igumen Andronik [Trubachev], "P. A. Florenskii. Zhiznennyi put'," in Hagemeister and Kauchtschischwili, *P. A. Florenskii i kul'tura ego vremeni,* 10.

15. Natalia K. Bonetskaia, "Ob odnom skachke v russkom filosofskom iazykoznanii," in Hagemeister and Kauchtschischwili, *P. A. Florenskii i kul'tura ego vremeni,* 258.

nonetheless is an intriguing liminal figure who preserved significant elements of extra-ecclesiastical Silver Age culture throughout his theological writings, even as he later tragically had to accommodate his priestly identity with the Soviet regime.[16] Tensions such as these are particularly apparent in his views on language.

The idea of language was central to all these endeavors, but Florenskii's particular conception of language cannot be understood apart from his metaphysics, in which he undertakes a fervent effort to establish a radical, ontologically unassailable concept of truth—of which language will then be made an exemplar.

Florenskii's metaphysics begins in a critique of rationalism, which he mounts in the general spirit of Vladimir Solov'ev's *Kritika otvlechennykh nachal* (A criticism of abstract principles) of 1877–80, while attacking some of Solov'ev's views and pointedly avoiding terminology that might suggest homage to him (in particular Florenskii rejected the key Solov'evian term "all-unity" because he felt that Solov'ev's writings constituted yet another speculative philosophical project undertaken in a typically neo-European, specifically German, spirit).[17] Much of this critique is contained in *Stolp i utverzhdenie,* where Florenskii casts his argument in the guise of a logical critique of the post-Enlightenment principle of empirical self-evidence but in fact offers a covert defense of *a priori* metaphysical assumptions, even an argument against the very principle of presuppositionless reasoning. The problem with dominant schools of philosophy in the early twentieth century, he argues, is that their version of truth relies on naked givenness (his main targets are empiricism, "transcendental rationalism," by which he perhaps means phenomenology, and mysticism of the unreasoning variety). They conceive of truth as something external to the perceiver, mechanistic, blind, and therefore—and this is the principal concern—contingent. What reason fails to perceive in this version of truth, however, is any form of *inner necessity* (here Florenskii uses the Russian *"razum"* for reason rather than *"rassudok,"* or mere ratiocination). When asked what the reason of such self-identical immediate givenness consists of, these schools are able to answer only this: "in the fact that givenness is itself: every A is A." Expressed in the quasi-mathematical formula "A = A," this assertion epitomizes for

16. Rosenthal, "Pavel Florensky as a 'God-Seeker,' " 70.
17. Khoruzhii, "O filosofii sviashchenika Pavla Florenskogo," xiii.

Florenskii the "law of identity" at the heart of Western rationalism and the modern forms of thought deriving from it.[18]

But the formula "A = A" is a tautology, Florenskii rebuts. It is a lifeless equation that "mechanically closes our mouths" and condemns us to live in the realm of the finite and therefore of randomness (there are not-so-distant echoes here of Dostoevsky's Underground Man, with his rebellion against the formula "$2 \times 2 = 4$"). The law of identity cannot answer the question "Why?": out of the "there is" of givenness one can in no way derive an "it must be so." This is where the work reveals itself as a theodicy, a search for a necessary and just order of things. Since every "A" excludes all other elements, he continues, it is also in turn excluded by them. If for "A" all other elements in the world are only "not-A," then "A" in its opposition to "not-A" can itself be only "not-not-A," that is, it cannot itself represent anything positive (a view distinctly at odds, one notes, with Saussurian structuralism, according to which elements of language are determined precisely and exclusively by their opposition to other elements). Hence if one accepts the law of identity, then all being, even as it seeks to affirm itself, in fact only destroys itself, turning itself into a mere sum of elements, each of which is nothing but the focus of a series of negations (presumably because no element can ever escape definition as "not-something"—a slightly odd line of argument given the apophatic theology traditional for Eastern Orthodoxy). "All being," he concludes, "is thus turned into nothing but negation, one great 'Not.' " "The law of identity is the spirit of death, emptiness, and nothingness."[19]

What Florenskii has done in these ruminations, of course, is to shift the ground of discourse from logic to metaphysics, a tactic that renders the argument specious without making the thought any less interesting.[20] Florenskii labels this pernicious form of rationalism "*epoche*" (from the Greek for stoppage, pause, suppression—it is the term Husserl uses for the logical

18. The quasi-mathematical nature of the formula is perhaps not by chance: in the encyclopedia entry of 1925–26 Florenskii asserts that his "worldview formed itself for the most part on the basis of mathematics and is suffused with its principles even though it does not use the language of mathematics" (quoted in Polovinkin, "P. A. Florenskii," 8).

19. Florenskii, *Stolp i utverzhdenie (I)*, 25–27; for similar arguments regarding the role perspectivalism plays in Western post-renaissance painting, in contrast to the aesthetics of the icon, see his *Ikonostas*, 47, 97.

20. One is reminded of the assessment offered in 1908 by N. N. Luzin of some of Florenskii's "contributions" to mathematics, that they amount to "hints, beautiful similes—something intoxicating and promising, irritating, alluring, and futile" (quoted in Sergei S. Demidov, "O matematike v tvorchestve P. A. Florenskogo," in Hagemeister and Kauchtschischwili, *P. A. Florenskii i kul'tura ego vremeni*, 178). Regarding this trait in Sergei Bulgakov, Evtuhov comments: "There is a clear break in Bulgakov's argumentation: in confronting the question of faith, his work ceases to be philosophy and shifts from argument by logical sequence to metaphor" (*Cross and the Sickle*, 170). She then observes that "religious philosophy is a qualitatively different enterprise from philosophy proper" (171 n. 25).

operation of "bracketing" or suspension of reference to the given world) and, in a manner familiar among eastward-leaning Russian writers since Solov'ev, treats it as a state of fallenness. "*Epoche*" is a position of skepticism, of "absolute doubt."[21] It postpones affirmative statement until propositions have been proven absolutely, but the contingent nature of all earthly knowledge condemns it to an untranscendable condition of "abstention from all judgment." It leads in effect to the assertion of nothing.[22]

To escape the impasse represented by *epoche*, Florenskii proposes in *Stolp i utverzhdenie* to travel by "touch and feel," guided not by skepticism but by "instinct," toward the concept of truth (the *istina* of Florenskii's title, transcendent truth, which term I have in mind throughout this discussion, rather than *pravda* or mere factual truth).[23] If *epoche* yields only knowledge of negation and fragmentation, then its restorative antithesis must lie in the proposition of essence and wholeness. Truth is therefore "essential [or genuinely existing] all-unity," he asserts—"as the philosopher defines it."[24] The philosopher and argument in question turn out to be, as a footnote indicates, Solov'ev and the ruminations offered in his *Kritika otvlechennykh nachal* on the logical necessity of truth being both "essence, that which genuinely exists" and a principle of oneness or unity (this was the core of Solov'ev's philosophy, deeply indebted to Pythagoras, Plato, and the Neoplatonists, and one of the key tenets of Russian idealism in Florenskii's youth). But what is significant about Florenskii's argument in the present context is less its validity or lack thereof than the distinct linguistic turn his reasoning takes, consonant with the broader turn toward questions of language that is a hallmark of twentieth-century European philosophy in general, from Russell and Wittgenstein through Heidegger and even to Derrida. For Florenskii augments Solov'ev's argument with a lengthy excursus into the etymology of the Russian "*istina*," and of the parallel words for "truth" in Greek, Hebrew, and Latin.[25]

---

21. Florenskii, *Stolp i utverzhdenie (I)*, 35.
22. Ibid., 35.
23. Ibid., 41.
24. Ibid., 15.
25. In pursuit of his own definition of 'Being' Heidegger also explores the grammar and etymology of the word 'Being' (*Sein*) itself. He glimpses a shadow of Being's portrait in the ancient Greek grammatical terms *ptosis* ("case," but etymologically a "fall"—cf. Russian *padezh*) and *enklisis* (declension, i.e., a "leaning"). Out of these meanings he conjures an archetypal scene of Being as presence. Since both terms refer to some kind of falling, tipping, or inclining, they imply the existence of something that otherwise stands upright. "Whatever thus stands is constant in itself and thereby freely and on its own runs up against the necessity of its limit, *peras*," which, he adds, is not imposed from without. "Instead, the self-restraining hold that comes from a limit, the having-of-itself wherein the constant holds itself, is the Being of beings; it is what first makes a being a being as opposed to a non-being. . . . Whatever places itself into and thereby enacts its limit [*ergrenzend*], and thus stands, has *morphe*"; Heidegger, *Introduction to Metaphysics*, 62–63.

The Russian term, Florenskii claims, derives from "*estina*," the nominal form of the verb "*est*" (to be), and thus denotes "that which is." It therefore can be taken to denote "that which genuinely exists, as opposed to that which is illusory, and implies 'absolute self-identity.' "[26] The Greek "*aleteia*" similarly refers to "that which endures, is not forgotten" (*a-leteia*: that which escapes oblivion, Lethe; the Latin and Hebrew Florenskii finds less philosophical, involving socially determined notions of fear/awe and promise/surety).[27] Whatever the ultimate accuracy of these etymological forays, Florenskii's unexpected turn toward linguistic meaning is characteristic in its own right and reveals a rich complex of attitudes.[28] Florenskii is motivated by the intuition that in language we find not aporia but authoritative meanings. If entities like "truth" and "being" are affirmed in some significant way in language, then they must be genuine. Moreover there is an implicit appeal to self-evidence in Florenskii's etymological arguments: he recurs to the inner meaning of words in order to remind us of what meaning we intend, and therefore at some level already know, when we use a word like "*istina*"—and in using a key word like *istina* one is not just deploying a sign but *saying* something, voicing a proposition (see Florenskii's remark in "Dialektika" [The dialectic] that "words are unfolded thoughts").[29] For Florenskii, language in its development takes no wrong turns. In effect he appropriates the nineteenth century's interest in exploring etymology but uses it to find not the traits of national psychology but a record of carefully sifted metaphysical propositions whose endurance marks them as at least partially true. And in a more general way this impulse to look toward language in order to learn about essence explains why the philosophy of language occupies such an important place in Florenskii's writings, and why those writings so often reward comparison with other twentieth-century philosophers like Heidegger and Wittgenstein.[30]

Given this ontological conception of truth as that which genuinely exists, only judgments pertaining to essence can be held to have any validity at all, Florenskii argues. Statements pertaining to non-essence ("*ne-sushchee*," or in the Greek term current among Russian modernists, "*to me on*") are not even judgments as such in the philosophical sense; they are mere

26. Florenskii, *Stolp i utverzhdenie (I)*, 15–16.

27. Ibid., 15–22.

28. On the validity or lack thereof in Florenskii's etymologies, see Viacheslav Vsevolodovich Ivanov, "O lingvisticheskikh issledovaniiakh P. A. Florenskogo," *Voprosy iazykoznaniia* 6 (1988): 69–87, and his "P. A. Florenskii i problema iazyka," in *P. A. Florenskii i kul'tura ego vremeni*, 207–51.

29. P. A. Florenskii, "Dialektika," in his *U vodorazdelov mysli*, 143.

30. On Heidegger, see S. S. Averintsev et al., notes to P. A. Florenskii, "Stroenie slova," in *U vodorazdelov mysli*, 370, n. 3; on Wittgenstein see Ivanov, "P. A. Florenskii i problema iazyka," in Hagemeister and Kauchtschischwili, *P. A. Florenskii i kul'tura ego vremeni*, 207.

"*doxa*" or opinion (a view perhaps consonant with the Orthodox tendency to define evil not as any genuinely existing thing but as the absence of good).[31] In fact Florenskii speaks of truth less as a proposition than as an *entity* or even a *being*, his remarks amounting to a kind of dream of truth beyond human philosophizing. Heidegger was to offer a strikingly similar concept, some twenty years later, of truth as the uncovering of essence rather than a correspondence between propositions.[32] Unlike "opinion," this kind of truth requires no justification other than itself.[33] It is "self-proving" and entirely autonomous, not dependent upon us for its inherence—and therefore, he reasons, a *subject* in its own right: "a Subject *qui per se ipsum concipitur et demonstratur,* which obtains itself and proves itself through itself."[34] This form of givenness derives from genuine reason, as opposed to the inert law of identity "A = A." As a "self-proven Subject" it is "*causa sui* with respect to essence as well as to existence, that is, it not only *per se concipitur et demonstratur* but also *per se est*" (this, he notes, was well understood by the Scholastics).[35] Needless to say, this view of the subject as a bastion of ontological certitude is radically at odds with much twentieth-century thought, especially in the West. But in Florenskii's scheme of things selfhood thus turns out to be inherent in essence, and he uses an awareness of this principle as a litmus test for worldviews. Rationalism, he claims, treats everything in the world as *res,* as 'thing,' and therefore can only attribute an external unity to objects (somewhat later in *Stolp i utverzhdenie* he similarly suggests that contemporary "scientific psychology," progeny of Enlightenment empiricism, knows no synthetic self, only a bundle of psychological states); the opposing view (which at this point he defines as "Orthodox" and categorizes as a form of "love") sees a principle of personhood underlying the world's phenomena, together with internal unity and self-positing (here he cites Fichte's self-positing "I").[36]

Taking his point of departure again from Solov'ev, and from an impulse toward mathematical gnosis that runs from Pythagoras to the Neoplatonists,

---

31. Florenskii, *Stolp i utverzhdenie (I),* 29.

32. Martin Heidegger, *Being and Time,* trans. Joan Stambaugh (Albany: State University of New York Press, 1996), 201–2. Robert Bird reports the following improbable but interesting claim of a *reverse* influence, that is, of Florenskii's ideas on Heidegger: "In a letter to Ol'ga Short (Deschartes) of 28 February 1933 Evsei Shor claimed that he had told Heidegger of Florenskii's philosophical analysis of truth, that Heidegger had expressed great interest, and that he had proceeded to use Florenskii's arguments in his own lectures without attribution (Rome Archive of Viacheslav Ivanov, reported to the author by A. B. Shishkin)"; Robert Bird, "Martin Heidegger and Russian Symbolist Philosophy," *Studies in East European Thought* 51 (1999): 103 n. 4.

33. Florenskii, *Stolp i utverzhdenie (I),* 30.

34. Ibid., 44.

35. Ibid., 45.

36. Ibid., 173, 78.

Florenskii next argues that this truth-as-subject must also be "actual infinity," the infinite thought of as something "co-herent" ("*tselo-kupnoe*," that is, "gathered into a whole"—the hyphenation is Florenskii's): it is "the infinite conceived as co-herent Unity, as a single Subject complete within itself."[37] The motivations behind this statement become clear as Florenskii's ruminations on the numerical bases of ontology unfold into a quasi-mathematical demonstration of the logical necessity of the Trinity as it is understood in Eastern Orthodoxy, a line of argument which replicates key points in a philosophical legacy that encompasses Plato, Alexandrian Neoplatonism, and the doctrinal debates over the nature of the Trinity in the early Church (it is by no means insignificant in this connection that Florenskii was after all a priest at the St. Sergius–*Holy Trinity* monastery, seat of the Russian Orthodox Church; he explicitly reviews the doctrinal part of this legacy).

"How is it possible," Florenskii asks, reproducing some of the argument from Plato's *Parmenides,* "that temporal-spatial plurality does not destroy identity?" It avoids doing so only when the plurality of elements is absolutely synthesized within (final) truth, so that what one initially encounters as "other" turns out *sub specie aeternitatis* to be "not other."[38] In other words, the mathematical phenomenon of infinity guarantees that in the overall scheme of things, otherness, "not-A," will—at some point, time, place—be recuperated as a part of us, of "A." "A is A because eternally abiding as not-A it finds in this not-A its affirmation as A."[39] This "higher form of the law of identity," with its echoes of the Orthodox belief in the ultimate redemption of the fallen world, is the rapturous ethico-logical vision Florenskii claims to have drawn from a work entitled *Opyt sistemy khristianskoi filosofii* (An attempt at a systematic Christian philosophy) by Archimandrite Serapion Mashkin, one of his teachers at the Moscow Theological Academy.[40] With his attraction to mysticism, which is particularly evident in *Stolp i utverzhdenie,* Florenskii describes the mind's encounter with contradiction as a form of the "organized amazement" that is the essence of philosophy, a "forever-amazed view of life": at the moment of concentration

37. Ibid., 43. Again, this metaphorical use of mathematical concepts is one of the hallmarks of Florenskii's early intellectual career. In an autobiography written in 1927 Florenskii speaks of his early conviction that all possible laws of being are already contained in mathematics (Igumen Andronik [Trubachev], "P. A. Florenskii. Zhiznennyi put'," in Hagemeister and Kauchtschischwili, *P. A. Florenskii i kul'tura ego vremeni,* 3).

38. Florenskii, *Stolp i utverzhdenie (I),* 46.

39. Ibid., 47. Florenskii also compares—not entirely lucidly—the "supra-rational synthesis" of truth-*istina,* which lies beyond rational thought and transcends logical contradictions with irrational numbers in mathematics; *Stolp i utverzhdenie (II),* prilozhenie k zhurnalu *Voprosy filosofii* (Moscow: Pravda, 1990), 506.

40. *Stolp i utverzhdenie (II),* 619–21.

the philosopher "exits his mind, that is, steps out of his usual condition . . . experiences ec-stasy."[41] In philosophy, thought asks over and over, "What is this [that amazes me]?"; it receives an answer in the form of a name, then asks again, and so forth; thus "develops a 'song of Songs' between thought and mystery."[42] That a doctrine of selfhood stands behind these remarks becomes clear when Florenskii translates this recuperation of otherness within infinity into explicitly personalizing terms. The self-proving and self-establishing aspects of truth, he claims, are in fact the relation of an "I" toward a "He" via a "Thou." Through this "Thou" the subjective "I" becomes an objective "He" and finds in the latter an affirmation and object-ness that establish it in the world. "He" is not an estranged other, not a "not-A," but an "I" made manifest to me (Florenskii introduces an ethical dimension into this discussion in the seventh "letter" of *Stolp i utverzhdenie,* where he identifies as the root of all evil the refusal to exit a state of self-identity, of "I = I," of self-affirmation without relations to another; in differing ways one is reminded here of Martin Buber and Mikhail Bakhtin).[43] "Truth contemplates itself through an Other in a Third: Father, Son, Spirit. Therefore," Florenskii concludes, "truth is unified essence in three hypostases."[44]

Florenskii declares this concept of truth, which he labels with the Greek term *homoousious* ("of one substance") and embodies in the formula "a Trinity of one essence and indivisible, a tri-hypostatic unity eternally co-existing," to be the only logical scheme capable of resolving the impasse of "*epoche*" typical of Western rationalism.[45] It is also, of course, precisely the doctrine of the Trinity arrived at in the early Church debates and affirmed at the General Council of Nicea in 325 in order to assert the consubstantiality of the Father and the Son, in particular so as to exclude the doctrine of Arianism, which held that Christ had been *created* by the Father (albeit before all other creatures and therefore enjoying elevated status).[46] Florenskii characterizes it as a "spiritual" philosophy capable of establishing truth as such. He identifies it with Orthodox and even more specifically Russian thought, as opposed to the rationalistic and therefore skeptical philosophy of the post-Renaissance West, which he declares to be the philosophy only of fallen flesh and labels with the Greek term *homoiousios*—"of *like* (rather than one) substance," the term used by early Christian theologians who

41. *Stolp i utverzhdenie (I),* 133, 135.
42. Ibid., 144.
43. Ibid., 177.
44. Ibid., 48–49.
45. Ibid., 51.
46. F. L. Cross and E. A. Livingstone, eds., *The Oxford Dictionary of the Christian Church* (Oxford: Oxford University Press, 1997), s.v. "Arianism."

promoted an ontologically looser definition of the Trinity.[47] In a series of
remarks appended to the main text of *Stolp i utverzhdenie* he further argues
that evidence for the Trinity abounds in the created world, revealing to us
that "threeness is the most widespread characteristic of being": in grammar
there are three persons; the self consists of physical, mental, and spiritual dimensions; logic operates with thesis, antithesis, and synthesis; and so
forth.[48] In fact Florenskii calls the denial of the Trinity a state of fallenness
(in this case, specifically from truth as "essence") and defines evil itself as
consisting in a denial of the principle of *homoousious*—"and only in this."[49]
Stolp i utverzhdenie really counts as a "theodicy," as Florenskii calls it, only
if one understands that he defines evil ultimately in this intellectual or doctrinal rather than ethical way.

Clearly what Florenskii offers in these central philosophical passages of
Stolp i utverzhdenie is not so much a logical definition of "truth" as an entire cosmology in which truth (the highest entity one can ultimately know)
and essence (the most authentic form of being) have been revealed as the
person of the Trinity. He has constructed his "inquiry" into logic in order
to arrive at the "conclusion" that not only does the Trinity as Godhead inhere in the world but that the ontological principle of *homoousious* ultimately underlies and defines relations among phenomena in empirical
reality (to give just one example, in the realm of psychology the principle of
homoousious assures us that the self transcends its apparent status as a mere
"bundle of psychological states" and exists in a state of wholeness). To put
it a little more brusquely, what Florenskii gets out of these ruminations is a
worldview in which personhood turns out to be the appropriate category in
which to treat life's phenomena because it is an emanation of the originating principle of all that exists (language will turn out to be a key example).
It is the desire to construe matters this way that has dictated the course of
Florenskii's "reasoning" on these issues, including his firm rejection of materialism, positivism, Machism, neo-Kantianism, and so forth. One is perhaps reminded of the account Florenskii himself offers in "Ikonostas" of the
way in which entire dreams with complex plots can paradoxically *culminate*
in a replay of the very stimulus that actually prompted them in the first
place (say, a door slamming, which becomes a shot providing the climax to
an involved oneiric plot).[50] Florenskii's claims are unquestionably dogmatic
and apodictic rather than analytical; but they may also be characterized as

47. Florenskii, *Stolp i utverzhdenie (I)*, 79. Florenskii (54) says that this view cannot guarantee
the numerical unity central to the true doctrine of the Trinity. On the theological issues, see *Oxford Dictionary of the Christian Church*, s.v. "Arianism."
48. Florenskii, *Stolp i utverzhdenie (II)*, 596–97.
49. Florenskii, *Stolp i utverzhdenie (I)*, 213.
50. Florenskii, "Ikonostas," in his *Ikonostas*, 14–15.

novelizing, as seeking not to deduce but to elaborate for us a potential vision of the world that we are implicitly urged to accept on aesthetic or moral or spiritual, rather than logical, grounds.[51] In this Florenskii is very Russian, and very closely allied with his novelistic predecessors in the nineteenth century. His method is justifiable or at least consistent when one recalls that he begins *Stolp i utverzhdenie* by distinguishing between science, which uses reason to deal with particulars, and philosophy, which seeks to address underlying principles in a state of perpetual amazement; and that for him logic has no authority superseding the doctrines of the Eastern Orthodox Church.

The concept of language plays a vital role within this worldview, and receives particularly extensive treatment in the works Florenskii gathered in *Mysl' i iazyk* (Thought and language—the title a patent homage to Potebnia), a collection he intended as part of a larger volume, ultimately unpublished, to be called *U vodorazdelov mysli* (At the watersheds of thought).[52] Florenskii's interest in language is closely involved with his gnostic yearnings, and the impulse to turn to language for evidence of the nature of being manifests itself everywhere in his works. Hence, as suggested above, his frequent recourse to etymologies in order to retrieve authentic concepts and his related habit of dissecting verbs, reminiscent of both Bakhtin and Heidegger. Hence also his tendency to seek truth-values in sentences. Truth becomes mine, is absorbed by me, through an act of judgment, Florenskii observes early in *Stolp i utverzhdenie,* and he later enlarges on this claim by remarking that knowledge always takes the form of a judgment, which itself exists in the form of the synthesis of some subject S and predicate P— that is, in the form of a sentence.[53] As I have commented above, in this "linguistic turn" Florenskii resembles some other well-known positions in twentieth-century philosophy of language, such as Austin's "ordinary language philosophy"—save that for Florenskii language in certain ways provides direct evidence of being, rather than merely the accumulated wisdom of humankind (much as he argues in *"Ikonostas"* that icons are direct

---

51. For a similar comment regarding the works of Aleksei Losev, see Vladimir Marchenkov, "Aleksei Losev and His Theory of Myth," introduction to Aleksei Fyodorovich Losev, *The Dialectics of Myth,* trans. Vladimir Marchenkov (London: Routledge, 2003), 33.

52. N. K. Bonetskaia notes that in Russian philosophy at the beginning of the twentieth century the "problem of the word" was considered the most fundamental question for any worldview; "O filologicheskoi shkole P. A. Florenskogo. *Filosofiia imeni* A. F. Loseva i *Filosofiia imeni* S. N. Bulgakova," *Studia Slavia Academiae Scientarium Hungaricae* 37 (1991–92): 123.

53. Florenskii, *Stolp i utverzhdenie (I),* 24, 146.

manifestations of their prototypes and not merely images that remind us of them). Florenskii's interest in sentence structure also recalls the view of both Russell and Wittgenstein that in its basic structural unit, the sentence, language manifests the underlying laws of logic (indeed Florenskii cites Russell and Whitehead in the bibliography of *Stolp i utverzhdenie*). In still more striking manner the claims Florenskii makes in "Nauka kak sim-volicheskoe opisanie" (Science as symbolic description) that scientific the-ories are just languages constructed in a certain way, and not repositories of absolute truths, recalls Wittgenstein's meditations on "language games" (though this is a much-abused term) and the "bewitchment of human thought with language"—or perhaps, as Ivanov further suggests, Niels Bohr's notion that the mathematical language of physics represents the per-fection of natural language.[54]

At their furthest implicative reach Florenskii's ideas might even be con-strued as anticipating certain post-structuralist beliefs (Soviet structuralists having already embraced him as a precursor). It is important to distinguish, however, between the idea that truth is entirely contingent, unknowable, or artificially constructed, together with its attendant emphasis on indetermi-nacy, uncertainty, and incompleteness as constituents of human experience, and Florenskii's view, which is more limited. He does not argue that no truth exists, only that it cannot be embedded in the fallible form of scien-tific theory—because to declare scientific theory to be "truth" would be to usurp the claims of what he calls "mystery," a realm of higher knowledge that can only be intimated in philosophy. The awareness of indeterminacy is linked with the "pathos of cognition" in Florenskii, in ways that run quite deep.[55] Thus, in the first "letter" of *Stolp i utverzhdenie* he defines the work as a "gnostic search for . . . the foundation of Truth" and even argues that the passage in Matthew 11:27, in which Jesus states that "no one knows the Son except the Father, and no one knows the Father except the Son and any one to whom the Son chooses to reveal him" (RSV), has a "predominantly *cognitive* meaning—I would dare to say a *theoretico-cognitive,* gnoseological one . . . the subject of the entire eleventh chapter of Matthew is the issue of cognition."[56] Yet the complex probings of knowledge in his works are car-ried out in a strikingly consistent mode of apocalypticism (or perhaps one

54. Viacheslav Vsevolodovich Ivanov, "P.A. Florenskii i problema iazyka," 227. In "Dialektika," the essay that follows "Nauka kak simvolicheskoe opisanie" in *Mysl' i iazyk,* Florenskii contrasts science to philosophy. Science, despite its illusion of abiding premises, classifications, terminol-ogy, and so on, only deals with symbols of reality; philosophy, on the other hand, is capable of truly "explaining" reality because it is a continual experiment with it; *U vodorazdelov mysli,* 131–32.

55. Bonetskaia, "Ob odnom skachke," in Hagemeister and Kauchtschischwili, *P. A. Florenskii i kul'tura ego vremeni,* 258.

56. Florenskii, *Stolp i utverzhdenie (I),* 12.

should call it pre-eschatologism): a desire to keep it all in play, prior to the advent of the New Jerusalem, lest any form of knowledge now available to us be mistaken for absolute knowledge of the All. As he argues in the fifth letter of *Stolp i utverzhdenie,* to assume that one had obtained full knowledge of how to purify one's flesh would signal "that perversion of the whole of human nature that goes by the name of 'seduction' (*prel'shcheniem*) or 'charm' (*prelest'iu*)" (Florenskii has in mind the etymological basis of these words in roots meaning "pride" and "[self-]flattery").[57] It is in this sense that Florenskii approaches philosophy as a form of "direct experimentation with reality," full of play and amazement not because reality is ultimately indeterminate but because to offer as final any specific (scientific or scholarly) account of the world would close off prematurely our anticipation of the second coming. The tendencies in both directions, toward essentialism and indeterminacy, mark Florenskii as a quintessential liminal figure of Russia's early twentieth century. The reader who assumes that Florenskii is a brooding provincial theologian is surprised to discover the richly informed bibliography of *Stolp i utverzhdenie,* which is open to a great deal of contemporary European thought; the reader who wants to construct a bridge from Florenskii's mediations on indeterminacy to such doctrines as deconstruction and postmodernism quickly discovers in him an essentialist and an Orthodox theologian.

One of the most important—and, at least outwardly, modern—ways in which language for Florenskii reflects the tentative nature of our pre-eschatological existence is in its various manifestations of the principle of logical "antinomy": its incorporation of unresolvably contradictory tendencies or phenomena, such as the opposition between objective and subjective aspects of the word, between uttered speech and mental understanding, or between individual and national dimensions of language.[58]

In *Stolp i utverzhdenie* Florenskii credits Kant and his *Critique of Pure Reason* with having introduced the term "antinomy" into modern philosophical

---

57. Ibid., 112.

58. Florenskii's examples, which he extends considerably beyond these, are drawn largely from Humboldt, Steinthal, and Potebnia, as well as from Victor Henry's 1896 *Antinomies linguistiques;* "Antinomiia iazyka," in *U vodorazdelov mysli,* 155–56; he treats antinomy in general in the sixth letter of *Stolp i utverzhdenie* entitled "Protivorechie," and linguistic antinomy in particular in the essay "Antinomiia iazyka," in the section entitled "Mysl' i iazyk" of the collection *U vodorazdelov mysli* that he assembled in 1918. There is an interesting Bakhtinian moment Florenskii quotes in which Henry says that ancient languages can be learned, though their material for us is already a "finished, closed-off whole"; "Antinomiia iazyka," in *U vodorazdelov mysli,* 158.

discourse, but he also cites a long list of precursors and contemporaries whose writings testify that antinomy has long been recognized as a constituent of human experience, from Plato's dialogues (he cites the debate over natural versus cultural origins of language in the *Cratylus* as the ultimate progenitor of the idea of linguistic antinomy) to Nicholas Cusanus (with his idea of *coincidentia oppositorum,* the coincidence within God of contradictory definitions) and on to more recent linguists and philosophers of language (Potebnia, Humboldt, Steinthal, and in particular Victor Henry's 1896 *Antinomies linguistiques*), mathematicians (Bolzano's *Paradoxen das unendlichen* of 1851), philosophers (Nietzsche's idea of "tragic optimism"), and physicists.[59] In connection with language, however, this antinomial thesis is best understood as an updating of the doctrine of linguistic indeterminacy elaborated by Humboldt and introduced into the Russian context by Potebnia—that is, of Humboldt's Romantic emphasis on the dynamic nature of linguistic phenomena that reveals the inherence of subjectivity in language (for Humboldt, if language is not actually a self proper, it at least behaves in the same manner as a self).

As we saw in Chapter 1, the key antinomy in Humboldt's account of language is that between the principles of *ergon* or thingness and *energeia* or activeness. Florenskii places himself decidedly in this tradition when he asserts that, on the one hand, everything in language is in motion, flows, and is created from moment to moment by humans, while, on the other hand, language comes to us as something "monumental," handed down to us as a set of fixed, ready-made words and grammatical relations.[60] He observes that the "monumental" part of this doctrine was not all that striking in the mid-nineteenth century because it had already served as dogma for both eighteenth-century proponents of rational language and for theologians who understood language exclusively as a divine gift; but the thesis of linguistic activity was truly innovative and astutely identified the living nature of language. Nonetheless, Florenskii revises Humboldt and Potebnia—and

59. Florenskii, *Stolp i utverzhdenie (I)*, 154, 147, 156; and *Stolp i utverzhdenie (II)*, 686–87, n. 208. Kant's first *Critique* shows that contradictory conclusions about the world as a whole can be drawn with equal propriety, such as the thesis that the world has a beginning in time and is limited in space, as well as its antithesis that it has no beginnings and no limits. Kant's point, however, is epistemological rather than ontological, as it is in Florenskii: the conflict of reason with itself shows us that the principles of reasoning that we use are not constitutive, showing us how the world is, but regulative, embodying injunctions about how we are to think about it (Blackburn, *Oxford Dictionary of Philosophy*, s.v., "antinomy").

60. Florenskii, "Antinomiia iazyka," in *U vodorazdelov mysli*, 154–55. This essentially Kantian distinction, which the neo-Kantian Herman Cohen turned into the slogan *"Die Welt ist nicht gegeben, aber ausgegeben,"* also appears in Bakhtin's opposition between that which is "given" and that which is "assigned" to us in life (*dan/zadan*), which in turn became a "rallying cry of the Bakhtin circle"; see Katerina Clark and Michael Holquist, *Mikhail Bakhtin* (Cambridge: Harvard University Press, 1984), 59.

reveals himself to be a *post*-romantic Modernist—by shifting emphasis to the simultaneous inherence of *ergon* and *energeia* in language.[61] In Humboldt the "monumental" aspect of language is the mere givenness of its historical form; the genuine essence of language inheres rather in the mental activity that he sometimes suggests exists prior to any concrete, realized speech. But in Florenskii's account both thesis and antithesis, in their contradictory simultaneity, are essential to "truth," so that in effect he asserts a kind of "meta-*energeia*" with regard to language, in which the vitality of language arises not out of the principle of *energeia* alone but out of a second-order flux between it and its opposite, between linguistic monumentality and activity. For Florenskii language inheres not in the transcendence of givenness in activity but in the living oscillation between *ergon* and *energeia*, between "thing" and "life." We treasure language as something objective, imposed on us by the conditions of life, he remarks, but we also recreate it when we speak—all the while continuing to believe in its objectivity.[62] These mutually exclusive tendencies form a pair, a syzygy, and it is their antinomial relation that enables or even generates language. Language arises out of, and does not exist prior to or apart from, these tensions.[63]

In the essay "Stroenie slova" (The structure of the word) Florenskii illustrates the phenomenon of linguistic antinomy by turning to the domain of semantics, or more accurately to the speaker's psychological experience in the course of invoking linguistic meaning. The guiding precept is, again, the Humboldt/Potebnia thesis—banner for semantic contingency—that "all understanding is misunderstanding" (Florenskii quotes Potebnia paraphrasing Humboldt on this); but here again Florenskii revises his sources.[64] He offers his own version of Potebnia's tripartite word (or trichotomous, as he calls it) in which the word consists of an outer form comprising the phoneme and morpheme, together with an inner form comprising its sememe.[65] He draws

---

61. See Bonetskaia's comment that the nineteenth century meets the twentieth in Florenskii's reception of Potebnia ("O filologicheskoi shkole P. A. Florenskogo," 253n).

62. Florenskii, "Antinomiia iazyka," in *U vodorazdelov mysli*, 163.

63. Florenskii, "Termin," in *U vodorazdelov mysli*, 200.

64. Florenskii, "Stroenie slova," in *U vodorazdelov mysli*, 236.

65. See also his description, reminiscent of Lockean psychology as well as of Benveniste's model of the successively determining layers of linguistic structure, of the phoneme as the symbol of the morpheme, and the morpheme in turn as the symbol of the sememe. What this means, Florenskii explains, is that the sememe is the sense of the morpheme, while the morpheme is the sense and goal of the phoneme. In more overtly psychological terms he also describes the phoneme as the spirit's reaction to an external impression and therefore the process by which the impression is recognized, so that the morpheme is spirit's reaction to an already (re)cognized impression, therefore the process by which a concept is formed; the sememe then is the spirit's reaction to a concept, which serves the formation of specific ideas. In other words a phoneme is the impression of an impression or a sensation; a morpheme is the sensation of a sensation or a concept; a sememe is the concept of a concept or an idea (ibid., 240).

an analogy between this structure and the skeleton, tissues, and mind of the human organism, and in support invokes the hermeneutics of the kabbalistic and Alexandrian schools (in other words Philo) which held that scriptural sense consists in sound, concept, and idea.[66] But even in this context he finds the lure of binary opposition hard to resist. The phenomenon of verbal form or structuredness only arises, he tells us, at that moment when, as it is being used, a word conjoins the antinomial principles of monumentality and receptivity.[67] At the moment of speech the word's "outer form," the sequence of phonemes and graphemes we would recognize as a dictionary entry, constitutes the given material that precedes speech proper; it is transmitted to the individual speaker by the collective or nation as a whole.[68] But the word also possesses "inner form," the domain in which the speaker creates new meaning at the very moment of speech.[69] Another (psychological) way of stating it: at the moment of speech we experience the word as a concept or representation, in which regard it becomes object-like for us (Florenskii emphasizes the etymology of this very term, ob-ject, something tossed in before our eyes, "*pred-met,* 'metaetsia pred' *nami*"), while at the same time we encounter the word's sememe in a state of flux, shaped by intonational and contextual nuances at the moment it is deployed.[70] The word is thus the meeting ground of two energies: in the process of speech the speaker joins up with a transindividual, collective (*sobornoe*) unity, and the energy of an individual spirit and that of the collective mutually grow into one another.[71] It is in this way, Florenskii remarks in "Antinomiia iazyka," that our thought comes to rely not on isolated ratiocination but on Collective Reason, on universal *Logos.*[72] Outer form is the unchanging, firm "body" of the word, inner form the constantly changing, direct manifestation of spirit. Words in this account exist simultaneously as prior empirical facts of language and as instances of my own spiritual life.

66. Ibid., 241.

67. Ibid., 232.

68. Ibid., 234.

69. As Steven Cassedy points out, this significantly revises Potebnia's association of inner form with etymology, which ethnic history of usage Florenskii relegates to outer form—though both Florenskii and Potebnia assert that inner form is the realm of creativity through which the word resembles a miniature work of art; Steven Cassedy, "Florenskij and Philosophy of Language in the Twentieth Century," in *P. A. Florenskii i kul'tura ego vremeni,* 290–91. For a comparison of Potebnia and Florenskii see also Bonetskaia, "Ob odnom skachke v russkom fiilosofskom iazykoznanii," in Hagemeister and Kauchtschischwili, *P. A. Florenskii i kul'tura ego vremeni,* 254–55. As the first chapter of this study makes clear, I disagree with Bonetskaia's definition of Potebnia as an "empirical psychologist" (versus the ontologist Florenskii) for whom the word is not much more than an acoustic sign for the trait of some object registered in the mind (ibid., 262).

70. Florenskii, "Stroenie slova," in *U vodorazdelov mysli,* 235–36.

71. Ibid., 234.

72. Florenskii, "Antinomiia iazyka," in *U vodorazdelov mysli,* 163.

Florenskii uses this notion of "antinomy" to gauge some of the most prominent manifestations of Modernist culture that surround him, arranging a series of contemporary treatises on language and poetic manifestos along an axis running from *ergon* to *energeia*. Though language conjoins these two poles, it is possible, Florenskii remarks, to find situations in which one or the other predominates (cf. Potebnia's similar remarks on the relative dominance in some cases of "poetic" versus "prosaic" tendencies in language). Artificial languages like Esperanto represent the predominance of *ergon* or thingness. Arising out of rationalist impulses (a striving for "philosophical language," the ascendancy of *a priori* logical categories over expressive forms), they in fact usurp and petrify real language.[73] His example of this impulse in the Russian context is none other than Lintsbakh's *Printsipy filosofskogo iazyka,* whose appearance he attributes to its author's dissatisfaction with language in any of its historically given forms, which Lintsbakh rejects as flawed in their "irrationality." This dissatisfaction then spawns the desire to replace language altogether with Lintsbakh's own invention. But in fact rather than being unprecedented and utopian, Lintsbakh's project is a derivative echo of French thought of the eighteenth century: anti-organic, mechanistic, convinced that everything results from social convention rather than nature (hence his premise that our ancestors "invented language," which is therefore by definition artificial).[74] The hyper-symmetrical, hyper-rational language Lintsbakh invents in the end represents a "monstrous assault on life" of a sort that "not even Marat" had contemplated.[75] At the other pole for Florenskii stands Futurism, which, for all its avant-garde demeanor represents a retrograde effort to recover the pre-logical chaos of language.[76] Futurist *zaum* represents an overemphasis on *energeia* in language, motivated by a sense that language must be something purely elemental. But even *zaum* requires *Logos,* Florenskii warns, otherwise it is like demon's gold that in the light of day turns out to be feces.[77] If schemes for artificial, "philosophical" languages represent a disbelief in the essentiality of already-given words, the Futurist experimentation represents a disbelief in the Word's inherent rationality.[78] Both these tendencies within Russia's Modernist culture are distortions of the principle of antinomy underpinning language—which must by implication find its true embodiment somewhere else.

---

73. Ibid., 164–65.
74. Ibid., 186–93.
75. Ibid., 192.
76. Ibid., 187.
77. Ibid., 185.
78. Ibid., 166.

"Antinomy" is thus a characteristically complex notion in Florenskii's thought, a part of his narrative about language rather than analysis of it. In one respect it represents a quasi-vitalist celebration of the subjectivity inherent in language—its resemblance to a living thing which reassures us that subjects themselves are dynamic, fluid, and unfinalized. On the other hand the discussions of "antinomy" in Florenskii also add up to a portrait of gnoseological indeterminacy, a sense that no sooner do we identify a definite characteristic of language than we must immediately also recognize the inherence of its opposite. Again, for Florenskii this is so because we must forestall, at least for now, any absolute knowledge or meaning, including that of language. Already in the sixth letter of *Stolp i utverzhdenie* entitled "Protivorechie" ("Contradiction") he declares that we live in a postlapsarian state of "fragmentation" (this a favorite notion of Solov'ev and his followers). "There, in heaven, there is one Truth; here on earth we have a multitude of truths, shards of Truth which are incongruent with one another."[79] Yet for a Russian paradoxicalist and apophatic theologian like Florenskii the very impossibility of logical resolution becomes a guarantee of the existence on a higher level of unifying Truth. The only way for *istina* to escape the vicissitudes of life, he argues in *Stolp i utverzhdenie,* is for it to rise above them and encompass its own contradiction. It must form a "self-contradictory judgment."[80] Logic deems this kind of formation a contradiction, but thesis and antithesis must both inhere in truth, which "is an antinomy, and cannot not be one."[81] This is the same mindset that celebrates the seemingly self-contradictory doctrine of the Trinity as evidence of its transcendent authenticity. It is the *form* of Modernist thought endowed with a radically un-Modernist content.

The paradox of Florenskii's protean thought is that even as he insists on the seemingly indeterminate, antinomial nature of language and reality, he also offers an essentialist vision of ontological certitude (whether this paradox is ultimately, as Struve suggests, the product of his psychological fragility and divided worldview, which hesitates between scientism and mysticism, is a matter for further debate).[82] In this complementary ontological or essentialist mode of his thought, Florenskii treats language as a reification of the order underlying the cosmos that is capable of providing

79. Florenskii, *Stolp i utverzhdenie (I),* 158.

80. Ibid., 147. It is interesting that in Florenskii's definition heresy is essentially a logical rather than a moral or spiritual failing, the seizing on one side of a truth rather than both its thesis and antithesis (161).

81. Ibid., 147.

82. Nikita Struve, "Florenskii i Khomiakov," in Hagemeister and Kauchtschischwili, *P. A. Florenskii i kul'tura ego vremeni,* 87.

proto-realizations of transcendence.[83] It is here, too, that his theory of language most clearly responds to the anxieties underlying revived Russian idealism in the early twentieth century by envisioning the word as a sort of unperplexed realization of the self.

One way in which language instantiates cosmic order is through the workings of human reason (again, in the sense of *razum* rather than mere ratiocination), which Florenskii holds to be capable of involving us directly in the realm of *Logos*-ordered being—because like others in the tradition of "Orthodox philosophy of language" outlined by Prat, Florenskii professes a *Logos*-based worldview that regards the created world as emanating from the mind of God and therefore at root rule-governed and harmonious.[84] Illusionism and alogism are the result, he argues, of the belief that reason does not take part in being. But once we recognize that it does take part, the act of cognition becomes not only gnoseological but ontological as well: "Cognition is the actual exiting of the cognizer from his own self, or, what amounts to the same thing, the actual entry of the cognized into the cognizer, the actual unification of the cognizer and the cognized."[85] To understand a word amounts to being conveyed, via a kind of Platonic mysticism, toward literal contact (*soprikosnovenie*) with the word's referent, an experience that is impossible, Florenskii remarks, if one believes that we are spiritually isolated from being.[86] As Slesinski points out, this notion is subtended in Florenskii by the conviction that the world is *homoousious* rather than *homoiousian,* which he derives from Orthodox Trinitarianism: that it is of the same, rather than merely similar, substance as the self, and therefore the self can experience communion with it.[87] Again, there is an ethical implication. One effect of this connectedness provided by the word is that it brings us *volens-nolens* out of our individual selves and into contact with the collective (or, ultimately, the Church). "In the word I exit the bounds of my own limitedness and merge with the historically manifested will of

---

83. In this respect at least Florenskii's thought resembles that of Roman Jakobson, whose understanding of language is everywhere subtended by the vision of a non-arbitrary, quasi-mathematical or geometrical order underlying life's phenomena or at the very least the products of human culture. See Holenstein's comparison of Jakobson's concept of wholes and their unity versus Wittgenstein's considerably looser concept of "family resemblances": "What distinguishes Jakobson from Wittgenstein is the non-arbitrariness, the strictly ordered presence and absence of features. Features are not arbitrarily present or absent; their presence or absence depends on the presence or absence of other features"; Elmar Holenstein, "Jakobson's Contribution to Phenomenology," in Daniel Armstrong and C. H. Van Schooneveld, eds., *Roman Jakobson. Echoes of His Scholarship* (Lisse: Peter de Ridder Press, 1977), 154.

84. Florenskii, *Stolp i utverzhdenie (I),* 126.

85. Ibid., 73.

86. Florenskii, "Termin," in *U vodorazdelov mysli,* 212.

87. Robert Slesinski, "The Metaphysics of Pan-Unity in Pavel A. Florenskij: A World View," in Hagemeister and Kauchtschischwili, *P. A. Florenskii i kul'tura ego vremeni,* 467.

the people, which has cumulatively registered itself in the formation of precisely this sememe of the given word."[88]

Moreover, in Florenskii's view to name an object is not merely to attach an identifying tag to it but also to elevate it to the level of *logos,* thereby rescuing it from randomness and non-being. In "Termin" (The term) he cites a passage from Lotze's *Microcosm* to the effect that we are never satisfied with the naked perception of an object but always want to draw it into the world of thought by naming it.[89] To *name,* therefore, is not to assign an arbitrary sound to some perception but (here he paraphrases Humboldt) to approach in one's thoughts the thoughts of the human race, with the result that the word now appears to embody a consistent, inwardly necessary link between external expression and internal content. Name conveys us to essence. This inwardly necessary link makes of the word or name a "symbol," Florenskii asserts. Florenskii's frequent etymological excurses work toward this end: they provide essentialist histories of words, rescuing them from arbitrariness (since the meaning of a word is made to appear not random or conventional but inevitable), while at the same time preserving their aura of mystery (since the underlying meaning is never fully transparent but must be excavated, interpreted, apperceived using a hermeneutic approach akin to that applied to sacred texts). Indeed, Florenskii's etymologies often seem to attribute a kind of intentionality to the word, as if the word had sought out its own semantic development.

For an example of how Florenskii turns an etymological excursus (be it accurate or fanciful) into a demonstration of semiotic inevitability, so that the word's form becomes the perfectly adequate iconic fulfillment of its meaning (this strategy explicitly recalling Potebnia's idea of word as miniature work of art—"the word is a myth, the seed of mythopoesis," as Florenskii paraphrases at one point—consider his "analysis" of the Russian *kipiatok* (boiling water) in "Stroenie slova."[90] Florenskii first analyzes the phonetic qualities of the word, discovering a rising tone in its sequence of two unstressed syllables followed by a stressed one; even within the syllable "*kip-*" he detects "the natural sound of a leap." He then offers historical-semantic comments linking its root and cognates to the meanings "to come into motion, to leap, to hop," concluding that the root itself denotes "a determined upward movement."[91] Ultimately the word *kipiatok* is revealed, in both form and meaning, to constitute "an entire little poem" on the theme

88. Florenskii, "Termin," in *U vodorazdelov mysli,* 263.

89. Ibid., 211. Florenskii may in fact have taken this example from Potebnia, who cites the Lotze passage in his *Mysl' i iazyk,* in *Estetika i poetika,* 164.

90. Florenskii, "Stroenie slova," in *U vodorazdelov mysli,* 247.

91. Ibid., 245–46.

of leaping and liveliness—and Florenskii then asserts the word's prominent role in the Gospel text in which Jesus tells the Samaritan woman at the well that the spiritual water that he offers "will become . . . a spring of water *welling up* to eternal life" (John 4:14, RSV; Florenskii quotes from a thirteenth-century Russian manuscript in which the word rendered in the RSV as "welling" is "*k″ipiashcha*," lit. 'boiling [up]'). He also asserts its etymological link with the Greek root for "Pegasus." Instead of a casual example of how sound and meaning condition one another as they evolve, the etymology Florenskii derives for *kipiatok* turns out to be an icon for life itself, conceived and represented as an upward striving of the spirit.

As the remarks on "names" cited above suggest, for Florenskii there exist certain types of words that provide even more immediate access to essence than others. His hierarchy of these is loose and inconsistent, but the impulse to find a quintessence, some form that epitomizes language in its highest function, is clear. At the lowest end stand his remarks on technical terms (*termin*), a "synthetic" form of the word that, unlike the avant-garde experiments Florenskii reviews, stands at the harmonious middle between being "already finished" (they reflect the "certain existential judgment" that humanity has passed on the phenomenon in question) and being "plastic" and responsive to the movements of the individual soul.[92] At the next level of essentiality comes the symbol, though Florenskii's use of this word can vary from essay to essay (see, for example, his disparaging of mechanical models in physics as "nothing more than symbols, capable only in some respects of replacing the phenomena they represent").[93] Symbols to Florenskii are words or other signs that manifest a consistent, inwardly necessary link between external expression and internal content.[94] They embody a principle of conceptual unity within the multiplicity of possible traits they connote, and in this regard are the same phenomenon that Plato called "idea" or "type," that Goethe called "*das Protophaenomen*," and Viacheslav Ivanov called "symbol."[95] Echoes of Symbolist doctrine, in particular of the notion that symbols provide contact with the transcendent realm, are also discernible in his remarks that the symbol "leads an existence larger than itself": it is something that through itself manifests something that is not itself.[96]

At the highest level of essentiality, however, stands the name (especially the personal name, though designative names—"*imia naritsatel'noe*" in

---

92. Florenskii, "Termin," in *U vodorazdelov mysli*, 208, 202.
93. Florenskii, "Nauka kak simvolicheskoe opisanie," in *U vodorazdelov mysli*, 119.
94. Florenskii, "Termin," in *U vodorazdelov mysli*, 211.
95. Florenskii, "Dialektika," in *U vodorazdelov mysli*, 145–46.
96. Florenskii, "Imiaslavie kak filosofskaia predposylka," in *U vodorazdelov mysli*, 287.

Russian—already stand out from the mass of ordinary words), which becomes the focus of Florenskii's strongest claims regarding language, being, and the self. A name, he remarks in "Imiaslavie kak filosofskaia predposylka" (Onomatodoxy as a philosophical presupposition) represents "a more concentrated center of energies than a mere word."[97] In their cognitive function—that is, for us as receivers and interpreters of names—names serve as the focus of their bearers' qualities. The first proof Florenskii offers of this in his extended essay "Imena" (Names), which he intended to include as one of the sections of *U vodorazdelov mysli,* is, interestingly, the literary text.[98] His example is Pushkin's *Tsygany* (The gypsies), whose various themes he finds concentrated in the name of the mother of the heroine, Zemfira, Mariula—down to the level of the individual letters forming her name.[99] In the world of the text, Florenskii suggests, names possess an "inner necessity" on a par with that of symbols proper.[100] But—and this is a key assumption—for Florenskii reality as a whole is constructed according to the same kind of intentionalist principles as those organizing the artistic text (in a prestructuralist sense, according to which there is an intender behind the text, someone who *means*), with the result that we can also regard a personal name as providing a "formula of personality/selfhood."[101] The name not only tells us what its bearer is like; it expresses the "type of self" its bearer is, nothing less than his or her "ontological form."[102] In a certain measure the name even *determines* the person its bearer becomes: "The name predetermines the self and indicates the ideal boundaries of its life."[103]

97. Ibid., 294.

98. Florenskii worked on this essay throughout the 1910s, planned to include it in the larger work ca. 1917, and revised it in the early 1920s. See Igumen Andronik (Trubachev), "Kniga *Imena* Sviashchenika Pavla Florenskogo (istokovedcheskii obzor)," in P. A. Florenskii, *Imena. Maloe sobranie sochinenii,* vypusk 1 (n.p.: Kupina, 1993), 310, 314.

99. Bonetskaia points out that Florenskii cites kabbalistic sources in *Stolp i utverzhdenie,* in particular a work by the eighteenth-century Antoine Fabre-d'Olivier, whose *Kosmogoniia Moiseia* had been published in 1911 in Russia ("O filologicheskoi shkole P. A. Florenskogo," 178).

100. Florenskii, *Imena,* 25.

101. Ibid., 29.

102. Ibid., 70.

103. Ibid., 90. In "Magichnost' slova" Florenskii remarks that personal names have always played an important incantatory role in magic; in *U vodorazdelov mysli,* 265. Note that Florenskii's view of names is radically opposed to that of analytic philosophers such as Bertrand Russell, who claims that what makes names distinct from other linguistic signs is their circularity: "there are many dogs called *Fido* but they do not share any property of 'Fidoness' " (paraphrased in Roman Jakobson, "Shifters, Verbal Categories, and the Russian Verb," in his *Selected Writings,* vol. 2 [The Hague: Mouton, 1971], 131). Florenskii's claim is precisely that names do denote such an abstract quality.

While Florenskii's ideas about symbols, terms, and personal names clearly echo the Silver Age's general exaltation of the word and its powers, his thought on the nature of language nonetheless stands out for its far more serious engagement of Orthodox theology and that theology's tendencies toward ontological literalism. In the case of language this literalism manifests itself most visibly in his concept of linguistic form, and in Florenskii's writings it is the idea of form that most clearly reveals the self-like nature of language. In this metaphysical context the notion of form that Florenskii deploys differs from the more conventionally linguistic terms he uses in, say, "Stroenie slova," where he speaks of the word's fixed "outer form" (phoneme and morpheme) and fluid "inner form" (sememe). When Florenskii speaks of "form" in this philosophical sense, it is as an essential precondition of ontology. "Everything that is has form and every form contains within itself a certain 'there is' [*est'*]; there is no being without form and no form without a being formed by it," he argues in "Dialektika."[104] A rose petal is at once the containing envelope and its visible contents: what the world consists of is phenomena, self-manifesting noumenality, and to perceive form is to be assured of the existence of this kind of ontological reality. In his preface to *U vodorazdelov mysli* he even states that the entire book has been elaborated around the concept of "form," understood as organic unity, as developed in Platonic-Aristotelian idealism, in medieval Realism, and in the latter day writings of Goethe, Schelling, and Novalis.[105]

Through a kind of metalinguistic metaphor Florenskii introduces the idea of form into the concept of the word itself, implying that an awareness of form is what enables consciousness and speech. In his discussion of technical terms as a type of synthetic word he embarks on a characteristic etymological and semantic (he calls it "semasiological") analysis of the very word "*termin*" (term). He points out that this Russian word is a borrowing from Latin *terminus,* which he glosses as "termin, *inis*" or "*termo, inis*" and derives from the root **ter,* meaning to step across, especially in order to reach a goal on the other side of some line. Originally this was imagined as a physical boundary, Florenskii claims, so the word originally meant a border post, stone, or sign in general (he further traces the word back to Greek *oros,* which derives from a word meaning furrow or border).[106] These were primarily boundaries of fields, of family plots. In their original form, however, these boundaries were symbolic rather than physical barriers. The space inside was presided over by family gods; along the boundary line the

---

104. Florenskii, "Dialektika," in *U vodorazdelov mysli,* 149.
105. Florenskii, "Puti i sredotochiia," in *U vodorazdelov mysli,* 32.
106. Florenskii, "Termin," in *U vodorazdelov mysli,* 218. Florenskii says that John the Damascene also notes the derivation of "term" from earthen boundaries (222).

owner placed marker stones or logs that were called "*termes.*"[107] Thus "*termin*" originally arises as the guardian of a threshold, of a sacred plot of ground, of everything within the delineated space. In other words, in its original sense it is a preserver of cultural boundaries, providing life with discreteness and structure, establishing the immovability of life's basic articulations.[108] The very notion of "word" or "term" thus turns out (according to the deterministic logic of Florenskii's etymologies) to contain the idea of boundary and enclosure, moreover of something spiritual or sacred by something physical and symbolic. This "discovery" is underscored when Florenskii argues that in philosophy the "term" provides certain "furrows for thought."[109] In the undefined field of possibilities that precedes thought the term establishes certain lines of definiteness; these enable consciousness. According to many contemporary psychologists, Florenskii states, consciousness arises from the arresting of the otherwise continuous stream of our psychic life; things flow along, until we "stumble" upon the unexpected and consciousness arises (Shklovsky had made this the basis for a Formalist theory of art a few years earlier, in "Iskusstvo, kak priem"). The "term" thus constitutes a boundary by means of which thought defines itself and in so doing becomes aware of itself (it "defines itself and therefore becomes aware of itself").[110] In its role as establisher of boundary or form, it is the precondition for knowledge and selfhood. The existence of perceptible form enables thought, consciousness, and life.

This image of inner content residing in outer form, of a sacred plot surrounded by boundary markers, also suggests in a way reminiscent of Potebnia the body-inhabiting self, and Florenskii's insistence on the importance of form as such may be seen as deriving from an Orthodox anthropology which insists that the flesh is a necessary part of creation—at any rate flesh that is not mere thing or *res* but has been uplifted into subjectivity and the life of the spirit. The human person is "given" to us in many senses, Florenskii begins in the ninth letter of *Stolp i utverzhdenie,* devoted to a defense of "*tvar',*" the created world, before the claims of Catholicism and neo-Kantianism; but it is first of all given to us as a body (the rest of the letter expands this into a defense of the role natural sciences should play within a genuinely Orthodox culture).[111] The body constitutes human form, not just its outward contours but the disposition/arrangement of everything in

---

107. Ibid., 219.

108. Ibid., 221.

109. Ibid., 225. The remark about furrows is perhaps meant to echo Viacheslav Ivanov's title *Borozdy i mezhi (Furrows and Boundaries,* 1916).

110. Ibid., 226.

111. Florenskii, *Stolp i utverzhdenie (I),* 264.

a human being.[112] As such it is also a guarantee of the unity of the self, and Florenskii even postulates that this principle of unity exists concretely within the body, as its "body within the body."[113]

In keeping with this anthropology Florenskii's reflections on both literal bodies and linguistic form are further characterized by a tendency toward an allegorical, or more accurately a homological, vision of the world, strongly reminiscent of medieval scholasticism. The letter of *Stolp i utverzhdenie* devoted to the created world, for example, explores a series of symmetries supposedly obtaining within the human body and structuring its various systems (nervous system, musculature, organs, even diseases), which render its upper half a mirror image of its lower half. In a footnote he appends a schematic diagram of this self-mirroring body—whose source he identifies simply as "mysticism"—and in an addendum presents a series of detailed tables listing specific parallels between upper and lower body, such as kidneys/lungs, anus/nasal opening.[114] This passage is followed by an etymological excursus into the meaning of the Russian word for heart (*serdtse*) as denoting something placed in the middle and therefore inward and central.[115] Florenskii even finds a place in this homotypical scheme for words.[116] If the upper and lower parts of the body mirror each other, he reasons, then the excretions of the lower part—semen—must have their counterpart in excretions of the upper—the production of speech.[117] Thus word is analogous with semen, verbal culture (*slovesnost'*) with sexuality, the act of speaking with male initiative, that of listening with female passivity.[118] He links this idea with the "eroticism of knowledge" developed by Socrates and Plato, and insists that for Plato the parallels were not metaphorical but amounted to an essential "semen-like nature of the word" ("*semennost' slova*"; the idea of "spermatic *logoi*" goes back to Philo and the Neoplatonists, as Florenskii likely knew from Trubetskoi's work). But he also points out that according to Jesus in the parable of the sower the "seed" is the

---

112. Ibid., 264.

113. Ibid., 265.

114. See *Stolp i utverzhdenie (II)*, 730, n. 457; 588–92. Bodily exercises focussing on the navel and specific patterns of breathing were also important to the monks of the *imiaslavie* movement in their trance-inducing recitations of the so-called Jesus prayer.

115. Ibid., 269.

116. Gadamer points out that the analogy between meaning in speech and the body goes back to classical rhetoric. The "circular relationship between the whole and the parts [i.e., the idea that the meaning of the whole guides understanding of individual passages, whose cumulative meanings guide understanding of the whole] is not new. It was already known to classical rhetoric, which compares perfect speech with the organic body, with the relationship between head and limbs" (*Truth and Method*, 175). According to Gadamer, Luther and his successors transferred this concept from classical rhetoric to the process of understanding in general.

117. Florenskii, "Magichnost' slova," in *U vodorazdelov mysli*, 272.

118. Ibid., 271.

"word." The point about sperm, Florenskii says, is that it is not just a drop of liquid, but an "intelligent essence" containing the pattern and potential of its future development. "In other words," he comments, "the sperm contains its own morpheme, phoneme, and sememe: it is a word establishing genealogical linkage primarily with respect to human essence (here Florenskii uses *ousia,* the Greek term used for the essence of the Godhead in the Trinity).[119] In "Magichnost' slova" (The word's magic), Florenskii asserts that the word itself is an "acoustical process distinct from the rest of nature, possessing the subtlest histological and aerial-histological structure" and therefore an organism in its own right: "the word is a self-contained little world, an organism."[120]

The most striking development of this idea of homotopy in Florenskii's writings can be found in his 1919 essay "Organoproektsiia" (Organoprojection), which begins with an examination of the relation of human beings to technology and ends in a cosmology centered on the structures of the human body.[121] Noting that the Greek *organ* means both "constituent of the body" and "instrument," he invokes Ernst Mapp's notion of "organoprojection" (from an 1877 essay on the philosophy of technology) to claim that instruments and machines can all be thought of as extensions of the human body. This is true not in the mechanistic sense characteristic of the eighteenth century, which regards the body as a well-designed machine (but thereby, according to Florenskii, turns life into something automatic and schematized); rather it is the parts of the human body that serve as the "organic prototypes" for the machines we make.[122] Thus, the *camera obscura* and its descendants are projections of the human eye, the fortepiano of the human ear (*sic,* because the seemingly passive apparatus of the inner ear is in fact designed to reproduce sounds via vibration, as does the piano), and electrical devices are extensions of the human nervous system. At the apex of these projections of the human body stands the house, the human domicile, which, filled with all the other instruments humans have devised, replicates the whole of the human body with its organs (commutatively, he calls the body the "domicile of the soul").[123] As Kaukhchishvili notes, Florenskii's vision is ultimately one of an essential inner bond between man as

119. Ibid., 272.

120. Ibid., 261.

121. Evtuhov notes that analogies with the human body reminiscent of medieval organic metaphors appear in discussions of Church authority held during the All-Russian Church Council in August of 1917 (*Cross and the Sickle,* 209).

122. P. A. Florenskii, "Organoproektsiia," *Dekorativnoe iskusstvo SSSR* 145 (1969), 12: 40.

123. Ibid., 41.

physico-biological being and the spatial world—at the center of which moves human selfhood with its creative potential.[124]

To have form, in other words, is to be the realization of a harmonious, self-reflecting scheme. It is the idea of structured regularity in everyday things, Florenskii remarks, that leads us to perceive the universality of *Logos*.[125] Moreover, it is precisely in the possession of such a body that we resemble God and have been created in the divine image, and Florenskii cites in support the patristic testimony of Tertullian and Augustine (and throwing in for further proof the vigor of this idea among the Russian people, as seen for example in their fierce resistance to Peter the Great's decree that nobles shave their beards). The body as an ordered structure indwelt by spirit is therefore the prototype of all created things, and Florenskii enthusiastically mentions Tertullian's belief that it was humans who were created as *foreimages* of the Son of God, rather than Christ who assumed ready-made, inferior human form when he appeared on earth.[126] Verbal form is simply the replication of this principle within language.

The *summa* of Florenskii's doctrine of language/word/name in its correlation with selfhood is found in his ideas concerning the name of God, where he argues that words (or names) do not just adhere to form in a manner characteristic of the created world in general; they are exemplars of divine incarnation whose prototype is the person of Christ. In articulating these ideas Florenskii was not so much dredging up elements of the patristic heritage as he was responding to the contemporary event of the so-called "*imiaslavie* debate," perhaps the most potent irruption of Neoplatonist Orthodoxy into Russian culture in the modern era, whose repercussions, as we have seen in the preceding chapter, spread far beyond religious circles (Losev, who was to dwell on these matters in even more detail than Florenskii, glosses the Russian *imiaslavie* as "onomatodoxy," or "worship of the name").

The doctrine over which the *imiaslavie* debate was to rage arose in the early twentieth century among monks on Mt. Athos, led by a Russian monk named Antonii (Bulatovich). Another Russian monk living on Athos named Ilarion outlined its precepts in 1907, in a work bearing the prolix title *Na gorakh Kavkaza. Beseda dvukh startsev podvizhnikov o vnutrennem edinenii nashikh serdets chrez molitvu Iisusu Khristovu ili dukhovnaia deiatel'nost' sovremennykh pustynnikov* (On the mountains of the Caucasus. A conversation of two elder monks on the inner unification of our hearts through

---

124. Nina M. Kaukhchishvili, "P. A. Florenskii ot drevnosti k stiliu modern," in Hagemeister and Kauchtschischwili, *P. A. Florenskii i kul'tura ego vremeni*, 44.

125. Florenskii, *Stolp i utverzhdenie (I)*, 286.

126. Ibid., 746.

prayer to Jesus Christ or the spiritual activity of modern anchorites). In it he called for a revival of devotional life centered on recitation, so as to invoke directly the presence of God, of the so-called Jesus prayer, which in its entirety consists of the words, "Lord Jesus Christ, Son of God, have mercy on me, a sinner!"[127] The practice was based on the supposed divine origins of the very name "Jesus" and the belief that "the name of God is God himself," so that its recitation brought about His immediate presence. Already on Athos there appeared opponents, especially among the administration, who held that the name of God was nothing but an empty sound of human provenance and could not therefore be used in this incantatory manner (the opponents were headed by Ieronim, the chief Russian hierarch on Mt. Athos, who was, however, deposed by the adherents of *imiaslavie*).[128]

The debate on Mt. Athos heated up in earnest in September 1912, when the patriarch of Constantinople, Joachim III, declared the adherents of *imiaslavie* pagan pantheists, then in early 1913 banned them from conducting religious services. Not long after, the Holy Synod in St. Petersburg sent one Bishop Nikon to Athos with a military detachment, which forcibly turned out the thousand or so Russian monks who had allied themselves with the movement. The monks were dispatched to provincial outposts in Russia, with a repeated ban on performing religious services. Yet the position of the Russian Church as a whole was ambivalent. Independently of one another the metropolitans of Moscow and Kiev (Makarii and Flavian, respectively) officially requested that the monks be readmitted to monasteries without the need for repentance, because their teachings were "sympathetic with" Orthodoxy; and the Synod itself, despite declaring *imiaslavie* a form of "neo-Eunomianism," repeatedly postponed formulating any final resolution on the matter (Florenskii and Sergei Bulgakov were both to have been members of the commission assembled to do this) until in 1917, "owing to certain events" (as Aleksei Losev puts it), the Synod itself was closed down.[129] For its part the Soviet government (predictably) regarded the movement as a counterrevolutionary threat, which attitude may have played a role in Losev's later arrest in 1930.[130]

---

127. An excellent account of the debate from the opposing viewpoint of the official Church is found in Troitskii, *Ob imenakh bozhiikh i imiabozhnikakh.* For a bibliography of works on the debate see Florovskii, *Puti russkogo bogosloviia,* 571–72. The volume of Losev's works collected under the title *Imia* is a virtual encyclopedia of classical and patristic sources of nameworship, and of Losev's redactions of *imiaslavie* doctrine; see A. F. Losev, *Imia. Izbrannye raboty, perevody, besedy, issledovaniia, arkhivnye materialy,* ed. A. A. Takho-Godi (St. Petersburg: Aleteia, 1997).

128. See Evtuhov, *Cross and the Sickle,* 210.

129. Troitskii, *Ob imenakh bozhiikh,* 48–49. See also Losev, "Imiaslavie," in *Imia,* 11–13.

130. L. A. Gogotishvili, "Religiozno-filosofskii status iazyka," in Aleksei Fedorovich Losev, *Bytie. Imia. Kosmos* (Moscow: Mysl', 1993), 909. See also Marchenkov, "Aleksei Losev and His Theory of Myth," introduction to Losev, *Dialectics of Myth,* 13–15.

While the debate raged on Athos in the early 1910s it was widely discussed in the Russian press, so that in absorbing some of its tenets figures like Florenskii, Bulgakov, and Losev were responding not only to patristic doctrines but also to their modern paraphrases and reformulations (as Bonetskaia observes, the *imiaslavie* debate was recognized as a reprise of the medieval debates between realist and nominalists, but was also quickly appropriated by thinkers opposed to both positivism and neo-Kantianism).[131] In addition to Florenskii the movement found intellectual support in Vladimir Ern (who believed that the official Church's condemnation was due to its being infiltrated by phenomenologists), Sergei Bulgakov, and, later, Aleksei Losev.[132]

Florenskii outlines his response to the Mt. Athos debate most fully in the essay "Imiaslavia kak filosofskaia predposylka," which set the precedent within modern Russian culture for revising an understanding of signs, especially verbal signs, in the direction of Orthodox ontologism—though as Bonetskaia points out, the Athos debate acted as a catalyst for ideas on language that Florenskii had already been developing for several years.[133] Florenskii proposes to redefine the relations between the word and its referent, as well as the (for him) cognate relations between subject and object, in light of the concepts of "essence" and "energy" as they had been developed within a long intellectual lineage extending back from the *imiaslavie* movement, to fourteenth-century debates within Eastern Orthodoxy regarding the nature of the light that shone from the transfigured Jesus on Mt. Tabor, to medieval realism, and ultimately to pre-Christian Neoplatonism—a series, Florenskii asserts, that evolved as a reaction against "theological illusionism and subjectivism."[134] Simply stated, the doctrine at the center of this tradition holds that the cosmos consists of entities—essences—that willfully exit themselves in order to create within the world some tangible manifestation or "energy." Florenskii defines a "word" as any outward manifestation of our essence, the aim of which is to introduce some meaning

131. Bonetskaia, "O filologicheskoi shkole P. A. Florenskogo," 154.

132. See L. A. Gogotishvili, "Religiozno-filosofskii status iazyka," in *Aleksei Fedorovich Losev, Bytie. Imia. Kosmos* (Moscow: Mysl', 1993), 909.

133. Bonetskaia, "Ob odnom skachke v russkom filosofskom iazykoznanii," in Hagemeister and Kauchtschischwili, *P. A. Florenskii i kul'tura ego vremeni*, 270.

134. Florenskii, "Imiaslavie kak filosofskaia predposylka," in *U vodorazdelov mysli*, 281. Florenskii offers a table categorizing the most significant schools of contemporary philosophy (immanentism, positivism, Kantianism, Platonism) according to the relationship they posit between appearance and essence; ibid., 304. As Evtuhov notes, Russian intellectuals and theologians alike recognized immediately that the *imiaslavie* debate recapitulated both the Western medieval controversy between nominalism and realism and the "Eastern hesychast controversy" over the divine energies between Gregory of Palamas and the Barlaamites (*Cross and the Sickle*, 211). These issues are examined more closely in the next chapter.

hitherto interior to us into the trans-subjective world.[135] In this expressive act we transcend the dualism of our consciousness (I/world) and gain an intimation of cosmic unity.[136] It is in this context that Florenskii speaks of the word as the basis—he actually calls it the "organ"—for a bond between the cognizer and the cognized, and of cognition as leading to a joining of existences.[137] Indeed, he asserts that the relation between subject and object of cognition is precisely that of the theological formula "*nesliianno i nerazdel'no*" used to describe the relation among the members of the Trinity. This is how the uttered word meets our inner longing for reality.[138]

There are, again, evident sympathies between these ideas and Viacheslav Ivanov's theories of the symbol, but Florenskii is less interested in endowing art with quasi-mystical qualities than in using the doctrine of essence/energy to outline a concept of the linguistic sign as a form of incarnation.[139] To this end he invokes the central tenet of the Athos name-worshipers, who held that "the name of God is God and God himself but God is not his name."[140] This is so, Florenskii explains, because the energy in question (the name "Jesus") is a direct manifestation of the divine essence—in this sense it "is" God himself, is ontologically coextensive with him—without, however, exhausting or comprehending it. There are direct and conscious parallels between this onomatological thesis and the theology of icons in the Eastern Church, and in "Ikonostas" Florenskii calls icons "the Name of God written in paints."[141] In this view both icons and names serve principally as signs of a self. Florenskii claims that the "stability" of the name-worshipers' formula rests on humankind's general conviction that "phenomena bear forth that which is manifest, and are therefore rightly called by its name" (the Russian phrase is a minuet of near-tautology: "*iavleniia iavliaiut iavliaemoe i potomu po spravedlivosti mogut imenovat'sia imenem poslednego*").[142] But the name of God is merely

---

135. Florenskii, "Imiaslavie kak filosofskaia predposylka," in *U vodorazdelov mysli*, 289.

136. Ibid., 284.

137. Ibid., 289, 286.

138. Ibid., 291.

139. For example, Ivanov's claim that symbols are not mere conventional signs but instruments for revealing the inner essence of things, and that what genuine art strives for is to express the parallelism of the phenomenal and noumenal realms, the points of inherence within the constituents of external reality (*realia*) of their correspondents within higher reality (*realiora*). See Viacheslav Ivanov, "Simvolizm," in his *Sobranie sochinenii*, vol. 2 (Brussels: Foyer Oriental Chrètien, 1974), 664; and "Zavety simvolizma," ibid., 597.

140. Florenskii, "Imiaslavie kak filosofskaia predposylka," in *U vodorazdelov mysli*, 300. In the addendum to the essay he also cites such related doctrinal episodes as disputes over the Filioque, and Gregory of Palamas's interpretation of the light revealed on Mt. Tabor (327). Losev, again, was to make still more of these precedents.

141. Ibid., 47.

142. Ibid., 301.

the paradigmatic, sacred example of what names in general are: tangible vessels (it is here that considerations of bodily "form" enter in) that import the "essence" of their referents into the world. The process by which they do this may be imperfect and incomplete—he suggests that the essence of the referent may only inhere in the name via "peripheral thinking," by analogy with peripheral vision (one thinks here of Bakhtin's words with sidelong glances)—but the name nonetheless leads us to perception of the individual form or "quiddity" of its sememe, its "etost'," *haecceitas, Diesheit*.[143] A name is thus more than itself, more than a mere formal sign. In the light of *imiaslavie* doctrine it both reveals and *is* what it denotes, and in this regard it epitomizes the phenomenon of manifestation characteristic of the cosmos as a whole.[144] It is ultimately not an instrument of communication but a self modeled on the divine self that assumed form within the created world.

Florenskii's vision of the name as an exemplar of divine incarnation found an immediate successor in the writings of Sergei Bulgakov. Bulgakov ultimately belongs to the same religiously oriented current of neo-idealism in which Florenskii's ideas developed—a branch of the early-twentieth-century Russian religious renaissance—but he arrived there by a distinctly different path marked by more radical turnings. Where Florenskii had emerged from the metaphysical interests of Symbolist culture, which he simply retheologized, Bulgakov began his intellectual career as a Marxist materialist, one of the so-called "legal Marxists" whose publications were tolerated by the tsarist regime in the 1890s. Following a serious engagement with the thought of Kant, however, whose philosophy "dissolved" the tenets of Marxism for him, at the turn of the century he converted to philosophical idealism, joining several other prominent thinkers whose similar change of course registered itself in such celebrated manifestoes of neo-idealism as *Problemy idealizma* (Problems of idealism [1902]), *Vekhi* (Signposts [1909]),

---

143. Ibid., 295, 297.

144. As Kish argues, Florenskii believes in a dynamic unity of sign and object derived from the sacramental use of icons. In the Western tradition the post-Enlightenment notion of the sign is that it *replaces* something else, substitutes for it, and exists in a relation of similarity to the object it replaces; but in the Orthodox sense Florenskii adheres to, sign and referent exist in a relation of identity and contiguity; they are *edinosushchny, homoousious*. It is in this sense that Florenskii's concept of the sign may be characterized as Eastern and ontological versus Western and instrumental (Ilona Kish, "Vidna-li neveruiushchemu Troitsa Rubleva? K voprosu o poniatii ikonnogo znaka v 'Ikonostase' P. A. Florenskogo," in Hagemeister and Kauchtschischwili, *P. A. Florenskii i kul'tura ego vremeni*, 402–5).

and later *Iz glubiny* (From out of the depths [1918]).[145] Not long after his Kantian phase he took the further step of converting, or perhaps it was really a returning, to a fervent and even mystical belief in Russian Orthodoxy. The ultimate extension of this last stage was his writings, much influenced by Solov'ev, on the notion of the Divine Sophia, which in his treatment went beyond the teachings of the official Church and was finally declared heretical by all the branches of Russian Orthodoxy.[146]

Like Florenskii's, the philosophical projects Bulgakov pursued following his conversion to idealism center on the search for a doctrine that would mitigate between the "two nightmares of contemporary philosophy," the mechanistic materialism of his early Marxist phase and the idealistic subjectivism of Kant and neo-Kantianism that he also eventually rejected.[147] But one could also view Bulgakov's philosophical wanderings more specifically as the search for an ontologically secure foundation for selfhood, one that ends up reaffirming certain Orthodox tenets (albeit enhanced with insights from other doctrines) in order to counter Marxism's threat of imprisoning the self in impersonal matter as well as the neo-Kantian dangers of solipsism and ephemeral subjectivity. As Evtuhov suggests, among Russian thinkers on the eve of 1905 the urge to translate the ethical principles of idealism into politics became a way of affirming the sovereignty of the individual. The point of Bulgakov's most significant philosophical work, *Filosofiia khoziaistva* (The philosophy of economics [1912]), in which he revisits from an idealist standpoint the Marxist issue of human collectivity and its role in history, is thus to reinterpret the relationship between the thinking subject and the external world, particularly through a critique of the post-Cartesian rationalist conception of the being as "thought thinking itself in a closed and self-sufficient system."[148] Bulgakov's writings on language belong very much to this project.

Although older than Florenskii (whom he met in 1905, in an organization called the Brotherhood of Christian Struggle), Bulgakov was the

145. L. A. Zander, *Bog i mir. Mirosozertsanie ottsa Sergiia Bulgakova*, vol. 1 (Paris: YMCA Press, 1948), 436; Evtuhov, *Cross and the Sickle,* 8–9. Bulgakov published his 1897 *O zakonomernosti sotsial'nykh iavlenii* in the journal *Voprosy filosofii i psikhologii,* organ of the Moscow Psychological Society and one of the principal loci of the new idealist movement in early-twentieth-century Russia (ibid., 37).

146. N. O. Losskii, *Istoriia russkoi filosofii* (Moscow: Vysshaia shkola, 1991), 296; Bonetskaia, "O filologicheskoi shkole P. A. Florenskogo," 157. Among other prominent "Sophiologists" in Bulgakov's day were Florenskii, Dmitrii Merezhkovskii, and Evgenii Trubetskoi.

147. Evtuhov, *Cross and the Sickle,* 128.

148. Ibid., 76, 159. Very similar issues were to concern Gustav Shpet a decade or so later, under Soviet conditions. One wonders whether Bulgakov's critique of Marxist economics through a reinterpretation of "*khoziaistvo*" or ownership does not later influence Shpet's critique of individualistic "proprietary" notions of human consciousness, as undertaken in, e.g., "Soznanie i ego sobstvennik," in his *Filosofskie etiudy* (Moscow: Progress, 1994), 20–116.

student in their relationship and elaborated his treatise on language, *Filo-sofiia imeni* (The philosophy of the name), very much in the spirit of Flo-renskii's adaptations of ideas connected with the *imiaslavie* movement.[149] The treatise would not merit more than a brief discussion as an extension of Florenskii's ideas were it not for the fact that, begun in Russia in 1917 but only completed in Paris in 1942, it often seems to be responding to a differ-ent, later set of European influences that either postdate or were unavailable to Florenskii. Bulgakov is also more attuned to linguistics proper than is Florenskii.

Like Florenskii, Bulgakov was scheduled to play an official role in the Church's sorting out of the Mt. Athos scandal, his assignment having been to outline for the 1917 All-Russian Church Council a stand on the relevant Christological issues. *Filosofiia imeni* grew out of this assignment.[150] Per-haps as a result, his "philosophy" of language is less philosophy in the ana-lytical sense than it is an exercise in finding within linguistics and other writings on the nature of language elements that could be assimilated to an *a priori* Orthodox Neoplatonism. It is an attempt to find philosophical jus-tification for his particular redaction of the *imiaslavie* doctrine in which he ultimately aims to hold up the phenomenon of language as further evidence of an Orthodox cosmology (Bonetskaia speaks of Bulgakov's "myth of the living, speaking cosmos").[151] The apparent self-contradictions in Bul-gakov's discussion typically resolve themselves in reference to this underly-ing agenda. Evtuhov remarks that "there is a clear break in Bulgakov's argumentation: in confronting the question of faith, his work ceases to be philosophy and shifts from argument by logical sequence to metaphor"— but this is the same as what I have called the "novelizing" tendencies in Flo-renskii, and something very similar could be said of a philosopher like Heidegger.[152] At root is not Russian intellectual naivete but something more like the often-noted difference in manner between "continental" and Anglo-American analytical philosophy.

Filosofiia imeni begins by reciting what by then had come to be the ex-pected premises for a neo-idealist and post-Symbolist treatment of lan-guage: it invokes the Humboldtian doctrine of the inseparability of language and thought that places language at the center of human con-sciousness ("human knowledge finds completion in and through words, thought is inseparable from the word"; "*die Sprache ist das Bildene Organ der*

149. Evtuhov, *Cross and the Sickle*, 129. Bonetskaia claims that Bulgakov's writings on language as well as those by Losev constitute a "philological school" based on Florenskii's ideas; "O filo-logicheskoi shkole P. A. Florenskogo," 115–16.

150. Evtuhov, *Cross and the Sickle*, 210, 244.

151. Bonetskaia, "O filologicheskoi shkole P. A. Florenskogo," 168.

152. Evtuhov, *Cross and the Sickle*, 170.

Gedanken," he cites; "thoughts do not exist without words," "thought born in a word and a word expressing thought are the dual unity [*dvuedinstvo*] of *logos*; *logos* is at once thought and word") while dismissing psychological explanations that might reduce language to an emanation of the mental life of the subject ("psychological absolutism," as Bulgakov calls it).[153] Language is thus affirmed as something autonomous—which is to say, actually existing in itself—yet central to selfhood and self-understanding (as his student Lev Zander notes, Bulgakov invoked this Humboldtian and Potebnian tradition specifically to counter the Kantian view of language as a mere instrument of thought).[154] The post-Symbolist lineage of Bulgakov's thought is also evident in his mention of the notion, beloved of both the Symbolist Andrei Bely and the Futurist Velemir Khlebnikov, of the incantatory "magic of words"—that dream of a tangible force residing in language, its potential for acting on the world. He invokes the "magic" of words most immediately in reference to poetry ("the word has a symbolic nature, which manifests itself in poetry, for there the word appears as an autonomous essence and force. . . . Poetry borders on the magic of words") but also, interestingly, as an explanation of what "various political parties" perversely attempt to accomplish by printing slogans on banners: these are "dead and impoverished," as compared with the "holy and living" inscriptions in churches, on which they perhaps indeed were modeled in the Russian context.[155]

Beyond this recycling of familiar ideas, however, Bulgakov defines the central task of his treatise as the more challenging effort to establish an ontology of language—and Evtuhov's statement that, when Bulgakov responded to the Church council's request by writing *Filosofiia imeni*, "it was on the poets' theories of language and symbol that he drew" actually applies only in part.[156] What is a word? he asks in his opening paragraph, and his immediate identification of language, speech, and linguistic phenomena in general with the discrete entity of the "word" already places him in the postromantic Russian tradition of thought on language that Potebnia had set in motion. Beyond the kinds of things linguistics and psychology can tell us about the structure of language or its place in our mental life, what is the essence (*eidos*) of the word, that without which the word does not exist? What does it mean that words have meaning?[157] He indicates a provisional answer by identifying the object of his inquiry as "*logos*—word—thought"

153. Prot. S. Bulgakov, *Filosofiia imeni* (Paris: YMCA Press, 1953), 7, 8, 18–19, 17.
154. Zander, *Bog i mir*, vol. 1, 442.
155. Bulgakov, *Filosofiia imeni*, 126–29, 147, 150.
156. Evtuhov, *Cross and the Sickle*, 244.
157. Bulgakov, *Filosofiia imeni*, 16.

in itself, apart from any questions of its origins or historical development.[158] The tendency to cite ancient Greek concepts such as *logos* and
eidos already suggests that the direction in which the inquiry will unfold will
be the Neoplatonist one entrenched in Russia, but Bulgakov's opening also
bears a striking resemblance to that of Heidegger's *Sein und Zeit* (1927;
Being and Time), which he may well have read. Heidegger's work opens by
"retrieving" the seemingly empty question of what "being" is (or, as he asks
in the 1935 *Introduction to Metaphysics*, "Why are there beings at all, instead
of nothing?") and in a manner similar to Bulgakov's casts its eye back
toward ancient Greek sources.[159] Be it paraphrase or chance resemblance,
the parallel indicates that the issues taken up by Bulgakov and other Russians had currency in far wider circles than those of the Russian religious
renaissance.

In a similar ontological vein, when Bulgakov poses the question of how
the "embodiment of sense" that characterizes language comes about, he
notes that this is not the same as our general ability to speak or the closely
related issue, "customary for philology, but lately rejected with irritation, of
the origins of language" (in other words, the tradition of Herder, Condillac, and Rousseau). Instead, what Bulgakov wants to know is what are the
"root elements" present in speech that enable meaning.[160] He rejects the
notion that language in this essential sense arises within society—and with
that rejects also the whole Steinthal/Wundt school of "psychological linguistics" that established itself as successor to Humboldt, as well as the Marxist
tenet that meaning in human life has social determinants.

Instead Bulgakov asserts the primordial nature of language as something
that preexists not only human society but even human being itself: "Language is not created by, it is realized within, society; it is language that con-
nects and provides a foundation for society" and not the other way

158. Ibid., 9.
159. Heidegger, *Being and Time*, 1; and *Introduction to Metaphysics*, 1. Bulgakov does not cite
Heidegger anywhere in his treatise, referring instead to the kinds of German sources one would
expect from someone following Potebnia: Humboldt, Steinthal, Wundt, and so forth. The
chronology that might support the claim of his response to Heidegger is also tricky, because it is
not clear how much of *Filosofiia imeni* was completed by 1918, when Bulgakov fled Russia, and
how much might have been worked out in the 1930s and 1940s, during which time he would almost certainly have become aware of Heidegger's *magnum opus*. One of the earliest Russian responses to *Sein und Zeit* is a review by Vasilii Sezeman in *Put'* 1928, no. 14. Semen Frank
(*Nepostizhimoe, Real'nost' i chelovek*), Boris Vysheslavtsev (*Etika preobrazhennogo erosa*), Nikolai
Berdiaev (*Ia i mir ob"ektov, Tsarstvo dukha i tsarstvo kesaria*), and Lev Shestov (*Kirkegard i ekzis-
tentsial'naia filosofiia*) also register responses to Heidegger. See also Maryse Dennes, *Husserl-Heidegger. Influence de leur oeuvre en Russie* (Paris and Montreal: L'Harmattan, 1998). I am indebted
to Galin Tihanov for these bibliographical references.
160. Bulgakov, *Filosofiia imeni*, 27.

around.[161] He posits the existence of "word-ideas," which preexist words in natural language in the form of certain ideal potentialities capable of creating their own acoustical "bodies" in the form of words.[162] As such they reveal humanity's own relation to the cosmos. For Bulgakov words are cosmic in nature; they form the language of things themselves, "their own ideation."[163] In fact, we do not speak words, rather they speak themselves within us.[164] They represent the "self-evidence of the cosmos within our spirit."[165] Words even "give birth to themselves," an event that takes place within the microcosm of the human mind in order that the cosmos might manifest itself and thereby come to know itself.[166] This is a mystical, not just metaphysical, account of language, reliant on Neoplatonist concepts of procession and embodiment—though at times Bulgakov's account of the origins of language has a distinctly phenomenological ring to it, suggesting the ideal entities that Husserl claimed we have access to in thought and thereby lighting a philosophical path that leads back to shared sources in Neoplatonism—perhaps even disclosing kindred aims (in fact this tendency to echo or approximate other philosophies without invoking them seems characteristic of Bulgakov). "Words are born in the depths of human consciousness as the voices of things themselves which give notice of those things themselves—not the least bit 'subjective' but having universal meaning and for that very reason being capable of being communicated."[167]

The words to which Bulgakov attributes this nature, however, are not the same as the empirical constituents of natural languages. Rather, he claims that there exists a "meta-logos" or *noumen* transcending all languages and inhering in different guises in all of them.[168] This meta-language possesses no concrete phenomenal form and is essentially undiscoverable by philology. It is nothing less than the pre-Babel language-as-such whose existence lies hidden beneath the post-Babel jumble of particular natural languages—which jumble, however, in no way alters this ontological unity of language.[169] Although it is more literal-minded, Bulgakov's view is not so different from that of the Port Royal linguists and Humboldt, for whom

---

161. Ibid., 22.

162. Ibid., 23.

163. Ibid., 24.

164. In a less mystical vein Gadamer also notes that the fact that each speaker encounters language as something preexisting, that language is the conscious creation of no one person or group, means that in essence it "speaks itself" through us and not the other way around; *Truth and Method*, 463.

165. Bulgakov, *Filosofiia imeni*, 15.

166. Ibid., 30.

167. Ibid., 118.

168. Ibid., 38.

169. Ibid., 38, 44. See also Zander, *Bog i mir*, vol. 1, 447–48.

language evinces principles of universal grammar representative of the laws of thinking common to all humanity; or from Chomsky, for whom those same principles serve as evidence that the human mind is "hardwired" with linguistic structure. Though Bulgakov does not identify them, he even posits the existence within each natural language of a set of "primordial words" (*pervo-slova*) constituting a "language proper within language" and forming a certain primary givenness out of which other words are made.[170] These words are "living verbal myths about the cosmos," imprinted with "cosmic events" (Bulgakov's position is close to that expressed at one point in Plato's *Cratylus* that things in the cosmos become manifest "through being imitated by letters and syllables").[171]

Paradoxically, the most interesting sections of *Filosofiia imeni* from a philosophical perspective are those in which Bulgakov undertakes a gnoseological inquiry into some of the more conventional objects of linguistic inquiry, that is, into those components of language dealt with in linguistics as elements of mere structure.[172] Saussure's celebrated opposition between *langue* and *parole,* for example, is discernible behind the similar opposition Bulgakov proposes between "*rech'*" (roughly the speech context) and "*slovo*" (the individual word). The word never exists independently, he tells us; in addition to its direct, denotative meaning it also acquires indirect, connotative ones from its place within larger units of speech, the most important of which is the sentence.[173] But Bulgakov quickly turns this kind of Saussurian precept toward gnoseological ends. The contextual use of a word is significant not as what finally determines its meaning but as the reification (*opredmechennost'*) of a transcendent idea, "its being in a certain object."[174] Moreover, in its referential function every use of a word (in particular a noun, on which more below) is attended by a connotative statement concerning existence: it performs the ontological gesture of stating "this is."[175]

170. Bulgakov, *Filosofiia imeni,* 31.

171. Ibid., 32. Plato, *Cratylus,* 368.

172. Steven Cassedy makes the interesting suggestion that Bulgakov is able to exploit a certain ambivalence between linguistics and theology in part because the word "*imia*" (name) in Russian, used prolifically in the theology of the divine names (e.g., *imiaslavie*), also figures in grammatical terminology more directly than it does in English. Thus "the expression for 'noun' in Russian . . . means something like 'essential name' or 'being-name' (*imja suščestvitel'noe*)"; in his *Flight from Eden. The Origins of Modern Literary Criticism and Theory* (Berkeley: University of California Press, 1990), 112–13.

173. Bulgakov, *Filosofiia imeni,* 45–46.

174. Ibid., 48.

175. Ibid., 48.

Every act of linguistic reference is thus predicated on an affirmative epistemology. The only reason we even consider speaking, in Bulgakov's view, is
that we know the cosmos exists and that it has made itself known to us as
it truly is. This referential event is not without its effect in the speaker as
well. Every act of naming together with its hidden existential judgment
brings about a mystical event in which the subject leaves its isolation to
enter the cosmos, and the cosmos enters the subject (as we have seen, Florenskii makes a similar claim). The name is the site where consciousness and
being come together.[176]

One of the most interesting of these intersections of conventional linguistics with Bulgakov's metaphysical ideas in *Filosofiia imeni* is Part III, devoted to what he calls "philosophical grammar." Bulgakov cites the German
idealist philosophers Hamann, Jakobi, and Herder as his sources (all of
them, incidentally, critical in one way or another of Kant),[177] but his inquiry into the propositional implications of grammatical forms, which is to
say, into what they might tell us about the nature of being, is cognate with
and possibly influenced by one of the most significant tendencies in twentieth-century European philosophy, which Wittgenstein labeled its "linguistic turn." The tendency was to advance the post-Kantian claim that human
thought or knowledge is significantly dependent on language, or, in more
extreme versions, that thought is completely subsumed within it—or "be-
witched" by it, in Wittgenstein's celebrated phrase.

Among the more likely influences on Bulgakov in this regard, given their
importance for Russia's Silver Age culture, are the French idealist philosophers of the early twentieth century (notably Henri Bergson, but also Leon
Brunschvicg and F. L. Pogson) who had indicted the "crystallizations of
meanings into congealed words" as one of the sources of the "substantialist
illusion" in modern philosophy (that is, our susceptibility to believe that
something exists as a discrete entity simply because our language denotes it
with a noun).[178] But there are also general affinities between Bulgakov's examination of grammar and the ideas of Wittgenstein, who had questioned
the conditions under which a signifying system could represent a state of affairs in the world, and the British philosophers influenced by him (Russell,
Moore, Austin, Ryle) who turned philosophy into a critique of language
aimed at eliminating mismatches between the superficial grammatical
structure of propositions and their underlying conceptual structure (Ayer,
Ryle; this is also essentially what Condillac was up to in the eighteenth

---

176. Ibid., 52.

177. Ibid., 243, n. 69.

178. Oswald Ducrot and Tzvetan Todorov, *Encyclopedic Dictionary of the Sciences of Language*,
trans. Catherine Porter (Baltimore: Johns Hopkins University Press, 1979), 92–93.

century), or who rejected the artificial language of formal logic in favor of the nuances of meaning embedded in the statements of natural speech (Austin and "ordinary language philosophy" at postwar Oxford). The common impulse in these cases is to assume that it is not language as such that misleads, only the specialized, artificial uses of it that have come to dominate philosophy and other sciences. But language as such remained culpable in the twentieth century, and at the extreme end of the line begun by the French idealists stands the Whorf-Sapir hypothesis, which argues that worldview is conditioned or perhaps even wholly determined by grammar, especially grammatical categories.

On this map Bulgakov stands closer to the Wittgenstein of the "Tractarian" period (that is, the positions articulated in the early *Tractatus Logico-Philosophicus* but renounced in the later works) than to the linguistic relativists, closer to the Wittgenstein who held that the structure of language reveals the structure of the world; but he stands still closer, again, to Heidegger, who turns in *Being and Time* to Greek grammatical terms for evidence of the nature of Being. In his effort to discover an "ontologically more primordial basis for language," Heidegger takes up the epistemology of parts of speech.[179] The question of whether the primordial form of the word is the noun (substantive) or verb, he remarks, "coincides with the question of the originary character of speech and speaking" and ultimately with that of the origin of language.[180] For Heidegger the verb is primordial, though not in its infinitive form (for example "*sein*"), which usage has transformed into a deverbal substantive and therefore an "empty" form (it is also, he points out, a relatively late addition to the set of parts of speech). Rather, the verbal form that has priority in the understanding of Being is the third-person present indicative, "is."[181]

Bulgakov arrives at an interpretation of the parts of speech that superficially appears the opposite of Heidegger's but in fact makes the same fundamental claim about language: namely, that in one of its particular forms language registers the essence of being. Bulgakov claims that the distinction between noun and verb (or in their syntactic roles, between subject and predicate) embodies the primal act of cognition from which a genuinely critical gnoseology must begin.[182] As we have seen, a noun for Bulgakov is really an ontological gesture predicating that its referent exists; a noun states with regard to its referent "this exists" ("*eto est*").[183] Even more radical in

179. Heidegger, *Introduction to Metaphysics*, 43.
180. Ibid., 59.
181. Ibid., 96.
182. Bulgakov, *Filosofiia imeni*, 49.
183. Ibid., 49.

its gnoseological import, however, is the first-person pronoun. It is the very root of language because it has no content other than testimony to its own existence (a view strikingly close, incidentally, to Jakobson's discussion of pronouns as "shifters," that is, parts of speech lacking fixed referentiality save to participants in a given act of speech—"I" denotes no concept save "person now speaking").[184] It is the principal realization within language of subjectivity, and as such the ontological frame into which the whole of being may be placed; it names the absolutely unnameable, which is to say the mystery of the human self; it is essence (*ousia*) itself, revealed in phenomena as primordial energy.[185] The first-person pronoun thus constitutes the first "hypostasis" of language, within which the second, the word proper, is born.[186] Nouns then arise as "realizations" of ideas, which in turn are "verbal images" of being.[187] Verbs are reduced in Bulgakov's account to the means by which nouns are modified within sentences, that is, by which the name of a thing is propositionally extended (he even claims that verbs do not truly indicate tense, since what a Russian sentence like "*ia byl*" ["I was"] really expresses is "*ia esm' byvshii*" [something like, "I am a person that has been"]).[188] The verb is mere phenomenon in relation to the noun's noumenon, its *ergon* belonging to the world of being and forms.[189] This is why it is given to verb forms to express spatiality and temporality.[190] The syntactic link between (grammatical) subject and predicate, however, overcomes the Kantian divide between (metaphysical) subject and object because all speech takes the form of the predication "A *is* B."[191] Moreover,

184. See Jakobson, "Shifters," 132–33. Benveniste describes pronouns as unique in having only "une 'réalité de discours' " and of the first-person pronoun in particular as having no linguistic existence "que dans l'acte de parole qui la profère"; Emile Benveniste, "La Nature des Pronoms," in Morris Halle et al., eds., *For Roman Jakobson: Essays on the Occasion of His Sixtieth Birthday, 11 October 1956* (The Hague: Mouton, 1956), 35. Bonetskaia calls the "philosophy of the 'I' "the center of Bulgakov's thought and the epitome of his interweaving of philological with ontological concerns ("O filologicheskoi shkole P. A. Florenskogo," 173–74).

185. Bulgakov, *Filosofiia imeni*, 54.

186. Ibid., 55.

187. Ibid., 60. It is in this context that Bulgakov also invokes Potebnia's idea that tropes, which are an esthetic act, serve as the basis for all verbal reference. The fact that language abounds in tropes indicates the magnitude of the gnoseological task set before language, he suggests (65). Tropes are therefore not the exclusive province of poets but characterize the workings of language in general (66). Onomatopoeia is simply a more conscious, reflexive form of the activity carried out throughout naming/language in general (though Bulgakov treats Potebnia's idea of "inner forms" as a purely historical matter). Regarding the idea that the elements of language constitute a set of philosophical propositions, Bulgakov cites a comment by the nineteenth-century German linguist Max Mueller that "language contains its own petrified philosophy" (64).

188. Ibid., 96.

189. Ibid., 69.

190. Ibid., 93.

191. Ibid., 88.

there is a direct link between this understanding of parts of speech and the concept of selfhood: from the premise that all thought and language turns out to be a predicate of "I" it follows, in Bulgakov's scheme, that language exists principally as a medium for the "I's" self-discovery.[192] Behind this there stands the analogy—though not the identity—of the "Absolute I" that is the property of God, the ideal subject, whose extension into the created world is everything knowable that might constitute the referent of a word.[193] In this vein Bulgakov even suggests that the triad of speech parts pronoun-noun-predicate manifests the principle of Trinitarianism within language.[194]

Bulgakov's inquiry into the meanings of grammar finds its polemical point in an attack on Kant, *bête noir* of subjectivism in his eyes. The form his critique of Kant takes in this instance is that of a hypothetical grammatical analysis of Kant's writings in order to reveal their unsuspecting dependence on language—something the French linguist Emile Benveniste was to do with Aristotle roughly a decade and a half after Bulgakov's work was published (in Paris, albeit in Russian).[195] Bulgakov accuses Kant of having failed in his account of human knowledge to subject language itself to a critique. He "walked right past" the question of language while unwittingly and ineluctably using it as a basis for his assertions. But "one cannot escape the power of language or the influence of grammar," Bulgakov remarks.[196] The guiding principle of the analysis Bulgakov proposes would be the properties of "Graeco-Latin grammar," which he asserts underlies all European languages as either model or anti-model.[197] What such an analysis would reveal is that Kant's categories or forms of knowledge (such as spatiality,

192. Zander, *Bog i mir,* vol. 1, 457.
193. Ibid., 458.
194. Bulgakov, *Filosofiia imeni,* 55.
195. In Chapter 6 of his *Problems of General Linguistics,* Benveniste begins by posing the question of the interrelation of thought and language. Whatever its independent status, the content of our thoughts "has to pass through language and conform to its framework" if it is to be articulated; yet there remains the possibility that there exist in thought some characteristics that "owe nothing to linguistic expression"; Emile Benveniste, *Problems in General Linguistics,* Miami Linguistics no. 8, trans. Mary Elizabeth Meek (Coral Gables: University of Miami Press, 1971), 56. He proposes approaching the problem through the intermediary of "categories," which can be found in both language and thought, and turns to the specific historical example of Aristotle's categories. Aristotle's categories are "the totality of predications that can be made about a being" but they turn out, on Benveniste's closer inspection, to be explainable as recodings of the categories of Greek grammar (thus Aristotle's "substance" is a transposition of the linguistic category of substantive, his "what, in what number"—of the adjective, his "where" and "when"—of adverbs of place and time, and so forth (57, 60). "No matter how much validity Aristotle's categories have as categories of thought," Benveniste concludes, "they turn out to be transposed from categories of language" (61).
196. Bulgakov, *Filosofiia imeni,* 89.
197. Ibid., 90.

temporality, quantity, quality, modality, and so forth) are simply attributes of the grammatical predicate.[198] The grammatical meanings on which Kant's propositions necessarily rely contradict the very claims those propositions make—and constitute the truth Kant tries hard to suppress. Whatever Kant's conscious intentions might have been, Bulgakov argues, his *Critique of Pure Reason* turns out to be essentially nothing but a "gnoseological commentary" on language.[199]

For all its suggestive parallels with secular (analytical, skeptical) European thought, Bulgakov's ontology of language nonetheless remains rooted in a doctrine of names as manifestations of divine essence and analogues of incarnation that he had derived from Florenskii's interpretations of the *imiaslavie* movement, though given the homiletic aims of Bulgakov's treatise it perhaps makes as much sense to accuse him of being derivative as it does to accuse the author of a sermon of plagiarizing the Bible.

The premise of Bulgakov's account is once again the doctrine of *energetika,* of the divine energies and their emanations. According to Bulgakov, the primary emanation of the Godhead is Sophia, which takes the form of the sphere of pure ideas (though, again, Bulgakov's ideas about Sophia or Divine Wisdom were later declared heretical by the Orthodox Church).[200] These ideas are instances of "sense" because they represent the meanings of the entities making up the created world, and they exist as *logoi* or "rays" emanating from the Divine *Logos,* which is itself the creative realization of the Divinity.[201] The words of natural languages are then understood as hybrids of these *logoi* and the formal elements of human speech.[202] No pure words are available to us in this world, at least not within particular natural languages, just as there are no sinless people; but when words "speak themselves" in us, their transcendent sense enters the domain of our otherwise fallible psyche, even if we need to be aware that their form is an imperfect one.[203]

198. Ibid., 103.

199. Ibid., 105. In the same passage Bulgakov makes the interesting remark that any philosophical system can be regarded as a "sentence," just as any sentence can be read as a miniature philosophical system; thus in Bulgakov's view uttering a sentence (or, within language, the endowing of a sentence with meaning) amounts to the same activity as elaborating an entire philosophical system.

200. In a postscriptum to *Filosofiia imeni* Bulgakov ties his concept of language to that of Sophia; ibid., 217–25.

201. Ibid., 119.

202. Ibid., 127.

203. Ibid., 129–30.

Following Florenskii, Bulgakov locates the quintessence of the word in proper names, which of all linguistic forms most clearly demonstrate the essential link between a verbal sign and its referent. In this version of neo-realism the name represents the Platonic idea, the *eidos,* of its bearer. It is a force residing at the root of individual being, for whom the name has a fatal and determining character.[204] All persons named "Sergei," for example, are somehow destined to make manifest the entelechy of that name, to bring forth "Sergei-ness."[205] In this vision of things, if linguistic signification is not arbitrary, neither is selfhood random, and Bulgakov offers a caustic moral and ontological critique of the kinds of neologisms that proliferated in Soviet Russia and of pseudonyms like "Lenin" and "Trotsky," which he treats as denials of their bearer's true identity.[206]

According to the doctrine of Divine energies, the reason that human names function in this way is that they exist in the image and likeness of the Divine incarnation and name.[207] Human names and the act of naming exist *because* there is divine naming, so all language arises out of the nature of God, specifically out of the fact of incarnation. Just as the *Logos* comes into being as the primary outflowing of energy from the Godhead, of which Christ's incarnation is itself an instance, so do all predicates attributable to God denote his outflowing, self-manifesting "properties" (Bulgakov cites both Dionysius the Areopagite and the Seventh Ecumenical council, staples of the *imiaslavie* doctrine, in support of this argument).[208] As Zander puts it, the incarnation of the *Logos,* which precedes and anticipates the creation of the physical world, is the "speech" of the otherwise silent God the Father; this is the link between gnoseology, as a doctrine of the word and reason or knowledge, and triadology, the doctrine of the *Logos*-Son's issuance within the Godhead.[209]

Bulgakov's version of the *imiaslavie* doctrine is particularly rich in its adaptations of linguistic phenomena to the idea of incarnation. He opens *Filosofiia imeni* by invoking the Stoic concept of the word's phonetic element as its "body," the material shell for the immaterial idea it "contains," a physicality we know all the more certainly for its being realized through the vocal organs of our own body.[210] Throughout the treatise he speaks of the word in terms of its "core" and "wrappings" (*iadro* and *obolochka*) and offers the Neoplatonic explanation that as "ideal potentials" words possess

204. Ibid., 158.
205. Ibid., 159–60.
206. Ibid., 160, 174.
207. Ibid., 178.
208. Ibid., 194, 195, 200, 178, 180–81.
209. Zander, *Bog i mir,* vol.1, 446–47.
210. Bulgakov, *Filosofiia imeni,* 9.

an inherent capacity for incarnation and "fashion bodies for themselves" in speech.[211] At one point he makes the seemingly naive suggestion that letters are the "primordial elements" out of which language is thus fashioned—but his source for this idea turns out to be the Jewish mystical tradition of the Kabbalah, which regards every letter of Scripture as having an absolute, immutable meaning and as being infused with the spirit of God.[212] As we have seen, in the Russian tradition it was Potebnia who adapted Humboldt's concept of "inner speech form" to concrete and incarnational ends by speaking of the inner form of the *word*; Bulgakov in effect turns Potebnia into a doctrine of Orthodox ontologism by translating a theory of the word's referentiality and structure into one of metaphysics (recall Potebnia's notions of etymological meaning, selected in an originary denotative act from among the variety of the referent's possible attributes). What forms the "*sub-jectum*," he claims, that which underlies the word, is the *ousia* or noumenon contained within it, while that through which it is named is a predicate, phenomenon, the *ergon* in relation to the inner entity's *energeia* (the latter are of course Humboldt's terms).[213]

Completing the Orthodox philosophical circle, Bulgakov compares words with icons. For Orthodoxy icons are not based on a principle of verisimilitude but of incarnation in which the given, material form of the icon exists in a direct ontological relation to its referent—it is an emanation of its referent's being (here Bulgakov cites as his authority the Second Council of Nicaea of 787, which dealt with the question of iconoclasm). The name of God, Bulgakov declares, is a verbal icon of God, and the true icon of God is his name.[214] He even proposes a series of analogic correspondences between the elements of icon painting (on which Florenskii had dwelt with such intensity) and those of language: to the paint and board of the icon corresponds the phoneme; to the hieroglyphic nature of the iconic model, the morpheme; and to its holy essence, the word's semantic content or inner form.[215] Bulgakov also places the name "Jesus Christ" at the apex of all the names revealing God's nature, as God's "proper name," so that in his account language supersedes even the holy images accorded such veneration in Orthodox worship.[216] Yet he is careful to point out, in contradistinction to the literalist wing of the *imiaslavie* movement, that the specific

211. Ibid., 23, 27.

212. Ibid., 42. Bonestkaia points out, however, that Bulgakov was ultimately more skeptical about kabbalistic claims than was Florenskii; "O filologicheskoi shkole P. A. Florenskogo," 180.

213. Bulgakov, *Filosofiia imeni*, 69.

214. Ibid., 184.

215. Ibid., 191.

216. Ibid., 204.

phonic sequence "*Iisus*" ("Jesus") is just the material wrapping of the name and not yet the divine name itself.[217] In the wider context of the *imiaslavie* movement what stands out in his thought is precisely this insistence on the human quality of the speech that conveys us to divine essence. For Bulgakov the sacred manifests itself in the imperfect medium of human language, just as the boards and paint of an icon are earthly materials shaped by fallible human hands.

217. Ibid., 211–12.

Chapter Four

Through the Prism of Phenomenology

WHERE FLORENSKII AND BULGAKOV conspicuously sought to
fuse the philosophy of language with Eastern Orthodox theology—and in
so doing made explicit some of the subtexts latent in Potebnia—the two
most extensive efforts to define selfhood in the context of language in twentieth-century Russia unfolded under the aegis of phenomenology. Phenomenology entered the Russian context during the turbulent period of the
1910s, and, like Nietzscheanism and Freudianism, is one of those doctrines
of European modernism whose influence on Russia's intellectual culture
was considerable in the early twentieth century but only belatedly acknowledged, in the aftermath of the Soviet era that suppressed it (and phenomenology continues to attract some of the best Russian philosophical minds,
as can be seen in the revived journal *Logos*).

The most ardent of these Russian thinkers to write on language in a phenomenological context was the philosopher Gustav Shpet (1879–1938).
Shpet belongs, broadly speaking, to the same current of neo-idealism that
produced Florenskii and Bulgakov (though he was adamantly secular), and
his central intellectual endeavor—an attempt to provide a definition of selfhood grounded in the forms of consciousness, and to establish its ontological certitude in opposition to both materialism and neo-Kantian
relativism—has its origins in the fertile controversies surrounding the issues
of consciousness, metaphysics, the nature of the self, and the nature of language that characterized early twentieth-century Russia.[1]

In fact, as Alexander Haardt points out, the milieu within which Shpet
moved was characterized by two opposing tendencies, both inimical to
materialism but significantly different from one another in cultural orientation. One looked almost exclusively toward contemporary European
thought and sought a return via neo-Kantianism to the Kantian critique
of knowledge.[2] Shpet often took neo-Kantianism to task for leading

---

1. Gidini, "Slovo i real'nost'," 52.
2. Alexander Haardt, *Husserl in Russland. Phänomenologie der Sprache und Kunst bei Gustav
Špet und Aleksej Losev* (Munich: Wilhelm Fink Verlag, 1992), 28.

philosophy down the path of illusionism and relativism, but he paid keen attention to developments in contemporary European philosophy, and neo-Kantianism in particular exerted an important (if reactive) influence on his thought. The other idealist tendency was characterized by efforts to revive pre-Kantian metaphysics, especially those of Plato, Aristotle, and Neoplatonism (which for many thinkers meant a revived union of Platonism and Christianity). Its center of gravity lay in the "Russian religious renaissance," some of whose key members (among them Sergei Bulgakov and Pavel Florenskii) were to become intellectual opponents of Soviet Marxism in its early phases. Shpet tended to distance himself from the religious leanings of the movement, identifying himself as "an advocate of philosophy as knowledge, not as morality," but at times his thought clearly reflects some of the movement's philosophical predilections, including its interest in Neoplatonism.[3]

The dividing line between these two subcurrents of Russian idealism (secular-epistemological and religious-metaphysical) ran through both of the country's capitals and their institutions. Thus at Moscow University S. N. Trubetskoi was prominent in the turn-of-the-century "metaphysical renaissance," while G. I. Chelpanov promoted neo-Kantianism; meanwhile in St. Petersburg metaphysics had its representative in the intuitivist N. O. Losskii, while neo-Kantianism found a parallel figure in A. I. Vvedenskii.[4] Or, to approach the issue through the more detailed prism of early influences on Shpet, one could consider Lev Mikhailovich Lopatin (1855–1910), who directed the Moscow Psychological Society from 1899 until its cessation following the Bolshevik Revolution of 1917, and who edited the journal *Voprosy filosofii i psikhologii,* in which Shpet published some of his early works.[5] A close friend of Vladimir Solov'ev, Lopatin criticized materialism and positivism from the standpoint of a peculiar metaphysical doctrine he had adapted from Christian Platonism and Leibnizian monadology.[6] Particularly influential on Shpet's thought were his reflections on the relation between the self and empirical reality: for Lopatin, the manifestations of psychological life change continuously, and, like everything else that takes place within time, "ceaselessly disappear"; but the "I" that experiences these psychological states remains identical to itself because it is a supratemporal substance—without which substance reality would dissipate into a myriad of disjoint worlds.[7]

3. Shpet is quoted in ibid., 52.
4. Ibid., 28 n. 37.
5. Gidini, "Slovo i real'nost'," 54.
6. Il'ichev, *Filosofskii entsiklopedicheskii slovar',* s.v. "Lopatin, Lev Mikhailovich."
7. Alekseev, *Filosofy Rossii XIX–XX stoletii,* 110–11.

An even more important early influence on Shpet, however—indeed, his mentor—was the philosopher and psychologist Georgii Ivanovich Chelpanov (1862–1936), who headed the department of philosophy at Moscow University from 1907 to 1923, and who in 1912 founded that institution's Psychological Institute, which he directed until his retirement in 1923 (and where Shpet worked from 1907 to 1912; Chelpanov also published in *Voprosy filosofii i psikhologii*).[8] Shpet attended Chelpanov's seminars in the philosophy department at the University of St. Vladimir in Kiev (whose faculty also included Evgenii Trubetskoi, later active in the Psychological Society of Moscow University and the "Solov'ev Religio-Philosophical Society," and Sergei Bulgakov) and then in Moscow, after Chelpanov transferred there in 1907. A student of the German philosopher and psychologist Wilhelm Wundt, Chelpanov was less interested in metaphysics than in the epistemological aspects of psychology, and he introduced into the Russian intellectual milieu such European figures as Wundt, Windelband, Sigwart, Steinthal, and Lazarus.[9] Moreover, it was Chelpanov who rediscovered the works of Potebnia and brought them to the wider attention of Russian intellectuals, and it was he who introduced Jakobson to "Husserl's psychology."[10]

Shpet belonged to the Moscow branch of this renascent Russian idealism and was conditioned by its stronger tendency toward anti-psychologism and anti-neo-Kantianism than that found in St. Petersburg, as well as by the attraction to Neoplatonism among philosophers at Moscow University.[11] For Shpet, Losev, and other Moscow intellectuals, anti-psychologism meant the conviction that the essence of selfhood could not be defined in terms of subjectively experienced or empirically observed states of mind; what they were after instead was an ontology of the self and its awareness.[12] It was this sense of anti-psychologism, in fact, that led to what was undoubtedly the most significant influence on Shpet's intellectual development: the "intense"

8. S. M. Polovinkin, "P. A. Florenskii: Logos protiv khaosa," *Filosofiia* 2 (1989): 3; Gidini, "Slovo i real'nost'," 54.

9. Joravsky, *Russian Psychology*, 107; Gidini, "Slovo i real'nost'," 54; Polovinkin, "P. A. Florenskii," 4. On the role played by psychology in general, and Wundt in particular, in the liberalization of philosophy and redefinition of selfhood in the years following the Great Reforms in Russia, see Joravsky, *Russian Psychology*, 92–95.

10. Jindřich Toman, *The Magic of a Common Language. Jakobson, Trubetzkoy, and the Prague Linguistic Circle* (Cambridge: MIT Press, 1995), 29.

11. Alexander Haardt, "*Appearance and Sense* and Phenomenology in Russia," in Gustav Shpet, *Appearance and Sense: Phenomenology as the Fundamental Science and Its Problems,* trans. Thomas Nemeth, Phaenomenologica 120 (Dordrecht: Kluwer Academic, 1991), xii.

12. Florovskii describes the philosophical activity of Vladimir Ern (1879–1917) as centering on the struggle against psychologism, in favor of ontologism, the latter represented in particular by the Platonists, Gregory of Nissius, and Dionysius the Areopagite; *Puti russkogo bogosloviia*, 489.

Moscow Husserlianism of the 1910s.[13] Echoes of Husserl's thought are detectable in the Russian milieu as early as 1906, in N. O. Losskii's *Grundlegung des Intuitivismus* (Foundations of intuitivism) and were disseminated from 1908 onward by Boris Iakovenko, "the most active propagator of Husserl's phenomenology in pre-1917 Russia," in the pages of *Voprosy filosofii i psikhologii* as part of a critique of Rickert's neo-Kantianism, then in the pages of the Russian edition of *Logos*.[14] Husserl's "Die Philosophie als strenge Wissenschaft" (Philosophy as a rigorous science) appeared in Russia in 1911, the same year in which it was published in Germany. A proseminar at Moscow University in 1914–15 on the problems of modern theoretical philosophy also examined Husserl's *Logische Untersuchungen* (*Logical Investigations*) and the first volume of his *Ideen zu einer reinen Phänomenologie und phänomenologischen Philosophie* (*Ideas Pertaining to a Pure Phenomenology and to a Phenomenological Philosophy*), both key influences on Shpet.[15] Husserl was also important specifically as an anti-psychologist to the Moscow linguists—Jakobson is another thinker profoundly affected by him—who had begun to regard the associationist psychology of Baudouin de Courtenay with skepticism and who found in Husserl sanction for rejecting psychology as a tool of explanation in the study of language.[16] Shpet himself spent 1912–13 studying with Husserl in Göttingen, and Husserl considered him one of his best disciples.[17]

One of the striking aspects of this idealist milieu in early-twentieth-century Russian thought is its syncretism and the hybrid forms of thought that it produced. Thus, the meeting of ancient metaphysics and neo-Kantianism translated into attempts at reconciling questions of "true being" ("*istinno sushchee*," a concept with theological overtones in the Russian context) with a modern critique of knowledge (*Erkenntniskritik*).[18] In this atmosphere Husserl could be transformed into a quasi-religious doctrine (imported into this scene, he was interpreted in light of the Metaphysical Renaissance's Platonic leanings as an ontologist rather than a theoretician of transcendental

13. Toman, *Magic of a Common Language*, 30.

14. Ibid., 33; Boris Jakowenko, "Ed. Husserl und die russische Philosophie," *Die russische Gedanke* 1929/30: 210–13.

15. Haardt, *Husserl in Russland*, 23.

16. Haardt, "*Appearance and Sense* and Phenomenology in Russia," xxi; Toman, *Magic of a Common Language*, 28. Jakobson seems to have adopted Husserl's logic of parts and wholes from the *Logical Investigations*; see Toman, *Magic of a Common Language*, 32. Regarding Husserl's influence on Jakobson see Elmar Holenstein, "Jakobson und Husserl," in Herman Parret, ed., *History of Linguistic Thought and Contemporary Linguistics* (Berlin: Walter de Gruyter, 1976), 772–810; and his "Jakobson's Contribution to Phenomenology," 145–62; also Stephen Rudy, "Jakobsonian Poetics of the Moscow and Prague Periods" (Ph.D. diss., Yale University, 1978).

17. Polovinkin, "P. A. Florenskii," 3; see also Ed. Gusserl, "Pis'ma E. Gusserla k Shpetu," *Logos* 1 (1992) 3: 233–42.

18. Haardt, *Husserl in Russland*, 28.

subjectivity), and even the works of Rickert and Cohen could be read as if they were ascetic treatises.[19] What Shpet offers as his contribution to these debates, as his own antidote to the bad choice between materialism and subjectivism, is an ontology of reason as something resident in and manifested through language and language-like phenomena. He writes as an academic philosopher and custodian of the discipline of philosophy who at first glance adheres almost slavishly to a Husserlian phenomenological framework; but he turns out on closer reading to emphasize certain elements of Husserl's thought over others in order to establish an *ontology* of consciousness as the embodiment of reason and cosmic unity.[20] In other words, he embraces Husserl as much as an antidote to the skepticism and fragmentation that he believed afflicted contemporary philosophy as for phenomenological doctrine per se. For Shpet, phenomenology represented a "living, concrete, and total philosophy, based on the evident givenness of inner experience," a view influenced less by Husserl's German context than by such Russian figures as Solov'ev, Iurkevich, Lopatin, and S. Trubetskoi and redolent of the Russian "philosophy of all-unity."[21] Another distinctly Russian moment in Shpet's thought may be seen in the way he insists, to a degree that suggests he is warding off an insidious awareness of it as chaos and disorder, on the inherently rational nature of the cosmos (and of consciousness, the human response to it): most of Shpet's writing was completed in the time of the revolution and its immediate aftermath.

Despite the fact that his published remarks on Potebnia range from the neglectful to the dismissive, in many ways Shpet can be viewed as one of the most conscious successors to Potebnia's work on the philosophy of language in Russia. Following Humboldt, Potebnia had insisted on the organic link between language and thought, the important consequence of which was to absorb language within the sphere of subjectivity. In his theory of the tripartite form of the word he then posited a structure that at once characterized language and the self, and in so doing he combined a complex series of influences from German linguistics to Orthodox doctrines of Christology, Trinitology, and icons. Like Potebnia, Shpet elaborates a concept of the inner structure of language as the context within which to examine issues directly implicating the self (such as consciousness and being), and like

19. Ibid., 63; Florovskii, *Puti russkogo bogosloviia,* 484–85.

20. Haardt, *"Appearance and Sense* and Phenomenology in Russia," 25.

21. Ibid., xxiii. On the philosophy of "all-unity," see V. N. Akulinin, *Filosofiia vseedinstva. Ot V. S. Solov'eva k P. A. Florenskomu* (Novosibirsk: Nauka, 1990).

Potebnia's his model of language can ultimately be read as a metaphorical version of a self.

What intervenes, vigorously, between these two otherwise related Russian explorations of language and selfhood is the Husserlian phenomenology to which Shpet had been exposed in the 1910s (though this intervention was in a sense not arbitrary, since Humboldt, the principal philosophical influence on Potebnia, was a significant source of ideas for Husserl as well). Because the works of Shpet and Losev remain opaque if read outside the context of phenomenology, some overview of Husserl's key concepts is called for here. I concentrate on the *Logical Investigations* of 1900, and the first volume of *Ideas Pertaining to a Pure Phenomenology and to a Phenomenological Philosophy*, because these were the most influential works in Russia and for Shpet in particular.[22]

Husserlian phenomenology proposed to study spirit rationally and scientifically by producing a philosophical account of the essence (or essences) underlying, or transcending, or not held hostage to, the constituents of reality immediately surrounding us.[23] What phenomenology did in the event was to discuss at great length the methodology through which this account might be produced and to advance claims about what the nature of that essence must be (though Husserl felt that such discussion was not propaedeutic to philosophy, it was philosophy);[24] but even in its incompleteness it held enormous attraction for Russian thinkers like Shpet and Aleksei Losev, who sought to resist the claims of *both* materialism (which denied the autonomy of spirit and thought) *and* radical subjectivism (which turned the knowable world into an illusion). In phenomenology this apperception of essence would be arrived at via the celebrated operation of "*epoché*" or bracketing: phenomenological analysis strives to set aside all elements of the empirical, factual, natural world so that the mind can "seize on essence originarily."[25] In Husserl's slogan, phenomenology was to be a "presupposition-less philosophy." Husserl did not deny the existence or knowability of the empirical realm, but he countered the assumption that only the physical could be real or have explanatory power (an attitude he termed "naturalism") by rejecting the empirical as the source of any kind of authentic

22. I have used the following English translations: Edmund Husserl, *Logical Investigations,* 2 vols., trans. J. N. Findlay (New York: Humanities Press, 1970); and Edmund Husserl, *Ideas Pertaining to a Pure Phenomenology and to a Phenomenological Philosophy: First Book,* trans. F. Kersten (The Hague: Martinus Nijhoff, 1983).

23. See Quentin Lauer's characterization of phenomenology in his "Introduction" in Edmund Husserl, *Phenomenology and the Crisis of Philosophy,* trans. Quentin Lauer (New York: Harper and Row, 1965), 16.

24. Ibid., 44.

25. Husserl, *Logical Investigations,* 832, 862; and Husserl, *Ideas,* xxii, 60.

insight into essences (his division of the cosmos into realms of existence versus essence echoing Plato's becoming versus being). "We do not give up the positing [of the natural order] we effected, but we 'put it out of action,' 'exclude it,' 'parenthesize it.' . . . No proposition about actualities of this world is accepted until parentheses have been put around it."[26] In this sense phenomenology actually privileges the "irreal" over the (merely) "real."[27] "Pure eidetic truths contain not the slightest assertions about facts," he states in *Ideas,* using the Platonic term *eidos* or underlying form, while in the *Logical Investigations* he goes so far as to declare that "Nature with all its physical laws is a fact that could well have been otherwise."[28]

It is of defining importance to Husserl's philosophy that this "seizing on originary essence" takes place within consciousness. Husserl believed that Descartes's *Meditations* had revealed the possibility of seeking a rational science of being by turning from consideration of the objective world to a reflective consideration of the thinking subject, and it is in this Kantian sense that phenomenology is "transcendental": it attends to our experiencing of the object, rather than to the object or *noumenon* directly.[29] The natural attitude is suspended for the sake of examining not some ideal realm separate from the observer but essences as they are given to us—as they appear to us, hence "phenomenology"—within our minds. "[I]f knowledge theory will nevertheless investigate the problems of the relationship between consciousness and being," Husserl wrote in an early, programmatic statement, "it can have before its eyes only being as the correlate of consciousness, as something 'intended' after the manner of consciousness: as perceived, remembered, expected, represented pictorially, imagined, identified, believed, opined, evaluated, etc."[30]

Husserl's important precursor in this regard is Franz Brentano, who had argued in his 1874 *Psychologie vom empirischen Standpunkt* that it is the nature of mental acts or experiences to be about something, directed toward something, in this sense to contain an intended object.[31] What nonetheless rescues phenomenology from Kantian agnosticism is Husserl's conviction that the essence of things—what they are, if not they in themselves—is

26. Husserl, *Ideas,* 59, 62.

27. Ibid., xxi; Husserl, *Logical Investigations,* 185.

28. Husserl, *Ideas,* 11; Husserl, *Logical Investigations,* 486.

29. Lauer, "Introduction," 20; Marvin Farber, *The Aims of Phenomenology* (New York: Harper and Row, 1966), 15.

30. Husserl, "Philosophy as a Rigorous Science," in his *Phenomenology and the Crisis of Philosophy,* 89.

31. Robert Audi, ed., *The Cambridge Dictionary of Philosophy* (Cambridge: Cambridge University Press, 1995), s.v. "Brentano, Franz." As Husserl puts it in *Ideas,* "It belongs to the essence of every actional cogito to be consciousness of something" (73).

adequately given in consciousness.[32] The world is transcendent in relation
to consciousness, but every transcendent being is uniquely "constituted" in
the life of consciousness. Consciousness for Husserl carries within itself not
only the unity of meaning constituting the world, but also the world as
really existing.[33] Thus already within consciousness we have apodictic
evidence of essence and need look no further; it is in this sense that phenomenology deals in "ideal immanence."[34] The consciousness that is examined in this fashion, however, must be "pure" or eidetic consciousness,
because phenomenology rejects psychology and subjectivism along with the
natural attitude. Phenomenology is not about the mental experiences I
might at some moment be having but about what remains—the phenomenological *residuum*—after all such purely subjective factors, together with
considerations of the natural world, have been eliminated in a series of pro-
gressively refined bracketings.[35] Husserl also describes the moment in
which such essence is arrived at as one of "eidetic seeing" (*Wesenschau*) or
"immediate seeing," a moment of intuition achieved through an act of
mental focus, a direction of the mental gaze (*geistigen Blickes*) toward the
object as such as it appears in consciousness. Phenomenology thus works
toward a purely immanent, purely descriptive examination into the contents of consciousness.[36]

From this account of consciousness there follows an inference that was
important for Husserl but absolutely vital for the Russians influenced by
him, indeed the whole point of their borrowing from him, especially as they
increasingly had to defend their views against materialism: namely, that
these eidetic elements of consciousness *exist* and are objects in their own
right. "Consciousness has in itself a being of its own which in its own absolute essence is not touched by the phenomenological exclusion," Husserl
states in *Ideas*.[37] The essence (*Eidos*) that resides there is a new sort of
object, and by concentrating on it phenomenology has opened up a new
region of *being* never before delineated in its peculiarity, that of the world
as *Eidos*.[38] Indeed, for Husserl only the phenomenal—the "irreal" rather
than the "real"—is given absolutely, because in it no contingency or facts
play a role.[39] As examples of "ideal affairs" that nonetheless "are 'objects,' "

32. Lauer, "Introduction," 21.
33. Farber, *Aims of Phenomenology,* 55–56.
34. Husserl, *Logical Investigations,* 99.
35. Ibid., 858. It is hard to overlook the certain affinity in Husserl for the apophatic thought
embraced by Orthodoxy: essence is arrived at via a series not of positings but of negations. See
also echoes of this idea in Husserl, *Ideas,* 258, and Husserl, *Logical Investigations,* 523.
36. Husserl, *Ideas,* 8, 36, 71; Husserl, *Logical Investigations,* 862.
37. Husserl, *Ideas,* 65.
38. Ibid., 9, 63.
39. Lauer, "Introduction," 26.

Husserl offers "the tone-quality *c,* which is a numerically unique member of the tonal scale, the number two, in the series of cardinal numbers, the figure in the ideal world of geometrical constructs, and any propositions in the 'world' of propositions."[40] He insists that this conception of the nature of "realities" does not turn the world into a subjective illusion or commit one to "Berkeleyan idealism."[41] Apodictic evidence for essence may be provided in mental acts of advertence to the object, but this does not mean that such essence arises solely out of those acts. Locke had mistakenly assumed that "the species" (that which can be generalized from individual sense perceptions) exists only in thought and has no known authentic existence in the world—and the "modern nominalism" of certain of Husserl's contemporaries is but an exaggerated reaction to this Lockean doctrine.[42] But Locke forgets, rejoins Husserl, that "mental existence is also real existence."[43] At the same time, however, Husserl rejected the "hypostatization" of essences in Platonic realism—the doctrine from which his metaphysics ultimately descends—because it would ascribe to essences "actual (veritable) being" and erroneously suggest that the species exists externally to thought.[44]

Moreover, and this is another moment important to his Russian followers, for Husserl the apodictic knowledge available to consciousness is not of randomness or irrationality, but of *Eidos,* the abstract forms that lend order to existence. What one perceives in the phenomenon is not just some mental entity, however authentic its existence, but more particularly the "noematic" moment that endows it with meaning or sense. In this vein Husserl speaks of the "synthetic unity" which is not an invention of science but is "present in things," and of laws of "pure logic," which are *a priori* and justified by inner evidence.[45] In Husserl's interpretation of Brentano's "intentionality" it is the essence of every intentive mental process to include in itself something such as a sense.[46] To have sense or to "intend to" something (*etwas im Sinne zu haben*) is the fundamental characteristic of all consciousness, which, therefore, is not just any mental living (*Erlebnis*) whatever, but

---

40. Husserl, *Ideas,* 41. Husserl at one point calls phenomenology the "geometry" of mental processes, and Lauer remarks that "as a mathematician turned philosopher, Husserl was aware of the constitutive function exercised by the mind in regard to the mathematical 'essences,' " which are "not found in or abstracted from the world of things, and yet they are infallibly 'given' "; Lauer, "Introduction," 48. Mathematics was an important point of departure for Losev's thought, too.

41. *Ideas,* 129.

42. Husserl, *Logical Investigations,* 350, 368.

43. Ibid., 359.

44. Husserl, *Ideas,* 40; Husserl, *Logical Investigations,* 350.

45. Husserl, *Logical Investigations,* 62, 99.

46. Husserl, *Ideas,* 213.

rather one having sense, which is "noetic." It is this sense that is "separated by an abyss from all of Nature and physics and no less from all psychology."[47] As Husserl puts it in a particularly elegant example, a tree *simpliciter* can be burned up, but the sense of our perception of it cannot.[48] To arrive at the apperception of essence through phenomenological analysis is thus to hold in one's gaze the principle of reason at the core of being. Or, as Lauer suggests, in order that philosophy, as the "science of being," be rigorous, Husserl would make reason the very source of being itself.[49]

To many of Husserl's contemporaries, this doctrine appeared a throw-back to Scholasticism, from which tradition Husserl had indeed derived the terms he used for the complex structures and levels of consciousness.[50] However accurate a genealogy this charge represented in Husserl's case, for Russians like Shpet and in particular Losev, the gesture of reaching back to pre-Renaissance modes of thought about the world was a deeply sympathetic one. Indeed, it is not irrelevant to an understanding of Russian phenomenology that the Aristotelian concept of *substantia* taken over by the Scholastic philosophers—permanent, underlying reality as contrasted with its changing and perceptible accidents—had played a significant role since the Scholastics in theories of consciousness, language (the debate between realists and nominalists), and such theological issues as the nature of the Trinity and of Christ's inherence in the eucharist.[51]

The starting point for any consideration of Shpet's thought is his reception of this Husserlian phenomenology. Much of *Appearance and Sense* (*Iavlenie i smysl* [1914])—first fruit of the time Shpet spent with Husserl in Göttingen in 1912–13, and the beginning of productive extensions of Husserlian thought in Russia—is devoted to reiterating Husserl's explication in *Ideas* of phenomenology as a science of essences knowable via intuition.[52] Following Husserl, Shpet proposes that philosophy turn its attention away from the empirical realm of "being in the world" and direct it instead toward the eidetic realm of "being in an idea."[53] These are perfectly orthodox Husserlian statements, indeed, virtual translations, but the context in which Shpet frames them betrays characteristic Russian

47. Ibid., 216–17.
48. Ibid.
49. Lauer, "Introduction," 52.
50. Ibid., 24; Il'ichev, *Filosofskii entsiklopedicheskii slovar'*, s.v. "fenomenologiia."
51. Cross and Livingstone, *Oxford Dictionary of the Christian Church*, s.v. "Scholasticism," "substance."
52. Haardt, *Husserl in Russland*, 68.
53. Gustav Shpet, *Iavlenie i smysl. Fenomenologiia kak osnovnaia nauka i ee problemy* (Tomsk: Vodolei, 1996), 25.

concerns.[54] He offers phenomenology specifically as an antidote to what he terms "negative" philosophy, which denies the world's unity and fails in one way or another to address "the foundations of everything existing."[55] Among its representatives are the psychologists, with their interest in theories of knowledge rather than essence, and Kant, Hume, and Jacobi, whose writings Shpet considers little more than forms of skepticism.[56] But according to Shpet "positive" philosophy, too, has paid insufficient attention to the *being* of the cognizing subject and "the being of cognition in its essence"—concerns that, incidentally, Heidegger was to make central to his 1927 *Being and Time.*[57] Shpet is also subtly but tendentiously selective in what he emphasizes in Husserl's thought. For Husserl, ontological issues, important as they were, stood in the shadow of a critique of knowledge (*Erkenntniskritik*); but Shpet, influenced by the Russian "metaphysical renaissance," tends to interpret Husserl in the context of Platonism and to see in transcendental phenomenology primarily an ontology of the life of consciousness.[58]

The remedy Shpet prescribes for the shortcomings of contemporary philosophy closely follows the methodology Husserl had outlined for his "presuppositionless" science of essence: philosophers must take the "natural" attitude toward the world out of action, so that what remains is "the entire 'world as eidos.' "[59] Skepticism, of the kind espoused by the likes of Hume, arises out of concentration on the "accidental" factors of the object's appearances to us, while phenomenology proposes to deal with the non-accidental and necessary components of its essence, which the object retains throughout changing contexts and which enables us to recognize it as the same object "in spite of all the changes of the intentive mental processes and in spite of the fluctuation of the attentional acts of the pure Ego."[60]

---

54. A. E. Savin points out that Shpet's professed desire in *Iavlenie i smysl* merely to acquaint the reader with Husserl's thought is disingenuous, as Russian translations of Husserl's works already existed. Shpet's purpose, rather, was subtle revision and redirection; in "Interpretatsiia i kritika G. G. Shpetom filosofii Ed. Gusserlia," *G. G. Shpet/Comprehensio. Vtorye shpetovskie chteniia* (Tomsk: Vodolei, 1997), 24.

55. Shpet, *Iavlenie i smysl,* 22.

56. Ibid., 149.

57. Ibid., 24, 108.

58. Haardt, *Husserl in Russland,* 90, 63, 33. Haardt comments that Russian thinkers were correct in seeing Husserl as a Platonist insofar as they regarded his thought as a reconciliation of Platonic ontology with the contemporary principle of subjectivity (33). He also notes the possible "ontologizing" influence of the Göttingen circle of Husserl's followers on Shpet (92), and points out that one of Husserl's most ardent Russian disciples, Boris Iakovenko, pointedly did not read him in the light of Platonism. For a similar observation see Savin, "Interpretatsiia i kritika," 26–27.

59. Shpet, *Iavlenie i smysl,* 41.

60. Ibid., 58–59, 122.

"Physical things" are given to us only empirically, through "adumbrations in appearances," whereas immanent being is apprehended as an absolute.[61] As in Husserl, this absolute is apprehended by the inner eye. Phenomenology attains its aim, Shpet asserts, not through any mechanical process of abstraction but through an "advertence of vision."[62] The philosophical gaze or "regard" refuses to stop with the "experientially given" but penetrates through to essence.[63] Eidetic intuition is fulfilled when "the contemplated *itself* stands before us as "*ob*-ject," when it gives itself to us in its originary givenness (as we have seen, Florenskii was to use this same etymological play in his "Stroenie slova" of 1922).[64]

Shpet's paraphrase of these concepts seems almost slavish, but his agenda was subtly different from Husserl's, and one of the most significant ways in which it differed has to do with the relatively greater attention he devotes to the question of consciousness (an emphasis characteristic of the Russian context as a whole). Even a simple recitation of Husserlian concepts on this point, however, would have led Shpet into complicated terrain, whose ambiguities would be especially vexing for someone seeking to establish an ontology of selfhood that is neither materialist nor subjective-illusionist. In Husserl's case ambiguity arises when, in the course of his critique of neo-Kantian epistemology, he seeks to define the role the Cartesian ego plays in phenomenology (or, as it could be rephrased in the context of the present study, the status of the self in an eidetic account of the world). The claim Husserl offers against neo-Kantianism, that the world is adequately given in consciousness, is not free of problems because the proposition that phenomenology should apprehend pure essence is complicated by a Brentanian insistence on this essence being apprehended within the consciousness of a perceiving "I"—and it is ultimately from Brentano's doctrine of intentionality that the lengthy discussions in Husserl of "directed" and "attending" consciousness, "mental regard," and so forth, derive, as well as a certain tension in phenomenological thought in general between discussions of consciousness and discussions of the "world as eidos." Husserl asserts that the ego left over after the act of bracketing is not the natural, "psychological" self but the pure "I" (*rein Ich*); but its first-person presence is nonetheless ineradicable from the phenomenological residue. When the world has been "annihilated" through phenomenological reduction, what is left is "absolute consciousness," and even though "I, the human being" am excluded in the reduction, the "pure" subject remains in the act of reflection as a "ray"

61. Ibid., 44.
62. Ibid., 26.
63. Ibid., 28.
64. Ibid., 88.

emanating from the ego.[65] The lingering presence of this entity seems to compel Husserl to perform vaguely specious acts of doubling. Thus, next to the "empirical I" or "psychological ego," which is the immediate experiencer of perceptions, moods, and states of mind, Husserl posits the "pure I" or "transcendental ego," which is the owner or agent behind acts of eidetic seeing. A part of the world and inseparable from individuals, this agent is also supposed to represent a cognitive center that possesses or intends, and to that extent transcends, the world. In similar manner he posits the noematic domain, in which dwell essences as such, but parallel to it also the noetic, in which their corresponding representations appear to consciousness.[66] Something of the same tensions may be seen in the development of the phenomenological movement as a whole, when philosophers who had welcomed the analyses of the *Logical Investigations* balked at the "transcendental turn" and seemingly greater emphasis on subjectivity in *Ideas.*

At the early stage represented by *Iavlenie i smysl* Shpet adheres closely to the Husserlian position on the role of *ego cogito.* He asserts that "the Ego is present in all acts of consciousness as a manifestation of 'mental regard,' " cites Husserl's remarks in *Ideas* to the effect that when everything empirical has been bracketed, "pure consciousness" alone remains as the "phenomenological residuum," and reproduces the Brentanian insight that the essential trait of consciousness is to be intentional, in the sense of being consciousness of something, directed to something.[67] He even states that the sphere of investigation for phenomenology is pure consciousness alone, pure mental processes, albeit examined eidetically rather than psychologically.[68]

In a series of works written after *Iavlenie i smysl,* however, Shpet began to outline a dissenting theory of the collective nature of consciousness in which he undertakes to rescue such entities as consciousness and sense from the isolated sphere of individual subjectivity.[69] His 1916 essay "Soznanie i

---

65. Husserl, *Ideas*, 109, 190–91.

66. Blackburn, *Oxford Dictionary of Philosophy*, s.v. "noema," notes the confusion arising from these terms in Husserl.

67. Shpet, *Iavlenie i smysl*, 121, 41–42.

68. Ibid., 67.

69. Shpet's key works on the collective nature of consciousness indicate yet again the intellectual milieu in which his thought on these issues arose: "Soznanie i ego sobstvennik" (1916) first came out in a separate edition, but then was published in a *Festschrift* for Georgii Chelpanov organized by students of his Kiev and Moscow seminars of 1891 to 1916; Shpet, *Filosofskie etiudy* (Moscow: Progres, 1994), 338. "Vvedenie v etnicheskuiu psikhologiiu" appeared in *Psikhologicheskoe obozrenie* in 1919, then was expanded as a result of Shpet's involvement in 1920–21 in the Moscow Linguistic Society; Shpet, *Sochineniia*, prilozhenie k zhurnalu *Voprosy filosofii* (Moscow: Pravda, 1989), 475. Shpet also relies on S. N. Trubetskoi's "O prirode chelovecheskogo soznaniia" (1889–91) and in "Soznanie i ego sobstvennik" approvingly cites Plotinus; in his *Filosofskie etiudy* (Moscow: Progress, 1994), 41.

ego sobstvennik" (Consciousness and its proprietor) examines the shortcomings he perceives in the theories of consciousness offered by contemporary philosophy. First among these, of course, is the radical subjectivism of
the neo-Kantians, for whom the world is but a hypothesis of one's conscious
mind (Natorp is cited heavily in this section). Following S. N. Trubetskoi,
Shpet traces subjectivism's current dominance to the spread of "Protestant
philosophy" in European thought, and he commends Trubetskoi for pointing out the existence in antiquity and the Middle Ages of very different,
non-individualistic understandings of consciousness.[70] Shpet counters this
tendency by inquiring into the "eidetic" rather than subjective elements in
the "I" of consciousness. He admits that this represents a paradox, since the
"I" is something individual while the eidetic must be general; but he points
out that Plotinus had already spoken of "the idea [in the eidetic sense] of
the singular" and proceeds to a critique of something he had recently en-
dorsed: Husserl's concept of the transcendental ego, which he treats as a
false solution to the problem of consciousness.[71]

Shpet's charge now is that Husserl's concept is inconsistent. If Husserl
were faithfully to carry out the phenomenological reduction, Shpet argues,
he would be left with "I" as an ownerless object, not a subject; when he instead places the "I" at the center of consciousness (as he does, for example,
by defining the transcendental ego as the "subject of 'pure' experience of the
type 'cogito,' " or the "I" as "that which is identical in various acts of cogi-
tatio") he is simply yielding to the insidious temptations of subjectivism.[72]
To correct this misstep Shpet pursues one of Husserl's assertions down a different path. Husserl says that "I" as a form of transcendence must be
thought of as a "thing among other things." This is true, Shpet replies, but
only to the extent that the "things" we are talking about are social in nature—that is, are not natural objects but what we would now call social
constructs.[73] Our "I," Shpet asserts, is just such a "concrete social thing,"
constituted not only by the internal principle of unity of thoughts, perceptions, and so on that it manifests (and which Husserl is fond of mention-
ing) but equally by the social context that surrounds and determines it.[74]
Moreover, the form it takes is not just an aggregate "*obshchee*," something
statistically common among members of a group, but "*obshchnoe*," the
product of collective activity.[75] It is the "property" not of any individual but
of the socio-cultural community, the nation, as a whole. This is Shpet's

70. Shpet, "Soznanie i ego sobstvennik," in *Filosofskie etiudy*, 79, 86.
71. Ibid., 28, 41.
72. Ibid., 87–89.
73. Ibid., 90–91.
74. Ibid., 111.
75. Ibid., 115.

adaptation of the idea of "collective" or "communal" (*sobornoe*) consciousness presented in S. N. Trubetskoi's "O prirode chelovecheskogo soznaniia"
(On the nature of human consciousness [1889–91]), which had asserted the
existence of a sensitive cosmos and within it a "universal consciousness"
("*vselenskoe soznanie*," the Russian term carrying ecclesiastical overtones) ultimately embodied, for Trubetskoi, in the Church and united in love.[76] The
argument also turns in part on language: Shpet suggests that whenever we
use specific terms to denote objects we operate within a socially conditioned
reality, so that when we use phrases like "*my* native land" or "*my* moral consciousness" we point not to ourselves as proprietors of these things but to
the communal consciousness in which they have their genuine existence.[77]

The ontological events that establish "eidetic" consciousness, therefore,
originate outside any single conscious self. Shpet was to apply these arguments to cultural phenomena a decade later in "Vvedenie v etnicheskuiu
psikhologiiu" (Introduction to the psychology of ethnos [1926]), his extensive review of the field that had emerged from the thought of Herder and
Humboldt, then matured in the *Völkerpsychologie* of Steinthal and Lazarus
into studies of the forms of subjectivity expressed within national cultures
(in the early 1920s Shpet had organized the ethnic psychology section at
Moscow University).[78] In Shpet's account, ethnic psychology faces a crisis.
Its current notions threaten, like Husserl's transcendent ego, to collapse into
mere objectivity (by dealing with such cultural forms as myths, religions,
literature as mere artifacts, Humboldtian *ergoi* rather than as manifestations
of creative activity) or else to offer only weak analogies from individual psychology, complete with Herbartian retentions, mergings, apperceptions,
and so forth.[79] What a philosophically alert version of the field should instead recognize is that the reality with which it deals is "the collective," and
in examining the multifarious forms of cultural expression it should examine specifically their "collective nature," which consists in the structured
forms of meaning they contain.[80] In other words, the ontology of the
meanings we find in "words, drawings, buildings, fashion [*kostium*]" (n.b.,
this well in advance of Barthes), and so forth is *intrinsically* collective, so
that "the concrete form of individual mental [*dushevnoi*] life is unthinkable

76. Sergei Bulgakov in his *Filosofiia khoziaistva* of 1912 had also argued that the "transcendental subject of knowledge" must be "supraindividual" (see Evtuhov, *Cross and the Sickle*, 162).

77. Shpet, "Soznanie i ego sobstvennik," in his *Sochineniia*, prilozhenie k zhurnalu *Voprosy
filosofii* 90, 110.

78. Shpet, "Vvedenie v etnicheskuiu psikhologiiu," in his *Sochineniia*, prilozhenie k zhurnalu
Voprosy filosofii (Moscow: Pravda, 1989), 475.

79. Ibid., 487.

80. Ibid., 479, 563. At one point he declares that the basis for such a science of "expressed
meanings" might be found in Anton Marty's "universal semasiology" (527).

except in social form."[81] Shpet dismisses the German linguist Hermann Paul's assertion that the content of our concepts cannot really be transferred from one individual to another as deriving from a typically "proprietary" theory of consciousness, countering that "the *content* of mental representations . . . cannot be transferred from one individual to another . . . because it is not located in any individual—it is not "mine," not "his," it is no one's, it is *transcendent*."[82] The subjective experiences of individuals are quite real, but they are "predetermined by the entire mass of apperceptions of the species, both contemporary and past," which is to say that they are mere empirical, expressed versions of the eidetic collective forms that inhabit but also transcend the individual mind.[83]

Much has been made in the post-Soviet revival of interest in Shpet of this insistence on the collective nature of consciousness as evidence of the supposedly "Russian" versus "Western" leanings of his thought. The insistence is undeniably reminiscent of the fondness for anything "collective" or "communal" among representatives of the Russian religious renaissance and of the general intellectual emphases of the closely related "philosophy of all-unity," some of whose precepts Shpet openly invokes in his remarks on the need for "positive philosophy" at the beginning of *Iavlenie i smysl* (witness also his borrowing from Trubetskoi's essay on consciousness). An affinity with these intellectual movements is also evident in the ethical strain running through Shpet's works, which seems to prompt a rejection of individual consciousness as much for its hubristic and fragmenting elevation of the individual over the collective as for any metaphysical error it represents. In this line consider his assertion in "Iazyk i smysl" (Language and sense) that, because to deal with meaning one must always take into account links with a larger context, "the word" takes us outside the bounds of our immediately given experience, or his remark in the same essay that "every act of perception of verbal meaning is necessarily an act of co-perception [*so-vospriiatiia*]"—a reminder of how often Shpet echoes or anticipates Bakhtin, that other religiously inflected philosopher of language and self in the early Soviet context (see the latter's celebrated "*so-bytie*" and his ideas regarding the other's necessary role in completing our self-perception).[84] Among other

81. Ibid., 563, 528.

82. Ibid., 518.

83. Ibid., 565. Trubetskoi had also proposed the hereditary conditioning of consciousness; "O prirode chelovecheskogo soznaniia," in *Sochineniia,* Filosofskoe nasledie, t. 120 (1906; reprint, Moscow: Mysl', 1994), 512. Shpet also proposes a new object of study, the intersubjective or interpsychological interactions between individuals, which parallels or anticipates the later Husserl's interest in the same subject; Shpet, "Vvedenie v etnicheskuiu psikhologiiu," in *Sochineniia,* prilozhenie k zhurnalu *Voprosy filosofii* 540.

84. Shpet, "Iazyk i smysl," *Logos* 7 (1996): 94, 99.

things, this ethical strain may have allowed Shpet to retain a focus on self-hood while discussing what otherwise appear to be impersonal, public meaning-structures. Nor should one discount the precedent of Potebnia and Humboldt, both of whom insisted on the dialogic nature of speech.

But Shpet was not a religiously oriented thinker like Trubetskoi or Florenskii—he was in fact vocal in his antipathy toward their brand of philosophy—and in the end, other, for him more pressing, concerns are at work in his treatment of consciousness. What resounds everywhere in the philosophical scenarios Shpet considers, and then rejects, is the threat that the self will either be eliminated or will turn out to be insubstantial. One can sense this even in his remarks on the concept of intentionality, which almost seems more important to him as a kind of ontological guarantee than it does as an epistemic principle: in effect, if "consciousness points to something *of which* it is consciousness," then my awareness of such pointing is important precisely for the reassurance it offers—against, for example, the claims of the neo-Kantians—that its object of regard exists.[85] A similar reflex can be sensed in his statement that every positing act of consciousness posits "doxically," that is, such an act always posits something as existing (as we have seen, this idea was important for Bulgakov as well).[86] It is as if, for Shpet, the self would become too fragile, too ephemeral, if it were not secured in some more stable form (the social collective, for example), and this strain of ontological anxiety with regard to the self, together with the efforts it generates to locate forms of ontological security, represents one of the most significant ways in which his version of phenomenology departs from its Husserlian model. Husserl had been concerned to assert that the eidetic contents of consciousness actually *exist* and constitute objects in their own right—he claimed that phenomenology had "opened up a new region of *being* never before delineated in its peculiarity, that of the world as Eidos"—but the need to establish the being of consciousness is palpably more vital for Shpet, who I think precisely for this reason "ontologizes" and "platonizes" Husserl, as Haardt points out.[87]

Shpet's treatment of the complexities surrounding the concept of the "ego" in phenomenology also hint at an unexpected (and, for him, ironic) precedent, which I have already suggested plays a role in Potebnia's thought. The third chapter of *Iavlenie i smysl* begins with a discussion of how various intellectual disciplines ought to be divided into those of "fact," which treat only the natural world, and "eidetic" ones actually dealing with essence. The discussion is involved and technical, even hairsplitting, but Shpet's point is

85. Ibid., 114.
86. Ibid., 119.
87. Husserl, *Ideas*, 63; Haardt, *Husserl in Russland*, 93.

that even such seemingly "eidetic" disciplines as "formal theories of logic, algebra, and other mathematical disciplines" must be suspended during phenomenological analysis.[88] This is especially true in the case of the self, where a rigorous approach similarly dictates that such entities as "soul," "psychological response," and "properties of character" be bracketed out as belonging to the merely natural realm.[89] But when that has been done there remains the problem of the "pure I," which cannot be dispensed with because it forms the necessary point of unity in all the changing perceptions of consciousness. At this point Shpet is still willing to resolve the dilemma by embracing a Husserlian formula he was to mock only a couple of years later as a "mannered concatenation of Latin words": the "eidetic I" emerges as a peculiar kind of "transcendence in immanence," which therefore cannot be subjected to any phenomenological reduction.[90]

The conceptual precedent for Shpet's ruminations emerges in a wry observation he makes on this very formula. The strictness of the phenomenological method, he remarks, demanded that we exclude even God as absolute transcendent; why, then, do we leave in place another transcendent that resembles the first in its absoluteness?[91] As Shpet may or may not have been aware at this point, phenomenology may have bracketed "God" out of its analyses, but its myriad operations of sorting what is transcendent out from what is immanent, of determining which "essences" belong in the absolute and which belong to the merely natural world, and so forth—even much of the vocabulary used—bears an uncanny resemblance to debates in the early history of the Church over Christology and the nature of the Trinity.[92] When the early Church was working out its complex understanding of Christology the issues turned on how much "humanity" to include in Christ's nature and how to account for its relation to his divinity. For example, Arianus proposed in the fourth century that Christ be considered of lesser stature than the Father, a mere part of the created order—a move, Ware suggests, designed to "protect the uniqueness and transcendence of God" (in essence, "bracketing" Jesus out of the Godhead).[93] In the fifth

88. Shpet, *Iavlenie i smysl*, 60–61.

89. Ibid., 62, 65–66.

90. Ibid., 72; Shpet, "Soznanie i ego sobstvennik," in *Sochineniia*, prilozhenie k zhurnalu *Voprosy filosofii*, 91. Shpet may have been aware of Hermann Bahr's similar essay, "Das unrettbare Ich," in his *Dialog vom Tragischen* (Berlin: S. Fischer, 1904), 79–101.

91. Shpet, *Iavlenie i smysl*, 72.

92. Haardt comments that the peculiar quality of Shpet's phenomenology consists in the way he on the one hand participates in the "transcendental turn" documented in Husserl's *Ideas*, but on the other hand is so influenced by the Russian Metaphysical Renaissance and the Göttingen circle of Husserl's followers that he interprets transcendental phenomenology as an ontology of the life of consciousness (*Husserl in Russland*, 92).

93. Timothy Ware, *The Orthodox Church*, new ed. (New York: Penguin Putnam, 1997), 22.

century Nestorius complicated the issue of Christ's divinity by rejecting the title of "Theotokos" (Mother of God) for Mary (she must then have given birth to a mere mortal), the "Nestorians" who followed him teaching a duality of hypostases and natures in the one person of Christ.[94] The Monophysites meanwhile held that Christ had but one hypostasis and one nature. Eventually in A.D. 451 the Council of Calcedon affirmed the so-called "Formulary of Reunion," which asserted that Christ was "one in essence" (*homoousios,* consubstantial) with the Father and held that within his one person (or hypostasis, of the Trinity) there were two natures, "without confusion, without change."[95] In all this what the Church was working out was a theological formula for the Incarnate *Logos,* for God made flesh—that is, for transcendence in immanence. In the case of the Trinity, in order to preserve the distinctness of Father, Son, and Holy Spirit it was asserted that each was a hypostasis and not a mere "accidental power."[96] At the same time, to avoid the contrary pitfall of polytheism it was held that the three hypostases formed a single, undivided *ousia* or essence, within which the hypostases functioned as manifestations of personhood (here defined roughly as a distinguishing quality—"it is the 'person' of the hypostasis called Father to be unbegotten, that of the hypostasis called 'Son' to be begotten").

To the extent that the complexities Shpet considers are prefigured in Husserl one could argue that, as in Bakhtin's remark that literary genres have "memories," Husserl's formula of "transcendence in immanence" as a definition of consciousness retained the "memory" of its origins in early Christian thought (which is not to exclude the still earlier influence of Greek thought). At the very least the conceptual matters with which Shpet deals in *Iavlenie i smysl* are palpably cognate with the debates over Christology and the Trinity: each involves an attempt to reconcile transcendence and immanence within a model of personhood, and in each case it is imperative that being neither be reduced to matter nor turned into a phantom. In other words, whether or not he did so under the influence of the Russian religious renaissance, because Shpet was trying to articulate an ontology of consciousness within a framework of reaction to both materialism and neo-Kantianism, he found himself in a philosophical position ironically reminiscent of the early Church, which had to account for the simultaneous divinity and humanity of Christ. And the solution Shpet was eventually to offer to the dilemma of consciousness—which is arguably the most

94. Pelikan, *Spirit of Eastern Christendom,* 49.

95. Cross and Livingstone, *Oxford Dictionary of the Christian Church,* s.v., "Christology." See also Ware, *Orthodox Church,* 22–23, and Pelikan, *Spirit of Eastern Christendom,* 49–61.

96. Pelikan, *Spirit of Eastern Christendom,* 49.

important element of his thought—betrays the marked influence of Russia's culture of *logos,* even as it anticipates the later Husserl. Shpet locates the solution in a particular understanding of language.

The relatively greater attention he devotes to language marks another way in which Shpet departs from Husserl, and it is one that, again, may be related to the kind of ontological anxieties that characterize his works. In relation to Husserl, Shpet's writings take a marked "hermeneutic turn," from an emphasis on *eidos* or essence in general to the more specific concept of sense—that is, from operations of bracketing-to-reveal-essence, which establish the phenomenological method as a new way of conducting philosophy, to attempts at describing the complex meaning-structure that method reveals.[97] It is in this shift that issues of language enter into those of "eidetic seeing," and it is here that Shpet elaborates his doctrine of selfhood-in-language.[98]

Husserl never really provides a definitive statement on the relation of thought to speech. On the whole he treats them as closely linked but takes care to limit the nature of the link to "a certain parallelism between thinking and speaking" within which there is no assurance of a perfect, *a priori* correspondence.[99] Yet in other passages he assigns linguistic phenomena a privileged role in his account of noema and noesis. He mentions but sets aside Frege's celebrated distinction between *Sinn* and *Bedeutung* (that is,

97. This hermeneutic shift is already signaled in the title of Shpet's most Husserlian work, *Iavlenie i smysl.* Haardt notes that Shpet's development of the notion of "sense" is one of the ways in which he extended or revised Husserl, in whose *Ideas* the notion was only vaguely sketched out; *Husserl in Russland,* 93.

98. Haardt suggests that Shpet may have followed the development of Husserl's thought on language issues in reverse. Husserl sent Shpet a copy of the newly reprinted first five *Logical Investigations* in December 1913 while Shpet was revising *Iavlenie i smysl,* which is otherwise so heavily influenced by the later *Ideas.* Shpet then reworked his presentation to make more room for a doctrine of meaning (Haardt, *"Appearance and Sense* and Phenomenology in Russia," xxviii). Yet *Logical Investigations* had been available in Russian translation by E. A. Bershtein since 1909 and Shpet would surely have read the original during his time in Göttingen. In any event, Shpet's involvement in issues of language was significant. He was a member of the Moscow Linguistic Circle from 1920 until it dissolved itself in 1924—where his ideas influenced Jakobson, Vinokur, and others (Polovinkin, "P. A. Florenskii," 9)—after which he and other members transferred their activity (and the Linguistic Circle's library) to GAKhN, where Shpet headed the project on "Problems of Artistic Form" (Toman, *Magic of a Common Language,* 66; Haardt says that Shpet and his associates at GAKhN were interested in particular in the "Russian Humboldt tradition"; *"Appearance and Sense,"* xxi). See also Aage A. Hansen-Löve, *Der russische Formalismus. Methodologische Rekonstruktion seiner Entwicklung aus dem Prinzip der Verfremdung* (Vienna: Verlag der Österreichischen Akademie der Wissenschaften, 1978), 181–83.

99. Husserl, *Logical Investigations,* 257.

between sense and reference, according to which the same referent—
Venus—can be referred to in two senses, as "morning star" and "evening
star"), asserting that it is more important to phenomenology that an expression *has* meaning, that is, it constitutes a relation to an object.[100] The more
relevant distinction for Husserl is between *Ausdruck,* or the "articulate
sound-complex," roughly speaking the forms in which meanings are embodied; and *Bedeutung,* or sense-giving and sense-fulfilling acts, and it is the
latter that concern him specifically.[101] What we know about judgments, he
observes, is that they always take verbal form; the objects of pure logic come
embedded in concrete mental states that function as the "meaning fulfillment" of certain verbal expressions.[102] In *Ideas Pertaining to a Pure Phenomenology* he speaks of "expressive act-strata," whose form is linguistic, being
woven into the other strata of the noema/noesis. If our perception is "This
is white," he argues, even if we have not expressed this perception linguistically, if we have thought or asserted "This is white," then "a new stratum
is co-present" that involves language.[103] In other words, to hold in mental
regard, which is the essence of the phenomenological act, is to invoke linguistic or language-like forms, while the function of words themselves is to
awaken "sense-conferring acts" within us.[104] Moreover, even if he will not
quite define it, Husserl strongly suggests that there is something essential in
the relation between such "expressive" forms or strata and their eidetic
sense. The meaning-combinations we find in the expressive strata are gov-
erned by nothing less than "*a priori* laws of essence," he states, and in *Ideas*
he describes "the act-stratum of expressing" as a distinctive form to which
all other strata of the noema conform (that is, they are modeled after it) and
that raises the given sense "to the realm of 'Logos,' of the *conceptual* and, on
that account, the *universal.*"[105] Husserl states quite explicitly that what he
has done is to take the language-based notion of "expressing" and in "an important cognitive step . . . appl[ied] [it] to the whole noetic-noematic
sphere."[106] In so doing he also places his "form-theory of meanings" within
a philosophical tradition assuming an essential relation between language
and sense that reaches as far back as Aristotle (on whose *Organon,* with its
doctrine of complex versus uncomplex signs, Husserl draws directly in elaborating the distinction between categorematic and syncategorematic forms
in *Logical Investigations*); that was transmitted via the Middle Ages, where

100. Ibid., 292.
101. Ibid., 277, 280.
102. Ibid., 250.
103. Husserl, *Ideas,* 295.
104. Husserl, *Logical Investigations,* 282.
105. Ibid., 510; Husserl, *Ideas,* 295.
106. Husserl, *Ideas,* 294.

inter alia it was influenced by Augustine's theory of signs in *De doctrina christiana* and *De trinitate* (the latter of which makes the important assertion that "concepts are words at heart") and by a Neoplatonic tradition conveyed through Boethius's theological treatises; and that resurfaced in Locke and Leibniz (Husserl mentions "the undoubted soundness of the idea of a universal grammar conceived by the rationalists of the seventeenth and eighteenth centuries").[107]

In *Iavlenie i smysl* Shpet draws explicit attention to the fact that Husserl borrows a linguistic term to characterize the noematic-noetic sphere, and makes language and language-like phenomena unequivocally central to his version of phenomenology.[108] Shpet remarks that although one can approach eidos as a point of unity, as "simply the object," on closer examination one perceives it as a complex, multilayered structure: the "sense" (*smysl*) of an object is not the whole of its noema, but a "moment of sense-endowing" residing at its core.[109] Surrounding it are other layers forming a "logical" stratum of the noema that serves to "express" its core of sense. Shpet calls the relation between the two one of *sense* to *meaning* (*smysl/znachenie*, that is, through "meaning" the logical layer expresses the sense of the noema).[110] He explores at some length the problematic of distinguishing "sense" as such from the expressive structures that attend it, but what is clear is that, like Husserl, he has invoked a notion, ultimately deriving from ancient Greek concepts of *logos*, which holds that *essence* exists first and foremost as *articulable form*, and in this notion reside two key aspects of Shpet's phenomenology: the assumption or insistence that the world is rational—purposeful and structured—and the assumption that this order is inherently language-like. The relevant opposition for him is not form versus content but the Aristotelian one of inert matter (*hyle*) versus meaningful form (*morphe*).[111]

Toward the end of *Iavlenie i smysl* Shpet observes that within the act of "positing" there are certain subordinate acts that are directed not to the sense itself—they are not the "doxic" act as such—but to its expressive layers. These acts perceive the contents of the noema to be only a *sign* for its inner sense. "We can call these acts which enliven every positing *hermeneutic* acts,"

107. Husserl speaks of "form theory of meanings," ibid., 313; his comment on universal grammar is in *Logical Investigations*, 524. See Lamarque, ed., *Concise Encyclopedia of the Philosophy of Language*, 489. See also Jakobson's "One of the Speculative Anticipations" and the discussion in Chapter 1 of this study of the relations among ideas of godhood, linguistic structure, and essence. On language issues in Husserl see especially Part 4 of the *Logical Investigations*.

108. Shpet, *Iavlenie i smysl*, 120; see also Haardt, "*Appearance and Sense*," xxi.

109. Shpet, *Iavlenie i smysl*, 124.

110. Ibid., 158.

111. Husserl himself invokes this opposition in *Ideas*, 204.

he states, "and we can consider 'positing' not only as a unity of sense and certain thetic moments, but as their unity together with the unity of the entelechy and of hermeneutic moments, which unity constitutes the unity of the object with its living intimate sense."[112] In other words, for Shpet the noema turns out to be a complex structure consisting of the *eidos* itself (which his elaborating analysis essentially defers and leaves mysterious) plus certain structures that are required to articulate or manifest it. As a result essences are susceptible to but also, and of equal importance, demand hermeneutic acts for their realization.

To this theme of the *sign-like* nature of the noematic object Shpet devoted the popular essay "Mudrost' ili razum?" (1917; Wisdom or reason?), followed by the far more extensive *Germenevtika i ee problemy* (1918; *Hermeneutics and Its Problems*). The latter offers a detailed review of hermeneutics from antiquity to the early twentieth century, covering a range of thinkers from Augustine, Origen, Flacius, and medieval scholasticism through Reid, Harris, Locke, Berkeley, and on to Schleiermacher, Dilthey, and Husserl, the point of which is to show that hermeneutics is poised at last to enter a foreordained period of genuine philosophical inquiry. The survey's real aim, however, is to corroborate Shpet's phenomenological understanding of the world. Yet hermeneutics serves Shpet as more than just a springboard, because in the course of his historical review he works out his understanding of the role meaning-structures play in his broader conception of the world. For Shpet the interpretive act accomplishes what eidetic analysis was meant to in Husserlian phenomenology.

Shpet shows his phenomenological bias in *Germenevtika i ee problemy* by dismissing everything in the history of hermeneutics that could be deemed subjectivist, merely pragmatic, or philosophically unproductive. He waves away as merely fanciful accounts such as those in Herder, Rousseau, and Condillac of the origins of language (what discussions about the nature of language as being either *nomoi* or *physei* are really about, he remarks, is not how language arose but what the principles of referentiality are), and he repeatedly stresses the inadequacy of "psychological" accounts of how we understand or interpret words. The fact that reference and meaning are invoked in dialogue, he argues, tells us that speech is a social phenomenon irreducible to purely subjective mental states, and the fact that we are able to communicate not just names of things but meanings points to the transindividual "*sui generis* being of ideas."[113] Instead, Shpet sees hermeneutics as dealing with its proper subject when it concerns itself with the

112. Shpet, *Iavlenie i smysl*, 164–65.
113. Shpet, *Germenevtika i ee problemy*, in A. V. Mikhailov, ed., *Kontekst 1989* (Moscow: Nauka, 1989), 256, 259.

essential relation between sign and meaning. A historical survey of the field reveals it to be characterized by the gradual convergence of two lines of inquiry, that into signs together with the logic-based systems into which they are shaped, and that into concepts and the nature of understanding. Their eventual convergence was in fact "predestined" from the outset when early hermeneutics linked inquiry into the nature of the sign with the *scientiae sermocinales* of grammar, rhetoric, and logic.[114] In its contemporary version the near-convergence takes the form of the closely related problems of, on the one hand, "the sign together with its correlative meaning" (*znak/znachenie:* it may be significant that in Russian the second term derives morphologically from the first and thus appears naturally as its adjunct or projection—hence also perhaps Jakobson's fondness for the Latin *signans/signatum*); and on the other that of "the process of cognition as the act of moving from sign to meaning."[115] For Shpet the fated convergence of these issues is about to take place, and hermeneutics is poised at last to deal with "the problem of meaning as such."[116]

This is ultimately made possible for Shpet by the fact that "the act of understanding is the uncovering of sense in a sign" ("*raskrytie smysla v znake*").[117] In other words the decipherment which is the business of hermeneutics can lead to the apperception of "sense" (which for him is synonymous with eidetic essence), or, as he restates the same point later, "understanding is *sui generis* cognition."[118] The reason that the discipline of hermeneutics has a philosophically significant destiny is that, given the kinds of structures noemas represent (a core of sense embedded in expressive, logical, language-like layers), the processes of decipherment or interpretation with which hermeneutics has concerned itself turn out to replicate those by which we arrive, in what might be called noematic exegesis, at apperception, which is to say cognition—mental regard—of the eidetic object. Interpretation can lead us to being.

One interesting ambiguity that Shpet's formula fails to remove has to do with whether signs in relation to their meanings are to be regarded as *analogs* for eidetic objects (thus, for example, Shpet sometimes talks about the *parallelism* between speech and understanding, *rech'/ponimanie*), or as ontologically coextensive with them, indeed, prototypes of any such object.[119] Put another way, Shpet is even less concerned than Husserl had

114. Ibid., 249.
115. Ibid., 252.
116. Ibid.
117. Ibid., 248.
118. Shpet, *Germenevtika i ee problemy,* in A. V. Mikhailov, ed., *Kontekst 1991* (Moscow: Nauka, 1991), 221.
119. Shpet, *Germenevtika i ee problemy,* in *Kontekst 1989,* 243.

been to clarify whether he is saying that the movement of our mental regard from a sign to its meaning *mimics* the phenomenological approach to essence, or that the decoding of a sign directly *conveys* our mental regard not just to linguistic "meaning" but to "sense," understood as essence. At stake is the issue of how closely language is linked with authentic being. The basis for the analogy is the structural image of inner core of meaning wrapped in outer layers of expressive form: in both phenomenology and hermeneutics we move from the structured, empirically available, and often literally material givenness of the latter to the noncontingent, *a priori,* and transcendent former. It is in this sense that signs resemble, or are, eidetic objects, and in this way that decoding signs serves as a "prototype" for the cognizing of essence.

Where the ambiguity becomes productive is in its expansion into a vision of the whole of reality as "semasiological" in nature, and therefore susceptible to interpretation, its essence cognizable and therefore rational. In the act of cognition we can identify moments of both empirical and eidetic vision, Shpet states, but also a third one of "intelligible intuition"—the possibility not only of intellectual understanding but also of "rational comprehension of the very 'reason of things,' their rational foundation."[120] Given insight into the structured and sign-like nature of reality, we "now place on eidos the same demand we place on 'the word': we regard essence itself as a sign. . . . The semasiological approach to essence itself forces one *eo ipso* to search in it, as in a 'foundation,' for *sense,* which opens up before us as the rational basis deposited in essence itself; here essence in its content proceeds out of reason as out of its founding principle."[121] If hermeneutics has taught us how to decipher signs, it has also taught us how to understand existence itself.

Moreover, although Shpet is interested in a variety of sign systems, particularly aesthetic ones, for him it is language that serves as the prototype for them all (and, Shpet notes, it is contemporary linguistics that has given hermeneutics its productive interest in "semasiology").[122] "To a certain—profound—degree," he remarks in another work, "language is the natural and the closest prototype and representation of any expression which harbors *meaning.*"[123] Indeed Shpet often seems to identify language as *the* sign-system constituting the "expressive" layer of the noema that bears its sense to us. Whenever we allow our regard to pause on experience, he says, we

120. Shpet, "Mudrost' ili razum?" in his *Filosofskie etiudy,* 316.
121. Ibid., 315.
122. Shpet, *Germenevtika i ee problemy,* in A. V. Mikhailov, ed., *Kontekst 1992* (Moscow: Nauka, 1993), 275.
123. Shpet, "Vvedenie v etnicheskuiu psikhologiiu," in *Sochineniia,* prilozhenie k zhurnalu *Voprosy filosofii,* 515.

have to do not with a naked datum but one "vested in a word" (*"oblechen-noe v slovo"*), which is the very *principium cognescendi* of our knowledge.[124] It is through language that we communicate with one another. It is in the words of language that meaning, in the form of ideas, has its existence. In particular it is from language that we learn about the relation between external (acoustic, graphic) and inner (meaning-bearing) form: "in relation to things this form reveals itself as idea, that is, as inner form in relation to outer form, the difference being that inner form is free from matter while outer is linked to it. It is in this quality of inner form . . . that the specific being of ideas consists."[125] Or, as he puts it in a revealing passage in "Mudrost' ili razum?":

> In the concept [*poniatii*] as inwardly formulated word we see not only a "concept" [*kontsept*] but also . . . eidetic content, which comports the sense or meaning of the concept to which we penetrate not by means of some simple "apprehension" [*kontsipirovanie*] but through an act of establishing. Since in itself this is a mere formational act, it includes a *sui generis* act of "intelligible intuition" which gives us "understanding" of the corresponding sense. Thus for us the word-concept is not just a "volume" or "class" but also a *sign* demanding understanding, that is, penetration into a certain meaning, as if into something intimate, into the "living soul" of the word-concept. Put another way, the word-concept, the word as term (*terminirovannoe slovo*), demands *interpretation*.[126]

This "word-concept," or, as one might call it, "hermeneutic eidos," is the focus of Shpet's philosophy as a whole and embodies his specifying revision of the Husserlian noema. But it is essential to understand that the hermeneutic turn this concept involved, which was so richly productive within his philosophical career, represents not a reversal of the celebrated "transcendental" turn in Husserl's own thought (represented in the differing concerns of *Ideas* over the earlier *Logical Investigations*)—not, or not only, a departure from eidetic inquiry into the more accessible, "hyletic" realms of social and cultural phenomena—but in fact an intensification of his interest in consciousness and in particular the self.

Obviously, as a product of consciousness Shpet's "word-concept" is in some way contiguous with the self, but there remains a significant difference between examining some element of selfhood and mapping onto that element the essential features of the self as a whole, so that it becomes a

124. Shpet, "Mudrost' ili razum?" 293–94.

125. Shpet, *Germenevtika i ee problemy*, in *Kontekst 1989*, 260.

126. Shpet, "Mudrost' ili razum?" 310. I have followed Thomas Nemeth in translating Shpet's *kontsipirovanie*—Nemeth gives it as "*kontseptirovanie*"—as "apprehension." It is Shpet's equivalent for Husserl's *Auffassung*. See Shpet, *Appearance and Sense,* 182.

replica in miniature of that self. But this is precisely what Shpet does: he projects onto the "word-concept" selflike qualities that are by no means necessarily foreseen in Husserl, suggesting at once that our selves are structured like it and that it is a kind of self in its own right.

Even though in his description of the word-concept Shpet places the expression "living soul" in quotation marks, the idea that a hermeneutic decoding of sense conveys us to something selflike is not, for him, just metaphorical or ironic. As a particularly apt analogy for this aspect of sign/essence in *Germenevtika* he offers some remarks Wilhelm Dilthey makes on the possibility of "scientifically" cognizing the self as an other. "The being of the other" (*chuzhoe bytie*), Shpet paraphrases, is not exhausted by the sensually given phenomena we have as evidence for it, because it is an inner reality that inhabits sensory facts such as sounds, gestures—that is, signs of various sorts. For Dilthey, understanding (*ponimanie,* Shpet's act of hermeneutic deciphering) is the process through which external, sensory signs lead us to know (*poznaem*) that which is inner. Shpet then makes a remarkable statement about where that human *bytie* is ultimately lodged: "Only in language does human 'inwardness' find its completely exhaustive and objectively comprehensible expression."[127] Or, as he outlines the tasks before a phenomenologically reconceived hermeneutics in the work's conclusion, "the problem of understanding is nothing less than that of spirit [*dukh*]."[128]

To understand how this agenda of situating selfhood within language develops within Shpet's thought we can return to some of his remarks on the structure of the *eidos* or noema. Following Husserl, Shpet states that, for all its multilayered complexity, it is in the nature of the noema as a whole to possess unity. As the core of the noema, sense belongs first of all to "that which constantly abides in the object and which remains identical in spite of all the changes of the attentive mental processes and in spite of the fluctuation of the attentional acts of the pure Ego."[129] The unity of "thetic" moments and sense in the object arises out of its moment of sameness, its element that is constant from perception to perception, a "certain X as the bearer" of sense.[130] However, from this understanding of noematic unity *for us* (that is, as that constant X which we must recognize as stable from attentional act to attentional act, and which we must separate from everything changing and therefore non-eidetic), Shpet subtly shifts to one of noematic unity *for the object itself.* To perceive the sense of an object fully and

127. Shpet, *Germenevtika i ee problemy,* in *Kontekst 1991,* 252.
128. Ibid., 278.
129. Shpet, *Iavlenie i smysl,* 122.
130. Ibid., 137; on these matters in Husserl see especially Part 6 of *Logical Investigations.*

adequately, Shpet asserts, we must go beyond regarding it as pure abstraction and penetrate into its "inner intimate [space] (*vnutrennoe intimnoe*)," which requires perceiving it in its "rational motivation."[131] As a "useful analogy" for how this is done he again offers the example of our ability to unite all the threads of perception when we regard the whole constituted by another *self* (*chuzhoi individual'nosti*).[132]

To illustrate his point further he discusses an example drawn from Aristotle but so reminiscent of Potebnia's theory of etymology (as the historically established center of our perceptions of an object, through which we gain awareness of the unity of our sensory images of it) and of Potebnia's *ur*-source in Plato's *Cratylus* (where etymologies are traced in order show that names properly identify the qualities of things) as to suggest an unacknowledged influence. If we take the example of an axe (*sekira*), Shpet says, we find its inner sense in the idea "to chop" (*rubit'*), that is, in the intended use for which it exists ("or has been made" would be more accurate: Shpet interestingly, if inconsistently, sets aside objects in the natural rather than the social world as having "pure content" alone, at most a quasi-teleology).[133] In a post-Hegelian context the idea of a teleology resident in the object is already suggestive of selfhood, but is not all that remote from similar discussions in Husserl. Where Shpet's "self-ward" turn becomes conspicuous is in the unabashedly vitalist way in which he treats this teleological "inner sense." In the case of the axe, he states, "to chop" reveals itself to me as nothing less than the object's "soul" or entelechy—the Aristotelian concept of the principle or mode through which the essence of a thing is fully realized, its informing spirit.[134] This entelechy constitutes the "core of the very sense" of the object, and the object in its "defining qualification" exists for this entelechy as a mere external sign—which comes close to saying that the axe itself, as a physical object, exists in order to denote the idea of chopping.[135] Moreover, this entelechic core comes close to constituting the object as a *sui generis* being in its own right. If we wanted to define the sense in which the noema of an object consists as abstract form, Shpet says, we would have to "turn back to Aristotle's teaching in order to trace it back to Plato and then, skipping over the centuries, encounter an analogous

131. Shpet, *Iavlenie i smysl*, 159, 138.
132. Ibid., 147.
133. Ibid., 159, 162–63.
134. Ibid., 160. Blackburn, *Oxford Dictionary of Philosophy*, s.v. "entelechy." Husserl actually at one point refers to meaning as "ensouling" the sensual-linguistic side of objects (*Logical Investigations*, 289), but elsewhere emphatically asserts that "being is nothing *in* the object, no part of it, no moment tenanting it" (*Logical Investigations*, 780). Shpet's discussion works to suggest that, at least when the object is social in nature, especially when it is language, being does "tenant" it.
135. Shpet, *Iavlenie i smysl*, 160.

thought in Leibniz"—that of form understood as something which "animates what is dead."[136] He makes similar statements when rebutting the claim that the I by itself "creates" sense in the noemas it perceives: "the object with its noema would remain dead," he asserts, if it did not bear in itself its *own* "enlivening sense."[137]

The concept of intentionality that Brentano developed in his *Psychologie vom empirischen Standpunkt* (1874), which was so influential on Husserl, may well turn out to harbor similar impulses, and in his late essay on organicism Cassirer suggested much the same about structural linguistics. Be that as it may, in the case of Shpet the "Humboldtian meditations" offered in *Vnutrenniaia forma slova* (The inner form of the word) and the related comments on "inner form" in the earlier *Esteticheskie fragmenty* (Esthetic fragments [1918]) emerge as central to his thought. In effect what happens is that Shpet's hermeneutic revision of Husserl circles back at this point to contemplate its origins in Humboldt and—though here the relation becomes more complex—in the original Russian Humboldtian, Potebnia.

As the subtitle of *Vnutrenniaia forma slova* indicates—"Studies and Variations on Themes of Humboldt"—Shpet sets its discussion of selfhood and language squarely in the context of the seminal statement on those issues in German philosophy.[138] Shpet uses Humboldt, who already inheres as an important subtext in Husserlian thought, as something of a corrective to certain emphases in phenomenology (for example, by adopting the former's normative view of language and insistence that it is "the forming organ of thought"), even as he passes Humboldt's ideas through a Husserlian filter (criticizing certain of Humboldt's Kantian habits of thought and centering his review of Humboldtian ideas in a phenomenological understanding of

136. Ibid., 158.

137. Ibid., 122.

138. Humboldt himself was indebted to A. W. Schlegel and especially to Hegel; for example, the latter's notion of the spirit's movement into self-consciousness, as described in *The Phenomenology of the Spirit*—Shpet remarks that at times it seems as if Humboldt's philosophical system was called forth in order to complete Hegel's; in his *Vnutrenniaia forma slova,* 33. Noam Chomsky, however, places the origins of this tradition (which for him belongs to an era when linguistics, philosophy, and psychology had not yet diverged into separate disciplines) in Descartes, who emphasized the "creative language use" that sets humans apart from the beasts (*Cartesian Linguistics,* 76 nn. 4, 5). The Cartesian line is then developed by A. W. Schlegel, for whom language functions as "the organ of thought" (*als Gedankenorgans*) and receives its most forceful expression in Humboldt (*Cartesian Linguistics,* 19). Chomsky notes that over the history of this "Cartesian linguistics" the view changes from language as a medium for thought to language as having a constitutive function with respect to thought (Ibid., 30). He also notes that Humboldt's important concept of the "inner form of language" developed against the background of intensive discussion among the romantics (Schlegel, Coleridge) of the distinction between "mechanical form" (which is imparted from without, accidentally, like an imprint in wax) and "organic form" (which is innate and unfolds itself from within); ibid., 22.

Bedeutungsbewusstsein).[139] Nor is it insignificant when one considers Shpet in his historical context that by 1927 the kind of wholesale exploration of romantic-idealist thought that a work like *Vnutrenniaia forma slova* represents amounted to a remarkably defiant gesture in the officially materialist Soviet intellectual climate.

Shpet sets out in *Vnutrenniaia forma slova* to rescue a "genuine" and "eidetic" Humboldt from the "psychologically leveling" influences of his successor, Steinthal, and implicitly from Steinthal's Russian successor Potebnia.[140] Psychological factors are peripheral to the inner form of language, he states.[141] What he is after instead is "linguistic consciousness as such," a dynamic object that he claims is archetypal for all other forms of thought and cultural activity.[142] To describe it he reiterates Humboldt's rebuttal to the view of language as an inert object. Rather than busy itself classifying the empirical data of diverse natural languages, philosophy should examine language *as such* as the "organ of inner being, even that being itself, as that being gradually attains inner cognition and reveals itself."[143] Language is the "formative organ of thought" (this a direct quotation from Humboldt) and as such should be understood not as an inert product but production itself, "the eternally repeating work of the spirit."[144] More specifically, language represents a particular kind of intellectual activity in which thought encounters sound in order to generate articulate sound-forms: language is generated out of this "completely inner intellectual" element of an intention to mean, of "ideas directed toward language" (*der auf die Sprache Bezug habenden Ideen,* Shpet quoting Humboldt here).[145] For both Humboldt and Shpet this intention to mean is a persistent inner need of humans, and differs from the impulses producing, say, an animal cry or a musical tone (the latter remark a jab at Rousseau's *Essai sur l'origine des langues*).[146]

This activity of the spirit in the heart of language turns out to concentrate in itself the whole complex, dialectical interplay between subjectivity and objectivity in general. Language operates by transforming subjectivity (thought) into something objective (sound-forms). In language the activity of the senses synthetically joins that of the soul to create a mental representation, which then takes on audible form.[147] Moreover in our verbal activity

139. Haardt, *Husserl in Russland,* 175–78.
140. Shpet, *Vnutrenniaia forma slova,* 7.
141. Ibid., 102; see also Shpet, "Esteticheskie fragmenty," in *Sochineniia,* 428.
142. Shpet, *Vnutrenniaia forma slova,* 36.
143. Ibid., 11.
144. Ibid., 13, 15.
145. Ibid., 21.
146. Ibid., 17.
147. Ibid., 16.

we surround ourselves with a world of sounds in order to take up into ourselves (*vospriniat'*) and process the world of objects. This turns out to be a cognitively necessary element in our encounter with the world, because "without language no object can exist for the soul; even external objects receive full essentiality for the soul only thanks to the intermediary of language."[148] But the process by which this happens is imperfect and dialectical, because "the inner idea, in order to reveal itself (become manifest) must overcome a certain resistance [*zatrudnenie*] from the side of sound, which overcoming does not even always succeed."[149] The "spirit creates, but in that very act opposes what is created to itself, and the latter, as object, in its turn exerts influence on it."[150] Shpet's German-romantic subtext clearly shows through all this talk of spirit and its activities, but one cannot help but notice as well how the same lexicon of creation/incarnation/kenosis noted in Chapter 1 insinuates itself into these descriptions. Thus, Shpet's remark that "language enables spiritual strivings to force a path out via the lips, and returns this product to its own ears" suggests a descent into matter followed by redemptive return to mind, while he describes the inner form of language as inhabiting its "external" grammatical and lexical forms "in the manner of a soul" and states that sound-form can be thought of as a kind of building in which language takes up residence (*ustraivaetsia*).[151] The human use of language is ultimately, as Shpet puts it, a process of "spirit's incarnation in language" ("*voploshchenie dukha v iazyke*").[152]

But in what, specifically, does Shpet's concept of "inner form" consist? It is especially important for him that this *energeia* pulsating in the heart of language does not stop with some vague activity of spirit but yields determinate *form*, which in the end is the focus of his philosophical work as a whole. *Vnutrenniaia forma slova* is Shpet's attempt to situate his phenomenologically inspired account of language and subjectivity in a line of

---

148. Ibid.

149. Ibid., 21; cf. Humboldt, "The *making of language* in general must be seen as a *producing*, in which the inner idea, to make itself manifest, has a *difficulty* to conquer" (*On Language,* 77).

150. Shpet, *Vnutrenniaia forma slova,* 28.

151. Ibid., 16, 26, 20. Cf. Humboldt: "For in that the mental striving breaks out through the lips in language, the product of that striving returns back to the speaker's ear" (*On Language,* 56). Lest these ideas appear unprecedented, consider the sixteenth- or seventeenth-century manuscript presented by Jakobson in "One of the Speculative Anticipations": having first established an analogy between the Holy Trinity and the human faculties of soul, reason, and the word (for which parallels exist in Augustine, as the text's annotator, Harry Wolfson, points out [372]), the anonymous author goes on to assert that just as the Son is twice-born (an Orthodox doctrine), "our word, too, has its twofold birth; For first our word is born of the soul, through some incomprehensible birth, and abides unknown near the soul; and then, born again through a second, fleshy birth, it emerges from the lips and reveals itself by the voice to the hearing" (373). Wolfson points out a further parallel with the Stoic notion of an "internal" versus "uttered" *logos* (373 n. 5).

152. Shpet, *Vnutrenniaia forma slova,* 26.

thought extending from Plato through the Neoplatonist Plotinus and the Renaissance Neoplatonist Giordano Bruno that regarded "inner form" as the workings of *eidos* in the human mind.[153]

For Shpet "inner form" is not just "sense" itself, in some simple undeveloped form; nor is it a visual "image," a psychological mechanism of association and apperception, or the etymological meaning of the word (with this Shpet dispenses with the Potebnia-Herbart-Steinthal tradition). Rather, it is the "guiding law of the development of the word's sense."[154] The "general laws of language," which Shpet implies coincide with inner form, arise out of the workings of the intention to mean on the sound-forms available to it in a given national language.[155] The inner form of the word "is not the concept in its totality, nor some abstract mental content, but a certain rule of its formation, registered [*zapechatlennoe*] within the concept as a formal moment. This rule is none other than the device, method, and principle of selection [of those moments of sense important to the given thought]—the law and basis of verbal-logical creativity in the service of expression, communication, and the transmission of sense."[156] It is "not a scheme or formula but a device, means, or method for developing the form of word-concepts." It represents the dialectical relation arising "between external signifying form and the objective form of [the concept's] thing-content" ("*predmetnoi formy veshchnogo soderzhaniia*," essentially a phenomenological definition of noematic essence).[157]

Although he invokes relatively little of it in the 1927 monograph, Shpet had in fact outlined a more detailed account of "inner form" roughly a decade earlier in "Esteticheskie fragmenty." There he makes it clear that what he means by "inner form" is not to be identified directly with the grammatical or lexical elements of a given natural language but belongs to the realm of intellectual sense-expression, which makes use of these

---

153. Shpet distinguishes between two strands in the history of the idea of inner form. One, which he attributes to Goethe, understands inner form as a nothing more than a vague, metaphorical *vis vitalis* (*Vnutrenniaia forma slova*, 52). The other is a philosophically serious, "rationalized" concept whose lineage extends from Platonic *eidos* as the prototype of an object through Plotinus, who transferred *eidos* to the mind and called it "*logos*," down to the Renaissance Neoplatonist Giordano Bruno, for whom inner form was eternal and unchanging versus mutable outer forms, and the English Neoplatonist Shaftesbury, who distinguished between mere "dead forms" and "forming forms" which embody the "forming power of the mind" (ibid., 56).

154. Shpet, *Vnutrenniaia forma slova*, 106; see also his "Esteticheskie fragmenty," in *Sochineniia*, 443, 447.

155. Shpet, *Vnutrenniaia forma slova*, 15.

156. Ibid., 98.

157. Ibid., 117. Shpet's concept of inner form is thus analogous to, and obviously influenced by, the "*rein formalen Grammatik*" that Husserl proposes in the *Logical Investigations* as the central discipline in a formal theory of meaning; see also Haardt, *Husserl in Russland*, 35.

elements without being reduced to them.[158] Instead, at the center of inner form stands the object, phenomenologically understood, which Shpet defines as whatever is presupposed when N uses a word and I understand him.[159] At the same time—and it is this next step in the argument that is so characteristic of Shpet in contrast to Husserl—this "presupposition" forms only a starting point of attention, an assigned theme that must then be developed. It is this developing that generates "inner form," and it is the "inner forms" so generated that call for hermeneutics in order to be apperceived. Between the "ontic forms" of the object and the morphological forms of the given language there enters a new network of forms constituting the system of relations between the two of them.[160] Shpet calls these "logical forms," and says they should be imagined as lying between morphemes and ontic forms.[161] Morphological forms are "external," ontic ones are "pure," while it is the *intermediary* logical forms that Shpet here identifies with the Humboldtian "inner form" of speech.[162] Their relation to ontic forms remains important, however. A "close correspondence" obtains between the two, which means that translation from the language of logic into the language of ontology, and vice versa, is always possible.[163]

In Shpet's account the word's "inner form" thus emerges as a set of relational rules by which thought takes on expressive form and through which, and this is the phenomenological moment, the objective world is adequately given in consciousness. "Inner form" is the very "law of the formation of concepts."[164] As the locus of this phenomenon the word itself turns out to be "a kind of absolute form, a form of forms, the highest and final

158. In *Vnutrenniaia forma slova* Shpet accuses Humboldt of confusion in this regard (62–64) and remarks that while inner form always finds expression, it has no constant form of externality (80). In "Esteticheskie fragmenty," in *Sochineniia,* he explicitly separates syntax and morphology from inner form, and draws a distinction between a dictionary containing mere "lexis," a simple listing of the names found in a language, and the set of "*logoi*" which bear meaning-sense (390–91).

159. Shpet, "Esteticheskie fragmenty," 393.

160. Ibid., 398.

161. On the role of logical forms in the word, especially with regard to the issue of types of words that are names and types that are not, see Shpet's unfinished manuscript of circa 1922–27, "Iazyk i smysl."

162. Shpet, "Esteticheskie fragmenty," in *Sochineniia,* 157.

163. Ibid., 400. In Shpet's remarks in "Esteticheskie fragmenty" on the inner form of poetry, which anticipate much in the subsequent development of structuralism, these relational inner logical forms come into complex play with the syntax of the given language to produce "inner differential forms of language," which arise out of the play between syntagma and logical forms and constitute the inner forms of *poetic* speech (408).

164. Ibid., 117.

in a system and structure of verbal logical forms."[165] As such it constitutes "the only completely universal sign," capable of replacing any other sign, and provides the ontological prototype for every other social or cultural artifact.[166] For Shpet not only words as such but speech in general, books, literature, and languages, also constitute "words" possessing "inner form"— social manifestations are "always homologous to verbal structure," he remarks.[167] The word represents not just an "inviolable structural unity" but nothing less than a "*sui generis* mode of being of a social-cultural type."[168] Moreover, the process of its formation leads to something resembling Hegelian self-consciousness: "At its most profound level, linguistic consciousness is nothing less than the verbal-logical consciousness of the law-governed nature [*zakonomernosti*] of life and of the development of language as a whole."[169] The only movement left to consciousness beyond this point, Shpet declares, is toward an understanding of the very content of absolute forms.

If these claims exceed even those advanced by Humboldt on behalf of inner form, it is because Shpet has gone even farther than Humboldt in working out a philosophical theory that identifies selfhood with the structures of language. But Shpet has also followed Potebnia's concretizing revision of Humboldt and transferred inner form from language in general to the integral word, just as he has promoted "the word," as Chubarov suggests, into a surrogate for the Husserlian transcendental ego.[170] For Shpet the word harbors *the* algorithm for the being of consciousness in the world—not the activity or product of the individual psychological subject, but "the spontaneous process of sense itself in its movement."[171] As he puts it in a passage of "Esteticheskie fragmenty" on the hermeneutics of the literary work, when we read literature—it is hard to imagine he is not thinking of novels, in a manner strikingly parallel to Bakhtin—we begin to

165. Ibid., 101. Shpet is far more determinate in his conception of inner form than Humboldt, who repeatedly returns to the idea of the looseness and contingency involved in linguistic communication: for Humboldt, all understanding is to some degree misunderstanding, and the word does not so much convey a concept as provoke the listener to undertake an intellectual search analogous to that which has taken place in the speaker (*On Language*, 151–52). This is one instance where Shpet reveals the influence of phenomenology and its distance from Romanticism.

166. Shpet, "Esteticheskie fragmenty," in *Sochineniia*, 140.

167. Ibid., 381, 141. This is essentially the point behind the aesthetic explorations in "Esteticheskie fragmenty."

168. Ibid., 67.

169. Ibid., 128. Recall, too, Potebnia's claim that "in addition to the factual unity of the image the inner form also provides knowledge of that unity" (*Mysl' i iazyk*, 147).

170. I. M. Chubarov, "Modifikatsiia fenomenologicheskoi paradigmy ponimaniia soznaniia v proekte germenevticheskoi dialektiki G. G. Shpeta," in *G. G. Shpet/Comprehensio. Vtorye shpetovskie chteniia* (Tomsk: Vodolei, 1997), 32.

171. Shpet, "Esteticheskie fragmenty," in 141, 128.

discern behind every word a secondary sense that refers to nothing less than the author's self.[172] "On the whole the author's selfhood emerges as the analog of a word. Selfhood *is* a word and demands its own [form of] understanding."[173]

Shpet's works can appear steeped in abstruse technicalities, a legacy of his tutelage in Husserlian phenomenology. But the impulses behind them were far from idiosyncratic, and were by no means peculiarly Russian. In the philosophy of language Shpet's hermeneutical effort to identify being with meaning-structures is in fact most reminiscent, not of other Russian figures, but of Hans-Georg Gadamer's 1960 *Warheit und Methode* (*Truth and Method*)—though "reminiscent" is not the right term if one considers that Shpet wrote his works roughly forty years in advance of Gadamer. Gadamer departs from an analogous position (namely, that of having assimilated Husserl and Dilthey, as Shpet had) and arrives at strikingly similar conclusions regarding the role that meaning-structures play in the phenomenon of being—but does so having pursued a different path: not through the retrospective metaphysics of the Russian religious renaissance, but through Heidegger (who, however, had his own agenda for reviving Greek metaphysical thought).

Gadamer's primary criticism concerning the issue of language is that we have gone from the complete "unconsciousness" of language in classical Greece (that is, nonrecognition of its relevance to metaphysics) to an "instrumentalist devaluation of language in modern times" that extends roughly from the Renaissance to structuralist linguistics of the twentieth century.[174] The instrumentalist theories of signs that dominate latter-day European thought, which see words and concepts as mere tools, are not much better than the Greek avoidance of the problem of language because they have missed the point of hermeneutical phenomena and left us with a devalued notion of language.[175] Insight into those phenomena can be gained, however, by considering the ontology of the work of art. For Gadamer the work of art exists as a form of play (Kant and Huizinga figure here), but this play is in turn more accurately understood as a form of self-presentation.[176] Therefore "the specific mode of the work of art's presence is the coming-to-presentation of being," and the process of understanding that is the concern of hermeneutics is what renders this self-presentation present to us.[177] Moreover, the work of art turns out to be only a specific

---

172. In *Vnutrenniaia forma slova* Shpet refers to poetic forms as "objectified subject" (186).
173. Shpet, "Esteticheskie fragmenty," in *Sochineniia,* 471.
174. Gadamer, *Truth and Method,* 403–4.
175. Ibid., 403.
176. Ibid., 108.
177. Ibid., 159.

instance of hermeneutical phenomena that characterize being in general, and that are for him, as they are for Shpet, epitomized in *language:* language is the universal medium in which understanding occurs, Gadamer asserts.[178] He finds precedents for this view in Schleiermacher, who organized hermeneutics according to the normative example of language, because he believed that everything hermeneutics deals in is ultimately cast in language; in Dilthey, who saw the life-process as one of self-objectification in structures of meaning, which makes understanding the activity through which these objectifications are translated back into the spiritual life from which they emerged; and most of all in Heidegger, for whom understanding was not merely a philosophical ideal, but the original form of the realization of *Dasein*—that is to say, the very mode in which being takes place.[179]

What is even more striking about Gadamer's account, however, and what makes him an even more relevant figure to the Russians than Heidegger, is that he explicitly locates the origins of this corrective notion of language in Christian theology. In the development of European thought what finally did "justice to the being of language," he argues, was not the Greek *logos* but the Christian idea of incarnation that transformed it. In contrast to the Greek notion of embodiment, the sort that takes place in Greek myths when the gods assume human form, being and form in the doctrine of incarnation are not ontologically distinct from one another. Nor is the "form" involved in the Christian concept of incarnation the mere copy of an ideal, as in Platonic metaphysics. Rather, the incarnation/Word is an *event* in which being emerges in external forms, externalizes itself in utterance (the issuance of the Son/*Logos* from the Father). The form that serves to incarnate/reveal in this event is neither autonomous nor a mere husk or tool; it has its being in the act of revealing.[180] And for Gadamer the event of incarnation defines the ontology of human language as well:

> The mystery of the Trinity is mirrored in the miracle of language insofar as the word that is true, because it says what the thing is, is nothing by itself and does not seek to be anything. . . . It has its being in the revealing. Exactly the same thing is true of the mystery of the Trinity. Here, too, the important thing is not the earthly appearance of the Redeemer as such, but rather his complete divinity, his consubstantiality with God.[181]

178. Ibid., 389.
179. Ibid., 196, 66, 259.
180. Ibid., 418–19.
181. Ibid., 421.

It is this "penetration" of Greek logic by Christian theology, Gadamer remarks, that restores full validity to the medium of language.[182] Interpenetrations of this kind, which we have seen latent in Potebnia but patent in Florenskii and Bulgakov, inform Shpet's works in complex ways. They are everywhere present, but nearly everywhere disavowed; they were to reassert themselves again in explicit and luxuriant form in the works of Aleksei Fedorovich Losev (1893–1988). Losev is the second significant philosopher of language in early-twentieth-century Russia whose ideas were influenced by Husserlian phenomenology. A student of Shpet's at Moscow University, he was a noticeably less rigorous (and less western-oriented) philosopher who nonetheless produced a series of works in the 1920s that constitute one of the most fertile, complex, and erudite, but also abstruse and idiosyncratic documents of Russian thought in the Soviet era.[183] It is in Losev, far more than in Potebnia, Shpet, or even Florenskii, that the subterranean currents in Russian thinking about selfhood and language rise to the surface—that the Platonic, Neoplatonic, patristic, and German idealist antecedents together with the twentieth-century contexts of phenomenology, neo-Kantianism, and even Soviet Marxism are explicitly acknowledged and richly explored.

Losev's intellectual background was similar to Shpet's, and he passed through many of the same laboratories of psychological and philosophical exploration of selfhood in late Silver Age and early Soviet Russia. Already in his gymnasium in Novocherkassk in the south of Russia he received a sound introduction to classical philology—gateway to Platonism and Neoplatonism—and developed an attachment to the writings of Vladimir Solov'ev, whose interests in idealist philosophy, Platonism, and theology he sustains in his own writings (the gymnasium's director, F. K. Frolov, presented him with an eight-volume edition of Solov'ev at the beginning of Losev's last year, and Losev was later to write a book-length study of Solov'ev).[184] From 1911 to 1915 he studied at Moscow University, where, among other things,

182. Ibid., 428.

183. The celebrated eight books of Losev's earlier career are *Antichnyi kosmos i sovremennaia nauka* (The ancient cosmos and modern science [1927]), *Muzyka kak predmet logiki* (Music as a topic in logic [1927]), *Filosofiia imeni* (The philosophy of the name [1927]), *Dialektika khudozhestvennoi formy* (The dialectics of artistic form [1927]), *Dialektika chisla u Plotina* (The dialectics of number in Plotinus [1928]), *Kritika platonizma u Aristotelia* (Aristotle's critique of Platonism [1928]), the first volume of *Ocherki antichnogo simvolizma i mifologii* (Sketches on ancient symbolism and mythology [1930]), and *Dialektika mifa* (*The Dialectics of Myth* [1930]).

184. A. F. Losev, *Vladimir Solov'ev i ego vremia* (Moscow: Progress, 1990); see A. A. Takho-Godi, "Aleksei Fedorovich Losev," in A. F. Losev, *Bytie. Imia. Kosmos* (Moscow: Mysl', 1993), 6; also Marchenkov, "Aleksei Losev and His Theory of Myth," introduction to Losev, *Dialectics of Myth*, 4–12.

he became friends with the poet Boris Pasternak.[185] He enrolled simultaneously in the departments of classical philology and philosophy, in the latter
case under Lopatin, Chelpanov, and Shpet (his first published essay, "Eros
u Platona," appeared in the same festschrift for Chelpanov as did Shpet's
"Soznanie i ego sobstvennik").[186] He studied briefly in Berlin in 1914, but
was forced to return to Russia by the outbreak of war.

Losev also participated energetically in the assorted circles devoted to
philosophical and psychological themes that proliferated in Moscow in the
pre-Soviet era, usually by reading papers on ancient Greek philosophy.
From 1911, under Chelpanov's sponsorship, he attended the "Solov'ev Religious-Philosophical Society," where he met such leading figures of the Russian metaphysical renaissance as Nikolai Berdiaev, Evgenii Trubetskoi,
Semën Frank, Il'ia Il'in, Sergei Bulgakov, and Florenskii—as well as Viacheslav Ivanov, for whose Neoplatonic theories of symbol and myth he felt a
particular affinity. When that circle closed following the October Revolution in 1917, he joined Berdiaev's Free Academy of Spiritual Culture, until
it, too, closed in 1922. He participated in Moscow University's Psychological
Society until it in turn was closed in 1921, and in the "Lopatin Philosophical Circle."[187] In addition to classical philology and ancient philosophy
Losev closely followed developments in contemporary philosophy, both in
Russia and in western Europe (especially, but by no means only, neo-Kantianism and phenomenology) and maintained an abiding interest in mathematics and music, exploring the links among Neoplatonic philosophy, the
ideal nature of numerical relations, and the "eidetic completeness" of musical imagery.[188] Losev's father had been a math teacher and violinist (though
he abandoned the family when Losev was young), Losev's wife (to whom he
had been married, incidentally, by Florenskii) was a mathematician and as-
tronomer, while Losev himself wrote serious studies on both subjects—witness his *Muzyka kak predmet logiki* (Music as a topic in logic [1927]) and
Dialektika chisla u Plotina (The dialectic of numbers in Plotinus [1928])—
and from 1922 to 1930 held the position of professor of aesthetics in the
Moscow Conservatory. As Losev himself summarized his wide-ranging

185. L. A. Gogotishvili, "Rannii Losev," *Voprosy filosofii* 7 (1989): 133.
186. Haardt, *Husserl in Russland*, 187–88.
187. Takho-Godi, "Aleksei Fedorovich Losev," in Losev, *Bytie. Imia. Kosmos*, 7. Katerina Clark
notes the concerted press campaign in 1922 and 1923 against those in Soviet universities who were
still "proselytizing" for an idealist or religious worldview; see her "The 'Quiet Revolution' in Soviet Intellectual Life," in Sheila Fitzpatrick et al., eds., *Russia in the Era of NEP* (Bloomington: Indiana University Press, 1991), 220. Takho-Godi also points out that many of Losev's teachers were
forced, for similar reasons, to emigrate in 1922; in her "Tri pis'ma A. F. Loseva," *Voprosy filosofii* 7
(1989): 150.
188. Takho-Godi, "A. F. Losev—filosof imeni, chisla, mifa," in *A. F. Losev i kul'tura XX veka*
(Moscow: Nauka, 1991), 10.

intellectual interests, in a letter written from his labor camp to his wife in her labor camp, "Synthesized within my worldview are the ancient cosmos with its finite space—and Einstein, scholasticism and neo-Kantianism, the monastery and marital relations, the refinement of western subjectivism with its mathematical and musical element and eastern [Orthodox] palamite ontologism."[189] Or, as he had put it in an earlier letter to her, "Name, number, and myth—that is the element in which your and my life unfolded."[190]

The trajectory of Losev's professional career is lamentably familiar from the Soviet era, though his astonishing output under difficult conditions is exceptional by any measure. After spending the trying civil war years in Moscow poring over ancient Greek texts at a time when the Soviet government and its avant-garde allies were blaring their hostility toward the past and most of the rest of the city's inhabitants were busy procuring food, Losev took a position as professor of classical philology at the University of Nizhnii Novgorod from 1919 to 1921.[191] From 1921 to 1930 he headed the section on aesthetics at GAKhN (State Academy for the Artistic Sciences), where Shpet served as vice president until 1929, and from which Shpet was purged in 1930.[192] Losev himself incurred the wrath of the authorities in 1930 by publishing a work (*Dialektika mifa* [*The Dialectics of Myth*]) to which he had restored passages cut by the censors. The official charge leveled against him was plotting an armed uprising to restore the monarchy, and Losev's provocative act earned him public invective from no less than Lazar Kaganovich, at the Sixteenth Congress of the Communist Party, and Gor'kii, in the 12 December 1931 issues of both *Pravda* and *Izvestiia*).[193] After seventeen months in Liubianka prison he was sentenced to ten years hard labor and dispatched to work on the infamous White Sea–Baltic canal project. As the agent who had handled Losev's affairs with publishers, his wife, Valentina Mikhailovna, was also arrested and sentenced to five years' hard labor. Following the intervention of Lenin's sister and Gor'kii's wife, however, both were released early, in 1933. In the 1930s Losev taught philosophy in "peripheral" universities, until in 1942 he was finally allowed to take

189. A. F. Losev, "Pis'ma," *Voprosy filosofii* 7 (1989): 153.

190. Quoted in Takho-Godi, "Aleksei Fedorovich Losev," in Losev, *Bytie. Imia. Kosmos*, 5.

191. Ibid., 8.

192. For a very thorough, if still incomplete, survey of Losev's activities in GAKhN, see A. G. Dunaev, "Losev i GAKhN," in *A. F. Losev i kul'tura XX veka* (Moscow: Nauka, 1991), 197–220 (among other interesting details is the abstract of a paper Losev gave on Cassirer's work on symbolic forms, 216–17). On RAKhN/GAKhN (the name changed in 1925) see John E. Bowlt, "RAKhN on Trial: The Purge of Gustav Shpet," *Experiment. A Journal of Russian Culture*, vol. 3 (1997): 295–305.

193. Takho-Godi, "Aleksei Fedorovich Losev," in Losev, *Bytie. Imia. Kosmos*, 24.

up a position in logic at Moscow State University.[194] Following a long hiatus in publishing, during which he nonetheless wrote prolifically "for the drawer," as the Russian saying has it, Losev enjoyed a very productive second career from the 1950s until his death in the late 1980s, during *perestroika*. The works of that period, however, fall outside the bounds of the present study.

At first glance Husserlian phenomenology affords an odd departure point for an explication of Losev's philosophy of language. Husserl occupies a much lower profile in Losev's works than in those of Shpet, and in Russian discussions of Losev's work phenomenology tends to be mentioned only in passing, if at all (though Takho-Godi's claim that Losev became acquainted with Husserl only after completing *Filosofiia imeni* in 1923 is surely inaccurate).[195] But for all Losev's preoccupation with ancient philosophy it is important to remember the contemporary premises of his thought. As Haardt points out, the *Rezeptionshorizont* in which the young Losev began to formulate his ideas was essentially the same as that which had shaped Shpet, and it is hard to imagine that a precocious philosopher studying at Moscow University in the 1910s would have missed out on its most fervent period of Husserlianism.[196] It is through Husserl that we can identify in Losev a set of initial metaphysical aims—having to do with asserting the being of ideas, against various forms of skepticism and denial—which are very close to those in Shpet and Husserl. "The idea is a *something*. The idea is something *that exists*," Losev argues at one point in *Dialektika mifa*,[197] essentially paraphrasing Husserl's repeated assertions that *eidos* is a new sort of *object*, that "mental existence is also real existence," and that phenomenology has opened up a new region of *being* never before delineated in its peculiarity, that of the world as *eidos*.[198] In fact Losev was to claim in 1930 that his study of the Platonic terms *eidos* and *idea*, and his investigations of

194. Gogotishvili, "Rannii Losev," 136.

195. Takho-Godi, "Aleksei Fedorovich Losev," in Losev, *Bytie. Imia. Kosmos*, 12. Although the textological history of *Filosofiia imeni* may not be straightforward (Losev completed the work in 1923 but only published it in 1927), and therefore parts may have been added after the basic text was completed, Losev's explicit reference in his introductory remarks to "the two or three explications of Husserl's thought in Russia" suggests he was already quite familiar with Husserl when writing this work; *Filosofiia imeni* (Moscow: Izd. Moskovskogo un-ta, 1990), 35. See also his comment in *Ocherki antichnogo simvolizma i mifologii* that he had not been "close" to Husserlianism in 1915–18, which implies that he was at least familiar with it, and his statement that he had completed his analysis of Husserlian eidetic terminology by 1921; *Ocherki antichnogo simvolizma i mifologii* (Moscow: Mysl', 1993), 697. Among scholars, Haardt lays the greatest stress on Losev's identity as a phenomenologist, devoting the second half of his *Husserl in Russland* to him.

196. Haardt, *Husserl in Russland*, 187.

197. A. F. Losev, *Dialektika mifa*, in his *Iz rannikh proizvedenii*, prilozhenie k zhurnalu *Voprosy filosofii* (Moscow: Pravda, 1990), 517.

198. Husserl, *Ideas*, 9; Husserl, *Logical Investigations*, 359; Husserl, *Ideas*, 63.

Neoplatonism—both cornerstones of his thought in general—had been profoundly influenced by Husserl's *Ideas,* although he claimed that he remained free of the "Husserlian hypnosis."[199]

Hypnosis or not, a Husserlian presence is simply impossible to ignore in Losev's works of the 1920s. Both *Filosofiia imeni* and *Dialektika khudozhestvennoi formy* identify their method as "phenomenological-dialectical" and posit the phenomenological "construal of *eidos* out of its separate moments" as a necessary, if preliminary, stage of philosophical analysis (to the extent that Losev places greater emphasis on the subsequent "dialectical" stage, on which more below, he really presents himself as a post-Husserlian).[200] Probably the most visible evidence of Husserl's influence on Losev lies in the philosophical procedures followed in many of Losev's works, especially the operations of "bracketing" certain forms of empirical reality and the stratification of analysis so as to provide accounts that successively approach the ascertainment of essence (that is, the phenomenological *epoché* which in Husserl enables the mind to seize on essence originarily). *Filosofiia imeni,* the most Husserlian of Losev's works, is organized as a successive examination of the "pre-objective structure [*dopredmetnaia struktura*] of the word" followed by that of its "object-structure [*predmetnaia struktura*]." This choice of methodological model is somewhat unfortunate for Losev's reader because it yields a wearying succession of analytical steps—*Filosofiia imeni* puts forward no fewer than sixty-seven "moments" of analysis! (The Neoplatonic philosopher Proclus, with his relentless propagation of hierarchical levels of reality, may be another regrettable model here.)

Together with its baroque methodological apparatus, however, Losev also adopts phenomenology's drive toward essence. The project he announces in *Filosofiia imeni* involves taking what he calls the "symbolon" that is the word and casting off from it everything having to do with the phoneme, that is, with its purely physical, acoustical side, then discarding everything having to do with psychological aspects of its usage and reception.[201] What one is left with is a very Husserlian "pure noema of the word . . . given in the form of a certain correlate of the object in the sphere of understanding" (that Losev speaks from the outset about *words* rather than the consciousness and eidetic intuitions that are central to Husserl, is, of course, characteristic of the Russian tradition going back at least to Potebnia).[202] "Veshch' i imia" opens with the similarly Husserlian assertion that the essence of a

199. Losev, *Ocherki antichnogo simvolizma i mifologii,* 696–97.

200. Losev, *Dialektika khudozhestvennoi formy* (1927; reprint, Munich: Verlag Otto Sagner, 1983), 9.

201. Losev, *Filosofiia imeni,* 42.

202. Ibid., 46. See Haardt, *Husserl in Russland,* 234–36, for a comparison of the concept of "noema" in Husserl and Losev.

thing is not formed out of its features but lies deeper, in its sense, and as late as 1930 Losev would refer to a key proposition in one of his works as "the complete phenomenological uncovering of these terms."[203]

Husserlian concepts play an equally significant "meonic" (as Losev himself might have termed it) role in Losev's works, that is, as guides to what ideas should be avoided and as philosophical precedent for turning away from them. For the most part these dangers group themselves into the same Scylla of (neo)Kantianism and psychologism, and Charybdis of positivism and materialism, that Florenskii, Bulgakov, and Shpet had sought to steer between—a configuration that says much about the extent to which Losev emerged from the psychological discussion groups of the Moscow intellectual scene stamped, like Shpet, with the pro-Husserl anti-psychologism described by Toman.

In the provocatively titled introduction to *Filosofiia imeni* ("Phenomenology is not psychology") Losev follows Husserl in criticizing psychology for its preoccupation with empirical observations of particular mental states or perceptions, rather than with the apprehension of essences. "What is bad is that in psychology so far there reigns the old sentimental habit of 'observations' of 'life' apart from any preliminary analysis of psychological concepts," he remarks, and asserts that to reduce psychology to such an applied science is as absurd as talking about mechanics, astronomy, or mathematics without first establishing them as theoretical (abstract) sciences.[204] Later, declaring the centrality of apophatic thought to his concept of the word (which at this point he is calling "symbolism"), he says that to separate the two means either to fall into agnosticism with regard to Kantian "things-in-themselves," which supposedly no cognitive act of the human mind can touch (as a result of which all existence, he claims, turns into a "impenetrable murk of illusion"); or to fall into "ugly positivism," which takes every phenomenon to be an essence and thus deifies life's chance events.[205] In the case of neo-Kantianism Losev accuses the movement of merely replacing Kant's metaphysical dualism with a logical one (though in general he held the movement in much higher regard than Shpet had). The notion that one can suspend judgments about things and remain in a sphere of "principles" and "hypotheses" is not pernicious in itself, Losev says, but it is insufficient. "The chief error of neo-Kantian transcendentalism consists in its *not being immediate knowledge* and *not speaking of immediate being*. It repels itself from immediate being and casts it into its hated swamp of commonplace

203. Losev, "Veshch' i imia," in his *Bytie. Imia. Kosmos*, 803; Losev, *Dialektika mifa*, in his *Iz rannikh proizvedenii*, 578.

204. Losev, *Filosofiia imeni*, 34.

205. Ibid., 113.

perception of 'givenness.' [But] being does not just come into being and dissolve, it does not just flow, change, and recede. It also harbors in every moment of its process something structurally finished and whole."[206]

Husserl had developed phenomenology in part as a reaction against positivism and the late-nineteenth-century view of the natural sciences as guides to philosophical truth, convinced as he did so that he was reviving idealist initiatives first undertaken by Plato and then Kant. For Losev, writing in the Soviet 1920s, the situation was analogous but complicated by the ascendancy of the "scientific materialism" of Marxism-Leninism as the prescribed worldview of Soviet society—and Losev is far more direct in his engagement of this adversary than is Shpet. The very idealist bias of Losev's writings, with their focus on the word, the name, essence, idea, and so on (epitomized in such assertions as "the universe is name/word" and "everything is sense and its expression") is brazenly anti-materialist, with a polemical edge that cost Losev some years of his life.[207] Nor did Losev refrain from taunting his opponents. Examining in *Dialektika mifa* the Marxist slogan, threadbare even by then, that "being determines consciousness," Losev asks whether consciousness itself is not a form of being. If it is not, he argues, then what we are left with is "Kantian metaphysical dualism" dividing subjective consciousness, which is not truly "being," from authentic things-in-themselves about which consciousness can have no knowledge. The only viable alternative to this impasse, he asserts, is to regard consciousness as also a form of being "determined" by its own form of existence (after all, he points out in an ironically candid Leninist vein, the Revolution was the result of conscious action exerted upon social existence).[208]

There are also perhaps deeper intellectual affinities between Losev and Husserl than even their shared eidetic bent might suggest. I have already indicated the sympathetic parallel between Husserl's "bracketing" procedures, which sequentially pare away what is non-essential in the object as it presents itself to us in consciousness, and the apophatic theology of the Orthodox Church—which Losev explicitly embraces in some of his works and which underlies virtually all of them—with its hierarchy of negative statements about what an ultimately unknowable God is *not*. To this may be added the fact that both were, in a sense, "mathematician[s] turned philosophers" who were interested in mathematical issues specifically as examples of eidetic phenomena.[209] Husserl's first book was *The Philosophy of Arithmetic*

206. Losev, "Veshch' i imia," in *Bytie. Imia. Kosmos,* 865. For further discussion by Losev of propositions concerning essence, idea, being, and so on in "rationalist philosophy" (Descartes and Kant in particular), see ibid., 849–56.

207. Losev, *Filosofiia imeni,* 153.

208. Losev, *Dialektika mifa,* in *Iz rannikh proizvedenii,* 519.

209. See Lauer's comment on Husserl, in his "Introduction," 48.

(1891), while one of Losev's celebrated octet of books written in the 1920s was *Dialektika chisla u Plotina* (1928). One could also note that on the level of intellectual, or even perhaps spiritual, personality, the "apodictic inner evidence" on which Husserl repeatedly insists as vital to phenomenological analysis can sound strikingly similar to Losev's interest in the silent, inward "Jesus" prayer of the *imiaslavie* movement. In the end it may be affinities such as these that bind together the Russian thought on language this study explores, and even the much broader Neoplatonic tradition described by Prat.

For all Losev's debt to Husserl, however, phenomenology remained for him not an endowing "influence" but a project to be emulated in its fundamentals, then surpassed. Losev finds phenomenology deficient in two key areas: it is weak on ontology, and it is insufficiently dialectical. In his published works of the 1920s he affects to derive this insight out of strict methodological considerations and nothing more, and to offer his supplementations accordingly; but in fact his writings are underlaid from the start by an *a priori* project, harmonious with other strands in the Moscow intellectual context and cognate with the Russian writings on language examined in this study, which aims at producing a cosmology in which a theory of the name as *logos*—as personified word—occupies a central position, so that the essence of being and the essence of language turn out to be the same thing. In order to do this Losev embarks on a stunning, intentional revival of Neoplatonic philosophy and related teachings in Eastern Orthodoxy that is designed to remedy the shortcomings of contemporary idealist philosophy while utterly displacing the materialism of Soviet ideology, which he cleverly unmasks as but another cultural myth. This project is carried out over a large and variegated *oeuvre* in which, due to the conditions of Soviet censorship, Losev had to resort to aesopian means rather than discourse in the terms he actually had in mind (which is one thing in literature, quite another in philosophy—hence perhaps the tendency among scholars to search in his profuse and camouflaged works for a manageable paradigm that might serve as "key" to it all).[210] But its result—however ungainly, idiosyncratic, and sometimes brazenly partisan—is the richest, most explicit tapestry that we have of the various strands informing Russian thought on language in the early twentieth century.

---

210. See, for example, Gogotishvili, "Rannii Losev," 137. *Filosofiia imeni* is probably the most thoroughly camouflaged, and therefore most opaque on an initial reading. There are some interesting parallels between the shape of Losev's *oeuvre* and that of Shpet, suggesting a certain element of emulation: both applied their ideas to the realm of aesthetic theory (Shpet's *Esteticheskie fragmenty*, Losev's *Dialektika khudozhestvennoi formy*) and to myth (Shpet's "Vvedenie v etnicheskuiu psikhologiiu," Losev's *Dialektika mifa*).

Losev shared his impulse to ontologize Husserl's thought with Shpet, though his claims in this area are significantly bolder than those of his erstwhile professor. The point of contention has to do with the status of the eidetic realities presented to us through acts of intuition. Although Husserl claimed that phenomenology did not turn the world into a subjective allusion or commit one to "Berkeleyan idealism," he explicitly rejected a "Platonic hypostatization" of essences that would ascribe to them "actual (veritable) being," and stated that the error of Platonic realism was to assume that the species exists externally to thought.[211] Losev is not so troubled by the prospect of hypostatization, and worries rather that this rejection leaves phenomenology mired in the subjectivity and skepticism of Kant and Hume. In fact, he argues, Husserlianism ("but not Husserl") is much closer to neo-Kantianism than it cares to admit. Both inquire into structures of pure sense, rather than into "things" and "real being" (a distinction Husserl would hardly have drawn so confidently); both set fact and sense in opposition to each other, rather than exploring the forms of their mutual integration; both ask what being is only as it obtains in consciousness and thought, and thus both content themselves with mere "hypotheses" regarding the nature of the world.[212]

Losev presents his own philosophy as a recovery of this "thing" itself, and he accomplishes this by exchanging Husserl's still very-provisional, yet-to-be-analyzed essence for the rather exotic fruit of an elaborate cosmology derived from Neoplatonism.[213] His writings thus assimilate the concerns of the Husserl-Shpet-Potebnia-Humboldt line of inquiry into language and thought to the interest in Neoplatonism prevalent in certain Moscow intellectual circles—an assimilation, again, all the more provocative and subversive for having been carried out in the context of Marxist-Leninist materialism.[214] In this he may simply have been following a characteristic Russian tendency to interpret German philosophy in the context of the "mighty neo-Platonic stream" running from the Middle Ages through Hegel, and he was almost certainly responding to the impetus to overcome

211. Husserl, *Logical Investigations*, 129, 350; Husserl, *Ideas*, 40. Moreover, for Husserl philosophy is all metamethodology: discussing how you do phenomenology *is* doing phenomenology. Losev has other things on his agenda.

212. Losev, "Veshch' i imia," in *Bytie. Imia. Kosmos*, 863, 865–66. The same ontological turn registers itself in *Filosofiia imeni* when Losev states that if "noema" were all that words contain we would be isolated from the world within our own thought processes. "But the mystery of the word lies in the communion [it affords] with the object and with other people" (48). The word is neither simply noema, nor simply the object itself. It is the arena in which we meet the "inner life" of objects (49).

213. Losev, "Veshch' i imia," in *Bytie. Imia. Kosmos*, 871.

214. For Losev's own account of how his interest in Platonism and Neoplatonism unfolded in parallel with his interest in Husserl, see his *Ocherki antichnogo simvolizma i mifologii*, 694–708.

the "schism" between consciousness and being that motivated adherents of Solov'evian "philosophy of All-Unity."[215] His interest in Neoplatonism may also, however, be seen as a part of a larger rekindling of interest in the movement among twentieth-century European philosophers, exemplified in such works as Praechter's *Richtungen und Schulen im Neuplatonismus* (1910), Bidez's *Vie de Porphyre* (1913), Theiler's *Vorbereitung des Neuplatonismus* (1930), and Dodd's 1936 English edition of Proclus's *Elements of Theology.*[216] Indeed, if Neoplatonism can be described as an adaptation of the categories of Greek thought to the world of inner experience, Husserl himself swims in this current.[217]

The Neoplatonists derived their cosmology from Plato's *Timaeus,* which discusses being and becoming and the generation of the universe by the Demiurge, especially from a literalizing reading of the *Parmenides,* the Platonic dialogue in which Parmenides, Zeno, and Socrates discuss such questions as the nature of "the all" (is it one, or many?), of "the one" (does it partake of being? what is its relation with the other?), and the existence of abstract ideas. From the *Parmenides* Plotinus extracted his doctrine of the three hypostases, while Proclus derived his *Theology* from it, and it influenced such Christian Neoplatonists as Dionysius the Areopagite (an important source for Losev).[218] Central to the Neoplatonist development of Platonic ideas was a metaphysical hierarchy headed by a principle of unity and elaborated through successive levels of being in which proximity to the original unity meant greater ontological status.[219] It was a concept born out of a "systematisation of the Pythagorean-Platonic tradition's identification of goodness with order and form, measure and limit, which in their turn imply number and mathematical ration and hence ultimately the presence

215. Prat, "Orthodox Philosophy of Language," 1. Losev's interest in Neoplatonism may have been influenced by P. P. Blonskii's study of Plotinus, which argues that a whole series of philosophers, from Proclus and Augustine to Luther, Calvin, Berkeley, Leibniz, Kant, Fichte, Schelling, and Hegel is "but separate moments in the development of a unified European philosophy based on Plotinus"; calls on philosophy to undertake a "rational reworking of myth"; and declares Plotinus to be "the basis of contemporary philosophy"; *Filosofiia Plotina* (Moscow: Tov. tipografiia A. I. Mamontova, 1918), 310–12. Losev and Blonskii were both students of Chelpanov, and maintained contact into the 1920s; see Takho-Godi, "A. F. Losev i G. I. Chelpanov," 37.

216. R. T. Wallis, *Neoplatonism* (New York: Charles Scribner's Sons, 1972), 175.

217. Ibid., 6. See also the recently published Porphyry, *Porphyry Introduction,* trans. with commentary by Jonathan Barnes (Oxford: Oxford University Press, 2003).

218. See Il'ichev, *Filosofskii entsiklopedicheskii slovar',* s.v. "Parmenid." On the conceptual complexities of *Parmenides,* see H. N. Fowler, "Introduction to the *Parmenides,*" in Plato, *Cratylus,* 195–97. On Neoplatonism in general, see Wallis, *Neoplatonism*; A. H. Armstrong, ed., *The Cambridge History of Later Greek and Early Medieval Philosophy* (Cambridge: Cambridge University Press, 1967); and C. Bigg, *Neoplatonism* (London: Society for Promoting Christian Knowledge, 1895).

219. Wallis, *Neoplatonism,* 56, 62.

of an organising unity."[220] At its apex stood a trinity of hypostases, of which the most important was "the One," an unknowable and unnamable entity, which was accessible only in a state of ecstasy and expressible only in the negative terms of apophatic theology (though one could refer to it as the Good or even God), but which, standing as a kind of ideal point outside the realm of existence, served as the cause of everything else.[221] Thus Plotinus, in his famous disquisition on "the Good or the One," asserts that things must be "one" in order to exist—this is a favorite notion of Losev's—and elsewhere suggests that the Greek word for "being," "*einai*," derives from the word for "one," "*hen.*"[222] Proclus similarly claims that "all that exists proceeds from a single cause."[223] Next in the Neoplatonic trinity came the Intelligence (*nous*), which represented the One's turning on itself in knowledge of itself (or, alternatively, the *nous* constituted itself by returning in vision or contemplation upon the One), then the Soul (*psyche*), the hypostasis turned both to mind and to the sensible cosmos.[224] These hypostases were believed to exist not just in nature but also in the human mind.[225] From this trinity there systematically derived successively lower levels on the scale of being, such as (in Proclus, whose entire theology is presented as the logical deduction of all these levels from the principle of unity) the "extant gods" (which included *nous* and being), followed by angels and demons, followed in turn by "particular souls" that inhabit bodies, such as the human soul, and so on down to the lowest level, which is matter. From this schema also derive the notion of intermediary powers between the cosmos and God (as in Philo) and assorted chains or ladders of being, which served the important purpose of bridging between the transcendent and the revealed worlds. This Neoplatonist cosmology is also, one notes, emphatically vitalist, the tale of an intelligible cosmos that is alive, a point of particular significance for Losev.

For the Neoplatonists the key principle—but also the paradox—informing the cosmos was the fact that this hierarchical, multiform, ramifying cosmos existed because the One did not remain in itself but exited from itself and its state of absolute unity, generating plurality and successively lower

220. Ibid., 48; or, as A. H. Armstrong puts it, this was a "curious Neopythagorean exegesis of the *Parmenides*"; See his "The One and Intellect," in Armstrong, *Cambridge History of Later Greek and Early Medieval Philosophy*, 237.

221. Bigg, *Neoplatonism*, 124.

222. Plotinus, *Ennead VI. 6–9*, Loeb Classical Library, vol. 468 (Cambridge: Harvard University Press, 1988), 303; and *Ennead V*, Loeb Classical Library, vol. 444 (Cambridge: Harvard University Press, 1984), 171.

223. Proclus, *The Elements of Theology. A Revised Text*, 2nd ed., trans. E. R. Dodds (Oxford: Oxford University Press, 1963), 13.

224. Plotinus, *Ennead V*, 35 n. 1.

225. Wallis, *Neoplatonism*, 2.

orders of existence. This exiting took the form of an exuding of energy, in which the One produced a series of external images of its own inwardness in a spontaneous outflow that could not terminate until everything that could possibly be—all the Aristotelian *potentia*—had come into being.[226] Echoing this idea Proclus, for example, states that whatever is complete proceeds to generate those things it is capable of producing, imitating in its turn the one originative principle of the universe.[227] The paradox lay in the fact that this outflow of energy was also its squandering since, as an imitation of its prior, but also therefore a mere image of it, each successive level of reality represented degradation and descent into an inferior order of being.[228] Hence the One's journey outward was also a downward one into darkness, until the lowest form of darkness is reached in matter. Losev, more influenced by early Christian adaptations of Neoplatonism, tends instead to emphasize the radiant, divine source of the manifest cosmos. But he was clearly attracted by the mystical bent in Neoplatonism, which arose out of its adherents' belief that eventually everything must return to its cause, and that it lay before the soul, therefore, to undertake an introspective journey back up the levels of being until it was reunited with the Intelligence and, ultimately, the One. "The soul must let go of all outward things and turn altogether to what is within [and] ignoring all things . . . and even ignoring itself, come to be in contemplation of the One," Plotinus instructs.[229]

A good deal of Losev's *oeuvre*, at least in the 1920s, can be thought of as an adaptation of this Neoplatonic cosmology to a series of "studies" of mathematics, music, ancient myth, language, aesthetic form, and so forth. He sticks remarkably close to his ancient sources, copiously citing and even translating them throughout *Antichnyi kosmos i sovremennaia nauka* (The ancient cosmos and modern science, his most elaborate, Proclus-like derivation of a metaphysical hierarchy), invoking them throughout footnotes in works like *Dialektika khudozhestvennoi formy* and *Filosofiia imeni* and adducing them implicitly in *Ocherki antichnogo simvolizma i mifologii*, which presents itself as an exercise in historical philology. The most explicitly Neoplatonic point of departure in his works, the proposition from which his other statements on the nature of being, myth, language, and so on are

---

226. Ibid., 61, 65. With its antonym of "potential," the term "energeia" also allowed Aristotle to use the notion of "becoming" in order to bridge the gap between what is, *on*, and what is not, *me on*, since becoming is conceived of as a transition between the two; Il'ichev, *Filosofskii entsiklopedicheskii slovar'*, s.v. "akt i potentsiia." On the Neoplatonist doctrine of emanation see in particular Armstrong, "The One and Intellect," in Armstrong, *Cambridge History of Later Greek and Early Medieval Philosophy*, 236–49.

227. Proclus, *Elements of Theology*, 29.

228. Wallis, *Neoplatonism*, 5.

229. Plotinus, *Ennead VI. 6–9*, 329.

recurringly deduced, is the concept of the "One" in its dialectical relation with the "other." Before we know or can judge of anything, Losev asserts at the beginning of *Dialektika khudozhestvennoi formy,* we have knowledge of "the One" or of the quality of unity (he offers the mundane example of looking at a clock and knowing at the very least that it is a "one" of something—an intentional verbal paradox because in Russian, as for example in German, the word for "clock," "*chasy,*" is plural).[230] Fundamental to any further thought at all is the positing of this "One" and the assumption of its existence, the fact of which, he argues, means that this "One" delineates itself against the background of other things, that is, of otherness to it in general. Synonyms or functional equivalents of the terms "one" and "other" can appear, depending on the context of the given work, but in each case what Losev offers is a principle of transcendent unity discernible within the given object and generative of it. In discussing artistic form, for example, he states that if a thing expresses something, that means there "rests" (*pochiet*) on it some sense, which is embodied in it.[231] Artistic form also presupposes a prototype (*pervoobraz*) that serves as its archetype (*praobraz*).[232] "Essence" (*sushchnost'*) or "the extant" (*sushchee*) can play a similar role, as when Losev says that "expression" is the form of essence.[233] He also speaks of *eidos*—the Platonic concept of underlying form—as engaging in dialectical relations with "otherness" (*inobytie*) analogous to those of "the one" and accomplishing the manifestation of "primal unity, the extant" (*pervo-edinoe, sushchee*).[234] In *Filosofiia imeni* he terms the same argument the "problematic of the mutual definition of the extant [*sushchee*] and the other [*inoe*]."[235]

Losev's insistence that it is not from the "One" alone but from its relation with its opposite that subordinate concepts must derive—the dialectical moment in this scheme—marks his second major supplementation of phenomenology and one of the defining features of his thought. We know something exists, Losev argues, only if it distinguishes itself from and does not merge with otherness. If some "one–extant" (*odno-sushchee*) exists, its pure other cannot be just another object but "the non-extant" itself (*ne-sushchee*) or "*meon*" (Greek for "non-being"; this is, incidentally, the way the Neoplatonists conceived of matter). This "other" or "otherness" is not some negative *thing*—to assume that would be to fall into "naturalistic

230. Losev, *Dialektika khudozhestvennoi formy,* 9–10.

231. Ibid., 12. Losev's statement is in direct contradiction, incidentally, to Husserl's assertion that "being is nothing *in* the object, no part of it, no moment tenanting it"; *Logical Investigations,* 780.

232. Losev, *Dialektika khudozhestvennoi formy,* 65.

233. Ibid., 12.

234. Ibid., 29.

235. Losev, *Filosofiia imeni,* 54.

metaphysics"—but a "moment" of necessary otherness inhering in and instantiating the extant. Moreover, if the extant is the foundation of that which is sense-ful (*smyslovoe*) and rational, the *meon* must be the beginning of the irrational, the dialectically necessary irrational moment in the very rationality of that which exists.[236] Losev explicitly criticizes both Husserl and Shpet for failing to understand their "eidology" dialectically, noting in particular their resulting inability to explain how sensual *hyle* and intentional *morphe* are connected to each other, and invoking Plato, Plotinus, and Hegel as his corrective sources.[237]

If Losev's dialecticalism is responsible in some of his works for turning what would have been succinct philosophical argument into elephantine structures, as he successively runs each postulate through seemingly interminable stages of negation and synthesis (which for the reader at least can replicate the soul's arduous, multileveled journey up from darkness), it also constitutes the distinctly modern element in his thought, something like his own version of Heisenberg's Uncertainty Principle or Florenskii's antinomies. Unlike other Russian ontologists, Shpet among them, Losev refuses to see "essence" or "idea" as reposing in tranquility, insisting instead on its interaction with the irrational and darkness. Heidegger, too, was to show that "the question of being includes the question of nothingness," and it may be a general characteristic of Russian thought in this period to be at once retrospective and modern.[238] But Losev may also have developed his notion of the dialectic as an ironic counterpoint to a heated debate over Marxist dialectics that erupted in the Institute for Scientific Philosophy in May 1926 in connection with a discussion of Bergson and the Theory of Relativity, and which continued in the Soviet press until 1929.[239] On one side were the "dialecticians," consisting of A. M. Deborin and his followers, who argued that the dialectic had to be included in fundamental postulates that precede experience; on the other were the "mechanists," led by L. I. Aksel'rod, for whom the dialectic was merely derived after the event from

236. Ibid., 54.

237. Losev, *Antichnyi kosmos i sovremennaia nauka,* in his *Bytie. Imia. Kosmos* (Moscow: Mysl', 1993), 331, n. 10. In a footnote to *Filosofiia imeni* (225 n. 5) Losev says that he has already explained twice the dialectical relation between the one and otherness: in *Antichnyi kosmos i sovremennaia nauka* (59–62 and 73–86 in the 1927 edition, which apparently correspond to 115–20 and 131–45 in the 1993 reprint) and in *Dialektika khudozhestvennoi formy,* nn. 4, 5 (137–38), where he cites the relevant passages in Plato, Plotinus, and Hegel and discusses elements of dialectical thinking in the neo-Kantianism of Cohen and Natorp. See also Dunaev, "Losev i GAKhN," for synopses of papers Losev read on Proclus and Hegel, the dialectic in German aesthetics of the late eighteenth century, and the dialectical structure of the symbol (214–16).

238. Heidegger is paraphrased in Gadamer, *Truth and Method,* 257.

239. Losev mentions the debate directly in *Dialektika mifa,* in *Iz rannikh proizvedenii,* 512.

experiential data.[240] Though it is impossible to verify, Haardt's suggestion is intriguing: that what allowed Losev to publish such unabashedly idealist works in the late 1920s was the apparent sympathy between his views and the Hegelianizing "dialectic" camp among Soviet ideologists.[241]

Following the Neoplatonists Losev invokes the Aristotelian concept of *energeia* to explain the event of the "one's" exit from itself into dialectical engagement with otherness.[242] Nor should one forget, given that this all leads in Losev's thought to a philosophy of language, that "*energeia*" had also figured importantly in Humboldt, where it was glossed as "activity" in opposition to *ergon* or product, and used to promote a theory of language as expression rather than representation, as a bringing forth of speech out of an inner need.[243] Here again Losev was responding to both his modern milieu and its ancient antecedents.

In *Antichnyi kosmos i sovremennaia nauka* Losev thus speaks of the "energy of essence" as the striving of pure mind "to affirm itself against the background of the other, the different, in darkness"; it is a "becoming" (*stanovlenie*, a key term for Losev, especially in this heavily Neoplatonic work) which the "second nature strives to affirm in the process of self-differentiation from that which is other [*inogo*], from darkness."[244] Things arise when this energy exuded by essence becomes embodied in some kind of form: "a *thing* arising out of the embodiment of the energy of essence and therefore having a different nature to it [*inobytiinoe ei*] is different from it and thus is not it itself. But at the same time the thing gains sense [*osmyslivaetsia*], that is, receives its existence, exclusively via the energy of essence, and for this reason a thing is the energy of essence—but one having a different nature from the essence itself."[245] Or again, "the energetically

240. See notes in Losev, *Iz rannikh proizvedenii*, 606 (notes to pp. 14 and 18) and 640 (note to p. 512). The mechanists were sharply criticized at the Second All-Union Conference of Marxist-Leninist Institutions in 1929, but the dialecticians were also eventually debunked in 1930–31 when Stalin labeled them "menshevik-ing idealists" (ibid., 640). See also Gogotishvili, "Rannii Losev," 144. The original version of "Veshch' i imia" directly invokes this debate in its preface; in Losev, *Imia*, 168–71. This version differs somewhat from the revision Losev prepared, in the hope of having it published, after his return from the camps (for which see Losev, *Bytie. Imie. Kosmos*, 802–80).

241. Haardt, *Husserl in Russland*, 188.

242. See Losev, *Dialektika khudozhestvennoi formy*, 155–57. See also Losev's "interpretive translation" of Plotinus's "On Potential and Energy" in *Antichnyi kosmos i sovremennaia nauka*, 307–15.

243. For further interesting discussion of related Greek terms, in particular of *logos* as intellect versus *ergon* as the intractable world, see Parry, *Logos and Ergon in Thucydides*, 13, 15–21, 83–86.

244. Losev, *Antichnyi kosmos i sovremennaia nauka*, 156.

245. Ibid., 439. Regarding the "dialectical" manner in which the identity of essence is preserved within difference, see Losev's long footnote on the concept of "quiddity" in Aristotle, in *Antichnyi kosmos i sovremennaia nauka*, 557–63; also "Veshch' i imia," in *Bytie. Imia. Kosmos*, 873. Losev also argues that the doctrine of energy explains such phenomena as sameness versus difference, and generality versus specificity, which he says are analogous to potential/energy; see *Antichnyi kosmos i sovremennaia nauka*, 561.

existing [*energiino-sushchee*] is an extant [*sushchee*] which has manifested itself in time and decisively revealed its image [*lik*]."[246]

For Losev this Aristotelian-Neoplatonic metaphysics of energy resolves
such problems as the Kantian dilemma of the inaccessible thing-in-itself, ultimately explaining how and why the cosmos is knowable (the obvious contemporary target here being neo-Kantianism).[247] If essence *is*, Losev argues
in *Dialektika mifa*, then it is something, it has some feature that distinguishes it from everything else. Therefore it is knowable. It in some way *appears* (*iavliaetsia*) or *manifests itself* (*proiavliaetsia*). If on the other hand
there is no manifestation of essence, then there is nothing to be said about
essence at all ("Thus does the Kantian metaphysic of the 'thing-in-itself'
crumble at the slightest touch of the dialectic," he confidently asserts).[248]
Essence may be an apophatic concept, Losev comments in "Veshch' i imia,"
because it refers to something absolutely unknowable under any conditions;
but the dialectic demands that essence manifest itself in otherness. As it
does so it crosses over into the realm of appearance, creating a third term in
which essence and appearance merge in an indivisible whole. This term is
"the energy of essence" or "expression."[249] Similarly in *Filosofiia imeni* he
defines "*energema*" as the appearance or manifestation of essence.[250] The
very process by which energy acts in "otherness" is that of a form-giving,
sense-endowing appropriation (*okhvatyvanie*) of darkness, which leads ultimately to a formal *logos*—that is, the discursive intellection of reality.[251] Or,
projecting this idea onto language, Losev remarks that the word is not just
sense but sense given in otherness; this givenness in otherness is its energy,
inseparable from essence but distinguishable, because separable, from its
apophatic core.[252] Turning such insights toward the opposite pole of philosophical resistance, Losev identifies materialism in *Dialektika mifa* as a doctrine that erroneously takes matter to be essence, when in fact it is mere
emanation.[253]

246. Ibid., 440. For more on Losev's dialectic of being, in particular on the connections between his Neoplatonic scheme and the Christian doctrine of the Trinity, see the fragment, unpublished in his lifetime but apparently written around the time of *Dialektia mifa*, "Absoliutnaia
dialektika = absoliutnaia mifologiia," in *Imia*, 140–67.

247. Gogotishvili remarks that Losev's doctrine of "*energetizm*" resolves the conflict between
absolute dualism and crude monism: for him God and the created world are separated ontologically by a dualist abyss (i.e., their natures are distinct), but "energically" (i.e., in the form of emanations) there exists a monistic link between them; Losev, *Ocherki antichnogo simvolizma i
mifologii*, 925.

248. Losev, *Dialektika mifa*, in *Iz rannikh proizvedenii*, 519.

249. Losev, "Veshch' i imia," in *Bytie. Imia. Kosmos*, 875–76.

250. Losev, *Filosofiia imeni*, 62.

251. Ibid., 115.

252. Ibid., 162.

253. Losev, *Dialektika mifa*, in *Iz rannikh proizvedenii*, 520.

If the doctrine of "energy" explains the phenomenon of becoming, "*stanovlenie*," as the paradoxical moment of identity between essence and otherness, what does this becoming in turn dialectically generate? Something that has already come about (*stavshee*), Losev answers in *Dialektika khudozhestvennoi formy,* a fact, a presence (*nalichnost'*).[254] This phase of the dialectic is of pivotal importance to him, and in the form of one of its synonyms, "expression," provides the meeting site for the concepts of being and language in his works as well as the rationale for the whole series of Neoplatonic redefinitions of philosophical, linguistic, and aesthetic terms he undertakes.[255] Expression or form is "essence in the process of becoming in the medium of the other, unchangeably streaming in its semantic energies. . . . In general, expression is a *symbol.*"[256] It is "that element which results from the embodiment [*voploshchenie*] of eidos in the realm of otherness"; as the "synthesis of eidos and its other-being" it is a complex phenomenon, incorporating meonic moments.[257] "Veshch' i imia" presents the same concept in a dramatically anthropomorphic form that hints at some of the sources Losev clearly had in mind but suppressed out of concern for censorship:

> It is necessary for substance to pour itself out into sense and for sense to materialize, to become substance. But this means to cross over into a new category which is neither simply substance nor simply its sense. This new category is the expression of substance, the *energic expression* of substance, understood and rationalized [*urazumevaemaia*] substance, a *word* about substance, the name of substance. . . . Pure sense becomes substantialized: this means that it goes from being something stable and purely inner, purely essential to being mobile, moving outward and therefore forward, moving *from within to the outside,* becoming *expressed.*[258]

This is precisely the point at which it becomes clear that Losev is not just reproducing Neoplatonist doctrines but applying them to very definite, contemporary aims. On the one hand in Losev's works the concept of "expression" derives from the way he uses Neoplatonic cosmology to supplement the phenomenological view in order to explain the nature of a certain class of objects. If the knowable world consists of phenomena, and these are to be understood as the sensually given emanations of underlying essences, then language and words and related things like artistic forms are best understood as having the same nature. In each case a sensually given form

---

254. Losev, *Dialektika khudozhestvennoi formy,* 10–11.

255. On the concept of "expression" see V. V. Bychkov, "Vyrazhenie kak glavnyi printsip estetiki A. F. Loseva," in *A. F. Losev i kul'tura XX veka,* 29–37.

256. Losev, *Dialektika khudozhestvennoi formy,* 13.

257. Ibid., 17.

258. Losev, "Veshch' i imia," 843–44.

points to a transcendent essence or sense residing within it. This vein of thought in Losev, in other words, works to establish a synonymy between language and the metaphysical principle of "expression" understood as Neoplatonic emanation. Much of *Filosofiia imeni,* with its delineations of preobjective and objective structures of the name, of "sememic," "poemic," and "noematic" levels within the name, and so forth, is taken up with this kind of effort to determine the eidetic/essential structure of the word; the same could be said of the whole of *Dialektika khudozhestvennoi formy.* In these works Losev's use of the concept "word" by and large coincides with the common understanding of it as a lexical or semantic unit of language. The thrust of his argument on this level can be understood as simultaneously anti-neo-Kantian and anti-Marxist, or, in the case of *Dialektika khudozhestvennoi formy,* anti-Formalist (since that work demonstrates that in the aesthetic object form is the mere emanation of a more important, indwelling essence). Words lend themselves readily to this view because they can be thought of as having an "external" phonic or graphic form that refers to an originary inner core of meaning. It is a view of language that harmonizes well with Husserlian intuitions of eidetic essence, Potebnia's etymological core of essential meaning, and Shpet's inner architecture of expressive forms.[259]

But something more specific is involved here than just providing a dialectical account of the eidetic essence resident in the word in order to resolve aporia that, as Losev would have it, stumped Kant and his modern successors; because in addition to telling us that words should be understood as emanations of essence Losev also wants to convince us that the cosmos is a mind that expresses itself, which is to say, a word; that words are typified in names; and that names enjoy an essential link with the intelligent essence they denote. At this point Losev's Neoplatonic theory of language turns into a vision of names as emblematic forms of personhood, symptoms of a cosmos that is itself personal. If in the vein mentioned above Losev's assertion may be summarized in the statement, "Words should be understood as examples of 'expression' or 'emanation,' " then here that assertion is modified to state that "emanation—which is to say, in Losev's scheme of thing, everything that exists—should be understood as a word."[260] As Gadamer was to put it later, in a passage in *Truth and Method*

259. In a clear nod to Potebnia, Losev in *Filosofiia imeni* discusses the "etymon" as the "original embryo of the word," the point at which it first becomes a "word" as such (38), but also cautions against taking it to be eidetic essence (41).

260. Gogotishvili identifies a similar stratification of Losev's thought on language into "ontology proper," on which level he defines language without reference to the human subject, and "subjective ontology," in which he considers the implications for us of knowledge that our word is the "energy" of the original cosmic name ("Rannii Losev," 912–16).

that could serve as commentary to Losev, "the coming into language of meaning points to a universal ontological structure, namely to the basic nature of everything toward which understanding can be directed. *Being that can be understood is language.*"[261]

The reason this modification is significant is that, unlike other conceivable forms of emanation, words are inherently the products of intentional acts by a self. In this regard emanation or expression for Losev is closely linked with the concept of "intellection." The Neoplatonists considered the One to be beyond all knowledge and language, but they held that in a moment of division and self-reflection it generated the Intellect, which was the hypostasis of self-knowledge. This Intellect in turn generated and found reflection in the soul, and the most significant moments in this soul's existence involved a turning back toward contemplation of its source.[262] Thus the very process of emanation that accounts for the existence of the cosmos establishes that cosmos as a sentient being.

In Losev's description it is essence's act of flowing outward from itself into nonbeing, and once there dialectically merging with nonbeing to produce an expressive form—this very act being synonymous with life—that instantiates knowledge, reason, and intellection. The dialectical confrontation of essence with *meon* establishes essence's boundary, and therefore its definition, and therefore its self-knowledge. "The word is . . . pure intellection, distinguishing itself from pure *meon,* or darkness, and thereby naming itself. The word is the form of the object's self-knowledge, which is gained in an absolute formation of its sense (for the *meon* is the formation of the object)."[263] Alive with this kind of self-defining dialectical interchange with otherness, the cosmos is by its very nature rational, meaningful, "intelligent": What *is* has come to be solely through an act of self-reflexive knowledge. Once we understand "symbol" in terms of the ontology of expression, Losev remarks in *Filosofiia imeni,* "we cross over . . . into the sphere of truly linguistic phenomena. . . . Language is the objective establishing of being, and this establishing is one of sense, or more accurately an expressive establishing, and still more accurately, a symbolic one. Every energy of essence is therefore a language in which essence converses with its surroundings."[264] In other words, and this could be taken as the central tenet of Losev's philosophy of language, since being is an expressive form, everything in the cosmos is therefore a form of "language" or indeed a single universal Word.

261. Gadamer, *Truth and Method,* 474.
262. See for example Plotinus, *Ennead V,* 33–35, 75. Solov'ev's concept of Divine Wisdom or "Sophia" owes a good deal to this point in Neoplatonist thought.
263. Losev, *Antichnyi kosmos i sovremennaia nauka,* 173.
264. Losev, *Filosofiia imeni,* 98.

Everything that exists is some form of sense and its expression. "If essence is a name or word," he states in *Filosofiia imeni,* "then that means that the entire world, the universe is also a name or a word, or names and words. All being consists of more or less living words. . . . Everything lives through the word and gives testimony in it."[265] Where Shpet had been careful to limit his vitalist account of expressive structures to the products of human culture, Losev claims this "verbal" nature even for inanimate physical reality— "for it means something, it is something comprehensible" even if it is "a hardened, petrified word and name, something cold and bereft of soul."[266] Moreover, without the name, Losev tells us, the universe would turn into a "deep abyss of darkness and chaos."[267]

Far from being the inert, conventionalized elements of communicative code that they are in a Saussurian view of language (or in what Gadamer calls the "modern instrumental theory of language"), then, words in Losev's account are organically connected with the rational life of things themselves.[268] Because words are the "energy of thought" and a "sense-endowing force" they are not static but always in motion. They exist in a state of intellectual activity.[269] At one point he goes so far as to call them biological entities, "vegetable-animal organisms" ("*rastitel'no-zhivotnyi organizm*").[270] This view amounts to a hyperbolic version of Humboldt's claim that language is not a mere instrument but the organ of thought, in which the vitalism that had characterized, say, Shpet's account of "inner form," is promoted to outright anthropomorphism. In his discussions of intellection (where "word" is defined as the key moment in thought's coming-into-being or "*stanovlenie*"), Losev often leaves out direct reference to human agency, rendering ambiguous the issue of whether he is describing, in some Husserlian vein, the eidetic qualities of the thought in which human subjects engage, or the dialectic process of intellection pervading the cosmos as a whole (actually, in Neoplatonic terms there is no necessary contradiction here: for Plotinus, my intellection is a moment in the Intellect's self-knowing).[271] The phenomenology of thought, he states in *Filosofiia imeni,* consists in the fact that "*knowledge thinks itself by itself from within. . . . At the level of thought the word is knowledge of itself and knowledge of the fact of that knowledge, that is, self-consciousness.*"[272]

265. Ibid., 153.
266. Ibid., 66.
267. Losev, "Veshch' i imia," in *Bytie. Imia. Kosmos,* 880.
268. Gadamer, *Truth and Method,* 418.
269. Losev, "Veshch' i imia," in *Bytie. Imia. Kosmos,* 831–32.
270. Losev, *Filosofiia imeni,* 69.
271. Plotinus, *Ennead V,* 89, 293, 299.
272. Losev, *Filosofiia imeni,* 74.

Potebnia had asserted that it is in words that human thought arrives at self-consciousness; but Losev transfers a Neoplatonic understanding of mind to a definition of words and claims that these "words" have knowledge, not just as agents for human understanding, as in Humboldt and Potebnia, but also *for themselves.* "The word is the form of the object's self-knowledge, which is gained in an absolute formation of its sense."[273] Soon after in the same work he states that "the name of essence is not the means for understanding essence but *the organ of self-consciousness for essence itself.*"[274] In "Veshch' i imia" the same idea appears with added emphasis on the notion of manifestation: "The name of the thing is its maximal conceptual and mental manifestation—the name of the thing is the very sense of the thing, the reason of the thing consciously projecting itself outward and rationally directing its bottomless depths toward the light of lucid consciousness."[275] Or again, in *Dialektika mifa,* with characteristic ambiguity regarding agency, "In the word consciousness attains the level of self-consciousness. In the word sense expresses itself as the organ of self-consciousness and, consequently, of the opposition of itself to everything else. The word is not only nature understood but also nature having understood itself, rationally conceived and rationally conceiving nature."[276]

Where there is selfhood in this degree, other self-related matters like ethics are not far behind. Here again one is reminded of the early Bakhtin, save that in Losev the ethical relations are as often described as arising within words themselves as they are attributed to the subjects who deploy them. Speech is inherently a form of dialogue for Losev, because the generation of form out of essence requires the act of emergence from the confines of the self to engage with others (an idea, as we have seen, that was important to Florenskii and Shpet as well). To speak (*zagovorit'*) means not only to exist and have some image of oneself, but to direct that image outward, Losev remarks in "Veshch' i imia." Only when "reality" genuinely speaks out (*zagovorit*) does it become possible for someone to know and understand it.[277] Through its name reality opens itself to the eye of reason and permits itself to be understood.[278] The word is more than pure noema, he asserts in *Filosofiia imeni.* It is "a bridge between the subject and the object," the arena in which perceiver and perceived, knower and known, meet; it is the arena

273. Losev, *Antichnyi kosmos i sovremennaia nauka,* 155.

274. Ibid., 173.

275. Losev, "Veshch' i imia," in *Bytie. Imia. Kosmos,* 845.

276. Losev, *Dialektika mifa,* in *Iz rannikh proizvedenii,* 534.

277. Losev, "Veshch' i imia," in *Bytie. Imia. Kosmos,* 808–9.

278. Losev, "Dialektika imeni," 142. This brief work was apparently intended as part of "Veshch' i imia" but was deleted by Losev when, after his return from the labor camp, he hoped to publish a toned-down version of the work. See commentary by Takho-Godi in Losev, *Imia,* xiv–xvi.

in which we meet the "inner life" of objects.[279] The name elevates into consciousness the object to which it belongs and endows it with sense.[280]

Although he sometimes uses the terms "word" and "name" synonymously, in Losev's account it is the latter that most fully bears these qualities of selfhood (and here in particular Losev is indebted to Florenskii). Names are not just another form of the word but word's epitome, and Losev summarizes his "ontology of the name" in the phrase, "the name of the thing is the thing itself," a self-conscious secularization of the *imiaslavie* credo regarding the name of God.[281] Names do not just proceed out of the essence of the thing as its concrete manifestation, as the doctrine of "expression" instructs;[282] they mark the very endpoint in the Neoplatonic journey outward into otherness that for Losev defines existence: "The name of the thing . . . is the terminal boundary of all its intellectual self-manifestations and self-expressions, if one approaches it from the side of its inner depths."[283] In this scheme the process of naming involves, again, the *referent's* acquiring knowledge of itself, as something distinct from all else ("This knowledge of oneself as distinct from everything else is precisely what *naming* is").[284] The name of a thing is the energy of its self-understanding.[285] As such the name always refers to a self (*lichnost'*) or "at least is interpreted as a self, as intellection, as an inner inspiriting/animation and self-consciousness."[286] At one point Losev even claims that when we use a name, the object to which it refers hears that name, responds to the call we have issued in uttering it, empathizes with it, corresponds with it, and responds to it![287] Thus does Losev arrive at a radically "realist" answer to the debate between realism and nominalism that has smoldered since the Middle Ages. As the constitutive factor of the thing, without which the thing would not be what it is, the name enjoys the most essential link possible with its referent and is fully appropriate to it.[288] The level of ontological anxiety is

279. Losev, *Filosofiia imeni*, 48–49.

280. Losev, "Veshch' i imia," in *Bytie. Imia. Kosmos,* 817.

281. Ibid., 810. Though see the fleeting distinction Losev draws between "*imia*" and "*nazvanie*" in "Veshch' i imia," in *Bytie. Imia. Kosmos,* 820.

282. See Losev, "Dialektika imeni," 143.

283. Losev, "Veshch' i imia," in *Bytie. Imia. Kosmos,* 844.

284. Ibid., 809.

285. Ibid., 838.

286. Ibid., 840.

287. Ibid., 829.

288. Ibid., 817–18. Losev handles the issue of natural languages having different names for things by calling the language-specific, etymologically encoded characterization of a thing its "concept" (*poniatie*) while defining "meaning" (*slovesnoe znachenie veshchi*) as the abstract sense universal to all languages; when we hear the German word "*Kunst,*" for example, fused in our reception of it are the abstract meaning of "art" and the local German emphasis, added to its expression, on the notion of will (because of the word's derivation from "*können*"); ibid., 822.

palpably lower in Losev than it is in Shpet, but his doctrine of the name accomplishes something similar: an ontologically secure and even idealized
version of the self has been spun off in a motion of its own, independent of
the vicissitudes afflicting more human subjects in the politically unsettled
era of the Soviet 1920s.

The manner in which Losev's key ideas, his peculiar merging of Neoplatonism with phenomenology, transcend the particular subject matter of the
studies in which they are presented justifies a reading of all his texts, or at
least those of the 1920s, as if they were one text appearing in a variety of top-
ical guises.[289] Nonetheless to gain a fuller sense of how Losev's doctrine of
the (cosmic) name as a form of personhood underlies the apparently idiosyncratic manner of the texts' ostensible terms, it bears looking more closely
at a single work. One of the fullest accounts he gave of his doctrine was the
fatefully self-published *Dialektika mifa* of 1927, which anyway merits closer
examination as one of the most interesting intellectual documents of the
early Soviet era.

Despite having been written at a time when the Soviet regime was increasingly insistent on ideological conformity—witness its attacks on the
Formalists—*Dialektika mifa* blithely invokes such notions as the Orthodox
understanding of communion and the incantatory qualities of names, and
in many passages affects a kind of naive anachronism, as if it had been written in 1910 as a contribution to Russia's religious renaissance. Yet it cun-
ningly engages its context, on the one hand offering an account of
materialist philosophy as nothing but a myth of matter as "dead Leviathan,"
based on the erroneous assumption that matter is essence rather than appearance, while on the other pretending to accept a definition of Christianity, too, as nothing but myth—only to show how meaning-laden and
central to human experience "myth" is.[290] As in the case of terms like
"word" or "name," in Losev's writings "myth" acquires an idiosyncratic definition that often seems remote from mythology in the anthropological
sense. *Dialektika mifa* can be read on one level as an analysis of myths as we
know them, and Losev makes occasional gestures in this direction; but it is

288. Ibid., 817–18. Losev handles the issue of natural languages having different names for
things by calling the language-specific, etymologically encoded characterization of a thing its
"concept" (*poniatie*) while defining "meaning" (*slovesnoe znachenie veshchi*) as the abstract sense
universal to all languages; when we hear the German word "*Kunst*," for example, fused in our reception of it are the abstract meaning of "art" and the local German emphasis, added to its expression, on the notion of will (because of the word's derivation from "*können*"); ibid., 822.

289. Gogotishvili, "Rannii Losev," 136–37.

290. See also Vladimir Marchenkov's discussion of Losev's concept of myth in connection with
Schelling's idea of a "new mythology," in his "Aleksei Losev and his Theory of Myth," introduction to Losev, *Dialectics of Myth*, 28, 38.

more accurately thought of as a treatise on expressive forms as exemplars of selfhood.

Losev begins *Dialektika mifa* with a discussion of his concept of "expression," which he defines here as "the active directing of that which is internal toward the external, a certain active self-transformation of the internal into the external" (from Potebnia onward metaphors of inwardness and outwardness have played an important role in Russian language-bound doctrines of selfhood). With characteristic fondness for dialectical paradox, he calls the resulting synthesis the "self-identical distinction of the internal from the external."[291] Words are precisely this kind of expressive entity, so they exemplify this "energic" synthesis of inner and outer. The examples Losev provides of larger verbal systems are mythology and poetry, which he further defines as forms of intellection, because they are animated or inspirited forms of expression—by which Losev seems to mean the Humboldtian notion that these are forms in which people think.[292] Myth is "the symbolically given intellection of life." Its "mythic" quality lies not in the object depicted but in the means by which it is expressed and comprehended.[293] Myth deals not in abstract ideas but in concrete gods, heroes, and actions; interpreted as Neoplatonic "expression," myth is therefore that "special sphere in which abstract concepts immerse themselves in order to transform themselves into living things of living perception."[294] But here Losev also defines selfhood (*lichnost'*) as "symbolically realized intellection," and modifies his definition of myth to take selfhood into account. Myth now becomes "the being of selfhood or, more precisely, the image of the being of selfhood, the form of selfhood, selfhood's image/face" ("*lik*").[295] Like all forms of essence, selfhood performs an act of expression in order to affirm itself, but the nature of this self-affirmation depends on the medium in which it occurs. When sought in its most fundamental existential roots, which Losev says lie "in eternity," the result is religion; but when it unfolds in history, the arena for Losev in which his cherished "energic or phenomenological coming-into-being of selfhood" takes place, the result is "myth."[296] Myth therefore represents the historical being of personhood, the verbal form of its self-consciousness in time.[297] Though Losev is drawing on a different set of sources here, this definition could also be read as a heavily Hegelian (re-)revision of the Marxist account of history.

291. Losev, *Dialektika mifa*, in *Iz rannikh proizvedenii*, 423.
292. Ibid., 444.
293. Ibid., 445.
294. Ibid., 456.
295. Ibid., 459. On how this is just the form of personhood and not its substance, see page 484.
296. Ibid., 481, 492.
297. Ibid., 536.

But how then to reconcile the antinomy between myth as conscious-verbal-personal form unfolding in history and our "lay" knowledge of it as tales about strange and supernatural events?[298] The synthesizing definition Losev offers at this point is that myth is a form of miracle.[299] This term he defines, seemingly idiosyncratically but almost certainly hinting at the Christological "miracle" of incarnation, as the unexpectedly complete correspondence in myth between the self's ideal prototype (*praobraz*) and its expressive, material, and historical, form.[300] "It is like the second incarnation of the idea, the first having taken place in the originary ideal archetype and paradigm, the other the incarnation of these in a real historical event" (*sobytii*, which here may have some of the overtones Bakhtin emphasized in the word, that is, a co-being).[301] Myth, then, is a word about a self, a word belonging to that self and expressing and manifesting its selfhood. It is therefore the proper word of a self or its *name* (*substvennoe slovo,* in the sense of exclusive belonging). "The name is that proper word about the self, that word which only it can give and reveal about itself. . . . In the name [there obtains] the dialectical synthesis of selfhood and its expressed-ness."[302] Because it incorporates a "miraculous" element, in the sense that its allegorical forms mimic the incarnation, it also creates miracles and is a "magical name" (an obvious allusion to Bely's "Magiia slov" and Florenskii's "Magichnost' slova"). At the same time, because it manifests itself in history, myth is an "unfolded magical name."[303] And if one speaks of something Losev calls "absolute mythology" rather than the particular mythologies of particular peoples, then myth is "an unfolded magical name taken in its absolute being," his summary definition of the term.[304]

Here Losev cannot help but disclose some of the intellectual agenda underlying his ostensible essay on "myth." First he argues that the dialectic of part and whole "dictates" the existence of the Church, because only in the Church are individual and community synthesized.[305] Then he cites with approval the kabbalistic notion that God manifests himself in Israel and

---

298. It is very likely that in his work on myth Losev was responding to intellectual debates in the 1920s over Levi-Bruhl's definition of myth as a form of primitive "prelogical" thought that was "indifferent to contradictions," in contrast to the concept-based logical thought of modern cultures. The debate was taken up in the Soviet press. See Gogotishvili, "Rannii Losev," 142–43. Given his "dialectical" bent, the putative relation between myth and logical contradictions would have been especially important for Losev.

299. Losev, *Dialektika mifa,* in *Iz rannikh proizvedenii,* 537.

300. Ibid., 550.

301. Ibid., 550–51.

302. Ibid., 579.

303. Ibid.; see also Losev, *Imia,* 159.

304. Losev, *Dialektika mifa,* in *Iz rannikh proizvedenii,* 595.

305. Ibid., 589.

becomes Israel for the sake of his own salvation.[306] In fact, he observes, something like theism or the immortality of the soul is required by the dialectic (*sic*; this in the late Soviet 1920s) because one could not expect an absolute idea to be sustained by "a divisible and mortal body."[307] The immortality of the soul thus turns out to be "the most primitive axiom of the dialectic," and since it has been shown that everything must find a consciousness adequate to it if it is to be known, then for the whole of being taken in its past, present, and future there must exist some "adequate universal [*vselenskaia*] consciousness," which "nothing prevents from being" a subject—whom Losev here openly labels "God."[308] But if "absolute mythology" is in fact a form of theism, positing the absolute existence outside the world of a single, personal God, then "mythology" admits only one complete and hypostatic manifestation of God in otherness, which is the Church.[309] All this is what Losev claims to have derived from an analysis of "myth."

At this point in Losev's thought—when he has asserted that the essence underlying the cosmos strives not only toward self-realization in otherness, but also toward self-understanding, thus self-naming, and thus an intensive form of communication with itself—a door opens onto a whole world of determining subtexts.[310] These are at best only hinted at in some of the works (though as we have seen, *Dialektika mifa* comes close to revealing them, as do parts of *Filosofiia imeni* and "Veshch' i imia") but they have come to light in the post-Soviet revival of interest in Losev. Like that of many a Soviet intellectual, Losev's life of the mind had a "basement" to it, a less public domain in which he pursued the interests genuinely closest to his heart, typically in the medium of "papers" read in small intellectual circles of close associates, or in letters and personal conversation.[311]

In Losev's case these interests are different from, but closely allied with, the Neoplatonism he does prolifically cite: they revolve around a series of Eastern Orthodox doctrines that turn out to provide the rationale for his entire *oeuvre* and the source of the boldly inductive cosmology just discussed. The published works of the 1920s present these doctrines in the camouflaged form of discussions of philosophy of language, mythology, mathematics, the culture of antiquity, and so on, and there is no doubt that

306. Ibid., 594.
307. Ibid., 595.
308. Ibid., 595–96.
309. Ibid., 597.
310. On these topics see also *Antichnyi kosmos i sovremennaia nauka*, 173.
311. See Takho-Godi, "Iz istorii sozdaniia i pechataniia rukopisei A. F. Loseva," in Losev, *Imia*, viii.

the need to do this imposed restraints on Losev's thought. *Filosofiia imeni* in particular suffered, and Losev purportedly told an associate in later years that while Sergei Bulgakov in *his* identically titled *Filosofiia imeni* had been able to say what he wanted, Losev had been forced to dissemble in order to evade the censor.[312] *Dialektika mifa* was to have been followed by a study in "angelology," which survived only in manuscript form,[313] and an essay offering philosophical justification for the doctrine of divine names was dropped from "Veshch' i imia," though whether by Losev or the censor is unclear.[314] But the form in which Losev's ideas are presented in his published works is incomplete or diverted rather than significantly altered (in many cases one would only have to add one more step in his cherished dialectic to bring the ideas into the domain of Church doctrine) and it is possible that Losev regarded their "essence" as being preserved despite their somewhat flawed "energic" realization.[315]

Orthodox sources are decisive for Losev because, for all his energetic excavations of Platonist and Neoplatonist sources, for him the ideas expressed in them remain pagan. In particular he denigrates the culture of antiquity for being "extrapersonal" (*vnelichnostnaia*) and holds that progress was made only when Philo of Alexandria recast the Platonic absolute as personhood (*lichnost'*) in his concept of the First-Unity.[316] He even criticizes Florenskii for "christianizing Plato."[317] For Losev it is ultimately not Neoplatonism but the Eastern Christian reworkings of it that provide insight into the nature of being, the self, and language, a fact that from the vantage point of cultural history shows how rooted Losev was—as opposed to a secularly oriented philosopher like Shpet—in the Russian religious renaissance of the early twentieth century, though he insisted on the rights of reason and philosophy as well. In a 1918 survey of Russian philosophy written for a German publication, Losev identified the quintessence of Russian

312. On truncations of *Filosofiia imeni* see Takho-Godi, "A. F. Losev—filosof imeni, chisla, mifa," 8, and "Aleksei Fedorovich Losev," 11–12. Losev's remark about the censor, made to S. B. Dzhimbinov sometime in the 1970s or 1980s, is cited in *Iz rannikh proizvedenii*, 611, note to p. 72.

313. Losev, "Pervozdannaia sushchnost'," in *Imia*, 101–26 (in it Losev suggests that key concepts in Kant, Hegel, Husserl, Cohen, and Natorp are nothing but "emptied out angelology" [103]); on the history of the manuscript, see xiii.

314. Losev, "Mif—razvernutoe magicheskoe imia," in *Imia*, 127–39; on its fate, see xiii.

315. Gogotishvili, "Rannii Losev," 144.

316. See G. K. Vagner, "Problema lichnosti v trudakh A. F. Loseva," in *A. F. Losev i kul'tura XX veka*, 24, 26. In this Losev was almost certainly following the arguments of S. N. Trubetskoi's "O prirode chelovecheskogo soznaniia," as the reference to Philo itself suggests.

317. Losev, *Ocherki antichnogo simvolizma i mifologii*, 705. Losev also offers a lengthy disquisition on the errors of Platonism (and Catholicism) vis-à-vis Eastern Orthodox thought (*vizantizm*), where he draws a distinction between hellenist and "Byzantine" (i.e., Eastern Orthodox) forms of Platonism; ibid., 865–904.

thought as lying in the struggle between Western *ratio* and the "Eastern Christian godmanhood of Logos,"[318] and the whole of his *oeuvre* can be thought of as a dialectical engagement of Orthodox doctrine in order to filter through it the history of culture and the contemporary world—in effect, a continuation of the Russian religious renaissance by other means, and in a decidedly riskier setting.[319]

The current of Eastern Orthodox thought on which Losev draws— which should not be confused with the whole of Orthodox doctrine or even its mainstream in the early twentieth century—is essentially a form of mystical ontologism, and can be labeled "Christian areopagitic Neoplatonism" or "Orthodox energism" ("*pravoslavnyi energetizm*"); or, as Losev himself identified it in a letter from the camps to his wife, "Eastern palamite ontologism" ("*vostochnyi palamitskii ontologizm*").[320] Its concern over the centuries has been to pursue a middle path between two crude forms of reductionism, one of which relegates God to the transcendent realm of abstract principle, denying his involvement in the world and any form in which He may be known (that way, for Losev, lay the Renaissance, Kantianism, and agnosticism); the other of which completely identifies soul with body, idea with matter, God with the created world, thereby reducing God to something creaturely and leading to various forms of pantheism or the deification of matter.[321] Orthodox ontologism resisted these complementary trends—which, one notes, closely parallel the neo-Kantianism and materialism of Russia's *fin-de-siècle*—by elaborating a vision of God's manifestation in the world via divine energies.

For Losev the most significant example of this line of thought was the *imiaslavie* movement discussed earlier in this study, that potent irruption of Neoplatonist Orthodoxy into modern Russian culture that the Soviet government, when it got around to it, regarded as a counterrevolutionary threat—an attitude that may have played a role in Losev's arrest in 1930.[322] Losev was personally involved in the *imiaslavie* debate and in the (fading) repercussions of it in Russian intellectual life of the 1920s. He made the acquaintance of Father David, one of the active promoters of the movement on Athos, and of another activist named Father Irinei, to whose corrections he submitted an outline of *imiaslavie* theses he intended to discuss with

318. Losev, "Russkaia filosofiia," in his *Strast' k dialektike*, 78. Losev refers in the same essay to "the great Russian problem of the Logos" as the focal point of Russian philosophy (101).

319. Gogotishvili, "Rannii Losev," 137.

320. Takho-Godi, "A. F. Losev—filosof imeni, chisla, mifa," 8; Gogotishvili, "Rannii Losev," 138; Takho-Godi, "Tri pis'ma A. F. Loseva," 153.

321. See Losev, *Iz rannikh proizvedenii*, 641, note to p. 523.

322. Gogotishvili, "Religiozno-filosofskii status iazyka," 909.

Florenskii in 1923.[323] So central was *imiaslavie* in the Losevs' lives that they would privately note whether friends did or did not qualify as genuine adherents of the movement (whether they were "*imiaslavets*" or "*imiaslavka*").[324] Indeed, *imiaslavie* has been claimed as the philosophical stimulus for all of Losev's writings of the 1920s, which in this view represent a concerted effort to sustain the movement's insights while providing a contemporary philosophical justification for them.[325] *Filosofiia imeni* and "Veshch' i imia" in particular are thinly veiled, "aesopian" contributions to this project, and "Dialektika imeni," the section cut from the latter prior to publication, proposes to discuss the relevant issues under the label of "onomatodoxy," Losev's Greek euphemism for "*imiaslavie.*"[326]

The *imiaslavie* doctrine is, in effect, an ultrapersonalized version of the cosmology presented in Losev's published works, whose formulations are readily arrived at by altering one or two of the cosmology's conspicuously theological terms; ultrapersonalized because it openly places at the head of a model that is already selfhood writ large (essence generating intelligence, which comes to know itself in otherness and so forth) the person of the Christian deity. The adherents of *imiaslavie* argued that "the name of God is God himself, but God is not his name." In Losev's expanded version this becomes: "The name of God is the energy of God, inseparable from the very essence of God, and therefore God Himself. . . . However, God is distinct from His energies and His name, and for that reason God is not his name and not a name at all."[327] In Losevian terms this is an "energic" explanation (and, equally, reassurance) of divine contact with the world. God transcends the created world together with the exudings of his energies, including even his own name, which is one of the forms of his self-knowledge; this is the apophatic sense of the formula's second half. But his manifestations, the deposits of the energies radiating from him, *are* present in the world and through them the believer can come into contact with God. Ontically and axiologically highest of these is the name of God—the term

323. Ibid.; "Tezisy ob imeni Bozhiem, napravlennye v 1923 g. o. P. A. Florenskomu," in Losev, *Imia*, 56–61.

324. Takho-Godi, "Iz istorii sozdaniia," in Losev, *Imia*, x.

325. Gogotishvili, "Religiozno-filosofskii status iazyka," 908. On Losev's philosophical updating of *imiaslavie*, see the remark in which he offers phenomenology as its "theoretical basis," because phenomenology freed logic from its accumulated naturalistic and abstract-metaphysical constructs ("Imiaslavie," in *Imia*, 16). Losev also claims that contemporary mathematicians had independently arrived at insights very close to those of *imiaslavie*, in particular in H. Kantor's set theory ("Imiaslavie," in *Imia*, 16). He also outlines some of the ways—oddly consonant in spirit with other maximally revisionist doctrines of the revolutionary era—in which *imiaslavie* would dictate global reconceptions of philosophy, chemistry, and biology (*Imia*, 71–72).

326. Losev, "Dialektika imeni," 147.

327. Losev, "Imiaslavie," in *Imia*, 15.

implied in all the secular substitutes Losev offers in his published works such as "word," "expression," or "symbol." The contact afforded through the divine name, Losev stresses, is "energic"—at a remove, mediated—and not "substantial" or direct, which is impossible; but it is no less real for that. The recited name of "God" can thus lead the believer to Him because it enjoys a relationship of contiguity with the very being of God. If this is true, then the same may be said of language, which the indirection of Losev's published writings, in which he cannot speak openly of God and his name and must resort to quasi-phenomenological discussions, ironically ends up deifying. Language proceeds out of divine essence. Or, to offer a slightly different paraphrase of the logic implied in Losev's thought, God must present some symbolic manifestation, some revelation of himself to the world; if we search among all the phenomena that might serve as this manifestation, the most privileged turns out to be language.

As a theory of language, *imiaslavie* had its roots in the teachings regarding the divine names of (pseudo)Dionysius the Areopagite, the Christian writer of the fifth and early sixth centuries who represented the height of Christian Neoplatonism (Losev twice translated the Areopagite corpus and twice lost his translation, once to the NKVD, the second time to a German bomb).[328] Dionysius insists that God "transcends any word and any knowledge, residing above all mind and essences and embracing all that exists" (Dionysius was the father of apophatic theology in the Church).[329] It is thus impossible to say or think anything of Him at all.[330] But the attributes through which God has manifested Himself in the world are knowable. In fact, the names for them have been recorded in scripture, and by studying them one can gain knowledge, if not of God in his essence, then at least of his revealed attributes. "We know God not from his nature, for that is unknowable and transcends all sense and mind, but from the arrangement of everything that exists, for that is his product, which preserves certain images [*obrazy* in the Russian translation; the Greek is *eikonas* or icons] and semblances of his divine prototypes."[331] If for Dionysius

328. Takho-Godi, "Aleksei Fedorovich Losev," in Losev, *Bytie. Imia. Kosmos,* 15. Actually the Areopagite corpus was probably not the work of St. Dionysius the Areopagite, whose conversion by Paul is mentioned in Acts 17:34, but of an unknown author who lived in Syria toward the end of the fifth century (Ware, *Orthodox Church,* 63). Paperno also mentions a fourth-century patristic debate over whether names are mere words or "Sophistic names" ("*sofiinye imena*") reflecting the essence of the things they depict ("O prirode poeticheskogo slova," 30).

329. Dionisii Areopagit, *O bozhestvennykh imenakh. O misticheskom bogoslovii* (St. Petersburg: Glagol, 1994), 29.

330. Ibid., 31.

331. Ibid., 245.

God in His essence is anonymous, in his manifestations He possesses multiple names.[332]

But for Losev a still more important source for an understanding of language than Dionysius's doctrine of divine names was hesychasm (Russian *isikhazm,* from Greek *esychia,* 'quietness'), a monastic movement that arose on Mt. Athos in the fourth and fifth centuries. Hesychasm experienced a vibrant and polemical revival in the fourteenth century, which furthered the split between the Eastern and Western Churches.[333] The Russian monks of the *imiaslavie* movement in fact saw themselves as revivers of hesychasm rather than initiators of anything new, and in his summaries of *imiaslavie* doctrine Losev repeatedly cites hesychasm as its most important antecedent.[334]

Like the adherents of *imiaslavie,* the hesychasts cultivated the practice of inner, mystical prayer, but for them this was potentially a means to something still more significant: the attainment within themselves of a divine light that they believed to be the same as that which had radiated from Christ during his transfiguration on Mt. Tabor (hence the label for this phenomenon, *"Favorskii svet,"* the "light of Tabor"). The hesychasts believed that this light persisted on earth and could be revealed to those who led the proper monastic life. From 1337 they came under attack from a philosopher-monk named Barlaam, who had been raised in the Greek colonies of Calabria ("a certain Calabrian emigrant," Losev disparagingly calls him).[335] Besides accusing the hesychasts of succumbing to fantasies, Barlaam argued

332. Ibid., 39. Losev finds further precedent for the *imiaslavie* teaching on names in Plato's *Cratylus,* or more accurately in Proclus's Neoplatonic commentary on it called *In Cratylum* (see *Antichnyi kosmos i sovremennaia nauka,* 151–74 and 393–400). He draws particular attention to Proclus's assertion that the names of the gods are "mysteriously embedded in the gods themselves" (*Antichnyi kosmos i sovremennaia nauka,* 393 n. 63) but are then dialectically revealed to mortals, and to the assertion that the divine mind contains within itself "icons and essential meanings [*smysly*] in sharply etched form, as if sculptures of essence" which are in turn "like names resembling numbers in their capacity as intelligent likenesses" (397 n. 65; Losev also cites Nicholas of Cusa's *De nomine Dei* on the unnameability of God himself, who as the "maximum" comprising all existence can have no consciousness other than himself capable of encompassing and naming him [398 n. 66 and 403 n. 73]). For an overview of Neoplatonist teachings on names see Maurus Hirschle, *Sprachphilosophie und Namenmagie im Neuplatonismus. Mit einem Exkurs zu 'Demokrit' B 142,* Beitraege zur klassischen Philologie, Heft 96 (Meisenheim an Glan: Verlag Anton Hain, 1979).

333. On hesychasm see Cross and Livingstone, *Oxford Dictionary of the Christian Church,* s.v. "Hesychasm"; Ware, *Orthodox Church,* 62–70; Pelikan, *Spirit of Eastern Christendom,* 261–70. There is also a hesychast movement in post-Soviet Russia; see Gogotishvili, "Losev, isikhazm i platonizm," in Losev, *Imia,* 551–79.

334. See, for example, Losev, "Imiaslavie," in *Imia,* 9, 14; and "O knige 'Na gorakh Kavkaza,' " ibid., 55.

335. Losev, *Ocherki antichnogo simvolizma i mifologii,* 865.

that the light on Mt. Tabor itself had been a purely physical phenomenon (*tvarnoi,* creaturely or created) which God had offered to the disciples as a mere sign; this was so because God is unknowable, and to argue that the light was divine would be to posit a divided God or admit to the existence of more than one deity. But an archbishop of Thessalonika named Gregory Palamas (1296–1359; hence the Russian term for this group of believers, "*palamity*" or "palamites") countered this "absolute apophatism," as Losev calls such forms of skepticism, with a doctrine of divine energies: the light of Tabor was not any created, material thing, nor was it the very essence of God, in the sense that God might have been contained in and circumscribed by it. It was "the divine energies, invisible to the natural eye," God's "essential energies" that were, however, not God himself;[336] or in Losev's paraphrase, "the energy of the Divine essence, distinct from that very essence but inseparable from it."[337] This palamite position was eventually adopted at the Councils of Constantinople in 1341, 1347, and 1351, and became an accepted part of Orthodox tradition.[338]

For Losev the importance of hesychast teaching is not merely dogmatic but bears directly on the philosophical and linguistic issues that dominate his works. From the standpoint of Orthodox mysticism, to denigrate the ontological meaning of something like the light of Tabor would be to deny that God had revealed himself to mankind, in effect to remove his presence from the world. To see this light in mystical experience, on the other hand, is to come into direct contact with the manifestation of a divine essence that is otherwise unknowable. But it is also highly relevant that this doctrine can be discussed in terms of signification, as when Barlaam denigrated the light of Tabor as a mere "symbol," because for Losev what might be called divine ontology had an immediate bearing on the semiosis that takes place in language.[339] In the somewhat Dostoevskian logic of his thought, the argument runs in effect as follows: if there exist what Barlaam calls mere symbols— words in the nominalist understanding of them, or Saussurian conventional signs—then we are condemned to Kantian skepticism (Losev called Barlaam "that Kantian of the fourteenth century") and with that to "all the

---

336. Sv. Grigorii Palama, *Triady v zashchitu sviashchennobezmolvstvuiushchikh* (Moscow: Kanon, 1996), 337, 287.

337. Losev, *Dialektika mifa,* in *Iz rannikh proizvedenii,* 610 n. 50; see also his *Ocherki antichnogo simvolizma i mifologii,* 865–66. In the Christian context the distinction between God's essence (*ousia*) and his energies goes back to the Cappadocian Fathers; see Ware, *Orthodox Church,* 68.

338. Cross and Livingstone, *Oxford Dictionary of the Christian Church,* s.v. "Hesychasm"; see also Losev's translation of relevant articles of the 1351 document in his *Ocherki antichnogo simvolizma i mifologii,* 894–99.

339. For Palamas's rebuttal of Barlaam's "symbolic" argument, see for example his *Triady,* 267–304.

apocalyptic convulsions of the Renaissance West."[340] But if the Orthodox doctrine of divine energies is true, then what the hesychasts believed about the divine light can be said, *mutatis mutandis,* about language in general.[341]

All these issues come to a head for Losev in the controversy surrounding the so-called "Filioque," in which the ideas of energies and emanation (and by extension expressive form in its relation to essence) are directly linked with the most authoritative model of selfhood of all, that of the Godhead; and it is in Losev's discussion of this controversy that the analogy between language and the divine self that had been suggested in Potebnia and Shpet becomes explicit. The Filioque is the Western doctrine of the Trinity that holds that the Holy Spirit proceeds from both the Father *and the Son,* "*ex Patre Filioque,*" rather than from the Father alone as taught in the Eastern Church (the phrase in question was inserted at the Third Council of Toledo in 589 into the Nicene-Constantinopolitan creed after the phrase "I believe in the Holy Spirit . . . who proceeds from the Father"; that this was done without ecumenical consultation was one of the Eastern Church's main objections).[342]

For the Eastern Church (and Losev) this question of procession is not an abstruse point of dogma but a fundamental tenet of faith on which an entire cosmology depends: from the time of Photius, a ninth-century Patriarch of Constantinople, it has been the focal point of contention for the Eastern Church in its theological disputes with the West and remains the chief theological barrier between the two branches of Christianity.[343] For Losev, if the Spirit does not proceed from the Father alone (whom the Eastern Church regards as sole *arche* or causal principle within the Godhead) but, at some sort of remove, also from the Son, then hierarchy has been introduced into the Trinity and the Holy Spirit has been demoted to an inferior role.[344] This kind of idea would not surprise us in a pagan like Plotinus, Losev remarks, who needed hierarchy in order to explain how the One

340. Losev's remark on Balaam is quoted in V. Veniaminov, "Kratkie svedeniia o zhitii i mysli sv. Grigoriia Palamy," in Palama, *Triady,* 353; Losev's remark on the Renaissance West is in his *Ocherki antichnogo simvolizma i mifologii,* 873.

341. Losev lists among the "energic manifestations" important to Palamas "light energies [*svetovye energii*], the word, grace, names"; *Ocherki antichnogo simvolizma i mifologii,* 873. The same meaning resides naturally, for Losev, in icons (which, however, have a much lower profile in this verbally oriented thinker than they do in the works of, say, Florenskii). In his overview of *imiaslavie* Losev identifies the eighth-century controversy over icons as a "great phenomenon of church history closely related to *imiaslavie,*" because to assert as the iconoclasts did that an "abyss" lies between "things-in-themselves" and their "appearances" is to profess Kantianism, whereas Platonist iconodules regard "appearances" as "revelations of essence"; Losev, "Imiaslavie," in *Imia,* 10.

342. Cross and Livingstone, *Oxford Dictionary of the Christian Church,* s.v. "Filioque"; Ware, *Orthodox Church,* 51.

343. Pelikan, *Spirit of Eastern Christendom,* 183–98; and Ware, *Orthodox Church,* 210–18.

344. Pelikan, *Spirit of Eastern Christendom,* 197.

generated lower levels of being; but for a Christian it introduces dangerous alterations in ontology. By denigrating the third hypostasis (Holy Spirit), the Filioque turns it into the merely empirical activity of God, even as it transforms the first (Father) into an abstract principle and the second (Son) into mere intellectual form (Losev calls this the "formalization and depletion of the first two Persons of the Godhead," their reduction to logical principles rather than persons).[345] In other words, to embrace the Filioque is to remove *personhood* from God.

In Losev's account all sorts of repercussions follow from this fateful error. He declares the Filioque to be the essence of the Western Church and source of everything pernicious in Catholicism, from indulgences to the authority of the Pope.[346] It commits one (somehow) to Arianism, the belief that the Son, too, is merely created and not divine. It fosters erroneous forms of devotional life, promoting a pagan-Platonist vision in which idea and matter fuse, and therefore the use of statuary in places of worship (whereas the East looks to the *mental* embodiment of apophatic essence in the word, and the embodiment of that word pictorially in the icon); and instead of the ringing of bells that one hears throughout the Orthodox lands (and which conveys to the believer "the apophatism of the inexhaustively outpouring energies of the First Essence") it bequeaths to the West only the "repressed-subjective triumph" of the pipe organ.[347] Indeed, wherever the Orthodox understanding of the Trinity fails to be upheld Losev sees the twin evils of abstraction (which as we have seen he often calls "Kantianism") and materialism. He even interprets the debate between "dialectical" and "mechanical" Marxists in these terms, suggesting the debate was "nothing other than" a secular updating of the theological dispute between the Eastern and Western Churches over the procession of the Holy Spirit and calling the mechanists "Catholic materialists" and the dialecticians "Orthodox materialists."[348] In the end for Losev all worldviews divide into two opposing camps: a "Byzantine-Muscovite" one upholding the doctrines of the *homoousious* Trinity, together

---

345. Losev, *Ocherki antichnogo simvolizma i mifologii*, 875. One finds similar comments on the "depersonalizing" effects of the Filioque even in the judicious Ware, who says that in the Western view "God is regarded too much in terms of abstract essence and too little in terms of specific personality" (*Orthodox Church*, 215) and in Pelikan, who notes that for the West the Holy Spirit becomes essentially a kind of principle of conjunction or communion between the Father and the Son, rather than an equivalent person (*Spirit of Eastern Christendom*, 196). Veniaminov notes that the early Church debates over the divine energies were aimed first and foremost at proving the unitary essence of the Trinity and the two natures of Christ—i.e., at preserving the personhood of the Christian deity ("Kratkie svedeniia," 360).

346. Losev, *Ocherki antichnogo simvolizma i mifologii*, 883–84.

347. Ibid., 883. See Florenskii's similar fulminations against the use of oil paint in western art, and organs in Catholic churches, in "Ikonostas," 90–91.

348. Losev, *Dialektika mifa*, in *Iz rannikh proizvedenii*, 512.

with diphysitism, iconodulism, hesychasm, and *imiaslavie*; and a godless alternative insisting on Arianism, monophysitism, iconoclasm, "Barlaam-
ism," and "onomatomachia" (*imiaborchestvo*).[349]

But the most pernicious corollary of all for Losev is the Filioque's necessary denigration of divine symbols, in the sense he so prolifically develops
of them as the manifest energies of divine essence. Because it disrupts the
ontological integrity of the Trinity, the Filioque cannot sustain a doctrine of
energies as the manifestation of God's person. It therefore denies that icons
are anything other than pictures and that the name of God is his "mental
revelation" to the world—and with all of this it denies the *ur*-example of energic manifestation, the very incarnation of Christ.[350] It was precisely to
counter the Filioque, Losev remarks, that the palamites found it necessary
to recognize the energy of the divine Essence as God himself; or, as Basil the
Great put it, there is no essence without energies, and no energies without
essence.[351]

Thus does Losev's conception of language come to be grounded in a doctrine of the divine Person and His incarnation.[352] What one finds in the
form of analogy in Potebnia is emphatically literalized in Losev, and language is "absolutized" to a degree few disciples of Potebnia would have anticipated, much less condoned. Most of Losev's works are "baggy monsters"
of treatises on language, myth, Greek philosophy, and so forth, and draw
prolifically on writers ranging from Plato through medieval scholasticism to
Cohen, Natorp, Husserl, and Cassirer; but in them any discussion of these
topics in their own terms, as they present themselves to us mundanely,
quickly folds in on itself and yields to eschatology. In this sense Losev is essentially useless to linguistics and philosophy as they have been understood
for most of the twentieth century. But what his works do offer is one of the
most forceful arguments elaborated in the Russian context for language or
word as a form of self. For Losev, the "meaningful" phenomena given to us
in this world are emanations of nothing less than the divine person, which
in philosophical terms are best described as forms of words, or, more accurately, names. The word is a self, because it is ontologically constituted as
an image of the incarnation. That is why it comprises all the important issues of selfhood, such as inwardness, outwardness, identity, self-knowledge,
causality, will, persistence, mutability, mortality, and immortality. To inquire into the nature of language is to discover not just Husserlian "essence"

349. Losev, *Ocherki antichnogo simvolizma i mifologii*, 900.
350. Ibid., 899–900.
351. Ibid., 893; Veniaminov, "Kratkie svedeniia," 359.
352. At one point Losev even refers his readers to section 13 of *Filosofiia imeni*, on "the dialectic of intelligence in the name," as an explication of the dialectical meaning of the Trinity (*Ocherki
antichnogo simvolizma i mifologii* 876)!

but revelation. And when we speak or write—and Losev's sense of such activities could only have been heightened by the hostile conditions of the Soviet era—we reify a part of the divine nature. One sometimes even gets the
sense from Losev's works that for him the fact that words exist, and have
been pondered in the ways they have by linguists and philosophers, sup-
ports the apophatic theology of the Eastern Church. This religious inclination unites Losev with Florenskii, Bulgakov, and a host of lesser figures in
Russia's religious renaissance. Yet as the example of Losev makes equally
clear, the most significant Russian intellectuals in this line arrived at their
position having first, as it were, worked their way through some of the
dominant movements in contemporary thought (in Losev's case, neo-Kantianism, phenomenology, and the Soviet brand of materialism). It was only
then, having absorbed and responded to those influences, that they set out
to develop their ideas within the framework of Orthodox theology.

Conclusion

A GUIDING ASSUMPTION OF THIS STUDY has been that the place occupied within a culture by such things as the writing of literature, pronouncements on what literature is for, the elaborating of literary theories, the study of linguistics and the philosophy of language, and so forth, is shaped by the broader understanding that culture maintains of what language is and the role it plays in human life. Very often this understanding subsists at a subliminal level and exerts its influence without being fully articulated. As we have seen, some of the most significant such endeavors in Russian culture of the late nineteenth and early twentieth centuries sought to draw the self into language, to define the self as something consisting of or inhering in words. The traumatic upheavals of the Soviet era, however, together with the persecution in Stalinist institutions of anything too evidently resembling philosophical idealism, made further work on the grand project of synthesizing Orthodox thought with modern philosophy virtually impossible (Losev's defiant gestures notwithstanding), and one can view the consolidation of Stalinist rule around 1930 as the outer temporal boundary to the project Potebnia set in motion in the 1860s. Yet by no means did this spell the end of all Russian interest in language as the site of selfhood. Just as Chapter 2 examined repercussions of Potebnia's ideas in the culture of Russian Modernism, this conclusion considers some of the ways in which the impulse to link language and self persists in works of the Soviet era—testimony to its enduring vitality within Russian culture of the twentieth century.

The psychologist Lev Vygotskii's *Myshlenie i rech'* (Thinking and speech [1934]) at first glance appears to be only tangentially related to the metaphysical ideas about language with which this study has dealt. It offers a psychological account of the role that speech plays in human consciousness, with an eye toward the development of speech in the child and its pedagogical implications (here oriented toward facilitating the assimilation of "systematic" scholarly knowledge in Soviet schools—presumably the Marxist-Leninist understanding of the world). But Vygotskii engages the psychological theories that concern him (principally those of Jean Piaget and

William Stern) in a distinctly Humboldtian context and, while reaching conclusions superficially at odds with Humboldt and Potebnia, ends up articulating a view of the self whose indebtedness to their line of thought about language is clear.

Vygotskii's very title announces this stance: an intentional echo of Potebnia's *Mysl' i iazyk,* it also alters each of its predecessor's terms in a way that emphasizes process over abstract entities (thus *myshlenie,* "thinking," and *rech',* "speech," though see the more evident *rapprochement* in the title of Chapter 7, "Mysl' i slovo" [Thought and word]). In the work itself he invokes the authority of Potebnia more than once, such as when he approvingly cites Potebnia's assertion (borrowed from Humboldt) that "language is a means for understanding oneself," or when he repeats the Humboldtian emphasis on process ("the relation of thought to the word is not a thing but a process") together with its rejection of a purely instrumental view of language ("thought is not expressed in a word, it completes itself in a word").[1] He also uses a largely Potebnian vocabulary to discuss the mental structure of the word, such as when he says that "meaning is the word itself, viewed from its inner side," or speaks of the word as having an inner, sense-possessing side, and an outer, audible side.[2] In *The Psychology of Art* he goes so far as to declare Potebnia's tripartite model of the word "the psychological system of philology."[3]

Potebnia's ideas nonetheless occupy the background of Vygotskii's study, which in a certain light can be read as a manifesto for dissolving the very bond between language and thought on which Humboldt and Potebnia had insisted so emphatically. Vygotskii seeks to identify a position midway between the extremes of complete identification and complete disjunction of thought and speech, but, perhaps because he is so aware that in Russia he works against the well-entrenched view that they are in essence the same phenomenon, the initial thrust of his argument is to show their disparate origins and natures. Psychological research, he remarks, shows that the developmental processes of language and thought proceed at separate paces and therefore must be distinct. Cries and babbling are clearly the origins of speech in the child, but they have nothing to do with thought, and Piaget's own research shows that grammatical development proceeds more rapidly in the child than does logic.[4] Thought and speech have completely different genetic roots and follow different paths of development.[5]

1. L. S. Vygotskii, *Myshlenie i rech'* (Moscow: Labirint, 1996), 165, 306, 308.
2. Ibid., 297, 306.
3. Lev Semenovich Vygotsky, *The Psychology of Art,* trans. Scripta Technica, Inc. (Cambridge: MIT Press, 1971), 30.
4. Vygotskii, *Myshlenie i rech',* 101, 103.
5. Ibid., 88, 107.

Moreover, in a gesture that would seem to distance him dramatically from Potebnia and his successors, Vygotskii militates against the "metaphysical concept of the self" that typically promotes the view of identity, attacking in particular William Stern's "monadological" reliance on the idea of a "holistic self" as something actually existing, as a "unique and self-valuable unity."[6] Rather, and here one senses the influence of his Soviet context, for Vygotskii speech and thought arise out of distinct but parallel processes of social conditioning. The child's need for logical thought develops out of its contacts with other consciousnesses, Vygotskii claims, here invoking Durkheim on the social conditioning of even such basic concepts as space and time; and he insists that linguistic thought is not a natural form of behavior but a social-historical one.[7]

Yet despite Vygotskii's vigorous assertion of the separate origins of speech and thought, when discussing the psychic life of adults he in effect treats them as identical because he argues that beyond a crucial point in childhood their development proceeds in tandem.[8] Indeed, he sees them as so inseparable that his favorite metaphor for their unity is that of water, whose constituents, hydrogen and oxygen, readily combust when separate but acquire entirely different properties when combined as H_2O.[9] At this point in his argument he rejects the instrumentalist view that speech somehow mirrors already-accomplished thought and offers the distinctly Potebnian remark that thought *completes itself* in language, that is, that apart from language thought—and that part of the self that depends on thought—remains inchoate.[10]

Despite Vygotskii's rejection of "metaphysical" notions of the self and his quasi-Marxist insistence on the social determinants of concepts and the language we use to express them (or, rather, bring them to completion), the idea of selfhood thus hovers over his remarks all the same. For the somewhat surprising focus of *Myshlenie i rech'* turns out to be the concept of "inner speech," a term redolent of Potebnia's "inner form of the word" as well as of some of its successors in the Russian tradition, such as Shpet's hermeneutic "inner form," the interiority of Florenskii's words-as-organisms, and Losev's self-unfolding Neoplatonic *logos*. Vygotskii's concern is to revise a theory of Piaget, according to which the egoistical speech of small children, who discourse volubly on the subject of themselves, is transcended and eventually disappears as the child matures and becomes socialized,

6. Ibid., 86–87.
7. Ibid., 70, 116.
8. Ibid., 103, 296.
9. Ibid., 11–12.
10. Ibid., 308.

especially by going to school. Paradoxically, given his emphasis on social determinants, Vygotskii rejects this view in favor of a theory that *preserves* the role egoistical speech plays in the life of consciousness: in his account egoistical speech does not disappear, it merely loses its vocalization and transforms itself into the phenomenon of "inner speech."[11] Vygotskii identifies certain structural and functional hallmarks of this speech, but his main concern is with the way this "inner speech" sustains a very Humboldtian conversation within us about the nature of our selves and the relation of those selves to the world outside us. Hence the approving invocation of Potebnia's claim that language is a means to self-understanding, together with the review of post-Lockean theories about the ways in which our knowledge of the world is processed into concepts and becomes available to our consciousness, as well as the ultimate insistence on the unity of thought and speech. As Caryl Emerson puts it, in Vygotskii's account by internalizing speech in this manner we become "[our] own best interlocutors."[12] While it is true that for Vygotskii, as for Bakhtin and such related thinkers as Trubetskoi and Shpet, the idea of an autonomous single consciousness is inherently self-contradictory because even internalized egocentric speech begins as a social phenomenon, in the pivotal passages of *Myshlenie i rech'* the emphasis is all on what transpires within an individual mind as it processes, for the sake of its own self-understanding, experience in the medium of words.[13]

Thus does Vygotskii requisition from Piaget what he had been reluctant to accept from Potebnia: a doctrine of "inwardness" that rests on the unity of self and language, however complex that unity may be. Nowhere is this appropriation clearer than in the work's concluding passage, in which Vygotskii summarizes his lengthy examination of Piaget's theory by stating that the key to human consciousness lies in the interrelation of thought and speech. What this means, he explains, is that speech is as old as consciousness, and the development of consciousness is linked throughout with the development of the word (and one notes that, just as Potebnia substitutes discussion of the "word" for what had been a discussion of "language" in Humboldt, so does Vygotskii here switch to speaking of the "word" rather than of "speech"). The resulting understanding is one in which all the tendencies toward concretization of linguistic essence, organicism (as Cassirer calls it), the staking of selfhood on something verbal, and even the transferal of qualities of selfhood to the word, which have characterized Russian

---

11. Ibid., 322.

12. Caryl Emerson, "The Outer Word and Inner Speech: Bakhtin, Vygotsky, and the Internalization of Language," *Critical Inquiry* 10: 2 (December 1983): 234.

13. Ibid., 248–49.

approaches to language from early on, suddenly come to the fore: "Consciousness is reflected in the word as the sun is in a tiny droplet of water. The word is related to consciousness as a small world to a large one, as a living cell to the organism, as an atom to the cosmos. [The word] *is* the little world of consciousness. The word endowed with sense [*osmyslennoe slovo*] is a microcosm of human consciousness."[14]

A work closely related in its interests to Vygotskii's *Myshlenie i rech'* is Valentin Voloshinov's *Marksizm i filosofiia iazyka* (1929), whose most significant aspect from the standpoint of the present study is the concerted effort it makes to draw Marxist cultural theory (back?) into the domain of language and language-related phenomena. It makes this effort in the very context we have been discussing: Voloshinov cites both Shpet and Losev as examples of recent interest, albeit non-Marxist, in the philosophy of language in Soviet Russia, and he notes that contemporary "bourgeois" philosophy is also developing "under the sign of the word." He further suggests that current debates over the nature of language parallel those in the Middle Ages between realism and nominalism.[15]

Voloshinov's main concern is to provide a semiotic reinterpretation of "ideology," that manifestation of the political in the realm of ideas that Marxist theory sees as the essence of the cultural "superstructure." Everything ideological has meaning, Voloshinov reasons, which means that it represents or stands for something else, that is, it is a sign.[16] Collectively these signs form a world of their own that exists in parallel with those of nature, technology, and so forth.[17] The mutual conditioning of "sign" by "ideology," moreover, is complete: where there is no sign, there is no ideology.[18] Just as Shpet had argued the centrality of language to hermeneutic phenomena, Voloshinov claims that the semiotic character of ideology expresses itself nowhere so clearly as in the word (n.b., reverting, in a characteristic Russian reflex, from discussion of "language" to the concrete "word"). "The word is the ideological phenomenon *par excellence.*"[19] Voloshinov suggests that this is because every manifestation of ideology is in fact a form of self-reflection or at least self-commentary on the part of the culture—and here we are clearly in the language-besotted world of the Bakhtin circle, with its vision of humanity's never-ending "dialogue" on the essential questions of life. The word is a necessary ingredient of every ideological creation, even nonverbal ones, Voloshinov asserts, because it accompanies

14. Vygotskii, *Myshlenie i rech'*, 362.
15. V. N. Voloshinov, *Marksizm i filosofiia iazyka* (Moscow: Labirint, 1993), 8 n. 4, 9.
16. Ibid., 13.
17. Ibid., 14.
18. Ibid., 13.
19. Ibid., 18.

and comments on every ideological act we might perform. This co-presence of the word is central to the very processes by which human culture works. "Every ideological refraction of the process of being, no matter what its signifying material, is accompanied by its refraction in the word as a necessary epiphenomenon."[20]

Among other things, what this account does is to make a language and the entities (such as "ideological acts") that are realized within it central to a Marxist philosophy of culture. As a historian of thought Voloshinov is also a remarkably astute interpreter of the implications intellectual movements can have for the philosophy of language, and in the second part of *Marksizm i filosofiia iazyka* he offers an incisive parsing of recent European thought into two broad camps. The first of these, which he labels "individual subjectivism," is represented by Humboldt and his successors (for example, Steinthal, Vossler, and Spitzer in Germany, Potebnia in Russia). It views the individual psyche as the source of language, the creation of which is analogous to artistic creation, and it sees the expression of the individual self as the primary function of language. The second tendency is that toward "abstract objectivism," represented by the linguistic theories of Saussure and Bally, which elevates the abstract normative system of language—in the independent reality of which it firmly believes—over any instances of individual expression (in Saussure's celebrated terms, *langue* over *parole*). In a biting and very Bakhtinian-sounding remark Voloshinov characterizes this approach to language as one shaped by the study of dead languages, which are inert and have nothing any longer to say, and whose meanings we can consider only through the reconstruction of their grammatical system. It is a "philosophy of the word of the other" (*filosofiia chuzhogo slova*).[21] What is remarkable about this account is less its sweeping characterization of language philosophy in terms of two fundamental attitudes than its use of the idea of selfhood as a heuristic principle: for the first tendency fails precisely in its hypertrophy of individualism, the second in its desiccation of the self.

This focus on selfhood is sustained in the main parts of Voloshinov's own argument, which mostly explore the role the ideologized word plays within the individual psyche, for in Voloshinov's account the sign turns out to be essential to consciousness as well as to ideology. "Consciousness can realize itself and become an actual fact only when incorporated in semiotic material," he tells us.[22] The reality of the inner psyche is the reality of the sign, and apart from semiotic material there is no psyche.[23] Now, it is true that

---

20. Ibid., 19–20.
21. Ibid., 81.
22. Ibid., 15.
23. Ibid., 31.

for Voloshinov this psyche is a social phenomenon ("The structure of the conscious individual self is every bit as social a structure as are collective experiences: it is a particular ideological interpretation of a complex but enduring social-economic situation that has been projected into an individual soul" [*sic*]); and it is true that its inner semiosis involves not the workings of individual subjectivism but a response to semiotic processes that have been drawn into the self from the public arena where they arose.[24] This "psyche" is a form of social property that we reproduce within ourselves, he explains, and thus the meeting site of our self and the world.[25] In fact, what Humboldt or Potebnia would have called "self-understanding" or "self-reflection" for Voloshinov more accurately involves figuring out the external origins of meanings we experience as inner words.[26] And, as one might expect from a product of the Bakhtin circle, *Marksizm i filosofiia iazyka* emphasizes dialogue: the word is essentially a two-sided act arising out of the interrelations between a speaker and a listener. It is therefore "a bridge spanning the distance between me and another."[27]

Yet for all these Bakhtinian-cum-Marxist strictures regarding collectivity (which after all already appear in Humboldt's successors Steinthal and Wundt, while in the Russian context Potebnia, Shpet, Bulgakov, and Florenskii all emphasize the dialogic nature of language), Voloshinov's contribution to Russian philosophy of language is, again, conspicuous in its swerve toward the notion of "inwardness." Thus the focus of much of his discussion is not the production of verbalized ideological structures on the public stage but the workings of something he calls, using the same term Vygotskii does, "inner speech." "Inner speech" is that domain within the individual in which social-ideological forms find their realization in words, and it is interesting that Voloshinov faults linguistics not for its neglect of the political domain but for overlooking this inner (semiotic and ideological) sphere. None of the categories of traditional linguistics can be applied to the phenomenon of inner speech, he cautions, a failure he attributes in part to the "abrupt wave of anti-psychologism" on which both Husserl and the modern discipline of linguistics rode into Russia.[28]

For all Voloshinov's perfectly earnest talk about the socio-ideological determinants of the individual psyche, in other words, for all his emphasis on the intersubjective subsistence of words and the selves they serve to define, his argument ultimately revolves around the problematic of how selves

24. Ibid., 98.
25. Ibid., 19, 31.
26. Ibid., 43.
27. Ibid., 94.
28. Ibid., 45, 37.

come to self-realization in language: "For apart from its disclosure in language, if only in inner speech, the self (*lichnost'*) is given neither to itself nor to others," he states categorically.[29] "The self comes into being in language, not, it is true, in its abstract forms so much as in its ideological themes. *From the standpoint of its inward subjective content the self is a theme in language. . . .* Consequently it is not the word which is the expression of an inner self but the inner self which is a word expressed or driven inward" (this, incidentally, well before Lacan claimed that the subconscious is structured like a language).[30] The whole idea of the self defining itself via language, moreover, is one that Voloshinov derives from the likes of Humboldt, Potebnia, Shpet, and Florenskii, rather than from any figure in the Marx-Engels-Plekhanov line. In Habermas's perceptive remark, *Marksizm i filosofiia iazyka* is essentially a Marxist interpretation of Humboldt.[31]

If Voloshinov's work bears the evident impress of the "Bakhtin circle," what of Bakhtin himself? With the possible exception of Roman Jakobson, Bakhtin is the best-known Russian writer on questions of language in the twentieth century. Indeed, his ideas concerning the nature of the novel, of medieval carnival, of the centrality of dialogue to human social life are familiar enough that they hardly require recitation here. The philosophical influences on Bakhtin and the intellectual milieu within which his ideas developed have also been well explored, including his close affinity with the Russian religious renaissance and its representatives, such as Florenskii, who are particularly relevant in the present context.[32] Rather than attempt an overview of Bakhtin's protean *oeuvre,* what I would like to do, drawing on this basic familiarity of his ideas, is to suggest how cognate they are with the focus of this study: the efforts to identify selfhood with language that characterized Russian thought in the late nineteenth and twentieth centuries.

Of all Bakhtin's works, the one containing the greatest number of ideas relevant to this topic is "Slovo v romane" (1934–35), which has entered the English-speaking world in Caryl Emerson's translation under the title "*Discourse* in the Novel." The broader, event-oriented term "discourse" is perfectly appropriate to the range of meanings Bakhtin associates with his subject, but it is important to recall that the literal translation of Bakhtin's

29. Ibid., 166.
30. Ibid., 167 (emphasis added).
31. Quoted in Tihanov, *Master and the Slave,* 197 n. 66.
32. See in particular Clark and Holquist, *Mikhail Bakhtin,* 120–45; Ruth Coates, *Christianity in Bakhtin: God and the Exiled Author* (Cambridge: Cambridge University Press, 1998); and Mihailovic, *Corporeal Words.*

title is "The *Word* in the Novel," which at least initially foregrounds a discrete object rather than a process and almost certainly, as Mihailovic co-
gently argues, carries connotations of the Johannine logos.[33] In this regard
it also suggests Bakhtin's dialogic engagement with the post-Potebnia tradition of thought on language in Russia.[34] But even prior to any close reading of Bakhtinian texts a simple enumeration of their familiar *topoi* already
reveals in them a kind of allegory of the self disposing itself within language:
his recurring themes are words that respond to other words, words that cast
sidelong glances, have intentions of one kind or another, that find loopholes, and so on. We tend to understand these characterizations metaphorically, but the anthropomorphizing metaphors are so persistent that they in
effect become one of the central assertions of his writings.

"Slovo v romane" sets forth Bakhtin's vision of the novel as the stage for
a polyphonous event in which diverse voices (or, as he calls them at one
point, "languages") representing diverse ideological positions interact in a
field unconstrained by authorial control.[35] Bakhtin writes as a dauntingly
erudite philologist, calling up an example from ancient Roman literature
here, an acute observation on an eighteenth-century British writer there,
but his essay is no more a "study" of the novel's evolution as a verbal genre
than, say, Derrida's "The Supplement of Copula" is a contribution to the
field of linguistics. Instead it is a "novel" in its own right, one concerned
with narrating the Hegelian drama of the word's fate within European history, its gradual coming to self-awareness in the era whose "verbal-ideolog-
ical life" begins to experience the breakdown of previous coercions toward
centralization and unity, followed by the word's gradual ascent toward autonomy and dialogic interchange with other voices within the uniquely
privileged genre of the novel.[36] Bakhtin's narration of this "plot" is, moreover, saturated with ethics (dialogue is beneficial or even necessary to the development of selves, monologic subordination of discourse is detrimental)
and epistemology (the "languages" incorporated within a novel constitute
specific points of view on the world; the word is an "intentional phenomenon").[37] Its descriptive manner is also unabashedly anthropomorphic, as
when, to take just one of myriad possible examples, Bakhtin says that the
word, "working its way toward its sense and its expression through an alien
verbal milieu with a diversity of accents manages in this dialogical process,

33. Mihailovic, *Corporeal Words*, 23–24, 40–41.

34. Mihailovic suggests that Bakhtin derives his lingua-centrism from Shpet, but this severely
limits the range of likely influences on him (ibid., 28).

35. M. Bakhtin, "Slovo v romane," in his *Voprosy literatury i estetiki. Issledovaniia raznykh let*
(Moscow: Khudozhestvennaia literatura, 1975), 76.

36. Ibid., 87. On Hegelian ideas in Bakhtin, see Tihanov, *Master and the Slave*, 24.

37. Bakhtin, "Slovo v romane," 104, 179.

through harmony or dissonance with these diverse moments, to formulate its stylistic appearance and tone"—in which passage we receive not just a description of stylistic attributes but an entire plot of self-realization.[38]

This is to say that "Discourse in the Novel" is in fact also a discourse about the self, something that should not surprise us if we reflect that Bakhtin's earliest known work posits the organic unity of the self (realized in the act of "responsibility," or "answerability," as the English translation has it) as an antidote to wholes formed through mere mechanical agglomeration of parts (the 1919 "Iskusstvo i otvetstvennost'" ["Art and Answerability"]). And when Bakhtin says that "the speaking person in the novel is always to greater or lesser degree an ideologue, whose word is always an ideologeme," what he is telling us is that selfhood always finds its most significant realization in language.[39] The verbal artifact that is the novel provides both the site and the record of humanity's most significant engagement with the world. Indeed, as Bakhtin puts it in one passage, human consciousness *lives* in language.[40] In broad terms this is the same conviction that we have seen in Shpet, Florenskii, and Losev—though Bakhtin is a Whorfian slightly *avant la lettre,* or at least a post-Wundtian, who insists on the independence of human thought from any one language that might be viewed as the "incontrovertible and sole embodiment of sense and truth," and who militates against any such verbal-utopian pretensions that might arise (as, for example, in poetry).[41] Nor should all the talk about polyphony in Bakhtin mislead us into seeing him as someone who rejects a metaphysical understanding of the self, for as Tihanov comments, "dialogue" in Bakhtin is not about increasing the number of distinct human voices and expanding their resonance in society; it is about widening the internal capacity of the self: "A follower of Plato rather than a predecessor of Habermas, Bakhtin's concern [in the early version of the Dostoevsky book, *Problems of Dostoevsky's Art*] is with the self, not with society."[42] That the capacity of the self widens within the realm of language is what makes Bakhtin the heir to ways of thinking about language, and the ways of investing hopes in language, that emerged in Russia following Potebnia.

If on reflection it causes little surprise to realize that the psychologizing Vygotskii and the philosophically inclined Voloshinov and Bakhtin express ideas cognate with the other writings on language that this study has examined, the structural linguistics of Roman Jakobson would appear to

---

38. Ibid., 91.
39. Ibid., 146.
40. Bakhtin's phrase is "iazyk dlia zhivushchego v nem soznaniia" (ibid., 106).
41. Ibid., 181, 211, 223. Bakhtin (181) cites Wundt, together with Steinthal and Lazarus.
42. Tihanov, *Master and the Slave,* 197.

epitomize the opposite of any metaphysical interest in language, indeed, to represent the apotheosis of the instrumentalist view that Gadamer laments of language as self-sufficient, objective form. Yet Jakobson's *oeuvre* developed under the influence of Moscow Husserlianism and has its own corresponding philosophical subtexts and agenda.

A particularly revealing example of these aspects of Jakobson's thought is his 1937 essay "The Statue in Puškin's Poetic Mythology," his exemplary investigation into recurring themes in the works of Russia's national poet and exemplar of what he termed "poetic mythology," the themes that organize and define a poet's *oeuvre*.[43] In this essay Jakobson examines the role sculptures of one kind or another play in some of Pushkin's later works, in particular *Mednyi vsadnik* (*The Bronze Horseman* [1833]), *Kamennyi gost'* (The stone guest [1830]), and *Skazka o zolotom petushke* (The fairytale of the golden cockerel [1834]). Not only do statues appear in these works, but they typically provide the actual versus apparent focus (as in *Kamennyi gost'*, which appears to be a version of the Don Juan tale while its real hero is a statue of the commander). As Jakobson points out, Pushkin's predilection for using titles to indicate the leading *dramatis personae* of his works suggests that the pointed reference to statues in these titles serves as an index to their conceptual centrality, with each title, moreover, adding an adjective indicating the material from which the statue is made.

Having noted the recurrence of statue motifs, Jakobson then finds a common "plot kernel" shared by all these works: a man is weary and longs for rest, and this motif is intertwined with desire for a woman. At this point there appears some kind of statue that exerts—or rather the being inseparably connected with the statue exerts—supernatural power over this woman. "After a vain resistance the man perishes through the intervention of the statue, which has miraculously set itself into motion, and the woman vanishes."[44] There are nuances to this "myth"—Jakobson traces three versions of it, identifies important intertextual links (for example, with the Polish poet Mickiewicz), finds corroborating evidence even in some of Pushkin's manuscript marginalia, offers brilliant conjectures (such as that the golden cockerel sitting atop its pin represents a sublimation of the famous Alexandrine column that was then being erected on St. Petersburg's Palace Square, and which Pushkin loathed)—but in each instance the myth's distinguishing feature is the ambivalent tension Pushkin creates between the paradoxically

43. My comments here are adapted from my article "Roman Jakobson's Sculptural Myth," *Annals of Scholarship* 14:2 (Fall 2000): 25–36.

44. Roman Jakobson, "The Statue in Puškin's Poetic Mythology," in *Puškin and His Sculptural Myth,* trans. and ed. John Burbank (The Hague: Mouton, 1975), 6.

moving statue (the statues in these works all come to life) and the equally paradoxical *immobile* being it represents.

In an innovative move that took Formalist analysis beyond the text
proper into what we would now call the "text" of the poet's life, Jakobson
also linked this sculptural myth with events in Pushkin's biography. Statues
start to appear only somewhat late in Pushkin's career, and in fact are concentrated in works, especially the three mentioned above, produced in the
three "Boldino autumns" Pushkin spent on his country estate of that name,
in 1830, 1833, and 1834 (hence the otherwise curious restriction of the statue
theme to later, longer, nonlyrical works). This happens to have coincided
with a period in Pushkin's life when he was weary and longed to marry Natalia Goncharova, but the marriage was delayed because his fiancée's mother
would not let her wed without a luxurious trousseau, and for this it was necessary to sell a gigantic bronze of Catherine the Great that had been cast by
Goncharova's grandfather—which sale required permission from the tsar
and therefore generated anxieties all around.

Now, what is curious about the essay is that Jakobson serves all this up
in the guise of a distributive study. He suggests that these insights into
Pushkin's statue motif have been arrived at inductively and empirically,
through an examination of the *oeuvre* that has noted a certain conspicuous
recurrence of themes and plot motifs and gone on from there to discover
parallel themes in the poet's life. Even as perceptive a student of Jakobson
as Stephen Rudy discusses the essay in terms similar to these, suggesting
that it "isolates and analyzes the thematic motif central to Pushkin's poetic
mythology" (but note, "the" and "central" here are already interesting).[45]
But there is more to this essay than meets the eye, and both the heuristic
procedure Jakobson deploys and the results it yields go further, and are ultimately far more interesting, than the scientific mask the essay assumes.
One can already sense this greater depth in Jakobson's discussion of "poetic
mythology," for in identifying the prominence of sculpture as a theme in
Pushkin's works and life he was not just claiming to have pointed out a sto-
chastic phenomenon but to have discovered one of the principles (or possibly "the" principle, as Rudy has it) according to which the works and the
life in their totality comprise a unified whole, a master text, which is held
together by certain recurring or invariable elements. According to this view
statue motifs do not just recur in Pushkin's *oeuvre*; they constitute "certain
organizing, cementing elements which are the vehicle of unity in the multiplicity of the poetic works."[46] To the extent that these elements are semantic or propositional in nature, they constitute a "myth," and this "myth"

45. Rudy, "Jakobsonian Poetics," 192.
46. Jakobson, "Statue in Puškin's Poetic Mythology," 1.

extends even into the non-artistic areas of the poet's life. In fact, for Jakobson it is in elements such as these that the *oeuvre,* as an organic, meaning-bearing whole (rather than a random collection of texts) inheres: such recurring motifs "make poems by Pushkin—Pushkin's, those by Mácha—truly Mácha's, those by Baudelaire—truly Baudelairean."[47]

A closer look at some of Jakobson's subtexts sheds light on the otherwise unmotivated appearance of this organic metaphor in his description of poetic *oeuvres* and helps to explain something of the essay's own *weltanschauung:* that is to say, the sort of benefit, in terms of a sense of what the world or human culture is about, that Jakobson seems to derive from his exploration of statues in Pushkin's works.

If the striking achievement of "The Statue in Puškin's Poetic Mythology" was its predication of this idea of "poetic mythology," that idea was not, for all its acuity, propounded *ab ovo* but derived from its intellectual context. The most significant influence on it, as indeed on much of Jakobson's cognate theory of language, was Husserl's phenomenology. As we have already noted, phenomenology swept Russian intellectual life in the 1910s, and Jakobson himself was later to name it as one of the significant sources of his linguistic theory, along with Baudoin de Courtenay, Saussure, and Russian avant-garde poetry.[48] Jakobson discovered Husserl's ideas in 1915–16, when he attended two seminars conducted by Chelpanov at the University's Psychological Institute (this during the war, so the seminar participants had to get their Husserl as contraband via Amsterdam). His exposure to Husserlian ideas would have been enhanced in the 1920s when Shpet began attending meetings of the Moscow Linguistic Circle, of which Jakobson was a prominent member. Jakobson's interest in Husserl may well have been rekindled in November 1935, just prior to the writing of the essay on statues in Pushkin, when Husserl came to Prague and at Jakobson's instigation read a lecture on "The Phenomenology of Language" at the Prague Linguistic Circle.[49]

What exactly constitutes the Husserlian moment in Jakobson's structural linguistics and its extensions into literary studies? Husserl's claim regarding language was that linguistic phenomena must have an *a priori* nature above and beyond any physiological, psychological, or cultural-historical determinants. He wanted to discover the universal forms immanent to all linguistic

---

47. Ibid.

48. Jakobson is quoted in Elmar Kholenshtain [Elmar Holenstein], "Iakobson i Gusserl (K voprosu o genezise strukturalizma)," *Logos* 7 (1996): 7.

49. Ibid., 12. Holenstein even suggests that Husserl's "On the Origins of Geometry" (1939, but apparently written a year after his visit to Prague) may have been influenced by a 1929 essay by Jakobson and P. Bogatyrev, "Folklore as a Special Form of Creativity," which argued the intersubjective constitution of cultural objects (ibid., 12, 24).

elements and to their relations with each other: before anything can be attributed to anything else, he believed, it must first be understood in terms of its own inner structure and then in its links with its context.[50] For Jakobson one of the most influential parts of Husserl's philosophy was the discussion in Section 3 of the *Logical Investigations* of parts and wholes and their interrelations. Jakobson's approach to phonology and morphology is everywhere informed by Husserl's insistence that every givenness is included within a context and can be understood only by taking into account its position within that context, and by the corresponding effort to determine the relations among the parts and between the parts and the whole.[51] This view rejects mechanistic causes. What it believes to produce change in, say, the phonological system of a language is something working within that phonological system and among its members. The discovery of such immanent, universal laws is the goal of Jakobsonian linguistics.[52]

Jakobson's treatment of these relations is intuitively phenomenological, moreover, because he examines the elements in question not only "in themselves" but as they are "given in the mind," "for us": thus, Jakobson's treatment of opposition (one of the fundamental kinds of relations binding parts into a whole) is not a logicistic one of exclusion but one of co-presentation, in which the excluded member of the opposition, and indeed the whole system of distinctive features, are included in the mind whenever any one element is present or invoked (for example, light/dark phonemes become perceptible only against each other's background).[53] Most noteworthy among the relations Jakobson posits for language is that of "markedness," a relation of implication in which one member of a pair indicates the presence of some feature, while the other conveys no specific information about the feature's presence or absence. Jakobson does not just enumerate properties that language treats as marked versus unmarked but looks for an "inner reason" for this signification (for example, he argues that compactness in vowels is unmarked because vowels themselves are compact, whereas the reverse is true for consonants).[54] He extends this understanding of how wholes or systems operate to dynamic (genetic) phenomena as well: a sound mutation is explained not primarily through external influences (physical, physiological) but through the structural pattern of the phonological system itself.[55]

50. Ibid., 9, 15.
51. Ibid., 16; Holenstein, "Jakobson's Contribution to Phenomenology," 146.
52. Holenstein, "Jakobson's Contribution to Phenomenology," 147.
53. Ibid.
54. Ibid., 149.
55. Ibid., 150.

In other words, this is how Jakobsonian linguistics produces "eidetic" analyses that strive toward the kind of cognition of essences that Husserl held to be the goal of genuine philosophy. As it happens, one of the most remarkable of Jakobson's "eidetic" studies is his 1936 "*Beitrag zur allgemeinen Kasuslehre*," in which he seeks to assess not only the syntactic functions of particular cases in Russian but also the "invariant" oppositional relations obtaining among them that are definitive, for Jakobson, of the Russian case system as a whole (this essay, incidentally, was written one year before the Pushkin essay and about the time of Husserl's stay in Prague).[56] To do this he examines the ways in which particular cases or pairs of cases realize, or fail to realize, such general meanings as "directedness," "quantification," or "marginality," his analysis leading to the apperception of a series of "isomorphic" relations among the cases.[57] In the end he presents these interrelations in the remarkably harmonious, complete, and three-dimensional geometric figure of a cube—or, he comes close to saying, the cube is the eidetic form of which the actual cases of modern Russian are realizations.[58] To get this eight-pointed figure out of the six cases of the Russian language requires the somewhat specious elevation to independent status of two "accessory" cases (genitive II and locative II) that many would consider simply variant endings—but so keen is Jakobson's desire to perceive the eidetic essence within the variety of Russian case endings that he is willing to fudge the definition of what constitutes a case.[59] The vision subtending this essay is one of a non-arbitrary, quasi-geometrical order underlying life's phenomena or at the very least the products of human culture.[60]

Nor is the geometrical figure with its implied spatiality incidental to the way Jakobson conceives eidetic wholes in general. In his well-known "Poetry of Grammar and Grammar of Poetry," in a section entitled "Grammar

56. Jakobson refers to the idea of invariance as "one of the fundamental concepts in the development of modern linguistics" and notes that its emergence in the Kazan' school in the 1870s paralleled "the success of the same idea in mathematics"—another "eidetic" field important to Husserl; in his "Morphological Observations on Slavic Declension (The Structure of Russian Case Forms)," in Roman Jakobson, *Russian and Slavic Grammar. Studies 1931–1981*, eds. Linda R. Waugh and Morris Halle (Berlin, New York, Amsterdam: Mouton, 1984), 106. For this discussion I have used this essay, which is a later and somewhat revised version of the "Beitrage."

57. Jakobson's statement of the "isomorphic relations" is "Instrumental: Nominative = Dative: Accusative = Locative: Genitive"; "Morphological Observations," 109.

58. Ibid., 126.

59. For insight into the cube's speciousness I am indebted to a lecture Richard D. Brecht gave at Cornell University, ca. 1980.

60. See Holenstein's comparison of Jakobson's concept of wholes and their unity versus Wittgenstein's considerably looser concept of "family resemblances": "What distinguishes Jakobson from Wittgenstein is the non-arbitrariness, the strictly ordered presence and absence of features. Features are not arbitrarily present or absent; their presence or absence depends on the presence or absence of other features" ("Jakobson's Contribution to Phenomenology," 154).

and Geometry," he argues that in poetry grammar is every bit as foundational to sense as geometry is to painting—it represents a similar "beautiful
necessity," an element with which the artist has no choice but to contend
but which also serves as the medium of artistic vision.[61] Jakobson points
out that the correspondence between the two fields has been noted since the
thirteenth century, and prompted Spinoza to treat grammar *more geomet-
rico.* He cites Panofsky citing Scholasticism and its classic *Summa* with its
three requirements of totality, arrangement according to a system of homologous parts, and deductive cogency.[62] Ultimately he attributes these parallels to "the abstractive power of human thought [that] superimposes simple
geometrical and grammatical patterns on the world of particular objects
and concrete words."[63]

Read in this light, the essay on statues in Pushkin's works emerges as another study of an eidetic whole that works toward apperception of the very
geometry of Pushkin's *oeuvre,* like the cube that for Jakobson "is" the inner
meaning of the Russian case system. This understanding of the essay already
indicates affinities with such concepts as Shpet's language-based structures
of sense, or Losev's incarnational dialectic realized within the *logos*—perhaps even, remotely, with the kind of structural metaphor important to
Potebnia ("inner form," "outer form," and so on). But the eidetic meaning
is not the only subtext in the essay, and it is the seemingly fortuitous focus
on statues in the Pushkin essay that discloses a deeper link between Jakobson and the other figures with whom this study has been concerned. For
Jakobson's focus on this thematic motif and its associated "plot kernel" is
not unpremeditated or simply occasional and certainly not, as the essay
might lead one to believe, the simple result of quantitative procedures applied dispassionately to Pushkin's works.

Jakobson himself indicates the privileged status the idea of sculpture enjoys in the essay, albeit indirectly, in the course of offering what look like
semiotic annotations to the larger study of statues in Pushkin's life and
works. He makes some fancy observations about poetic depictions of statues constituting "the sign of a sign or image of an image; in such a poem
the statue as sign [*signum*] becomes a theme or signified object [*signatum*]";[64] but more important is his suggestion that the sculptural sign is not
just any sign but a privileged one providing something like a minimal
instance of what signs in general represent: "A statue—in contrast to a

---

61. Roman Jakobson, "Poetry of Grammar and Grammar of Poetry," in his *Language in Literature* (Cambridge: Harvard University Press, 1987), 133.
62. Ibid., 134–35.
63. Ibid., 133.
64. Jakobson, "Statue in Puškin's Poetic Mythology," 31. *Ekphrasis* is the trope in question, and
its classical treatment is Lessing's *Laokoon.*

painting—so approximates its model in its three dimensionality that the in-
organic world is nearly cancelled out of its themes: a sculptural still life
would not provide the distinct antinomy between the representation and
the represented object that every artistic sign includes and cancels. Only the
opposition of the *dead, immobile matter* from which a statue is shaped and
the *mobile, animate being* which a statue represents provides a sufficient distance."[65] As a result of this "simultaneous identity and difference" of sign
and object signified, sculpture presents us with "one of the most dramatic
semiotic antinomies."[66]

There are two important ideas implied but not stated here. First, given
this virtually complete limitation to the human figure (minor exceptions
like equestrian statues and Pushkin's golden cockerel notwithstanding) the
statue emerges as the quintessential artistic sign for a (human) being—historically, statues have almost always represented persons. Second, under-
scoring the same point, the minimal antinomy on which the sculptural sign
relies for its effect foregrounds ontology: in the statue, according to Jakobson, we are forced to see the opposition between living being and dead matter, which is to say, the precise boundary of being. It is as if, in Jakobson's
treatment, the reduction of the sign to its minimal elements exposes its essential link with being. A sign emerges as the *form* of being, an idea very
close to Shpet.

This sculptural theme, which provides one of the unifying, "cementing"
elements in Pushkin's *oeuvre* (in the implicit terms of Jakobson's essay, it
contributes to the form which is that *oeuvre*'s *eidos*), and which therefore instantiates its identity (for it is such elements, Jakobson claims, that "make
poems by Pushkin—Pushkin's"), turns out itself to have a fairly long history
linking it with ideas about how intellectual essences assume tangible
form.[67] In antiquity, especially in Neoplatonism, statues were often cited as
privileged examples of the indwelling of idea or intelligence in matter. Plotinus, for example, discusses statues in connection with the concepts of "potential" and "energy" (roughly, idea/form as it exists apart from or prior to
its manifestation in matter, versus its extension into material form). He is
concerned to argue that when *eidos* takes form it becomes something intermediary, no longer pure *eidos* but also not mere matter. "This energically-
given is not matter, but it contains *eidos,* so that it is something between
pure *eidos* and pure matter. This holds even when one substance arises out

65. Ibid., 31–32. Rudy makes an interesting remark in this regard: "The specific nature of the
sculptural sign is only a particular, *and maximal,* case of the larger semiotic antinomy of sign and
object which is so crucial for art in general"; "Jakobsonian Poetics," 194 (emphasis added).
66. Jakobson, "Statue in Puškin's Poetic Mythology," 37.
67. Ibid., 1.

of another, as for example when out of bronze there arises a statue; for a statue is a different substance from bronze precisely as the union of bronze with a certain form."[68]

In the fourth *Ennead* Plotinus again speaks of statues in connection with the theurgic practice of animating them, an idea very close to Pushkin's use of the theme: "And I think that the wise men of old, who made temples and statues in the wish that the gods should be present to them, looking to the nature of the All, had in mind that the nature of souls is everywhere easy to attract, but that if someone were to construct something sympathetic to it and able to receive a part of it, it would of all things receive soul most easily."[69] That is to say, as material forms, statues are closest to, most fitted to, souls and therefore might be used to "lure" them into this world. In a related passage Plotinus remarks that "the souls of men see their images as if in the mirror of Dionysus"—an allusion to the Orphic story of the child Dionysus being lured by the Titans with a mirror so that they could tear him to pieces and eat him.[70] Proclus, too, argues in his commentary on Plato that "the mind contains icons and essential senses in neatly articulated form, as it were *sculptures of essence,* in a manner like names which imitate numbers in their role as intelligent images."[71]

Nor, as we have seen, were these ideas in any way remote from the intellectual context of Jakobson's youth in early twentieth-century Moscow, when the vogue for Neoplatonism rivaled that for phenomenology. Among the adherents of Neoplatonism Losev himself used the example of sculpture to define the difference between what he saw as the partial truth of ancient Platonism from what was for him the complete truth of Neoplatonism in its Eastern Orthodox redaction:

> What is Platonism? We have already had occasion to see that Platonism is the systematically developed intuition of the *body.* It does not know the ideal world in its pure ideality. It knows only the *identity* of the "ideal" and the "real," as a result of which the idea becomes something merely formal and the "real," the thing, grows cold. But this also means that Platonism is an absolute *monism* of the sensual and the supersensual. . . . In real-life terms, intuitively, what we have here is complete wholeness and identity, indissolvable unity, a *body,* a *statue.*"[72]

68. "O potentsii i energii" (On potential and energy), an "interpretive translation" of Plotinus's Treatise II.5, which Losev offers as an appendix to his own *Antichnyi kosmos i sovremennaia nauka* (309–11).

69. Plotinus, *Ennead IV. 1–9,* Loeb Classical Library 443 (Cambridge: Harvard University Press, 1984), 71.

70. Ibid., 73.

71. Proclus, *In Cratylum,* cited in Losev, *Antichnyi kosmos i sovremennaia nauka,* 397, n. 65.

72. Losev, *Ocherki antichnogo simvolizma i mifologii,* 868.

Or again:

> Paganism (and, as its clearest expression, Platonism) is based on a sculptural
> understanding of being, and by "sculpture" I mean that synthesis of pure
> idea/identity and pure materiality when the idea is expressed not absolutely,
> but only insofar as is necessary to endow a body with sense, and when the
> body or thing are taken not in themselves but only insofar as they manifest
> an idea.[73]

But it was none other than Potebnia who, in *Mysl' i iazyk*, had illustrated
his concept of the "inner form of the word" with the example of a marble
statue of justice, in which the statue itself represents external form, the abstract concept of "justice" represents the statue's content, while the specific
representation of "woman with scales and sword" constitutes its inner
form.[74] Furthermore, in *Iz zapisok po teorii slovesnosti* (Notes on a theory of
literature) Potebnia cites Lessing's *Laokoon* on the different representational
provinces of the arts (plastic arts like sculpture and painting portray only a
single moment of some event but possess spatial variety, whereas poetry
portrays temporal sequence) and then in a footnote to this passage illustrates how the sculptural representation of a single moment transforms
itself into narrative sequence when it enters the realm of poetry by mention-
ing Pushkin's poem on a Petersburg statue by N. Pimenov called "Igrok v
babki" (Youth playing knucklebones).[75] Jakobson cites this very poem
when discussing Pushkin's fascination with statues, and comments on it
very much in the vein of Potebnia and Lessing without, however, mention-
ing either (he instead footnotes Rodin): "The conventional space of the
statue merges with the real space into which the statue has been placed, and
despite its atemporal substance, an idea of something that has preceded the
represented state and of something that should follow it comes of itself to
mind: the statue is placed in temporal succession."[76]

In fact, the idea that statues are particularly apt metaphors for words
seems to have been common currency in some of the very writings on
language that we have considered earlier. Bal'mont, for example, in his
Poeziia kak volshebstvo, asserts that "every word is the speaking statue of an

---

73. Ibid., 882.

74. Potebnia, *Mysl' i iazyk,* in his *Estetika i poetika,* 175. Rudy mentions this example in his discussion of Jakobson's contexts and notes that it is in fact taken from the German linguist Heymann Steinthal, without, however, indicating exactly from where; "Jakobsonian Poetics," 31.

75. Potebnia, *Iz zapisok po teorii slovesnosti,* in his *Estetika i poetika,* 289–90, 453 n. 4. The
Pushkin poem is "Na statuiu igraiushchego v babki" (On a statue of a youth playing knucklebones):
    Iunosha trizhdy shagnul, naklonilsia, rukoi o koleno
    Bodro opersia, drugoi podnial metkuiu kost'.
    Vot uzh pritselilsia . . . proch'! razdaisia, narod liubopytnyi,
    Vroz' rasstupis'; ne meshai russkoi udaloi igre.

Egyptian temple" and claims that in order for "every sound-sculpture called the Word to reveal its secret voice and magically begin to speak to us we must find in ourselves the primordial power of incantation."[77] And Andrei Bely—interestingly, in his ecstatic review of Potebnia's legacy, which appeared in the phenomenologically oriented journal *Logos*—draws an analogy reminiscent of Plotinus's remarks (which he may well have read) when he speaks of statues as being "on the one hand, the incorporeal thought of the sculptor, obscure even to him and accessible to no one else; and on the other hand, a chunk of marble having nothing in common with this thought; but the statue is neither the thought nor the marble but something distinct from its producers and containing more than they."[78]

Why, then, does Jakobson seize on the theme of statues as the connective principle of Pushkin's works—especially when, as must be said, it is by no means immediately obvious that they indeed are the focus, or even a very significant element of, the *oeuvre* as a whole? I believe that he does so because statues serve as models of what from the outset he conceives Pushkin's *oeuvre* to be: a form coextensive with and adequate to a complex, abstract idea; moreover, an idea, as the instantiation of the literary entity that is "Pushkin," that can be thought of as constituting his literary "being." In other words sculpture, as a sign or form that receives the soul or identity, is not just a theme that happened to be significant for Pushkin; it is a synecdoche for Jakobson's own concept of poetic *oeuvres*. But that concept in turn is cognate with the other efforts to construct a simulacrum of selfhood within language that have been discussed in this book—and that is why, for Jakobson, it is statues, as representations of selves, that become the privileged example of the eidetic being-in-form that is poetic mythology.

The example of Jakobson even mirrors the confluence of impulses that lay behind those efforts. In his writings innovative linguistic theories come into contact with contemporary philosophy in the form of Husserl's phenomenology, but also link up with the enduring Neoplatonic thought of Eastern Orthodoxy. Some awareness of this very arcing of intellectual contexts seems to register itself in the Pushkin essay. At one point Jakobson comments regarding the "dramatic semiotic antinomy" embodied in statues: "It was precisely this antinomy that led to the bitter fights around iconoclasm."[79] As we have seen, some of the most significant modern Russian

76. Jakobson, "Statue in Puškin's Poetic Mythology," 32.

77. Bal'mont, *Poeziia kak volshebstvo*, 54–55.

78. Belyi, "Mysl' i iazyk. Filosofiia iazyka A. A. Potebni," 252.

79. Jakobson, "Statue in Puškin's Poetic Mythology," 37. Jakobson cites as his source on the icon controversies O. Ostrogorskii, "Gnoseologicheskie osnovy vizantiiskogo spora o sv. ikonakh," *Seminarium Kondakovianum*, 2, 47f. Internet searching reveals that vol. 2 was published in 1920, in Prague.

responses to Neoplatonism arose out of the controversy sparked on Mt. Athos by the Russian monks who attempted to revive the fourteenth-century doctrine of *imiaslavie,* and who relied precisely on the iconodule positions outlined in a still earlier (eighth century) controversy over icons. In the end it seems to be the case, as Jakobson suggests when explaining Pushkin's evident association of statues with idolatry, that, "whether it concerns the unbeliever Pushkin, the heretic Blok, or the anti-religious writings of Majakovskij, Russian poets have grown up in a world of Orthodox customs, and their work is unwittingly saturated with *the symbolism of the Eastern Church.*"[80]

80. Jakobson, "Statue in Puškin's Poetic Mythology," 40.

Selected Bibliography

Akulinin, V. N. *Filosofiia vseedinstva. Ot V. S. Solov'eva k P. A. Florenskomu.* Novosibirsk: Nauka, 1990.

Alekseev, P. V., et al. *Filosofy Rossii XIX–XX stoletii (biografii, idei, trudy).* Moscow: "Kniga i biznes," 1993.

Amirova, T. A., B. A. Ol'khovikov, and Iu. V. Rozhdestvenskii. *Ocherki po istorii lingvistiki.* Moscow: Nauka, 1975.

Arens, Katherine. *Structures of Knowing: Psychologies of the Nineteenth Century.* Boston Studies in the Philosophy of Science, 113. Dordrecht: Kluwer Academic, 1989.

Armstrong, A. H., ed. *The Cambridge History of Later Greek and Early Medieval Philosophy.* Cambridge: Cambridge University Press, 1967.

Audi, Robert, ed. *The Cambridge Dictionary of Philosophy.* Cambridge: Cambridge University Press, 1995.

Bahr, Hermann. "Das unrettbare Ich." In *Dialog vom Tragischen,* 79–101. Berlin: S. Fischer, 1904.

Bakhtin, M. "Slovo v romane." In *Voprosy literatury i estetiki. Issledovaniia raznykh let,* 72–233. Moscow: Khudozhestvennaia literatura, 1975.

——. *Problemy poetiki Dostoevskogo.* 4th ed. Moscow: Sovetskaia Rossiia, 1979.

——. *The Dialogic Imagination: Four Essays.* Ed. Michael Holquist. Trans. Caryl Emerson and Michael Holquist. University of Texas Press Slavic Series, no. 1. Austin: University of Texas Press, 1981.

——. "Iskusstvo i otvetstvennost'." In *M. M. Bakhtin. Raboty 20-kh godov,* 7–8. Kiev: "Next," 1994.

Bal'mont, Konstantin. *Poeziia kak volshebstvo.* Moscow, 1915. Reprint, Letchworth-Herts, England: Prideaux Press, 1973.

Batiushkov, F. "V bor'be so slovom." *Zhurnal ministerstva narodnogo prosveshcheniia* 1900. No. 2, otd. 2. 209–28.

Belyi, Andrei. *Simvolizm.* Moscow, 1910. Reprint, Slavische Propyläen. Band 62. Munich: Wilhelm Fink Verlag, 1969.

——. "Mysl' i iazyk. Filosofiia iazyka A. A. Potebni." *Logos* 1910: 240–58.

——. *Glossolaliia. Poema o zvuke.* Moscow/Berlin, 1917/1922. Reprint, Tomsk: Vodolei, 1994.

Benveniste, Emile. "La Nature des Pronoms." In *For Roman Jakobson. Essays on the Occasion of His Sixtieth Birthday. 11 October 1956,* ed. Morris Halle et al., 34–37. The Hague: Mouton, 1956.

——. *Problèmes de linguistique générale.* Vol. I. Paris: Gallimard, 1966.

——. *Problems in General Linguistics.* Trans. Mary Elizabeth Meek. Miami Linguistics no. 8. Coral Gables, Fla.: University of Miami Press, 1971.

Berezin, F. M. *Russkoe iazykoznanie kontsa XIX–nachala XX v.* Moscow: Nauka, 1976.

——, ed. *Khrestomatiia po istorii russkogo iazykoznaniia.* 2nd, corrected, ed. Moscow: Vysshaia shkola, 1977.

Bibikhin, V. "V poiskakh suti slova. Vnutrenniaiai forma u A. A. Potebni." *Novoe literaturnoe obozrenie* 14 (1995): 23–34.

Bigg, C. *Neoplatonism.* London: Society for Promoting Christian Knowledge, 1895.

Bird, Robert. "Martin Heidegger and Russian Symbolist Philosophy." *Studies in East European Thought* 51 (1999): 85–108.

Blackburn, Simon. *The Oxford Dictionary of Philosophy.* Oxford: Oxford University Press, 1994.

Blok, Aleksandr. "Poeziia zagovorov i zaklinanii." In *Sobranie sochinenii v vos'mi tomakh.* t. 5, 36–65. Moscow-Leningrad: Khudozhestvennaia literatura, 1962.

Blonskii, P. P. *Filosofiia Plotina.* Moscow: Tov. tipografiia A. I. Mamontova, 1918.

Bonetskaia, N. K. "O filologicheskoi shkole P. A. Florenskogo. *Filosofiia imeni* A. F. Loseva i *Filosofiia imeni* S. N. Bulgakova." *Studia Slavia Academiae Scientarium Hungaricae* 37 (1991–92): 113–89.

Bowlt, John E. "RAKhN on Trial: The Purge of Gustav Shpet." *Experiment: A Journal of Russian Culture* 3 (1997): 295–305.

Brown, Edward J. *Stankevich and His Moscow Circle, 1830–1840.* Stanford: Stanford University Press, 1966.

Bulgakov, Prot. S. *Filosofiia imeni.* Paris: YMCA Press, 1953.

Burke, Kenneth. *The Rhetoric of Religion: Studies in Logology.* Boston: Beacon Press, 1961.

Buzuk, P. A. *Ocherki po psikhologii iazyka.* Odessa: Knigoizdatel'stvo A. A. Ivasenko, 1918.

Bychkov, V. V. "Vyrazhenie kak glavnyi printsip estetiki A. F. Loseva." In *A. F. Losev i kul'tura XX veka. Losevskie chteniia,* 29–37. Moscow: Nauka, 1991.

Cassedy, Steven. *Flight from Eden: The Origins of Modern Literary Criticism and Theory.* Berkeley: University of California Press, 1990.

——. "Pavel Florenskij's Philosophy of Language: Its Contextuality and Its Context." *Slavic and East European Journal* 35, no. 4 (1991): 537–52.

——. "Florenskij and Philosophy of Language in the Twentieth Century." In *P. A. Florenskii i kultura ego vremeni/P. A. Florenskij e la cultura della sua epoca,* ed. Michael Hagemeister and Nina Kauchtschischwili, 289–93. Marburg: Blaue Hoerner Verlag, 1995.

Cassirer, Ernst A. "Structuralism in Modern Linguistics." *Word* 1 (April 1945): 99–120.

Chomsky, Noam. *Cartesian Linguistics. A Chapter in the History of Rationalist Thought.* 1966. Reprint, Lanham, Md.: University Press of America, 1983.

Chubarov, I. M. "Modifikatsiia fenomenologicheskoi paradigmy ponimaniia soznaniia v proekte germenevticheskoi dialektiki G. G. Shpeta." In *G. G. Shpet/Comprehensio. Vtorye shpetovskie chteniia,* 27–33. Tomsk: Vodolei, 1997.

Chudakov, A. P. "A. A. Potebnia." In *Akademicheskie shkoly v russkom literaturovedenii,* ed. P. A. Nikolaeva et al., 305–52. Moscow: Nauka, 1975.

Clark, Katerina. "The 'Quiet Revolution' in Soviet Intellectual Life." In *Russia in the Era of NEP,* ed. Sheila Fitzpatrick et al., 210–30. Bloomington: Indiana University Press, 1991.

Clark, Katerina, and Michael Holquist. *Mikhail Bakhtin.* Cambridge: Harvard University Press, 1984.

Coates, Ruth. *Christianity in Bakhtin: God and the Exiled Author.* Cambridge: Cambridge University Press, 1998.

Condillac, Étienne Bonnot de. *An Essay on the Origin of Human Knowledge: Being a Supplement to Mr. Locke's Essay on the Human Understanding (1746).* A facsimile reproduction of the translation of Thomas Nugent, with an introduction by Robert G. Weyant. Delmar, N.Y.: Scholars' Facsimiles and Reprints, 1971/1998.

Coseriu, Eugenio. "Semantik, Innere Sprachform und Tiefenstruktur." *Folia Linguistica. Acta Societatis Linguistica Europaeae* 4 (1970): 53–63.

Cross, F. L., and E. A. Livingstone, eds. *The Oxford Dictionary of the Christian Church.* Oxford: Oxford University Press, 1997.

Davies, Anna Morpurgo. *Nineteenth-Century Linguistics.* Vol. 4 of *History of Linguistics,* ed. Giulio Lepschy. London: Longman, 1998.

Dennes, Maryse. *Husserl-Heidegger. Influence de leur oeuvre en Russie.* Paris and Montreal: L'Harmattan, 1998.

Derrida, Jacques. "The Supplement of Copula: Philosophy *before* Linguistics." In *Textual Strategies: Perspectives in Post-Structuralist Criticism,* ed. Josue V. Harari. Ithaca, N.Y.: Cornell University Press, 1979.

Dionisii Areopagit. *O bozhestvennykh imenakh. O misticheskom bogoslovii.* St. Petersburg: Glagol, 1994.

Dodd, C. H. *Historical Tradition in the Fourth Gospel.* Cambridge: Cambridge University Press, 1963.

Ducrot, Oswald, and Tzvetan Todorov. *Encyclopedic Dictionary of the Sciences of Language.* Trans. Catherine Porter. Baltimore: Johns Hopkins University Press, 1979.

Dunaev, A. G. "Losev i GAKhN." In *A. F. Losev i kul'tura XX veka,* 197–220. Moscow: Nauka, 1991.

Emerson, Caryl. "The Outer Word and Inner Speech: Bakhtin, Vygotsky, and the Internalization of Language." *Critical Inquiry* 10, no. 2 (1983): 245–64.

Ern, Vladimir. *Bor'ba za Logos. Opyty filosofskie i kriticheskie.* Moscow: Put', 1911.

Evtuhov, Catherine. *The Cross and the Sickle: Sergei Bulgakov and the Fate of Russian Religious Philosophy, 1890–1920.* Ithaca, N.Y.: Cornell University Press, 1997.

Farber, Marvin. *The Aims of Phenomenology.* New York: Harper and Row, 1966.

Firth, J. R. *The Tongues of Men.* London: Watts, 1937.

Fizer, John. *Alexander A. Potebnja's Psycholinguistic Theory of Literature: A Metacritical Inquiry.* Harvard Ukrainian Research Institute Monograph Series. Cambridge: Harvard University Press, 1986.

Florenskii, P. A. "Organoproektsiia." *Dekorativnoe iskusstvo SSSR* 12, 145 (1969): 39–42.

———. *Sobranie sochinenii.* Ed. N. A. Struve. Tom I. *Stat'i po iskusstvu.* Paris: YMCA Press, 1985.

———. *Stolp i utverzhdenie istiny (I).* Prilozhenie k zhurnalu *Voprosy filosofii.* Tom 1. Moscow: Pravda, 1990.

———. *Stolp i utverzhdenie istiny (II).* Prilozhenie k zhurnalu *Voprosy filosofii.* Tom 1. Moscow: Pravda, 1990.

——. *U vodorazdelov mysli.* Prilozhenie k zhurnalu *Voprosy filosofii.* Tom 2. Moscow: Pravda, 1990.

——. *Ikonostas. Izbrannye trudy po iskusstvu.* St. Petersburg: Mirfil/Russkaia kniga, 1993.

——. *Imena. Maloe sobranie sochinenii.* Vypusk 1. n.p: Kupina, 1993.

Florovskii, Prot. Georgii. *Puti russkogo bogosloviia.* Paris, 1927. Reprint, Vilnius: Vil'niusskoe pravoslavnoe eparkhial'noe upravlenie, 1991.

Fowler, H. N. Introduction to the *Parmenides.* In Plato, *Cratylus, Parmenides, Greater Hippias, Lesser Hippias,* 195–97. Loeb Classical Library, vol. 167. Cambridge: Harvard University Press, 1992.

Freidin, Gregory. *A Coat of Many Colors: Osip Mandelstam and His Mythologies of Self-Presentation.* Berkeley: University of California Press, 1987.

Gadamer, Hans-Georg. *Truth and Method.* 2nd, revised, ed. Trans. Joel Weinsheimer and Donald G. Marshall. New York: Continuum, 1998.

Gaidenko, P. P. " 'Konkretnyi idealizm' S. N. Trubetskogo." In Sergei Nikolaevich Trubetskoi, *Sochineniia.* Filosofskoe nasledie, t. 120, 3–41. 1906. Reprint. Moscow: Mysl', 1994.

Gasparov, Boris M. "The Language Situation and the Linguistic Polemic in Mid-Nineteenth-Century Russia." In *Aspects of the Slavic Language Question,* ed. Riccardo Picchio and Harvey Goldblatt, vol. 2, *East Slavic,* 297–333. New Haven: Yale Concilium on International and Area Studies, 1984.

Gidini, M. K. "Slovo i real'nost'. K voprosu o rekonstruktsii filosofii iazyka Gustava Shpeta." In *G. G. Shpet/Comprehensio. Vtorye shpetovskie chteniia,* 51–98. Tomsk: Vodolei, 1997.

Gogotishvili, L. A. "Rannii Losev." *Voprosy filosofii* 7 (1989): 132–48.

——. "Platonizm v zazerkal'e XX veka, ili Vniz po lestnitse, vedushchei vverkh." In A. F. Losev, *Ocherki antichnogo simvolizma i mifologii,* ed. A. A. Takho-Godi and I. I. Makhan'kova. Moscow: Mysl', 1993.

——. "Religiozno-filosofskii status iazyka." In Aleksei Fedorovich Losev, *Bytie. Imia. Kosmos,* ed. A. A. Takho-Godi, 906–23. Moscow: Mysl', 1993.

——. "Losev, isikhazm i platonizm." In A. F. Losev, *Imia. Izbrannye raboty, perevody, besedy, issledovaniia, arkhivnye materialy,* ed. A. A. Takho-Godi, 551–79. St. Petersburg: Aleteiia, 1997.

Goldblatt, Harvey. "The Church Slavonic Language Question in the Fourteenth and Fifteenth Centuries: Constantin Kostenečki's *Skazánie izъjavljénno ō pismenex.*" In *Aspects of the Slavic Language Question,* ed. Riccardo Picchio and Harvey Goldblatt, vol. 1, *Church Slavonic—South Slavic—West Slavic,* 67–98. New Haven: Yale Concilium on International and Area Studies, 1984.

Gornfel'd, A. G. "Muki slova." *Russkoe bogatstvo* (1899): 73–110.

——. "Nauchnaia glossolaliia." In *Boevye otkliki na mirnye temy,* 140–54. Leningrad: Kolos, 1924.

Gumilev, Nikolai. *Stikhotvoreniia i poemy.* Biblioteka poeta. Bol'shaia seriia. 3rd ed. Leningrad: Sovetskii pisatel', 1988.

Gusserl, Ed. *See* Husserl, Edmund.

Haardt, Alexander. "*Appearance and Sense* and Phenomenology in Russia." In Gustav Shpet, *Appearance and Sense: Phenomenology as the Fundamental Science and Its Problems,* trans. Thomas Nemeth, i–xxxi. Phaenomenologica 120. Dordrecht: Kluwer Academic, 1991.

———. *Husserl in Russland. Phänomenologie der Sprache und Kunst bei Gustav Špet und Aleksej Losev.* Übergänge: Texte und Studien zu Handlung, Sprache und Lebenswelt. Band 25. Munich: Wilhelm Fink Verlag, 1992.

Hagemeister, Michael, and Nina Kauchtschischwili, eds. *P. A. Florenskii i kul'tura ego vremeni/P. A. Florenskij e la cultura della sua epoca.* Marburg: Blaue Hoerner Verlag, 1995.

Hansen-Löve, Aage A. *Der russische Formalismus. Methodologische Rekonstruktion seiner Entwicklung aus dem Prinzip der Verfremdung.* Vienna: Verlag der Österreichischen Akademie der Wissenschaften, 1978.

Hegel, [Georg Wilhelm Friedrich]. *The Philosophy of Hegel.* Ed. Carl J. Friedrich. New York: Modern Library, 1953.

———. *Hegel: Texts and Commentary.* Trans. and ed. Walter Kaufmann. Notre Dame: University of Notre Dame Press, 1977.

Heidegger, Martin. *Being and Time.* Trans. Joan Stambaugh. Albany: State University of New York Press, 1996.

———. *Introduction to Metaphysics.* Trans. Gregory Fried and Richard Polt. New Haven: Yale University Press, 2000.

Herbart, Johann Friedrich. *A Text-Book in Psychology.* Trans. Margaret K. Smith. New York: A. Appleton, 1891.

Herder, Johann Gottfried. "Essay on the Origin of Language." In *On the Origin of Language,* trans., with afterwords, by John H. Moran and Alexander Gode and introduction by Alexander Gode, 87–166. Chicago: University of Chicago Press, 1966.

Hirschle, Maurus. *Sprachphilosophie und Namenmagie im Neuplatonismus. Mit einem Exkurs zu 'Demokrit' B 142.* Beiträge zur klassischen Philologie. Heft 96. Meisenheim an Glan: Verlag Anton Hain, 1979.

Holenstein, Elmar. "Jakobson und Husserl." In *History of Linguistic Thought and Contemporary Linguistics,* ed. Herman Parret, 772–810. Berlin: Walter de Gruyter, 1976. [Also as Elmar Kholenshtain, "Iakobson i Gusserl (K voprosu o genezise strukturalizma)." *Logos* 7 (1996): 7–37.]

———. "Jakobson's Contribution to Phenomenology." In *Roman Jakobson: Echoes of His Scholarship,* ed. Daniel Armstrong and C. H. Van Schooneveld, 145–62. Lisse: Peter de Ridder Press, 1977.

Humboldt, Wilhelm von. *On Language: The Diversity of Human Language-Structure and Its Influence on the Mental Development of Mankind.* Trans. Peter Heath. Cambridge: Cambridge University Press, 1988.

Husserl, Edmund. *Phenomenology and the Crisis of Philosophy.* Trans. Quentin Lauer. New York: Harper and Row, 1965.

———. [Gusserl, Ed.] "Pis'ma E. Gusserla k Shpetu." *Logos* 1 (1992) 3: 233–42.

———. *Logical Investigations.* 2 vols. Trans. J. N. Findlay. New York: Humanities Press, 1970.

———. *Ideas Pertaining to a Pure Phenomenology and to a Phenomenological Philosophy. First Book.* Trans. F. Kersten. The Hague: Martinus Nijhoff, 1983.

Husserl, Edmund [Gusserl, Ed.], and G. Shpet. "Otvetnye pis'ma Gustava Shpeta." *Logos* 7 (1996): 123–33.

Iaroshevskii, M. G. "Poniatie vnutrennei formy slova u Potebni." *Izvestiia AN SSSR. Otdelenie literatury i iazyka.* Tom V, vypusk 5 (1946): 395–99.

Iartseva, V. N., et al. *Lingvisticheskii entsiklopedicheskii slovar'*. Moscow: Sovetskaia entsiklopediia, 1990.

Il'ichev, L. F., et al. *Filosofskii entsiklopedicheskii slovar'*. Moscow: Sovetskaia entsiklopediia, 1983.

Isupov, K. G., ed. *Florenskii: Pro et Contra. Lichnost' i tvorchestvo Pavla Florenskogo v otsenke russkikh myslitelei i issledovatelei*. St. Petersburg: Russkii Khristianskii gumanitarnyi universitet, 1996.

Ivanov, Viacheslav Ivanovich. *Sobranie sochinenii*. Vol. 2. Brussels: Foyer Oriental Chrétien, 1974.

Ivanov, Viacheslav Vsevolodovich. "O lingvisticheskikh issledovaniiakh P. A. Florenskogo." *Voprosy iazykoznaniia* 6 (1988): 69–87.

——. "P. A. Florenskii i problema iazyka." In *P. A. Florenskii i kul'tura ego vremeni/P. A. Florenskij e la cultura della sua epoca*, ed. Michael Hagemeister and Nina Kauchtschischwili, 207–51. Marburg: Blaue Hoerner Verlag, 1995.

Jagić, V. *Codex Slovenicus Rerum Grammaticarum*. Berlin, 1896. Reprint, Slavische Proplyäen. Band 25. Munich: Wilhelm Fink Verlag, 1968.

Jakobson, Roman. "Shifters, Verbal Categories, and the Russian Verb." In *Selected Writings*, 2:130–47. The Hague: Mouton, 1971.

——. "One of the Speculative Anticipations: An Old Russian Treatise on the Divine and Human Word." In *Selected Writings*, 2:369–74. The Hague: Mouton, 1971.

——. "The Statue in Puškin's Poetic Mythology." In *Puškin and His Sculptural Myth*, 1–44. Trans. and ed. John Burbank. The Hague: Mouton, 1975.

——. "Morphological Observations on Slavic Declension (The Structure of Russian Case Forms)." In *Russian and Slavic Grammar: Studies 1931–1981*, ed. Linda R. Waugh and Morris Halle, 105–33. Berlin, New York, Amsterdam: Mouton, 1984.

——. "Poetry of Grammar and Grammar of Poetry." In *Language in Literature*, 121–44. Cambridge: Harvard University Press, 1987.

Jakowenko, Boris. "Ed. Husserl und die russische Philosophie." *Die russische Gedanke* 1929/30: 210–13.

Joravsky, David. *Russian Psychology: A Critical History*. Oxford: Basil Blackwell, 1989.

Kalinichenko, V. "Gustav Shpet: ot fenomenologii k germenevtike." *Logos* 1 (1992) 3: 37–61.

Kazakova, N. A. *Antifeodal'nye ereticheskie dvizheniia na Rusi XIV–nachala XVI veka*. Leningrad: n.p., 1955.

Khlebnikov, Velemir. *Tvoreniia*. Moscow: Sovetskii pisatel', 1987.

Knobloch, Clemens. *Geschichte der psychologischen Sprachauffassung in Deutschland von 1850 bis 1920*. Reihe Germanistische Linguistik, 86. Tübingen: Max Niemeyer Verlag, 1988.

Kolesov, Vladimir V. "Traces of the Medieval Russian Language Question in the Russian *Azbukovniki*." In *Aspects of the Slavic Language Question*, ed. Riccardo Picchio and Harvey Goldblatt, vol. 2, *East Slavic*, 87–123. New Haven: Yale Concilium on International and Area Studies, 1984.

Konovalov, D. G. "Religioznyi ekstaz v russkom mysticheskom sektanstve." Chast' 1, vyp.1. "Fizicheskie iavleniia v kartine sektantskogo ekstaza." Reprint from *Bogoslovskii vestnik* (1907, 1908). Sergiev Posad: Tipografiia Sv.-Tr. Sergievoi Lavry, 1908.

Koubourlis, Demetrius J. *A Concordance to the Poems of Osip Mandelstam*. Ithaca, N.Y.: Cornell University Press, 1974.

Lamarque, Peter V., ed. *Concise Encyclopedia of Philosophy of Language.* Oxford: Elsevier Science/Pergamon, 1997.

Lauer, Quentin. Introduction to *Phenomenology and the Crisis of Philosophy,* by Edmund Husserl, 1–68. New York: Harper and Row, 1965.

Lintsbakh, Ia. *Printsipy filosofskogo iazyka.* Petrograd: n.p., 1916.

Losev, Aleksei Fedorovich. "Logika simvola." *Kontekst 1972,* 182–217. Moscow: Nauka, 1973.

——. *Dialektika khudozhestvennoi formy.* Moscow, 1927. Reprint, Specimina Philologiae Slavicae. Band 55. Munich: Verlag Otto Sagner, 1983.

——. "Pis'ma." *Voprosy filosofii* 7 (1989): 152–59.

——. *Filosofiia imeni.* Moscow: Izd. Moskovskogo universiteta, 1990.

——. *Iz rannikh proizvedenii.* Prilozhenie k zhurnalu *Voprosy filosofii.* Moscow: Pravda, 1990.

——. *Strast' k dialektike.* Moscow: Sovetskii pisatel', 1990.

——. *Vladimir Solov'ev i ego vremia.* Moscow: Progress, 1990.

——. *Antichnyi kosmos i sovremennaia nauka.* In his *Bytie. Imia. Kosmos,* ed. A. A. Takho-Godi, 61–612. Moscow: Mysl', 1993.

——. *Bytie. Imia. Kosmos.* Ed. A. A. Takho-Godi. Moscow: Mysl', 1993.

——. "Dialektika imeni." *Kontekst 1992.* Moscow: Nauka, 1993. 133–48.

——. *Ocherki antichnogo simvolizma i mifologii.* Ed. A. A. Takho-Godi and I. I. Makhan'kova. Moscow: Mysl', 1993.

——. *Imia. Izbrannye raboty, perevody, besedy, issledovaniia, arkhivnye materialy.* Ed. A. A. Takho-Godi. St. Petersburg: Aleteia, 1997.

——. *Samoe samo.* Ed. A. A. Takho-Godi and V. P. Troitskii. Moscow: Eksmo-Press, 1999.

Losev, Aleksei Fyodorovich. *The Dialectics of Myth.* Trans. Vladimir Marchenkov. London: Routledge, 2003.

Losskii, N. O. *Istoriia russkoi filosofii.* Moscow: Vysshaia shkola, 1991.

Lowry, Richard. *The Evolution of Psychological Theory. A Critical History of Concepts and Presuppositions.* 2nd ed. New York: Aldine, 1982.

Manchester, Martin L. *The Philosophical Foundations of Humboldt's Linguistic Doctrines.* Amsterdam Studies in the Theory and History of Linguistics Science. Studies in the History of the Language Sciences, vol. 32. Amsterdam: John Benjamins, 1985.

Mandel'shtam, Osip. *Sobranie sochinenii v trekh tomakh.* t. 2, *Proza.* 2nd ed. New York: Inter-Language Literary Associates, 1971.

Markov, Vladimir, ed. *Manifesty i programmy russkikh futuristov.* Slavische Propyläen. Munich: Wilhelm Fink Verlag, 1967.

——. *Russian Futurism. A History.* Berkeley: University of California Press, 1968.

Mathiesen, Robert. "The Church Slavonic Language Question: An Overview (IX–XX Centuries)." In *Aspects of the Slavic Language Question,* ed. Riccardo Picchio and Harvey Goldblatt, vol. 1, *Church Slavonic—South Slavic—West Slavic,* 45–65. New Haven: Yale Concilium on International and Area Studies, 1984.

Mihailovic, Alexandar. *Corporeal Words: Mikhail Bakhtin's Theology of Discourse.* Evanston: Northwestern University Press, 1997.

Moran, John H. "Afterword." In Johan Gottfried Herder and Jean-Jacques Rousseau, *On the Origin of Language,* trans. and afterwords John H. Moran and Alexander Gode, 75–83. Chicago: University of Chicago Press, 1966.

Morson, Gary Saul, and Caryl Emerson. *Mikhail Bakhtin: Creation of a Prosaics.* Stanford: Stanford University Press, 1990.

Nekrasov, P. A. *Moskovskaia filosofsko-matematicheskaia shkola i ee osnovateli.* Moscow: n.p., 1904.

Nikolaeva, P. A., et al., eds. *Akademicheskie shkoly v russkom literaturovedenii.* Moscow: Nauka, 1975.

Palama, Sv. Grigorii. *Triady v zashchitu sviashchennobezmolvstvuiushchikh.* Moscow: Kanon, 1996.

Paperno, I. "O prirode poeticheskogo slova. Bogoslovskie istochniki spora Mandel'shtama s simvolizmom." *Literaturnoe obozrenie* no. 1 (1991): 29–36. [Also as Irina Paperno, "On the Nature of the Word: Theological Sources of Mandel'stam's Dialogue with the Symbolists." In *Christianity and the Eastern Slavs,* ed. Boris Gasparov, Robert P. Hughes, Irina Paperno, and Olga Raevsky-Hughes. Vol. 2, *Russian Culture in Modern Times,* 287–310. Berkeley: University of California Press, 1994.]

Parry, Adam Millman. *Logos and Ergon in Thucydides.* New York: Arno Press, 1981.

Pasternak, E. V. "G. G. Shpet." In G. G. Shpet, *Sochineniia.* Prilozhenie k zhurnalu *Voprosy filosofii,* 3–8. Moscow: Pravda, 1989.

Pedersen, Holger. *Linguistic Science in the Nineteenth Century: Methods and Results.* Trans. John Webster Spargo. Cambridge: Harvard University Press, 1931.

Pelikan, Jaroslav. *The Spirit of Eastern Christendom (600–1700).* Vol. 2 of *The Christian Tradition.* Chicago: University of Chicago Press, 1974.

Penelhum, Terence. "Personal Identity." *Encyclopedia of Philosophy,* ed. Paul Edwards, 6:95–107. New York: Macmillan and Free Press, 1967.

Philo. *The Works of Philo: Complete and Unabridged.* Trans. C. D. Yonge. N.p.: Hendrickson, 1993.

Picchio, Riccardo. "Church Slavonic." In Alexander M. Schenker and Edward Stankiewicz, eds., *The Slavic Literary Languages: Formation and Development,* 1–33. New Haven: Yale Concilium on International and Area Studies, 1980.

Plato. *Cratylus.* In *The Works of Plato,* ed. George Burges, 3:281–395. London: Henry G. Bohn, 1850.

———. *Cratylus, Parmenides, Greater Hippias, Lesser Hippias.* Loeb Classical Library, vol. 167. Cambridge: Harvard University Press, 1992.

Plotin. *Sochineniia. Plotin v russkikh perevodakh.* St. Petersburg: Aleteia, 1995.

Plotinus. *Porphyry on Plotinus. Ennead I.* Loeb Classical Library, vol. 440. Cambridge: Harvard University Press, 1966.

———. *Ennead IV. 1–9.* Loeb Classical Library, vol. 443. Cambridge: Harvard University Press, 1984.

———. *Ennead V.* Loeb Classical Library, vol. 444. Cambridge: Harvard University Press, 1984.

———. *Ennead VI. 6–9.* Loeb Classical Library, vol. 468. Cambridge: Harvard University Press, 1988.

Plotnikov, I. " 'Obshchestvo izucheniia poeticheskogo iazyka' i Potebnia." *Pedagogicheskaia mysl'* 1 (1923): 31–40.

Pogodin, A. P. *Iazyk, kak tvorchestvo. Voprosy teorii i psikhologii tvorchestva.* t. 4. Khar'kov: n.p., 1913.

Polivanov, M. K. "Gustav Shet." In G. G. Shpet, *Filosofskie etiudy,* 3–19. Moscow: Progress, 1994.

Polovinkin, S. M. "P. A. Florenskii: Logos protiv khaosa." *Filosofiia* 2 (1989): 1–64.

Poole, Randall Allen. "The Moscow Psychological Society and the Neo-Idealist Development of Russian Liberalism." Ph.D. diss., University of Notre Dame, 1995.

Porphyry. *Porphyry Introduction.* Trans. with commentary by Jonathan Barnes. Oxford: Oxford University Press, 2003.

Portnov, A. N. *Iazyk i soznanie: osnovnye paradigmy issledovaniia problemy v filosofii XIX–XX vv.* Ivanovo: Ivanovskii gos. universitet, 1994.

Postovalova, V. I. "Posleslovie." In A. F. Losev, *Filosofiia imeni,* 228–58. Moscow: Izd. Moskovskogo universiteta, 1990.

Potebnia, A. A. *Estetika i poetika.* Moscow: Iskusstvo, 1976.

Prat, Naftali. "Orthodox Philosophy of Language in Russia." *Studies in Soviet Thought* 20 (1979): 1–21.

Presniakov, O. P. *A. A. Potebnia i russkoe literaturovedenie kontsa XIX–nachala XX veka.* Saratov: izd. Saratovskogo universiteta, 1978.

——. *Poetika poznaniia i tvorchestva. Teoriia slovesnosti A. A. Potebni.* Moscow: Khudozhestvennaia literatura, 1980.

Proclus. *The Elements of Theology: A Revised Text.* 2nd ed. Trans. E. R. Dodds. Oxford: Oxford University Press, 1963.

Rainov, T. *Aleksandr Afanas'evich Potebnia.* Petrograd: Kolos, 1924.

Rancour-Laferriere, Daniel. "Why the Formalists Had No Theory of the Literary Person." *Wiener Slawistischer Almanach.* Sonderband 31, 327–37. "Psychopoetik." 1992.

Robins, R. H. *A Short History of Linguistics.* 4th ed. London: Longman, 1997.

Rousseau, Jean-Jacques. "Essay on the Origin of Languages." In *On the Origin of Language,* trans., with afterwords, by John H. Moran and Alexander Gode, and introduction by Alexander Gode, 5–74. Chicago: University of Chicago Press, 1966.

Rudy, Stephen. "Jakobsonian Poetics of the Moscow and Prague Periods." Ph.D. diss. Yale University, 1978.

Salmon, Paul B. "Also Ran: Some Rivals of Herder in the Berlin Academy's 1770 Essay Competition on the Origin of Language." *Historiographia Linguistica* 16, no. 1/2 (1989): 25–48.

Savin, A. E. "Interpretatsiia i kritika G. G. Shpetom filosofii Ed. Gusserlia." In *G. G. Shpet/Comprehensio. Vtorye shpetovskie chteniia,* 24–27. Tomsk: Vodolei, 1997.

Schenker, Alexander M., and Edward Stankiewicz, eds. *The Slavic Literary Languages: Formation and Development.* New Haven: Yale Concilium on International and Area Studies, 1980.

Searle, John R. *The Rediscovery of the Mind.* Cambridge: MIT Press, 1998.

Seifrid, Thomas. "The Structure of the Self: Potebnia and Russian Philosophy of Language, 1860–1930." In *American Contributions to the Twelfth International Congress of Slavists,* 169–81. Columbus, Ohio: Slavica, 1998.

——. "Roman Jakobson's Sculptural Myth." *Annals of Scholarship* 14:2 (Fall 2000): 25–36.

——. "Khaidegger i russkie o iazyke i bytii." *Novoe literaturnoe obozrenie* 53:1 (2002): 64–74.

Shklovskii, Viktor. "O poezii i zaumnom iazyke." In *Poetika. Sborniki po teorii poeticheskogo iazyka,* 13–26. Petrograd: 18-ia Gosudarstvennaia tipografiia, 1919.

——. "Potebnia." In *Poetika. Sborniki po teorii poeticheskogo iazyka*, 3–6. Petrograd: 18-ia Gosudarstvennaia tipografiia, 1919.

——. "Voskreshenie slova." *Texte der Russischen Formalisten*. Band II, 2–17. Munich: Wilhelm Fink, Verlag, 1972.

Shpet, Gustav. *Vnutrenniaia forma slova (Etiudy i variatsii na temy Gumbol'dta)*. Moscow: Gos. akademiia khudozhestvennykh nauk, 1927.

——. *Sochineniia*. Prilozhenie k zhurnalu *Voprosy filosofii*. Moscow: Pravda, 1989.

——. *Appearance and Sense: Phenomenology as the Fundamental Science and Its Problems*. Trans. Thomas Nemeth. Phaenomenologica 120. Dordrecht: Kluwer Academic, 1991.

——. *Germenevtika i ee problemy*. In *Kontekst 1989*, ed. A. V. Mikhailov, 231–67. Moscow: Nauka, 1989. *Kontekst 1990*, ed. A. V. Mikhailov, 219–59. Moscow: Nauka, 1990. *Kontekst 1991*, ed. A. V. Mikhailov, 215–55. Moscow: Nauka, 1991. *Kontekst 1992*, ed. A. V. Mikhailov, 251–84. Moscow: Nauka, 1993.

——. *Filosofskie etiudy*. Moscow: Progress, 1994.

——. "Iazyk i smysl." *Logos* 7 (1996): 81–122.

——. *Iavlenie i smysl. Fenomenologiia kak osnovnaia nauka i ee problemy*. Tomsk: Vodolei, 1996.

Sreznevskii, I. I. *Mysli ob istorii russkogo iazyka. Chitano na akte Imp. S.-Peterburgskogo universiteta 8 fev. 1849 g*. Reprint, Moscow: Gos. uchebno-pedagogicheskoe izdatel'stvo, 1959.

Steiner, Peter. *Russian Formalism: A Metapoetics*. Ithaca, N.Y.: Cornell University Press, 1984.

——. "*Tropos Logikos*: Gustav Shpet's Philosophy of History." *Slavic Review* 62, no. 2 (Summer 2003): 343–58.

Steinthal, Heymann. *Grammatik, Logik und Psychologie, ihre Prinzipien und ihr Verhältnis zueinander*. 1855. Reprint, Hildesheim: Georg Olms Verlagsbuchhandlung, 1968.

Sukhov, A. D., ed. *Sto russkikh filosofov*. Moscow: Mirta, 1995.

Takho-Godi, A. A. "Tri pis'ma A. F. Loseva." *Voprosy filosofii* 7 (1989): 149–52.

——. "A. F. Losev—filosof imeni, chisla, mifa." In *A. F. Losev i kul'tura XX veka*, 3–23. Moscow: Nauka, 1991.

——. "Aleksei Fedorovich Losev." In A. F. Losev, *Bytie. Imia. Kosmos*, 5–30. Moscow: Mysl', 1993.

——. "A. F. Losev i G. I. Chelpanov." *Nachala* 1 (1994): 36–9.

——. "Iz istorii sozdaniia i pechataniia rukopisei A. F. Loseva." In A. F. Losev, *Imia. Izbrannye raboty, perevody, besedy, issledovaniia, arkhivnye materialy*, v–xxi. St. Petersburg: Aleteia, 1997.

Taylor, Charles. *Hegel*. Cambridge: Cambridge University Press, 1975.

Tihanov, Galin. *The Master and the Slave: Lukács, Bakhtin, and the Ideas of Their Time*. Oxford: Oxford University Press, 2000.

Toman, Jindřich. *The Magic of a Common Language: Jakobson, Trubetzkoy, and the Prague Linguistic Circle*. Cambridge: MIT Press, 1995.

Toscano, Silvia. "Orthodox Slavdom." In *History of Linguistics*, ed. Giulio Lepschy, 3: 123–48. Renaissance and Early Modern Linguistics. London: Longman, 1998.

Troitskii, S. V. *Ob imenakh bozhiikh i imiabozhnikakh*. St. Petersburg: Sinodal'naia tipografiia, 1914.

Troitskii, V. P. " 'Antichnyi kosmos i sovremennaia nauka' i sovremennaia nauka." In A. F. Losev, *Bytie. Imia. Kosmos,* 123–48. Moscow: Mysl', 1993.

Trubetskoi, Sergei Nikolaevich. *Uchenie o Logose v ego istorii.* In *Sochineniia.* Filosofskoe nasledie, t. 120, 43–480. 1906. Reprint, Moscow: Mysl', 1994.

———. "O prirode chelovecheskogo soznaniia." In *Sochineniia.* Filosofskoe nasledie, t. 120, 483–592. 1906. Reprint, Moscow: Mysl', 1994.

Vagner, G. K. "Problema lichnosti v trudakh A. F. Loseva." In *A. F. Losev i kul'tura XX veka. Losevskie chteniia,* 24–28. Moscow: Nauka, 1991.

Veniaminov, V. "Kratkie svedeniia o zhitii i mysli sv. Grigoriia Palamy." In Sv. Grigorii Palama, *Triady v zashchitu sviashchennobezmolvstvuiushchikh,* 344–81. Moscow: Kanon, 1996.

Vetukhov, A. A. A. *Potebnia (†29 noiabria 1891 g.).* Warsaw, 1898. Reprint from *Russkii filologicheskii vestnik.* Warsaw: Tipografiia Varshavskogo uchebnogo okruga, n. d.

Voloshinov, V. N. *Marksizm i filosofiia iazyka.* Moscow: Labirint, 1993.

Vygotskii, L. S. *Myshlenie i rech'.* Moscow: Labirint, 1996.

Vygotsky, Lev Semenovich. *The Psychology of Art.* Trans. Scripta Technica, Inc. Cambridge: MIT Press, 1971.

Walicki, Andrzej. *A History of Russian Thought from the Enlightenment to Marxism.* Trans. Hilda Andrews-Rusiecka. Stanford: Stanford University Press, 1979.

Wallis, R. T. *Neoplatonism.* New York: Charles Scribner's Sons, 1972.

Ware, Timothy. *The Orthodox Church.* New York: Penguin Putnam, 1997.

West, James. *Russian Symbolism: A Study of Vyacheslav Ivanov and the Russian Symbolist Aesthetic.* London: Methuen, 1970.

Wittgenstein, Ludwig. *Tractatus Logico-Philosophicus.* Trans. D. F. Pears and B. F. McGuiness. London: Routledge, 1974.

———. *Philosophical Investigations.* 3rd ed. Trans. G. E. M. Anscombe. Englewood Cliffs, N.J.: Prentice-Hall, 1958.

Wolfson, Harry Austryn. *The Philosophy of the Church Fathers.* Vol. 1. *Faith, Trinity, Incarnation.* Cambridge: Harvard University Press, 1964.

Worth, Dean S. *The Origins of Russian Grammar: Notes on the State of Russian Philology Before the Advent of Printed Grammars.* Columbus, Ohio: Slavica, 1983.

Zander, L. A. *Bog i mir. Mirosozertsanie ottsa Sergiia Bulgakova.* 2 vols. Paris: YMCA Press, 1948.

Zenkovsky, V. V. *A History of Russian Philosophy,* vol. 2. Trans. George L. Kline. New York: Columbia University Press, 1953.

Zernov, Nicolas. *The Russian Religious Renaissance of the Twentieth Century.* New York: Harper and Row, 1963.

Zhivov, V., and B. Uspenskii. "Grammatica sub specie Theologiae. Preteritnye formy glagola 'byti' v russkom iazykovom soznanii XVI–XVIII vekov." *Russian Linguistics* 10, no. 3 (1986): 259–79.

Zvegintsev, V. A. *Istoriia iazykoznaniia XIX–XX vekov v ocherkakh i izvlecheniiakh.* Chast' I. Moscow: Prosveshchenie, 1964.

Index